A New Introduction to Poverty

The Role of Race, Power, and Politics

EDITED BY

Louis Kushnick and James Jennings

New York University Press

NEW YORK AND LONDON

NEW YORK UNIVERSITY PRESS
New York and London

Copyright © 1999 by New York University

Library of Congress Cataloging-in-Publication Data

A new introduction to poverty: the role of race, power, and politics/edited
by Louis Kushnick and James Jennings
     p. cm.—
     Includes bibliographical references.
     ISBN 0-8147-4238-6 (clothbound: acid-free paper)
     ISBN 0-8147-4239-4 (paperbound: acid-free paper)
     1. Poverty—United States. 2. Poor—United States. 3. Power
(Social sciences)—United States. 4. Racism—United States.
     I. Kushnick, Louis. II. Jennings, James, 1949-
     HC110.P6 N394 1999
     305.8'00973—ddc21   98-40087

                                  CIP

"Brings to ⋯ ⋯ ⋯ ⋯ ⋯ ace,
gender, pol ⋯ ⋯ ook
is certain t ⋯ best
analysts of ⋯

⋯ ssor
⋯ ogy,
⋯ ter,
⋯ ork

20 3 02

"This impo ⋯ ⋯ ects
merely the ⋯ ⋯ hat
confrontin ⋯ g a
stacked dec ⋯ her
and the po ⋯ nal
priorities. I ⋯ ead
this book."

⋯ ary
⋯ ces

"Unlike in ⋯ ⋯ the
contributor ⋯ ain
how urban ⋯ rs,
and studen ⋯

⋯ ary
⋯ ing

To the memory of my friend and comrade Haywood Burns, who lived and died fighting for social and racial justice. He touched and influenced so many of us with his integrity, passion, and humanity. —LK

and

To the resurgence of struggles for social and economic justice and especially young people who must fashion the vision for a new democracy. —JJ

Contents

Acknowledgments

The editors would like to express gratitude and appreciation to several individuals who assisted with the publication of this book. Louisa Castner provided editorial assistance in the early stages of the manuscript's development. Her keen editorial eye helped us to develop an organizationally coherent document. Gemima Remy St. Louis, Yvonne Gomes-Santos, and Kimberly Moffitt also provided editorial assistance that contributed significantly to the strengths of this book. The Trotter Institute and its staff also provided key support and assistance in the completion of this manuscript.

The editors also acknowledge the invaluable contribution made by Benjamin P. Bowser, Jacqueline Ould, Patricia Kushnick, and their colleagues at the Institute of Race Relations, as well as the many individuals involved with antipoverty and anti-racist struggles in places like Boston, New York City, Chicago, and many other places in the international arena. Their work in opposing racism and working toward social and racial justice is to be applauded. Louis Kushnick and James Jennings would also like to acknowledge the financial assistance provided by the Centre for the Study of Globalisation, Eurocentrism, and Marginality and by the Department of Sociology at the University of Manchester, and especially the William Monroe Trotter Institute at the University of Massachusetts Boston.

We also express appreciation and thanks to the publishers and contributors who allowed us to reprint their work. These include Princeton University Press, Oxford University Press, Sage Race Relations Abstracts, New York University Press, Monthly Review Press, Macmillan Press, Ltd., and the Association for Evolutionary Economics.

Contributors

Mimi Abramovitz is Professor of Social Work at Hunter College and City University of New York. She has written extensively on women and the history and politics of welfare in the United States. She is the author of several books, including *Regulating the Lives of Women*.

Pete Alcock is Professor of Social Policy and Administration at the University of Birmingham in England. He is a member of the editorial boards of the *Journal of Social Policy* and *Benefits: A Journal of Social Security Research, Policy and Practice*. He has acted as adviser to the "Child Poverty Action Group." He is author of several books, including *Understanding Poverty* and *Social Policy in Britain*.

Bonnie Thornton Dill is Professor of Women's Studies and Director of the Research Consortium on Gender, Race, and Ethnicity at the University of Maryland at College Park. Her books include *Women of Color in U.S. Society* (coedited) and *Across the Boundaries of Race and Class: Work and Family among Black Female Domestic Servants*.

Raymond S. Franklin is Professor of Economics and Labor Studies at Queens College, CUNY, Professor of Sociology at CUNY Graduate Center, and also the former Director of the Michael Harrington Center for Democratic Values and Social Change in New York City. He is the author of *American Capitalism: Two Visions* and of numerous articles on socialism, economics, and urban affairs.

Hermon George Jr. is Professor of Black Studies at the University of Northern Colorado. He has written extensively on black politics in the United States and on the impact of globalization. He is author of *American Race Relations Theory: A Review of Four Models*.

James Jennings is Professor of Political Science and Director of the William Monroe Trotter Institute, University of Massachusetts Boston. He has published a number of articles and books on black and Latino politics in the United States, including *Puerto Rican Politics in Urban America*, *The Politics of Black Empowerment*, and *Race, Politics and Economic Development: Community Perspectives*. He is active in a range of community-based activities.

Michael B. Katz is Stanley I. Sheerr Professor of History at the University of Pennsylvania. He is the author of numerous books covering the areas of poverty, urban education, and social policy. He has published, *Improving Poor People: The Welfare State, the "Underclass," and Urban Schools as History*. His earlier books include *Beyond the Shadow of the Poorhouse: A Social History of Welfare in America* and, much earlier, *Class, Bureaucracy and Schools*.

Marlene Kim is Assistant Professor of Labor Studies at Rutgers University. Her research, focusing on the working poor and wage discrimination, has appeared in *Industrial Relations, Feminist Economics, Challenge, Journal of Economic Issues*, and many books.

Louis Kushnick is Senior Lecturer in American Studies at the University of Manchester, England, and has been the editor of *Sage Race Relations Abstracts* since 1980. He is Director of the Iqbal Ahmed Race Relations Archives and author of *Race, Class, and Struggle* and many articles and essays.

Rebecca Morales is a Research Associate at the Center for U.S.-Mexican Studies, University of California, San Diego. She is the author of *Flexible Production: Restructuring of the International Automobile Industry* and coeditor of *Latinos in a Changing U.S. Economy: Comparative Perspectives on Growing Inequality* and *Borderless Borders: U.S. Latinos, Latin Americans and the Paradox of Interdependence.*

Sandra Patton is a Post-doctoral Research Fellow at the Institute on Race and Poverty at the University of Minnesota. She is coauthor of *Feminism, Race, and Family Values*, as well as numerous essays and articles.

Valerie Polakow is Professor of Education at Eastern Michigan University. She is the author of *The Erosion of Childhood* and *Lives on the Edge: Single Mothers and their Children in the Other America*, which won the Phi Delta Kappa Book of the Year Award in 1994. She has written numerous articles about women and children in poverty, welfare policies, homelessness, and child care policy.

Jackie Pope is Associate Professor of Public Administration at Stockton State College. She is the author of *Biting the Hand That Feeds Them: Organizing Women on Welfare at the Grass Roots Level.* Her research on welfare reform policies has been published in the *Black Scholar* and other journals and anthologies.

Jill Quadagno is Professor of Sociology at Florida State University, where she also holds the Mildred and Claude Pepper Chair in Social Gerontology. She is the author of *The Transformation of Old Age Security.*

David C. Ranney is Associate Professor at the College of Urban Planning and Public Affairs, University of Illinois at Chicago. He has published widely on public policy including three books and numerous articles on issues of employment, labor and community organization, and city planning.

Barbara Ransby is Assistant Professor of African-American Studies and History at the University of Chicago, Illinois. She has written extensively on the relations between gender, race, and politics. She serves as an editor of *Race and Class.*

Maxine Baca Zinn is Professor of Sociology at Michigan State University where she is also Senior Research Associate at the Julian Samora Research Institute. She is coauthor of *Women of Color in U.S. Society* and *Diversity in Families*, currently in its fifth edition.

Poverty as Race, Power, and Wealth

James Jennings and Louis Kushnick

This anthology serves to introduce the topic of poverty in the United States within an institutional framework based on how power, race, and wealth interact with the maintenance of poverty. The major theme of this collection is that racial and gender hierarchies are important features for the maintenance of wealth and political power in this country. In addition, the collection reflects that poor people are not politically passive. The articles in this anthology illustrate in various ways that the persistence of poverty cannot be understood completely, nor can it be reduced significantly, without also examining the question of who has political influence in the United States. Specifically, we must examine how those with power use it to maintain the distribution patterns of wealth at the same time that millions of individuals and families continue in poverty. The unchanging distribution of wealth and power is the greatest determinant in the persistence of massive impoverization of some sectors in this society. Furthermore, the racializing of poverty serves to strengthen institutional arrangements and social relations that generally keep high proportions of women and people of color in economically vulnerable and impoverished positions.

It is the position of the contributors to this volume that the problem of poverty cannot be analyzed or responded to effectively if it is perceived simply as a behavioral issue for poor people or, in what William Ryan described several decades ago as a "blaming-the-victim" approach. We believe that persistent poverty, and poverty that is highly concentrated in some communities, reflects the interplay of an array of national and international factors, as well as specific economic arrangements that support social relations at least partially defined by race and gender. At a broad level, three factors contribute to continuing poverty and high rates of impoverization among certain groups: the increasing imbalance in the distribution of wealth, with the rich continually becoming richer; the unbridled mobility of capital, both in finance and in production; and the prevalence of low wages coupled with levels of relatively high unemployment among certain groups. These are the root causes of poverty in many societies.

These causes of poverty are exacerbated by national policies that allow corporate leaders to pursue profits without consideration of the social costs incurred by their strategies. Militarization also aggravates the causes of poverty by appropriating resources that could be utilized to expand socially beneficial productivity and using them instead to produce tools for human destruction. The major causes of poverty also contribute to the fiscal incapacity of national and local governments, at times raising the level of political and social tensions and popular dissatisfaction as a result. This particular point is argued by Rebecca Morales in her chapter, which illustrates how poverty is part of a broader problem of deteriorating urban living conditions.

In the United States, at least three mechanisms work to mute class tensions that arise from the subsidization of the rich by the working and middle-class sectors of the population. One ideological mechanism is the belief that diligent individuals can make it economically and achieve the good life if they work hard and put God and country above everything; this is the popular Horatio Alger myth. Second is the supply-side proposition, which maintains that economic development and progress will result from allowing wealthy interests to accumulate more wealth; policies that result in lower taxes and less regulation of income mean, according to this thinking, that the wealthy will have more resources to save and invest, raising the standard of living for everyone by producing a healthier economy.

Race is the third mechanism by which class tensions and popular dissatisfaction with economic policies have been managed by wealthy and powerful interests. Certain racial mechanisms have been manipulated by some interests to divide poor and working-class people who are black from poor and working-class people who are not black. Tools used for this purpose throughout U.S. history include segregation and discrimination; the belief and practices associated with the presumption of white cultural superiority; political and racial scapegoating; and even the public presentation and dialogue of welfare reform in the contemporary period. The media also contribute to this process by aggressively racializing poverty. Journalists and commentators frequently present the faces of poor people as black, Puerto Rican, or of other minority racial heritage, and focus on problems like teen births, family instability, crime and drug use, low educational achievement, and poor health attributes—as if poor whites did not exhibit similar characteristics. The racialization of poverty is strengthened and facilitated by private and public policies that continue to result in residential and educational segregation.

Indeed, there are significant historical and contemporary differences among black, white, Latino, Asian, and Native American poverty in this country. Black poverty tends to be more highly concentrated, and black people tend to be impoverished for longer periods of times than whites or some Latino groups. Black poor people also tend to be poorer than white poor people. Black children and youth, as well as some groups of Latino children, remain the most impoverished in this society. But the root causes of long-lasting and persistent poverty are linked directly to the political and economic factors suggested here. If poor people were politically capable of raising and sustaining alliances on the basis of their poverty, then these issues would be highlighted. In a few episodic cases, such alliances have actually been forged, as is shown in some of the selections in this anthology. It is precisely this political possibility, however, that is discouraged and resisted by political and economic leadership in response to the interests of wealth and corporate power.

To a large extent, the current literature and the public dialogue on poverty in the United States ignore the possibility that the poor might forge political alliances. There is generally an absence of a perspective that considers power or the relationship between racial hierarchy and divisions, poverty, and the distribution and management of wealth.

The connection between wealth and power, on the one hand, and poverty and powerlessness, on the other, has been ignored or overlooked by politicians, the media, and academe. Despite some important earlier works, such as that of Frances Fox Piven and Richard A. Cloward and that of other writers cited in this text, the role of politics and the distribution of power and wealth are minimized or ignored in much of the analysis of poverty and race today.

The work of some poverty researchers is myopic regarding political factors that have led to and that sustain persistent impoverishment for many Americans. But politics, as the contributors to this volume contend, is a major factor requiring examination by those seeking to determine the causes of poverty, as well as the means for its resolution, especially among communities of color in the United States. As James Jennings writes in this volume, politics is not "explored for its explanatory possibilities; it is merely assumed by some researchers that poverty has more to do with pathology among groups like Puerto Ricans and blacks, or with politically irrelevant structural cataclysmic changes in the economy, than with the lack of political power that characterizes impoverished groups in this nation." This assessment is also offered by the political scientist David C. Ranney in his chapter, "Class, Gender, and Poverty: A Critique of Contemporary Theories." The lack of political analysis regarding the problem of poverty on the part of the research community and the media encourages the use of the notion of dependency as a major, yet undefined, variable in explaining the nature of poverty. And yet this unexamined concept, Ranney argues, is consistently used in devising policy responses to poverty.

The myth of a dependency culture as created by income-transfer programs that benefit poor people became the new orthodoxy in mainstream media and intellectual circles, as reflected in the work of Thomas Sowell, George Gilder, Mickey Kaus, Charles Murray, and others. Yet, the policy initiatives of the current Democratic administration reflect the ideas and suggestions of these very same conservative writers. In fact, there has been little fundamental difference between Republicans and Democrats in how they approach the notions of work and personal responsibility. Both electoral camps ignore the basic causes of poverty and instead propose that this problem reflects the lack of a work ethic or a sense of personal responsibility among poor people. Although the problem of poverty has been presented and discussed in many sectors in terms of dependency or the absence of a work ethic, domestic poverty in the United States is in fact much more complex, reflecting the interplay of political and economic factors, rather than the particular behavior of poor people.

As a textbook, this anthology is designed to meet the following objectives: (1) to provide historical overviews of major ideological and political debates about the nature, causes, and responses to poverty in the United States; (2) to highlight concepts and models that are useful for the assessment and critique of antipoverty initiatives; and (3) to show the relationship among race, gender, and wealth inequality, highlighting in particular how poverty is racialized and perpetuated in ways that are oppressive to women. The editors believe that these kinds of topics are necessary for a full understanding of the *political* (rather than the *behavioral*) nature of the problem of poverty in the United States. While the dialogue generated by this anthology will remind readers of the short-lived debates about poverty during the civil rights and the Black Power movements, the articles also focus on developments in recent periods as well.

This textbook utilizes history and several disciplines, as well as the activist experiences of many of the authors, to examine the institutional and policy causes of poverty and how these are tied to the class interests of the powerful sectors of society at the expense of working-class and poor people. All the articles in this collection suggest that the nature of poverty and responses to it are determined by those with political and economic power in such ways as to conserve and expand the holding of such power. The chapters in this book explain but also challenge the myths and dominant perceptions that have characterized the literature and that are the basis of study and discourse in policy arenas regarding race and poverty in the United States. It is the purpose of this collection to contradict these myths by suggesting ideas, theories, and analytical frameworks to understand the causes of poverty and their relationship to the functioning of political and economic systems.

Collectively, the articles critique some of the major theoretical and historical assumptions of welfare reform in the current period. Historical overviews of major debates, philosophical positions, and policy strategies related to poverty in the United States are included here. Selections in the anthology discuss the tradition and history of political decision making as it pertains to poverty welfare reform and the connection between this process and the maintenance of the current distribution of power and wealth, as well as the justification of the increasing wealth inequality in U.S. society. The conceptual difference between poverty and welfare reform in the current period is also examined from various positions. Much of the recent welfare reform dialogue in the United States has overlooked the problem of poverty, instead focusing on welfare dependency. This is yet another mechanism that perpetuates the economic and social status quo.

The Causes and Extent of Poverty

The first chapter in this anthology, by James Jennings, reviews some of the literature that proposes to explain the nature and causes of poverty, as well as its persistent features. This opening chapter suggests that, since the end of World War II, poverty and poor people living in the United States have been a continuing focus of social anxiety, a source of public debate, and a target of ineffective federal policies in terms of reducing poverty for significant proportions of blacks and other people of color, particularly women in these sectors. The second chapter in Part I, by David C. Ranney, examines some of the theories offered to explain poverty and shows that the issue of the distribution of power, and how it is manifested politically and economically, is conceptually separated from the problem of poverty. But a latent function of such policies, viewed sociologically and historically, is to support the interests of the wealthy, rather than the well-being of poor people. Therefore, poverty will not be reduced by following the current thinking and implementing the currently popular approaches to this problem.

A NOTE ABOUT THE ABSENCE OF HISTORY

Despite the massive amount of material written in the past quarter of the twentieth century, the literature reflects significant oversights and weaknesses in several areas, as already mentioned. As the historian Michael B. Katz points out in his selection in Part II, one major flaw is the absence of a historical context in the analysis and dialogue about poverty in this country. The lack of such a context encourages the continual use of vague, undefined terms, such as *underclass, slum,* or *broken family,* in methodologies and analyses of the problem of poverty. Another historian, Jill Quadagno, illustrates how historical analysis can be used to understand the intellectual and political foundations of the welfare state in the United States, and the arguments about race offered to support these assumptions. Quadagno illustrates the historical bases of race as a political tool for dampening support for a racial welfare state with a strong commitment to equality. Her chapter is important because it raises the question as to whether some of the values and thinking about race that underlie current thinking about welfare reform are critically different from those underpinning the New Deal in the 1930s. The chapter in this section by James Jennings reiterates some of the concerns raised by Katz and Quadagno and outlines some of the major methodological problems associated with the study and analysis of poverty among Puerto Rican communities.

Poverty and Race as Functions of Economic and Political Power

Quadagno and Katz suggest that race is a fundamental feature of society, and both discuss how it influences the problem of poverty. What others have referred to as "racial hierarchy" or what Hermon George Jr. calls the "racial subordination process" serves a useful function for powerful and wealthy interests in society. Race has been utilized to detract attention from wealth inequality and from the consequence of poverty and economic dislocation for significant numbers of people. Thus, although poverty is not solely a "black" problem, it is politically effective (and perhaps even methodologically neater) to represent it as such because it serves to divert dialogue from issues related to the accumulation, management, and distribution of wealth. In fact, as Rebecca Morales shows in her essay in Part II, poverty must be viewed within the context of urban society. Morales focuses on a group, Latinos, that is experiencing persistent poverty and that is becoming rapidly more impoverished. She presents the problem of poverty within a broader issue of the urban life in the United States, illustrating that a behavioral approach to the problem of poverty that affects massive numbers of people and vast sections of some neighborhoods is illogical within a context of general social and economic decline of urban places. In other words, if problems in the areas of housing, lack of economic development, corporate downsizing, extensive poor health, deteriorating physical infrastructure, and others did not exist, then there might be justification for focusing on the behavior or attitudes of poor people. But clearly, given the context, there is little justification for not approaching poverty as more complex and as a phenomenon linked to social, economic, and political decisions and policies.

Raymond S. Franklin's chapter is useful in showing more specifically how poverty is linked to race. He reminds us that many of the behavioral characteristics associated with disfavored racial groups considered dysfunctional in popular contexts actually reflect class. This implies that these characteristics are found among poor people regardless of their racial or ethnic background; poverty is fundamentally a class issue. Historically, race and racial divisions have been fomented in order to keep people from realizing the political, or class, nature of persistent poverty in the United States.

The use of race and ethnicity as political dividers of working-class and poor people is also a common tactic in the current period. Some evidence for the usefulness of highlighting race and ethnicity to keep people divided is found in a *CBS News/New York Times Poll* reported on December 6-9, 1994:

> attitudes about the poor and about welfare recipients have a racial element: Americans are more likely to think that people on welfare (and all those who are poor in this country) are more likely to be black than they are to be white. And the characterizations of welfare recipients differ dramatically based on the racial images one has of them. Those who say welfare recipients are mostly white (18% say this) are more likely to think people on welfare want to work, that they are on welfare because of circumstances beyond their control, and that they really need help. On the other hand, people who think most welfare recipients are black (44%) say they're on welfare because of lack of effort, that they don't want to work, and that they could get along without welfare benefits.

This anthology reemphasizes what is illustrated in this survey—that is, that the racialization of poverty has been a central feature of the political delegitimation and pacification of poor people.

Distorted media images have been central to the attack on poor people and the few programs that even slightly benefit them, images of black and Puerto Rican women with loads of "illegitimate" children and of black and Latino men, lazy and dangerous, as suggested by Edward C. Banfield in *The Unheavenly City*;[1] frequent photos of poor black women with babies bolstering these myths in the *New York Times* and other major news outlets; and similar images that will continue to pervade the literature after the publication of this book. This catalog of distorted images was crucial in Ronald Reagan's presidential campaigns, as it was in the Ku Klux Klan spokesperson David Duke's gubernatorial and senatorial campaigns in Louisiana and in the right-wing politician Oval Fordyce's gubernatorial campaign in Mississippi. And such images continue to be useful for both Republicans and Democrats. The portrait of the *underclass*, a pejorative term used by conservatives and liberals alike, has been created as another myth to prove the deleterious consequences of programs that benefit the poor, thereby justifying policies of policing and containment and reminding good, normal, hard-working, middle-class citizens that they have nothing in common with "them."

Louis Kushnick's chapter in Part III shows how race is used to build a false consciousness on the part of the white working class vis-à-vis blacks and Latinos. As long as the system of wealth is successful in convincing white workers and white poor people that their whiteness is far more important than their exploitation as members of the working class, they will remain soldiers (albeit poorly paid ones) in keeping poor and working-class blacks and Latinos in their lower social and economic place. At times, this service is carried out in the political arena, but the use of violence, racial animosity, and hatred also permeates the history of the United States, as well as the contemporary period, as Kushnick points out.

Much of the information on and analysis of poverty presented by academic circles is based on and conceptually confined by both the liberal and conservative political and electoral camps in the United States. Many policy discussions about the relationship of race to the causes of poverty are essentially debates between theorists who advocate social welfare liberalism and those who espouse free-market conservatism. But these two schools of thought both approach the problem of poverty simplistically, focusing primarily if not completely on the behavioral characteristics of poor people, and both schools engage in analyses of poverty that result in similar public policies. For example, the Family Support Act of 1988 was supported by both the Republican President George Bush and many Democratic governors and congressional representatives. The Family Support Act, a national attempt to reform welfare for poor persons and families, reflected a particularly narrow, incomplete, and ahistorical view of the causes of persistent poverty. As Valerie Polakow explains in her chapter in Part III, the Personal Responsibility and Work Opportunity Act of 1996, which replaced the Family Support Act of 1988 and traditional welfare for poor people, is similarly flawed as welfare reform, as it represents a regurgitation of long-held conservative and reactionary responses to the status of poor people. It, too, is supported by both Republicans and Democrats at the national level.

One way of illustrating the complex political and economic factors in relation to poverty and race is to examine poverty in the international arena. If the behavior of poor people is the major cause of their impoverishment, then we can reasonably expect poverty experiences in the United States to be unique. The sociologist Peter Alcock, however, dampens this argument. He shows that the relationship emerging between race and poverty in England is remarkably similar to that in the United States as described by other contributors to this volume. This suggests that the problem of poverty in the United States is not unique and may have parallels in other societies. The political scientist Hermon George Jr. extends the suggestions raised in Alcock's chapter by describing how racial hierarchy exists in the international arena, focusing on its origins and its uses by interests with wealth and power.

Poverty, Race, and Gender Inequality

The chapter by Mimi Abramovitz, which opens Part IV, provides a historical context for understanding how women, especially women of color, have become marginalized and are kept in this status by government policies and corporate practices. Again, it is politics and the use of power that allow the maintenance of this exclusion. Abramovitz illustrates that women are not passive. Although the experiences of women differ, depending on their race and ethnicity, it is still possible to generate political mobilization that responds to the needs of poor and working-class women across these boundaries. The chapters by Valerie Polakow, Bonnie Thornton Dill et al., and Jackie Pope show that, although women have achieved some degree of political equality, there has not been a fundamental change in how they are economically exploited in the United States. The abolition of gender equality is still not a primary consideration on the part of those sectors of society, whether liberal or conservative, that control or design antipoverty policies.

Polakow reminds readers that the denial of the political nature of persistent poverty "permit[s] public denial of our social responsibility to poor mothers and their children." Thus, poor people and families have become delegitimized in the public arena, with a consequent loss of political support for the reduction of poverty through redistribution of social and economic resources.

Bonnie Thornton Dill, Maxine Baca Zinn, and Sandra L. Patton focus on the national debate on family values. The authors show how this debate is imbued with racial overtones. Furthermore, they point out, the issue is used to blame women, especially poor, black, and Latina women, for their own impoverishment. The discussion of family values also helps to maintain a class structure that determines in large part the formation of families rather than analyzing particular family structures that lead to poverty status, as has been noted by many conservative and liberal writers. Yet, on a positive note, women in many communities have successfully resisted this kind of exploitation. Women of color have been in the forefront of efforts to combat their own marginalization, as illustrated by Jackie Pope in her case study of the Brooklyn Welfare Action Council. Women have also fought against exploitation in the labor market and in the public assistance arena in many ways, including political organization. Pope explains that, through political mobilization, women of color have advanced their own economic interests, benefiting not just themselves but their families, communities, and other women. The examples described in this chapter are repeated in a growing number of studies, reflecting the political impact of women of color in the struggle to expand social welfare for children and families.

Poverty, Race, and Distribution of Economic Benefits

A number of observers, including George and Katz in this volume, have proposed that national and international economic developments point to an increasing social marginalization of black people and other people of color. Barbara Ransby examines this situation and shows that, since black poor people have become economically expendable, it is crucial for interests that represent wealth aggressively to discourage the politicization of this sector. The careful management and distribution of economic benefits, especially jobs, become crucial in the political struggle to maintain law and order.

Beginning Part V, the economist Marlene Kim shows that the marginalization of blacks and other minority groups is not the result of a lack of work ethic, thus discrediting the behavioral explanation. Instead, she maintains that the problem is more fundamentally one of national and international economic decisions that result in increasing wealth inequality, as argued by other contributors. But can government be used to change the marginalized status of black workers and poor people, especially women? The late David M. Gordon suggested that the answer is yes.[2] He offers a hopeful vision for challenging racial and gender oppression and the continuing impoverization of vast numbers of people. But Gordon and others remind readers that this vision requires the mobilization and exertion of political power on the part of poor people. As has been proven throughout the history of the United States, only until poor people organize themselves and challenge those responsible for justifying and maintaining the economic status quo is poverty reduced. We hope that this text will remind our readers that race and gender inequality have been implemented effectively in many periods, and in other societies, to prevent this kind of mobilization.

NOTES

1. Edward C. Banfield, *The Unheavenly City* (Boston: Little, Brown, 1973).
2. David M. Gordon, "Values That Work," *Nation* (June 17, 1996).

Part I

The Causes and Extent of Poverty

Chapter One

Persistent Poverty in the United States
Review of Theories and Explanations

James Jennings

> This association of poverty with progress is the great enigma of our times. It is the central fact from which spring industrial, social, and political difficulties that perplex the world, and with which statesmanship and philanthropy and education grapple in vain. From it come the clouds that overhang the future of the most progressive and self-reliant nations. It is the riddle which the Sphinx of Fate puts to our civilization and which not to answer is to be destroyed.
>
> —Henry George, *Progress and Poverty: An Inquiry into the Cause of Industrial Depressions and of Increase of Want with Increase of Wealth*, 1879

The enigma of poverty was foretold as a major philosophical and political question of our times by Karl Polanyi, who observed during World War II that the question "Where do the poor come from was raised by a bevy of pamphlets which grew thicker with the advancing century."[1] He wrote in *The Great Transformation*: "This apparent contradiction was destined to become to the next generation of Western humanity the most perplexing of all the recurrent phenomena in social life."[2] Polanyi's comment was anticipated by W. E. B. Du Bois a few years earlier during his commencement address to graduates of Fisk University in 1938:

> The most distressing fact in the present world is poverty; not absolute poverty, because some folks are rich and many are well-to-do; not poverty as great as some lands and other historical ages have known; but poverty more poignant and discouraging because it comes after a dream of wealth; of riotous, wasteful and even vulgar accumulation of individual riches, which suddenly leaves the majority of mankind today without enough to eat; without proper shelter; without sufficient clothing.[3]

Thus, the enigma described by Henry George in 1879 remained unresolved during the period of Du Bois and Polanyi in the Western world in 1938 and in 1944, and it continues to be unresolved today.

Frameworks for Understanding Explanations for Poverty

Many explanations for the existence of poverty have been offered in the literature. Two professors of city and regional planning, William W. Goldsmith and Edward J. Blakely, reduce theories and explanations of poverty to three categories: "poverty as pathology," "poverty as incident or accident," and "poverty as structure."[4] These categories can be reduced further into two points of view regarding people who are poor. The first is what Barry R. Schiller refers to as the "restricted opportunity" argument, and the second is the "flawed character" argument. In exploring this point, Schiller writes:

> The first perceives the incidence of poverty to be the natural concomitant of individual defects in aspiration or ability. In colonial times this perspective was aptly summarized by the puritanical Humane Society, which concluded that "by a just and inflexible law of Providence, misery is ordained to be the companion and punishment of vice." In more modern times theories of sin and immorality have not fared well.... Instead we speak in terms of "work ethic" and attribute individual impoverishment to a lack thereof.[5]

There is still much support for this paradigm today in the United States. As the political scientists Lee Sigelman and Susan Welch state:

> National surveys of the adult population...during the 1970s and 1980s, [hear] testimony to the prevailing American faith that in economic affairs "God helps those who help themselves."...This strong strain of individualism is evident in the underspread tendency to blame the poor for their poverty. Most Americans consider insufficient effort, lack of ability, weak motivation, and immoderation to be among the most important reasons for poverty in this country, and a sizeable minority would include "loose morals and drunkenness" as well.[6]

The other major perspective described by Schiller, "restricted opportunity," proposes that "the poor are poor because they do not have adequate access to good schools, jobs, and income, because they are discriminated against on the basis of color, sex, income, or class and because they are not furnished with a fair share of government protection, subsidy, or services."[7]

These explanations of poverty are reflected in the writings of many social welfare researchers. Michael Sherraden writes, for example, that "there are many elaborate theories, and variations of themes, on poverty. These can be simplistically lumped into two groups—theories that focus on individual behaviors and theories that focus on social structures."[8] Yet another writer who reiterates the conceptual dichotomy reflected in Schiller's work is the social welfare scholar Chaim I. Waxman: "There are among American sociologists and policy makers two major conceptualizations and explanations of poverty: one is known as the cultural perspective and the other as the situational perspective."[9]

The historian Jay R. Mandel, in *The Roots of Black Poverty*, provides a historical explanation for black poverty that is a variation of the restricted-opportunity thesis proposed by Schiller. Mandel correctly points out that black poverty certainly existed during slavery and has persisted continually since Emancipation. Family structure and group attitudes or attributes may have changed over generations, but poverty has consistently been more widespread and persistent in the black community than it has been among white Americans. Mandel explains continuing black poverty as a reflection and continuation of the effects of the plantation economy in the South that persisted for decades after the Civil War.[10] This echoes the analysis by W. E. B. Du Bois of Southern politics and economy in his classic work, *Black Reconstruction in America 1860-1880*: "It was the policy of the state to keep the Negro laborer poor, to confine him as far as possible to menial occupation, to make him a surplus labor reservoir and to force him into peonage and unpaid toil."[11] Blacks were in large part confined to the plantation economy in the last four decades of the nineteenth century, even while the industrialized North received fourteen million immigrants from Europe.

As Mandel posits, the long duration of the plantation economy in the South has had the effect of placing the "black working class in a difficult half-way position. Only one generation or so removed from the plantation economy, nothing like full occupational integration has occurred and the black working class remains disproportionately in low-wage jobs."[12] He argues that the effects of the plantation economy have prevented millions of blacks from developing the political tools and economic position they need to obtain control of parts of the emerging industrialized order. This situation prevents effective community-based responses to continual poverty for large sectors of the black community.

The black experience shares some commonalities with that of Puerto Ricans, another group with a migratory history and one in which significant numbers of individuals and families are impoverished in the United States. Many Puerto Ricans who have migrated to the United States since the early 1900s have been hampered in building political tools for group advancement in the occupational structure of Northeastern cities. The continual back-and-forth migration of Puerto Ricans between Puerto Rico and cities in the northeastern United States was one factor that inhibited opportunities for the building of a political base that could be used by this community to move up the social and economic ladder.[13]

The historian Elizabeth Pleck has examined black poverty and its causes in earlier periods. Her study provides an analysis of how blacks experienced poverty between 1865 and 1900 and concludes that there are two major explanations for black poverty during this period in places like Boston, Chicago, Cleveland, and Philadelphia. The explanations do not have to do with cultural or educational deficiencies on the part of blacks, she states; instead,

> the handicaps of black workers arose from the operation of two distinct racial barriers to be found within Boston, exclusion and unsuccessful competition. Exclusion, the first of these, involved entry-level racial barriers in hiring and the recruitment of new black arrivals into service jobs. As a consequence, most black newcomers entered menial work and stayed in it, becoming drifters between low-wage jobs and moving incessantly from one city to the next....aspiring entrepreneurs, professionals, clerks, and craftsmen confronted a second

barrier, unsuccessful competition, not because of some unique cultural deficiency but because race was used as a means of firing them or forcing them out.[14]

These kinds of explanation for black urban poverty in earlier periods, which have appeared in a range of literature focusing on the emergence of black communities in the American city, can be placed in the restricted-opportunity framework, rather than the flawed-character framework. Representative studies include Harold X. Connally's *A Ghetto Grows in Brooklyn*, Gilbert Osofsky's *Harlem: The Making of a Ghetto, Negro New York, 1890-1930*, and Kenneth L. Kusmer's *Black Cleveland: 1870-1930*.[15] A similar study that focuses on the emergence and the social life of the Puerto Rican community in New York City is *Memorias de Bernardo Vega*, by Cesar A. Iglesias.[16]

One work by Henry George, published in the mid-nineteenth century, states that poverty is a result of broad economic and social forces and the concomitant absence of a political base for impacted groups. During that period, George asserted that the existence of a poverty-stricken population was related to the rise in land values and the fact that poor people did not own land:

> The ownership of land is the great fundamental fact which ultimately determines the social, the political, and consequently the intellectual and moral condition of a people. And it must be so. For land is the habitation of man, the storehouse upon which he must draw for all his needs, the material to which his labor must be applied for the supply of all his desires; for even the products of the sea cannot be taken, the light of the sun enjoyed, or any of the forces of nature utilized, without the use of land or its products. On the land we are born, from it we live, to it we return again—children of the soil as truly as is the blade of grass or the flower of the field.[17]

George points out that land values usually rise with an increase in population density and urbanization, but the increase in value is rarely distributed to the population whose growth produced the rise in value. The "unearned increment" is almost always assigned to those lucky enough to have owned the land affected by the growth in population.

Stephen Thernstrom's *Poverty and Progress*, published in the mid-1960s, also suggests broad economic developments as the major explanation for poverty in nineteenth-century America. As he wrote in his case study of poverty in Newburyport, Massachusetts:

> Few students of nineteenth-century American communities have experienced much optimism about the economic situation of the urban working class during the 1850-1880 period. Wages for unskilled and semiskilled labor were never very high in the best of times, and unemployment was endemic to the economic system. These decades were punctuated by national financial panic in 1857, a postwar slump, and a prolonged depression in the 1870s.[18]

The kind of historical and social analysis developed by Mandel regarding black poverty and by George and Thernstrom in explaining poverty as a result of systemic forces in the nineteenth century is missing from many contemporary public and scholarly discussions on this topic.

The Human Capital Explanation

One school of thought that runs through the poverty literature focuses on limited "human capital" as an explanation for poverty. In other words, people are poor primarily because they lack education, training, job skills, or language proficiency, and this lack of human capital prevents economic mobility. While this explanation can be associated with restricted opportunity, it focuses on the weaknesses of the individual. There is a presumption that the economic system is effective for anyone who is properly skilled and educated; thus, poverty could be reduced significantly if only impoverished groups could obtain the skills necessary for the available jobs.

In Boston, Massachusetts, as in many other cities, for example, individuals who have not completed high school have been left out of many jobs in the changing labor market; presumably, the absence of skills, or the "skills mismatch," has increased this group's chances of living in poverty or near-poverty. During the 1970s and 1980s, the central cities lost hundreds of thousands of entry-level jobs that could have been filled by people without a high school diploma. This loss occurred simultaneously with an increase in the number of knowledge-intensive jobs requiring fourteen or more years of schooling. This pattern has been especially evident in many of the larger cities in the Northeast, but is also apparent in other regions.[19] The sociologist Vilma Ortiz reports the same pattern for New York City and Los Angeles: the number of jobs for the more educated tended to increase much faster than jobs for the less educated.[20]

Although these studies have formed many of the programmatic underpinnings for employment and training programs (that is, human capital programs) around the United States, several reports have pointed to an imprecise relationship between educational attainment and poverty, especially for blacks and Latinos.[21] While higher education does reduce the chances of being poor among blacks and Latinos, it does not necessarily lessen the poverty or income gap between these groups and whites. This point is illustrated in Table 1.1.

TABLE 1.1

Percentage of Household Heads below Poverty Line by Education and Race, 1985

Educational Attainment	Black	White	Difference
Fewer than 8 years*	34	23	11
8 years	37	13	24
High school, 1-3 years	36	15	21
High school, 4 years	27	7	20
College, 1 or more years	11	3	8

SOURCE: Gerald Jaynes and Robin Williams, "Poverty Rates and Distribution of Black and White Populations by Various Demographic Characteristics, 1985," in *A Common Destiny*, ed. Gerald Jaynes and Robin Williams (Washington, D.C.: National Academy Press, 1989), 288.

*Educational attainment of household heads, aged twenty-five and older.

The income gap among blacks, whites, and Latinos, even when the researcher controls for schooling, remains today. In 1990, while 22.6 percent of white families below the poverty level were headed by someone with fewer than eight years of schooling the figure for comparable black families was 38.7 percent, and for Latino families, 31.6 percent. While only 6.9 percent of all white heads of household who were high school graduates were living below the poverty level, for blacks and Latinos the comparative rates were 11.9 percent and 9.3 percent, respectively.[22] The gap in percentage points between blacks and whites below the poverty level actually *widens* as blacks obtain more education, up to one year of college. This relationship was also noted by Jose E. Cruz regarding Puerto Ricans: "Low educational attainment 'explains' poverty to some degree; yet Puerto Rican educational levels are higher than Mexican American, while the poverty level of the latter is less."[23]

Norman Fainstein also takes issue with the human capital or skills-mismatch explanation. He writes that "the mismatch diagnosis is inadequate and misleading. Urban blacks are not particularly dependent on a declining manufacturing sector; rather, they suffer from segmentation into low-wage employment in growth industries."[24] Fainstein implies that improving the skills of urban blacks may not necessarily produce more available jobs with above-poverty-level wages. I revisit this discussion in a later section of this essay.

Cultural, Moral, and Genetic Explanations

Another set of researchers and observers suggests that improper social and work attitudes, including lack of moral standards, dysfunctional cultural attributes, or particular personal dispositions, explain poverty and its persistence among some groups. These arguments reflect Schiller's flawed-character framework. There are two basic subsets to this school of thought. One liberal variant is reflected in the work of the sociologist Oscar Lewis. Lewis suggests that many Puerto Ricans in New York City are poor because they do not have middle-class norms and values; such norms, he argues, can be imparted to poor people through education and proper socialization.[25] Lewis's approach is tied to the restricted-opportunity viewpoint because it suggests that the poor have not been allowed to develop the proper values and behavior for achieving middle-class status in the United States.

A conservative strand of thinking within the cultural school is reflected in the political scientist Edward C. Banfield's widely read work *The Unheavenly City* (1973).[26] He argues that the innate "ethos" of some groups prevents them from acquiring the proper work habits, moral disposition, attitudes, and cultural norms necessary for social mobility, regardless of government attempts to achieve this. He suggests that government should not waste resources trying to change the innate cultural weaknesses of some people but, rather, should seek to constrain their physical mobility and their ability to damage the chances of others in the black community. George Gilder also emphasizes sexual immorality in his explanation of poverty: "Their problem is not poverty but a collapse of family discipline and sexual morality."[27] In a later work, Gilder proposes that poverty is inevitable for some in society and suggests that the chances of impoverishment are determined by an individual's moral character; those who get stuck in poverty have rejected hard work, marriage and family, and religious faith.[28] Manuel Carballo and Mary Jo Bane remind us that this has been a major explanation of poverty used by political conservatives:

> Conservatives from Hobbes to the present day have felt that the causes and cures of individual poverty are essentially not political or economic, but moral. Anyone willing to work hard can "make it." Therefore, those who have not made it must be unwilling to work and lazy. This theme has been behind every conservative solution to poverty from almshouses to "workfare."[29]

In an earlier work, *Wealth and Poverty*, Gilder does not delve deeply into whether the moral weaknesses of the poor are innate or whether they reflect a group "ethos," as is argued by Banfield, but he does concur with Banfield's general theme that poverty reflects immorality and a lack of hard work. Gilder's tone throughout this book is reflected in the following passage:

> The only dependable route from poverty is always work, family, and faith. The first principle is that in order to move up, the poor must not only work, they must work harder than the classes above them. Every previous generation of the lower class has made such efforts. But the current poor, white even more than black, are refusing to work hard....The key to the intractable poverty of the hardcore American poor is the dominance of single and separated men in poor communities....The problem is neither race nor matriarchy in any meaningful sense. It is familiar anarchy among the concentrated poor of the inner city, in which flamboyant and impulsive youths rather than responsible men provide the themes of aspiration. The result is that male sexual rhythms tend to prevail, and boys are brought up without authoritative fathers in the home to instill in them the values of responsible paternity: the provider role. "If she wants me, she'll pay," one young stud assured me in prison.[30]

Gilder suggests that the poor have a depraved morality that society can rectify by using draconian measures to punish and imprison the recalcitrant poor for a behavior considered negative by middle-class society.

While Banfield toys with the idea that poverty among blacks and Latinos may be related to low innate native intelligence and genetic inferiority, Lowell E. Galloway wholeheartedly embraces this proposition:

> If intelligence is treated as a physical aspect of man and economic rent is paid to those possessing unusual amounts of it, the very real possibility exists that poverty is transmitted from parent to child through the genetic mechanism. In the broadest sense, this implies that poverty is to some substantial extent hereditary in the physical sense....The thrust of our argument has been that a major source of the white-Negro income gap is probably differential endowments of genetic human capital.[31]

The claim of black genetic inferiority rests primarily on Galloway's sweeping contention that increasing educational expenditures have not been able to close the racial gap in educational achievement. As he argues, "What can explain the apparent lack of impact of per pupil expenditures on student performance? And, what are the implications of this in terms of the inheritance of poverty question? The answer to the first question may simply be that after some expenditure threshold is reached, the critical factor is the native ability (intelligence?) of the student population" (67). Galloway concludes that, given genetic ability as the major explanation for poverty status in the United States, the existence of poverty in society is quite "natural": "In assessing the nature of the poverty problem in the United States, we have placed great emphasis on the importance of differentials in the distribution of genetic human capital as a source of inequality in the distribution of income. This implies something 'natural' about the existence of relative poverty in this country" (159).

Challenging the "culture of poverty" ideas put forth by neoconservatives such as Charles Murray, Gilder, Banfield, and others, William J. Wilson argues that "the key theoretical concept...is not 'culture of poverty' but 'social isolation.'"[32] In essence, the poor may not conform to the norms of middle-class expectations because they have become detached from this sector and are therefore increasingly isolated from role models who reflect acceptable social behavior. One of the earliest yet still most powerful critiques of the utilization of cultural or genetic explanations for poverty is the sociologist Charles A. Valentine's *Culture and Poverty* (1968).[33] Valentine examines the literature that has used culture as an explanation of poverty up to the time of his book's publication and argues that E. Franklin Frazier's sociological work laid much of the foundation for the culture of poverty school. Valentine adds that those who propose cultural differences as an explanation for poverty have not proved their case analytically.

The cultural approach is easily espoused, however, because as Kenneth Clark suggests, "the cult of cultural deprivation...is seductive."[34] Valentine supports Clark's description of cultural explanations as a "subtle form of social class and racial snobbery and ignorance."[35] In the final chapter of his book, Valentine proposes that the reason that many social welfare programs aimed at eliminating or reducing poverty have not been effective is the presumption of cultural deprivation; these programs have not empowered poor people "to act in behalf of their own interests, either individually or collectively."[36] Valentine's work is relevant to issues of poverty in the current period. His recommendations call not merely for more social welfare programs but also for greater political mobilization on the part of poor people.

Two more recent critiques of the cultural explanation of black poverty include essays by the political economist Manning Marable (1987) and philosopher Cornel West (1987).[37] Both Marable and West argue that the many discussions on the presumed pathology of black culture have not actually reflected community experiences. Both suggest that intellectuals who focus on fatalistic or culture-focused models for explaining black poverty represent the interests of a political, social, economic, and cultural status quo that is antithetical to the well-being of poor people or to the elimination of poverty.

The Self-Serving Role of Public Assistance Bureaucracies as an Explanation

Another thread that runs through the poverty literature has focused on the roles of public assistance bureaucracies as an explanation for persistent poverty. This school also has two versions, each at a different end of the ideological spectrum. Some writers have proposed that the institutional inability to eliminate poverty can be explained in large part by the self-serving functions and roles of public assistance bureaucracies that have organizational interests in maintaining poverty.[38] This interpretation holds that poverty is functional for the political and organizational well-being of public assistance bureaucracies and necessary for the continuing careers of bureaucrats who administer services to the poor. It is argued, furthermore, that public assistance bureaucracies maintain poverty by inhibiting the natural entrepreneurial spirit of people who are poor.

Interestingly, both liberals and conservatives have identified the organizational nature and behavior of public assistance bureaucracies as major obstacles in reducing poverty.[39] The policies called for by these various authors, however, are quite different. Some propose the elimination of public assistance bureaucracies and an unfettering of the free market. Yet other writers argue that only by transferring power to the poor can society guarantee opportunities for their social and economic mobility.

Macroeconomic and Demographic Explanations

The impact of broad economic and demographic changes at both the national and the international levels is another explanation for the problem of poverty. Goldsmith and Blakely posit that poverty is partially a result of radical change and transformation in global and domestic economies. But they add that these changes have exacerbated the problem of poverty in the United States because of inadequate political responses on the part of government: "We believe, in fact, that the recent upsurge in urban poverty has been generated not simply by transformations in the structure of the global and domestic economies, but by a particular set of American political responses, which have also helped guide these transformations."[40] They add:

> Three features dominate the current situation: America is less influential in worldwide economic affairs; the international economy itself is less stable; and the landscape of domestic industry has been transformed. In these circumstances...it would be almost impossible to eradicate poverty by relying on the usual domestic economic policies, employment and training programs, or efforts that focus on jobs alone. Policies have not faced up to America's new place in the world.

The sociologist Stanley Lieberson draws upon a historical analysis of the structural changes in the U.S. economy to explain the different social and economic mobility patterns of blacks and Latinos, on the one hand, and white ethnics, on the other, throughout American history. He states that the structural occupational context for blacks and Latinos is dramatically different today from the way it was for the immigrant groups that entered America at the turn of the century.[41] There were more jobs available during the earlier period that permitted some degree of security and social mobility. Lieberson's thesis is similar to that of the political scientist Charles V. Hamilton, who proposes that

> before we look at the black and Hispanic situation, it is useful to see the context in which earlier ethnic politics in this country developed. Those groups began arriving in America when industrial expansion was taking off. They could not have been more timely. Periodic depressions notwithstanding, there was a continually growing private-sector economy that could accommodate, indeed welcomed, growing masses of unskilled labor. That labor came....The need was mutual and the relationship mutually beneficial.[42]

Another way in which the broader economic context was historically more advantageous to whites than blacks is illustrated by Gerald D. Suttles in *The Social Order of the Slum* (1968). He reminds us that, in earlier periods, greater proportions of poor blacks lived in Chicago public housing compared to poor Italians, who tended to live in their own private homes. This meant that Italians had an opportunity to use their property as venture capital, to make their homes profitable by performing economic tasks like renting or to use their homes as a basis for adding income to that received from outside salaried occupations. These kinds of opportunities were closed to many blacks due to both de facto and de jure segregation in American cities.[43]

In the decades of the 1970s and 1980s, the rapidly changing occupational structure of the national economy resulted in the increasing impoverization of the American city population. Mark Rosenman describes some of these changes:

> The occupational structure of our nation is changing rapidly. Each year, two to three million workers lose jobs because of structural factors, in both urban and rural areas. Since 1981, two million manufacturing jobs have been lost....over 40% fewer jobs were created during the 1980s than in the last half of the prior decade....Approximately half of recently created jobs are "contingent" positions from which workers are easily laid off. About 50% of new jobs created between 1979 and 1984 also paid less than $7000 a year.[44]

Dennis Gilbert and Joseph A. Kahl also list this changing occupational structure as one factor of central importance in explaining structural unemployment and the diminishing number of jobs that pay good living wages:

> The system of production was changing as factories became more automated. Manufacturing jobs for persons of low skill were shrinking as a proportion of the labor force, and many antiquated factories in the older cities were closing and shifting their production either to small towns or to foreign countries. Therefore, an excess of job seekers was competing for a diminishing supply of positions. A disproportionate number of those without jobs were from minority groups, American citizens living in the slums originally built for foreign immigrants.[45]

These kinds of discussions are related to Wilson's focus on the impact of broad economic changes on cities and neighborhoods as an explanation for the growth of persistent poverty among some groups.[46]

Economic downturn and the decline in manufacturing jobs as an explanation for poverty is also suggested by David Osborne, who argues that poverty and economic displacement reflect the general ill health of the economy and the increasing disconnection from the economy's mainstream of large numbers of people:

> Three groups are caught in the mismatch between available jobs and available workers: dislocated industrial workers; the urban poor; and the rural poor. Increasingly, these three groups live in isolated communities that have lost their connections to the economic mainstream. These communities are caught in a downward spiral of disinvestment, increasing poverty, and further disinvestment. A few of their members successfully make the jump into the economic mainstream, but as communities, they grow ever more isolated.[47]

The sociologist Vijai P. Singh summarizes this view as one of

two competing explanations for the persistence of poverty and the emergence of the underclass in the United States. The first position is that recent changes in the American economy have substantially contributed to the growth of the underclass population....The massive elimination of blue-collar, entry-level jobs and the emergence of knowledge-based jobs have not favored many blacks who did not possess sufficient levels of education, skill or work experience. Unemployment and growing isolation from the mainstream economy have led to unwed parenting, dependency, lawlessness, joblessness, and school failure among some blacks.[48]

This approach has been challenged in part by several studies that show that the relationship between economic growth and poverty may not be as strong for various demographic groups as has been assumed by some observers. The researchers Rebecca M. Blank and Alan S. Blinder report,

Poverty declined particularly rapidly during the boom years of 1965, 1966, and 1968 (which, of course, were also the years in which the Great Society programs were getting started) and then rose slightly during the mild recession of 1969-1970. When expansion resumed in 1971-1973, the poverty rate ratcheted down another notch—to 11.1 percent, its historic low; the deep recession of 1973-1975 pushed poverty back to 12.3 percent; the 1976-78 expansion trimmed the poverty rate once again; and back-to-back recessions in 1980 and 1981-82 raised poverty from 11.7 percent in 1979 to 15 percent in 1982. In 1982 and 1983 real GNP fell and then rose, the average unemployment rate was constant, and poverty crept upward to 15.2 percent.[49]

These findings support, in part, Osborne's argument. These authors also note, however, that "only among white male-headed households" is this relationship between economic fluctuation and poverty rates so clear.[50] Along this line, the researcher James Thornton and his colleagues conclude that the lack of national economic growth as an explanation for pockets of poverty "has been overstated."[51] Theodore Cross shows that the relationship of economic growth and declining poverty during the decade of the 1970s may have been clear-cut for whites, but not necessarily for blacks.[52] Does this critique hold true for the 1980s? In 1980, the gross national product was $3,187 billion (in constant 1982 dollars); by 1988, this figure increased by 29.2 percent, to $4,118 billion.[53] Reiterating Cross's query, did this rising wave of economic growth lift blacks and Latinos out of poverty? As was the case for the 1970s, the response is negative. As a matter of fact, according to the U.S. Bureau of the Census, an additional 214,000 white families became impoverished during this period. But for blacks and Latinos the situation was worse: an additional 257,000 black families became impoverished, while another 382,000 Latino families became impoverished during a period when the gross national product grew significantly. Table 1.2 illustrates these developments.

TABLE 1.2

Number of Families below Poverty Level by Race and Hispanic Origin: 1980-1988

	1980	1988	Percentage Change
Gross National Product	3,187[a]	4,118[a]	+29.2
Families below poverty level		(*in thousands*)	
Whites	4,195	4,409	+5.1
Blacks	1,820	2,077	+14.1
Hispanics	751	1,133	+50.8

SOURCE: Derived from U.S. Bureau of Economic Analysis, *Survey of Current Business*, April 1991 (Washington, D.C., 1991); and U.S. Bureau of the Census, *Statistical Abstract of the United States, 1992* (Washington, D.C., 1992), table 724.
[a]Billions of dollars, and in constant 1992 dollars.

Wilson and other writers, including Osborne, remind us, furthermore, that the poor are becoming more socially isolated as a result of the broad economic and demographic changes described earlier. Wilson and his coauthors offer statistics to illustrate the growing isolation of the poor by showing the change in the racial composition of the poor in U.S. cities from 1970 to 1980.[54] This study uses Chicago as a case study to describe the outmigration of the nonpoor from the city. The authors explain the social transformation that has occurred in inner cities that are characterized by increasing isolation: the poor are increasingly divorced from job networks and from individual and positive role models, as well as from community institutions. This suggestion has been challenged by several writers, who show that the alleged flight of the black middle class is not the major culprit for increasing levels of poverty in predominantly black and poor neighborhoods. Furthermore, the notion of a halcyon period of black ghetto life where the black middle class lived fruitfully with an impoverished stratum of people has been critiqued by Brett Williams as urban "mythic history."[55] She argues that convincing evidence for this notion has yet to be offered.

Employment Opportunities and Low Wages as Explanations

Low wages and a lack of jobs at decent wages may be among the most important causes for poverty for all groups. These were cited earlier as significant factors for the impoverishment of individuals and groups in Henry George's study in the mid-nineteenth century: "The cause which produces poverty in the midst of advancing wealth is evidently the cause which exhibits itself in the tendency, everywhere recognized, of wages being kept to a minimum."[56] One article that examines how some people were able to overcome poverty in the 1930s cited a study by the Research Department of the AFL-CIO that concluded that low wages were a major cause of poverty during the Great Depression. This study concludes that poverty during the Depression was reduced primarily by stabilizing and improving the wages and purchasing power of workers.[57] The report suggests that minimum-wage policies could be effective in preventing the impoverishment of workers.

One of the most comprehensive earlier studies of the relationship between income and poverty is that by the economist Gabriel Kolko.[58] Kolko identifies unemployment and low income, or "poverty wages," as the major causes of poverty. A study published in the early 1970s with a similar thesis regarding the relationship between poverty and low wages was done by the economist Barry Bluestone,[59] who illustrates the strong connection between poverty and low wages by highlighting and discussing the characteristics of the U.S. working poor. This idea was developed fully by Sar A. Levitan and Isaac Schapiro.[60] A more comprehensive study of the relationship between wages and poverty was a work sponsored by the Center on Budget and Policy Priorities and authored by Schapiro.[61]

A study by Linda R. Martin and Demetrios Giannaros, done in 1990, concludes that a major explanation for poverty rates among women is low wages: "The most important empirical conclusion of this study is that, in relative terms, the real minimum wage plays a major role in explaining the feminization of poverty."[62] These researchers compare the effects of government transfer payments, unemployment rates, and fluctuations in economic activity and find that the minimum wage levels set by the federal government had a major impact on the extent of poverty among families headed by women. A similar conclusion about poor families was reached by Ronald B. Mincy, whose study results "appear to favor a higher minimum wage, but caution is necessary. Despite its inefficiency in reaching the poor, a higher minimum wage would significantly reduce poverty among working families."[63]

Racism, Discrimination, and Segregation as Explanations

Racism and discrimination cannot be discounted or dismissed as explanations for persisting poverty in communities of color. In a report published in the 1960s, the political scientist Anthony Downs identifies several ways in which institutions discriminate against poor people and blacks in particular: by providing assistance in ways that emphasize dependency; by imposing higher costs for goods and services; by omitting impoverished people from social insurance schemes; by denying services (mortgage loans, credit, municipal services); and by maintaining public schools of lower quality.[64]

Manuel Carballo states that the failure to take account of racism and discrimination is a major weakness in how conservatives approach the problem of poverty:

The central mission element, by omission or commission, in the conservative view of poverty, drawn as it is from the intellectual roots of a then racially homogenous Great Britain, is its failure to grasp the basic relationship in multi-racial America between racism and poverty. While most of the poor are white, disproportionate numbers of the poor are black, Hispanic (that is, primarily mulatto or mestizo), and native American....Racism is by no means the sole or indeed perhaps even the primary cause of poverty among minorities....But racism does have a lot to do with the concentration of minorities in municipalities whose tax base cannot carry quality public education; in neighborhoods that make minorities the disproportionate victims of crime; in jobs that are part-time, low-wage, and without the benefits of health insurance, pensions, or even social security.[65]

Discrimination means that the skills necessary for economic mobility are inaccessible to people of color; it means that job promotions are unequally distributed on the basis of race and ethnicity; and it means that information about economic opportunities is not distributed uniformly or consistently.

The connections between discrimination and poverty are suggested in one case study of Massachusetts by the sociologist James E. Blackwell. He reviews the reasons for unemployment among black youth.[66] In his view, people of color are subject to discriminatory practices, both formal and informal, which have detrimental consequences in the following areas: skills/union apprenticeship programs; availability of mortgages; economic dislocation; job promotions; equity of wages; and availability of information and informational networks about employment opportunities.

Racial segregation, as suggested by the sociologists Douglas S. Massey and Nancy A. Denton and even earlier by Kenneth Clark, goes hand in hand with racism and discrimination. Massey and Denton's study "indicates that racial residential segregation is the principal structural feature of American society responsible for the perpetuation of urban poverty and represents a primary cause of racial inequality in the United States."[67] Elsewhere, Massey writes that continuing racial segregation

> acts to undermine the socioeconomic environment faced by poor blacks and leave their communities extremely vulnerable to any downturn in the economy. Under conditions of high racial segregation, a rise in the black poverty rates produces a dramatic loss in potential demand in poor black neighborhoods, leading to the withdrawal, deterioration, and outright elimination of goods and services distributed through the market.[68]

Racial segregation, in other words, exacerbates the ill effects of downturns in the economy or poverty increases among black individuals or families to a far greater extent than among whites. Understanding the relationship between racial segregation and poverty, according to Massey, provides insight into why the composition of the underclass is black and why this sector is concentrated in the Northeast and the Midwest. Massey posits that "segregation heightens and reinforces negative racial stereotypes by concentrating people who fit those stereotypes in a small number of highly visible minority neighborhoods—a structural version of 'blaming the victim'—thereby hardening prejudice, making discrimination more likely, and maintaining the motivation for segregation. The persistence of segregation, in turn, worsens the concentration of poverty."[69]

Family Structure as an Explanation

As suggested in many popular and academic forums, dysfunctional family structure is a popular explanation for poverty, and sometimes the so-called breakdown of the family is offered as a major reason that individuals and families fall into poverty; this belief persists despite overwhelming and growing evidence that this link is much more complex than is suggested by the claim. The demographer Mary Jo Bane writes: "It has become common knowledge—whether true or no—that family structure is important in explaining contemporary poverty....[But] in fact, previous research...indicates that a rather small percentage of the changes in the poverty level over the past few decades can be attributed to demographic change."[70] Bane concludes that a focus on family structure is erroneous: "The problem of poverty should be addressed by devoting attention to employment, wages, and the development of skills necessary for productive participation in the labor force rather than hand wringing about the decline of the family."[71]

Despite increasing evidence to support this view, however, the family structure explanation suggested by Daniel Patrick Moynihan and, much earlier, by the sociologist E. Franklin Frazier, not only remains conventionally popular but reflects much of current social welfare policies in the United States. The "feminization of poverty" has been turned to as a special feature of the relationship between family structure and poverty. This term, supposedly coined by Diana Pearce,[72] is used to indicate that female-headed families are more susceptible to poverty than male-headed or two-parent families. Although the term may be recent, Mimi Abramovitz shows that women's impoverishment dates back to colonial America, when from one-third to one-half of a town's poor were likely to be female.[73] Thus, the *feminization of poverty* may be a misnomer if it suggests that this is a new development in the national profile and history of poverty.

Bane provides a statistical overview of poverty characteristics and trends associated with female-headed households.[74] Barbara Ehrenreich and her associates (1983) discuss how women are particularly exploited in the United States. This qualitative study provides case studies and cameos of women who are experiencing poverty. One conclusion of the book is that "a job is not necessarily an antidote to poverty for women. On the contrary, the jobs available to women are part of the problem."[75] Women, according to these authors, are clustered in only 20 out of 420 occupations listed by the Bureau of Labor Statistics. These occupations tend to offer the lowest pay.

In her article, published in 1978, Pearce suggests that race is not as significant a factor as gender in explaining the depressed economic condition of poor women.[76] But, as shown by the extensive work of the political economist Julianne Malveaux and others, it is not accurate to dismiss important racial distinctions in the poverty experiences of women. Malveaux describes how the labor experiences of black and white women differ significantly.[77] Gertrude S. Goldberg and Eleanor Kremin respond to Pearce by writing that "in the United States, black and Hispanic single mothers suffer poverty rates 50 percent greater than their white counterparts, and black women are three times as likely as white women to be in the economically vulnerable position of single motherhood. Three-fifths of poor, single-mother families in the United States, moreover, are women of color and their children."[78]

A strong precedent for utilizing family structure as an explanation for poverty is the Moynihan Report, published in 1965, which proposed a link between the family structure of blacks and poverty:

> The circumstances of the Negro American community in recent years have probably been getting worse, not better....the fundamental problem, in which this is most clearly the case, is that of family structure...so long as this situation persists, the cycle of poverty and disadvantage will continue to repeat itself.[79]

Other observers, such as Banfield, have gone so far as to suggest a cultural predisposition on the part of lower-class groups not to maintain stable families, leading to greater levels of poverty among these groups.[80]

In a book based on an analysis of U.S. Bureau of the Census data for 1980, the researchers Reynolds Farley and Walter Allen conclude that

> the best single category of explanations for race differences in the organization of family life in contemporary U.S. society would seem to be those that attribute importance to race differences in functional relationship with the larger society and its institutions. Black-white differences in economic well-being, political power, and social standing—more so than differences in values and predispositions—explain the observed race differences in family organization and process.[81]

This finding has been confirmed by other studies. The Joint Center for Political and Economic Studies, for example, reports that

> while family structure is an important factor in determining whether a black child will be poor, the decline in marriage and the increased proportion of births occurring out of wedlock do not account fully for the decline in children's economic well-being. Indeed, the study revealed that the economic slippage experienced by all types of black families—whether headed by married couples, never-married women, or formerly married women—played at least as great a role as family structure change in the worsening status of black children.[82]

It is clear that single-female-headed households have a higher poverty rate than single-male-headed or two-parent households. But the implications of this relationship are not as clear and conclusive as some would contend. A clear and consistent poverty gap at the national level remains among black, white, and Latino families of similar composition. White families tend to be better off in economic terms than comparably structured black and Latino families. This fact tends to dampen the unqualified claim that "family breakup" causes poverty.

There are examples of other national social welfare systems that do not reflect a strong correlation between single, female heads of household and poverty status. Sweden is one such example. As Goldberg and Kremin write:

> In the United States it has long been assumed that there is a direct link between poverty and family composition or single motherhood. However, Sweden has gone far toward breaking this link—a notable achievement. Single motherhood is about as prevalent in Sweden as it is in the U.S. By using a combination of labor market and social policies...Sweden has achieved a relatively low rate of poverty for single parent families.[83]

As the case of Sweden suggests, the relationship between single female heads of households and poverty status is not pre-determined. Even in the United States, there are some periods when increasing the rate of labor-force participation for women, coupled with decent wages, has reduced poverty status for single-female-headed families. For example, in reviewing the immediate post-World War II period, Richard X. Chase reports that increasing labor force participation rates for women during that period resulted in some reduction in the poverty rate for female heads of households.[84] Chase's study shows that the incidence of poverty for all female-headed families was reduced from 51.5 percent in 1947 to 49.2 percent in 1956, and to 47.6 percent in 1963. These reductions were due to the increasing labor-participation rate of women earning wages that enabled them to live above the poverty level. During these same years, however, the incidence of poverty for male-headed families fell even more dramatically, from 29.9 percent in 1947 to 19.8 percent in 1956, and to 15.6 percent in 1963.

Dependency as an Explanation

Charles A. Murray (1984) proposes that the poor remain so because they have become psychologically and programmatically dependent on unjustifiably generous government largesse.[85] If such programs did not exist, he argues, then presumably the poor would be forced not only to look for work but also to maintain stable two-parent families, which would eventually enable them to move out of poverty. This belief is held widely by both blacks and whites, according to a survey reported by Sigelman and Welch. They report that 71 percent of blacks and 86 percent of whites believe that "welfare encourages people to work less."[86]

"Permissiveness" rather than generosity is the culprit in explaining welfare dependency, according to Lawrence M. Mead. He believes that poverty is perpetuated by the U.S. social welfare system because it permits people to receive benefits without demanding a return. Poor people should be encouraged to become independent and competent by first reflecting "good citizenship." This would reduce the number of unwed mothers and jobless men, Mead claims.[87] Arguments that the welfare system is a major cause of increases in the number of single female heads of household are not supported by hard data, as pointed out by Isabel V. Sawhill: "The literature on the relationship between the welfare system and the growth of female-headed families suggests that welfare can account for no more than 15 to 25 percent of the growth in the incidence of women heading families over this period, or—at most—for a 0.4 percentage-point increase in the poverty rate."[88]

The relatively high proportion and growth of single-female-headed households among blacks and Latinos should be of concern. But it cannot be shown definitively or analytically, according to the political scientist Adolph H. Reed,[89] that this growth reflects male irresponsibility or a pathological and pathetic dependency on public assistance, as has been argued by other writers cited earlier. The argument that dependency is caused by government handouts, although a popular and seductive explanation of persistent poverty, has little basis in hard evidence.

William J. Wilson and Kathryn M. Neckerman have reported that many studies that have focused on the relationship between welfare benefits and out-of-wedlock births show that there is no association between these two factors. Furthermore, there is no relationship between varying state AFDC benefit levels and states' out-of-wedlock birth rates.[90] According to these authors, one reason for the higher level of single female heads of household in black communities is that the pool of "marriageable" black men has declined rapidly in the past two to three decades.[91] This means that the availability of black men with jobs who could support a family has declined considerably since World War II. There are fewer and fewer black men who can support families as a result of continuing unemployment, hence the increase in black-female-headed families since that era. The Joint Center for Political and Economic Studies reported that "nationally, less than 40 percent of black males aged 16 to 64 years are working full time, compared with almost 55 percent of white males."[92] Table 1.3 illustrates further the disparate rates of labor-force participation for black and white males.

TABLE 1.3
Labor Force Participation Rates of Males, 16 to 34 Years, and by Race, 1950-80

	1950	1960	1970	1980
Black males (16-19 yrs)	55.8	42.4	35.8	36.5
White males (16-19 yrs)	51.5	51.1	48.9	55.5
Black males (20-24)	80.4	82.0	76.4	73.5
White males (20-24)	82.1	86.8	81.6	84.3
Black males (25-34)	86.2	88.5	87.6	83.5
White males (25-34)	92.8	95.7	94.7	94.3

SOURCE: William J. Wilson and Kathryn M. Neckerman, "Poverty and Family Structure: The Widening Gap between Evidence and Public Policy Issues," in *Fighting Poverty: What Works and What Doesn't*, ed. Sheldon H. Danziger and Daniel H. Weinberg (Cambridge, Mass.: Harvard University Press, 1986), table 10.4.

Wilson and Neckerman argue that black women with children are not marrying at a higher rate due to the relative lack of employed or employable, that is, marriageable, black men. The differences in the labor-force participation rate of black and of white males help to explain the greater proportion of single-female-headed families among blacks. Although this proposition was made in earlier studies, the continuing decline of black male participation in the labor market has revived it as an explanation for the changing structure of black families. Like Wilson and Neckerman, a report of the Center for the Study of Social Policy, issued in 1985, states:

> Census and labor force data show that nearly half of the black male population age 16-64 is either unemployed, out of the labor force, in prisons, or their labor force status cannot be determined by available data. In contrast, only 23 percent of white men age 16-64 are in a similar situation....[C]orresponding increases in the number of black female-headed families may be rooted in the fact that many black men are jobless and thus unable to support families.[93]

Along this line of thought, Wilson and Neckerman point out that

> in the 1960s scholars readily attributed black family deterioration to the problems of male joblessness. However, in the past ten to fifteen years, in the face of the overwhelming focus on welfare as the major source of black family break-up, concerns about the importance of male joblessness have receded into the background. We argue in this paper that the available evidence justifies renewed scholarly and public policy attention to the connection between the disintegration of poor families and black male prospects for stable employment.[94]

The economist William A. Darity Jr. and his colleagues focus on this lack of marriageable black men. In addition to considering declining labor-force participation as a cause, Darity et al. cite imprisonment, murder, suicide, drugs, and racial discrimination as major explanations for the relatively small pool of marriageable black men.[95]

One researcher who has identified the gender ratio in the black community as being related to family structure and economic consequences is the political economist Manning Marable. In an internationally recognized work, *How Capitalism Underdeveloped Black America*, he proposes that black men are being imprisoned at much higher rates than whites and that this is reflected in the deteriorating racial and economic development of the black community.[96] According to the political scientist Andrew Hacker, this situation is not improving: the availability of black men is decreasing, which means that the relatively large presence of single-black-female-headed households may be the norm for a long period. As Hacker writes:

> The pool of "marriageable" black men gets smaller every year....over half a million black men are in jails and prisons, and as many more could be sent or returned there if they violate their parole or probation....Another large group is debilitated by drugs or alcohol or mental illness. In addition, the death rates for younger men have reached terrifying levels.[97]

Lack of Political Empowerment as an Explanation

Lack of political power has been suggested as another explanation for the continuing status of poverty among some groups, especially those questionably labeled as the "black underclass." The social scientists Paul A. Baran and Paul M. Sweezy discussed the role of potential and economic power in maintaining poverty in the mid-1960s:

> The system has two poles: wealth, privilege, power at one; poverty, deprivation, powerlessness at the other....Today, Negroes are at the bottom, and there is neither room above nor anyone ready to take their place....For the many, nothing short of a complete change in the system—the abolition of both poles and the substitution of a society in which wealth and power are shared by all—can transform their condition.[98]

This theme is repeated by the black studies scholar Hermon George Jr.: "The subordination process is essentially a set of political-economic relationships which, dictated by U.S. capitalism, have determined the specific forms of inclusive exclusion which have characterized the histories of groups incorporated into the social order, in particular, people of African, Latin American, and Asian descent."[99] The political scientist Bette Woody also sees the political decisions of a conservative government as a major factor in the maintenance of poverty. She believes that an example of this is manifested by the government's refusal to respond to the negative impact of a changing economy on black income earners:

> Two political factors have hampered fuller recognition of the impact of a changing economy on black earners. One is the absence of government response to the massive shift in the economy from production to services and a corresponding changeover in the gender

composition of the American workforce. The second is the rise of an aggressive political conservatism in the United States, which uses selective indicators that emphasize social behavior as a cause of poverty.[100]

A political explanation for poverty and depressed economic opportunities for African American women is offered by F. I. Ajanaku et al., who argue that the underdevelopment of black women and their economic potential has taken place at the same time that capital accumulation has benefited European Americans. This imbalance has not been rectified by black women because they lack the political power to advocate effectively on their own behalf.[101]

Martin Luther King Jr. defined the nature of persistent poverty fundamentally as a reflection of the political power and moral will of the wealthy and better-off sectors in society.[102] He argued that only political power on the part of the poor can solve the problem of poverty in the United States—that only "power can transform the ghetto." According to King, resolving the problem of poverty also requires confronting the growing militarization and imperialism of the U.S. government. King believed, furthermore, that capitalism—or at least the excesses of U.S. capitalism rather than individual or group deficiencies—produces and is responsible for poverty.

The National Conference of Catholic Bishops issued a "Pastoral Letter on U.S. Economy" in November 1987, in which it implicitly endorsed King's earlier message regarding effective strategies for the elimination of poverty in American society. This letter calls for greater national emphasis on the problem of poverty:

> If the U.S. were a country in which poverty existed amidst relatively equitable income distribution, one might argue that we do not have the resources to provide everyone with an adequate living. But, in fact, this is a country marked by glaring inequitable distribution of wealth and necessities....[G]ross inequalities are morally unjustifiable, particularly when millions lack even the bare necessities of life. In our judgement, the distribution of income and wealth in the U.S. is so inequitable that it violates this minimum standard of distributive justice.[103]

This statement defines poverty and growing social inequality, as King had earlier, as a national economic and moral crisis, one that requires a political response on the part of the poor and their advocates.

Notes

This chapter appeared previously in *Understanding the Nature of Poverty in Urban America* (Westport, Conn.: Praeger, 1994).

1. Karl Polanyi, *The Great Transformation: The Political and Economic Origin of Our Time* (Boston: Beacon Press, 1944), 91.

2. Ibid., 93.

3. W. E. B. Du Bois, "The Revelation of Saint Orgne the Damned," in *W. E .B. Du Bois Speaks: Speeches and Addresses*, ed. Philip S. Foner (New York: Pathfinder Press, 1970), 107.

4. William W. Goldsmith and Edward J. Blakely, *Separate Societies: Poverty and Inequality in US Cities* (Philadelphia: Temple University Press, 1992).

5. Barry R. Schiller, *The Economics of Poverty and Discrimination* (Englewood Cliffs, N.J.: Prentice-Hall, 1976), 40.

6. Lee Sigelman and Susan Welch, *Black Americans' View of Racial Inequality: The Dream Deferred* (New York: Cambridge University Press, 1991), 86.

7. Schiller, *The Economics of Poverty and Discrimination*, 40.

8. Michael Sherraden, *Assets and the Poor* (Armonk, N.Y.: M. E. Sharpe, 1991), 35.

9. Chaim I. Waxman, *The Stigma of Poverty* (New York: Pergamon, 1983), 1.

10. Jay R. Mandel, *The Roots of Black Poverty: The Southern Plantation Economy after the Civil War* (Durham, N.C.: Duke University Press, 1978).

11. W. E. B. Du Bois, *Black Reconstruction in America, 1860-1880* (New York: Atheneum, 1985), 696. Originally published in 1935.

12. Mandel, *The Roots of Black Poverty*, 121.

13. James Jennings and Monte Rivera, eds., *Puerto Rican Politics in Urban America* (Westport, Conn.: Greenwood Press, 1984).

14. Elizabeth Pleck, *Black Migration and Poverty, Boston 1865-1900* (New York: Academic Press, 1979), 199.

15. Harold X. Connally, *A Ghetto Grows in Brooklyn* (New York: New York University Press, 1977); Gilbert Osofsky, *Harlem: The Making of a Ghetto* (New York: Harper and Row, 1966); and Kenneth L. Kusmer, *Black Cleveland: 1870-1930* (Chicago: University of Illinois Press, 1976).

16. Cesar A. Iglesias, *Memorias de Bernardo Vega* (Puerto Rico: Ediciones Huracan, 1980).

17. Henry George, *Progress and Poverty: An Inquiry into the Cause of Industrial Depressions and of Increase of Want with Increase of Wealth* (New York: Robert Schalkenbach Foundation, 1958), 296. Originally published in 1879.

18. Stephen Thernstrom, *Poverty and Progress: Social Mobility in a Nineteenth-Century City* (New York: Atheneum, 1969), 131.

19. William J. Wilson, *The Truly Disadvantaged: The Inner City, the Underclass and Public Policy* (Chicago: University of Chicago Press, 1987), 40. See also John D. Kasarda, "Urban Change and Minority Opportunities," in *The New Urban Poverty*, ed. Paul E. Peterson (Washington, D.C.: Brookings Institute, 1985), 50.

20. Vilma Ortiz, "Latinos and Industrial Change in New York and Los Angeles," in *Hispanics in the Labor Force*, ed. Edwin Melendez et al. (New York: Plenum, 1991), 125. See also Kasarda, "Urban Change and Minority Opportunities."

21. Jeanne E. Griffith, Mary J. Frasc, and John H. Ralph, *American Education: The Challenge of Change* (Washington, D.C.: Population on Reference Bureau, 1989), 9-10; Dawn M. Beskerville, "Poverty vs. Academic Achievement," *Black Enterprise* (March 1991): 37.

22. *Statistical Abstract of the United States: 1992*, 112th ed. (Washington, D.C.: U.S. Bureau of the Census), 459.

23. Jose E. Cruz, *Developing a Puerto Rican Agenda for Research and Research Advocacy* (Washington, D.C.: National Puerto Rican Coalition, 1992), 7.

24. Norman Fainstein, "The Underclass/Mismatch Hypothesis as an Explanation for Black Economic Deprivation," *Politics and Society* 15, no. 4 (1986-87): 403.

25. Oscar Lewis, *La Vida: A Puerto Rican Family in the Culture of Poverty* (New York: Random House, 1966).

26. Edward C. Banfield, *The Unheavenly City* (Boston: Little, Brown, 1973).

27. George Gilder, "The Collapse of the American Family," *Public Interest* 89 (Fall 1987): 20.

28. George Gilder, "The Nature of Poverty," in *Social Welfare Policy: Perspectives, Patterns and Insights*, ed. I. C. Colby (Chicago: Dorsey Press, 1989).

29. Manuel Carballo and Mary Jo Bane, *The State and the Poor in the 1980s* (Westport, Conn.: Auburn Publishing, 1984), xxi.

30. George Gilder, *Wealth and Poverty* (New York: Basic Books, 1981), 69, 71.

31. Lowell E. Galloway, *Poverty in America* (Columbus: Grid, 1973), 91.

32. William J. Wilson, "The Ghetto Underclass and the Social Transformation of the Inner City," *Black Scholar* 19, no. 3 (1988): 16.

33. Charles A. Valentine, *Culture and Poverty: Critique and Counter Proposals* (Chicago: University of Chicago Press, 1968).

34. Kenneth B. Clark, *Dark Ghetto* (New York: Harper and Row, 1965), 130.

35. Valentine, *Culture and Poverty*, 82.

36. Ibid., 155.

37. Manning Marable, "The Contradictory Contours of Black Political Culture," in *The Year Left 2*, ed. Mike Davis, Michael Sprinker, Manning Marable, and Fred Pfeil (London: Verso, 1987); Cornel West, "Race and Social Theory: Towards a Genealogical Materialist Analysis," in *The Year Left 2*, ed. Mike Davis, Michael Sprinker, Manning Marable, and Fred Pfeil (London: Verso, 1987).

38. Robert L. Woodson, *On the Road to Economic Freedom* (Washington, D.C.: Regnery Gateway, 1987); Nathan Glazer, *The Limits of Social Policy* (Cambridge, Mass.: Harvard University Press, 1989).

39. Francis Fox Piven and Richard A. Cloward, *Regulating the Poor* (New York: Pantheon, 1971); Charles V. Hamilton, "A Patron-Recipient Relationship and Minority Politics in New York City," *Political Science Quarterly* 94, no. 2 (1979).

40. Goldsmith and Blakely, *Separate Societies*, 11.

41. Stanley Lieberson, *A Piece of the Pie: Black and White Immigrants since 1880* (Berkeley and Los Angeles: University of California Press, 1980).

42. Charles V. Hamilton, "Political Access, Minority Participation, and the New Normalcy," in *Minority Report: What Has Happened to Blacks, Hispanics, American Indians, and Other Minorities in the Eighties*, ed. Leslie W. Dunbar (New York: Pantheon, 1984), 8.

43. Gerald D. Suttles, *The Social Order of the Slum* (Chicago: University of Chicago Press, 1968).

44. Mark Rosenman, "How the Poor Would Remedy Poverty: A Review Essay," *Social Policy* 18, no. 4 (1988): 62.

45. Dennis Gilbert and Joseph A. Kahl, eds., *The American Class Structure: A New Synthesis* (Chicago: Dorsey Press, 1987), 294.

46. Wilson, *The Truly Disadvantaged*.

47. David Osborne, *Laboratories of Democracy: A New Breed of Governor Creates Models for National Growth* (Cambridge, Mass.: Harvard Business School Press, 1990), 289.

48. Vijai P. Singh, "The Underclass in the United States: Some Correlates of Economic Change," *Sociological Inquiry* 61, no. 4 (1991): 509.

49. Rebecca M. Blank and Alan S. Blinder, "Macroeconomics, Income Distribution, and Poverty," in *Fighting Poverty: What Works and What Doesn't*, ed. Sheldon H. Danziger and Daniel H. Weinberg (Cambridge, Mass.: Harvard University Press, 1986), 189.

50. Ibid., 184.

51. James Thornton, Richard Agnello, and Charles Link, "Poverty and Economic Growth: Trickle Down Peters Out," *Economic Inquiry* 16, no. 3 (1978): 385-93.

52. Theodore Cross, *The Black Power Imperative* (New York: Faulkner, 1984).

53. U.S. Department of Commerce, Bureau of the Census, *Statistical Abstract of the United States, 1992* (Washington, D.C.: Government Printing Office, 1992), table 674.

54. William J. Wilson, Robert Aponte, Joleen Kirscheman, and Lois J. O. Wocquaint, "The Ghetto Underclass and the Changing Structure of Urban Poverty," in *Quiet Riots: Race and Poverty in the United States*, ed. Fred Harris and Roger Wilkins (New York: Pantheon, 1988).

55. Brett Williams, "Poverty among African-Americans in the United States," *Human Organizations* 51, no. 2 (1992): 167.

56. George, *Progress and Poverty*, 17.

57. American Federation of Labor and Congress of Industrial Organizations, "The Low-Paid Worker," in *Poverty in America*, ed. Louis A. Ferman, Joyce L. Kornbluh, and Alan Haber (Ann Arbor: University of Michigan Press, 1969), 190.

58. Gabriel Kolko, *Wealth and Power in America: An Analysis of Social Class and Income Distribution* (New York: Praeger, 1962).

59. Barry Bluestone "Lower-Income Workers and Marginal Industries," in *Poverty in America*, ed. Louis A. Ferman, Joyce L. Kornbluh, and Alan Haber (Ann Arbor: University of Michigan Press, 1969).

60. Sar A. Levitan and Isaac Schapiro, *Working but Poor: America's Contradiction* (Baltimore: Johns Hopkins University Press, 1987).

61. Isaac Schapiro, *No Escape: The Minimum Wage and Poverty* (Washington, D.C.: Center on Budget and Policy Priorities, 1987).

62. Linda R. Martin and Demetrios Giannaros, "Would a Higher Minimum Wage Help Poor Families Headed by Women?" *Monthly Labor Review* (August 1990): 36.

63. Ronald B. Mincy, "Raising the Minimum Wage: Effects on Family Policy," *Monthly Labor Review* (July 1990): 24.

64. Anthony Downs, *Who Are the Urban Poor?* (New York: Committee for Economic Development, 1970).

65. Carballo and Bane, *The State and the Poor in the 1980s*, xxii.

66. James E. Blackwell, *Youth Employment and Unemployment: Outreach Initiatives in Massachusetts and the City of Boston* (Boston: William M. Trotter Institute, University of Massachusetts, 1987).

67. Douglas S. Massey and Nancy A. Denton, *American Apartheid: Segregation and the Making of the Underclass* (Cambridge, Mass.: Harvard University Press, 1993), viii.

68. Douglas S. Massey, "American Apartheid: Segregation and the Making of the Underclass," *Poverty and Race* 1, no. 4 (1992): 2.

69. Ibid., 4.

70. Mary Jo Bane, "Household Composition and Poverty," in *Fighting Poverty: What Works and What Doesn't*, ed. Sheldon H. Danziger and Daniel H. Weinberg (Cambridge, Mass.: Harvard University Press, 1986), 209.

71. Ibid., 231.

72. Diana Pearce, "The Feminization of Poverty: Women, Work and Welfare," *Urban and Social Change Review* 11 (February 1978).

73. Mimi Abramovitz, *Regulating the Lives of Women: Social Welfare Policy from Colonial Times to Present* (Boston: South End Press, 1989), 76.

74. Mary Jo Bane, "Politics and Policies of Feminization of Poverty," in *The Politics of Social Policy in the U.S.*, ed. Margaret Weir, Ann S. Orloff, and Theda Skcopol (Princeton, N.J.: Princeton University Press, 1988).

75. Barbara Ehrenreich, Holly Sklar, and Karen Stallard, *Poverty in the American Dream: Women and Children First* (Boston: South End Press, 1983), 18.

76. Pearce, "The Feminization of Poverty," 34.

77. Julianne Malveaux, "The Political Economy of Black Women," in *Race, Politics and Economic Development: Community Perspective*, ed. James Jennings (London: Verso Press, 1992).

78. Gertrude S. Goldberg and Eleanor Kremin, *The Feminization of Poverty: Only in America?* (New York: Praeger, 1990), 5.

79. Daniel P. Moynihan, *The Negro Family, the Case for National Action* (Washington, D.C.: Government Printing Office, 1965), 30.

80. Banfield, *The Unheavenly City*.

81. Reynolds Farley and Walter Allen, *The Color Line and the Quality of Life in America* (New York: Oxford University Press, 1989), 187.

82. Cynthia Rexroat, *The Declining Economic Status of Black Children* (Washington, D.C.: Joint Center for Political and Economic Studies, 1990), 4.

83. Goldberg and Kremin, *The Feminization of Poverty*, 202.

84. Richard X. Chase, "Trends in Poverty Incidence and Its Rate of Reduction for Various Demographic Groups: 1947-1963," Ph.D. diss., University of Maryland, 1966; Peter Karsten, "A Quarter Century of Poverty in the US, 1947-1972: Definitions, Change, Continuity and the Future," in *Collected Papers on Poverty Issues*, ed. Doris Yokelson (New York: Hudson Institute, 1975).

85. Charles A. Murray, "The Two Wars against Poverty: Economic Growth and the Great Society," *Public Interest* 69 (Autumn 1982); Charles A. Murray, *Losing Ground: American Social Policy, 1950-1980* (New York: Basic Books, 1984).

86. Sigelman and Welch, *Black Americans' View of Racial Inequality*, 141.

87. Lawrence M. Mead, *Beyond Entitlement: The Social Obligations of Citizenship* (New York: Free Press, 1986).

88. Isabel Sawhill, "Poverty and the Underclass," in *Challenges to Leadership: Economic and Social Issues for the Next Decade* (Washington, D.C.: Urban Institute Press, 1988), 220.

89. Adolph H. Reed, "The Underclass as Myth and Symbol: The Poverty of Discourse about Poverty," *Radical America* 24, no. 1 (1991).

90. William J. Wilson and Kathryn M. Neckerman, "Poverty and Family Structure: The Widening Gap between Evidence and Public Policy Issues," in *Fighting Poverty: What Works and What Doesn't*, ed. Sheldon H. Danziger and Daniel H. Weinberg (Cambridge, Mass.: Harvard University Press, 1986), 248.

91. Ibid., 252-59.

92. Katherine McFate, *The Metropolitan Area Fact Book: Statistical Portrait of Blacks and Whites* (Washington, D.C.: Joint Center for Political and Economic Studies, 1988), 8.

93. Center for Social Policy, *The Flip Side of Female-headed Families: Black Adult Men* (Washington, D.C.: Center for Social Policy, 1985), i.

94. Wilson and Neckerman, "Poverty and Family Structure," 256.

95. William A. Darity Jr., Samuel L. Myers, William J. Sobol, and Emmett Carson, "How Useful Is the Black Underclass?" *Focus* 13, no. 2 (1991): 12; William P. O'Hare, Kelvin M. Pollard, Taynia L. Mann, and Mary M. Kent, *African Americans in the 1990s* (Washington, D.C.: Population Reference Bureau, 1991).

96. Manning Marable, *How Capitalism Underdeveloped Black America* (Boston: South End Press, 1983).

97. Andrew Hacker, *Two Nations: Black and White, Separate, Hostile, Unequal* (New York: Scribner's, 1992), 75.

98. Paul A. Baran and Paul M. Sweezy, *Monopoly Capital: An Essay on the American Economic and Social Order* (New York: Monthly Review Press, 1966), 279.

99. Hermon George Jr., "Black Americans, the 'Underclass' and the Subordination Process," *Black Scholar* 19, no. 3 (1988): 48.

100. Bette Woody, *Black Women in the Workplace: Impacts of Structural Change in the Economy* (Westport, Conn.: Greenwood Press, 1992), 9.

101. F. I. Ajanaku, M. L. Jackson, and T. S. Mosley, "Underdevelopment in the U.S. Labor Market: The Case of African American Female Workers," *Urban League Review* 14, no. 2 (1990): 29-41.

102. Martin Luther King Jr., *Where Do We Go from Here: Chaos or Community?* (Boston: Beacon Press, 1967).

103. National Conference of Catholic Bishops, "Pastoral Letter on U.S. Economy," *Economic Justice for All* (November 1987).

DISCUSSION QUESTIONS

1. What are the major explanations of persistent poverty in the United States; how are these explanations similar to or different from those that you have read or heard about earlier?

2. What is the validity of explanations of poverty that focus on individual behavior?

3. What is the validity of explanations of poverty that focus on social structures?

4. What are the major explanations of black poverty?

5. Evaluate the argument that the lack of political power is the major cause of poverty.

6. Assess the political implications of at least two different explanations of persistent poverty.

7. How is the relationship between political power and poverty explained?

FOR FURTHER READING

Abramovitz, Mimi (1989) *Regulating the Lives of Women: Social Welfare Policy from Colonial Times to Present*. Boston: South End Press.

Banfield, Edward C. (1973) *The Unheavenly City*. Boston: Little, Brown.

Baran, Paul A., and Paul M. Sweezy (1966) *Monopoly Capital: An Essay on the American Economic and Social Order*. New York: Monthly Review Press.

Clark, Kenneth B. (1965) *Dark Ghetto*. New York: Harper and Row.

Connally, Harold X. (1977) *A Ghetto Grows in Brooklyn*. New York: New York University Press.

Cross, Theodore (1984) *The Black Power Imperative*. New York: Faulkner.

Du Bois, W. E. B. (1935) *Black Reconstruction in America, 1860-1880*. New York: Atheneum (1985).

Ehrenreich, Barbara, Holly Sklar, and Karen Stallard (1983) *Poverty in the American Dream: Women and Children First*. Boston: South End Press.

Farley, Reynolds, and Walter Allen (1989) *The Color Line and the Quality of Life in America*. New York: Oxford University Press.

George, Henry (1879) *Progress and Poverty: An Inquiry into the Cause of Industrial Depressions and of Increase of Want with Increase of Wealth*. Reprint ed. (1958). New York: Robert Schalkenbach Foundation.

Gilder, George (1989) "The Nature of Poverty," in I. C. Colby (ed.), *Social Welfare Policy: Perspectives, Patterns and Insights*. Chicago: Dorsey Press.

Glazer, Nathan (1989) *The Limits of Social Policy*. Cambridge, Mass.: Harvard University Press.

Goldberg, Gertrude S., and Eleanor Kremin (1990) *The Feminization of Poverty: Only in America?* New York: Praeger.

Goldsmith, William W., and Edward J. Blakely (1992) *Separate Societies: Poverty and Inequality in U.S. Cities*. Philadelphia: Temple University Press.

Hacker, Andrew (1992) *Two Nations: Black and White, Separate, Hostile, Unequal*. New York: Charles Scribner's.

Hamilton, Charles V. (1979) "A Patron-Recipient Relationship and Minority Politics in New York City," *Political Science Quarterly* 94(2).

King, Martin Luther, Jr. (1967) *Where Do We Go from Here: Chaos or Community?* Boston: Beacon Press.

Lewis, Oscar (1966) *La Vida: A Puerto Rican Family in the Culture of Poverty*. New York: Random House.

Lieberson, Stanley (1980) *A Piece of the Pie: Black and White Immigrants since 1880*. Berkeley: University of California Press.

Malveaux, Julianne (1992) "The Political Economy of Black Women," in James Jennings (ed.), *Race, Politics and Economic Development: Community Perspective*. London: Verso Press.

Mandel, Jay R. (1978) *The Roots of Black Poverty: The Southern Plantation Economy after the Civil War*. Durham, N.C.: Duke University Press.

Massey, Douglas S., and Nancy Denton (1993) *American Apartheid: Segregation and the Making of the Underclass*. Cambridge, Mass.: Harvard University Press.

Moynihan, Daniel P. (1965) *The Negro Family: The Case for National Action*. Washington, D.C.: U.S. Government Printing Office.

Murray, Charles A. (1984) *Losing Ground: American Social Policy, 1950-1980*. New York: Basic Books.

Piven, Francis Fox, and Richard A. Cloward (1971) *Regulating the Poor*. New York: Pantheon.

Pleck, Elizabeth (1979) *Black Migration and Poverty, Boston 1865-1900*. New York: Academic Press.

Schapiro, Isaac (1987) *No Escape: The Minimum Wage and Poverty*. Washington, D.C.: Center on Budget and Policy Priorities.

Schiller, Barry R. (1976) *The Economics of Poverty and Discrimination*. Englewood Cliffs, N.J.: Prentice-Hall.

Sherraden, Michael (1991) *Assets and the Poor*. Armonk, N.Y.: M.E. Sharpe.

Wilson, William J. (1987) *The Truly Disadvantaged: The Inner City, the Underclass and Public Policy*. Chicago: University of Chicago Press.

Woodson, Robert L. (1987) *On the Road to Economic Freedom*. Washington, D.C.: Regnery Gateway.

Chapter Two

Class, Race, Gender, and Poverty
A Critique of Some Contemporary Theories

David C. Ranney

This essay critiques some of the theoretical underpinnings of a broad political consensus in the United States around the treatment of poverty. Under that consensus, poor people are being displaced from their homes as public housing and other income supports are being systematically removed. Inner-city communities where concentrations of poor black and Latino peoples live are being redeveloped into "mixed-income communities." Poor people are being told by government officials and politicians to find work and to find housing in the private sector. Yet there are neither enough jobs nor enough housing to accommodate people in need. Chicago is a case in point.

In 1997, the Chicago City Council passed a resolution that offered private real estate developers a subsidy worth $281 million to eliminate 974 public housing units for very low income families and to replace them with a mix of housing units for moderate and very high income people. There were only a few dissenting votes. The plan to redevelop the Cabrini-Green development in Chicago is part of a larger policy shift by the U.S. government's Department of Housing and Urban Development (HUD), which is eliminating public housing in favor of a voucher system that would enable poor people to try to find housing in the private sector. It is also part of the U.S. government's general effort at welfare "reform," which is dismantling the social safety net for those in poverty in order to force them into the labor market. While the city council vote indicates local political support for the plan to turn a large public housing development of black people into a "mixed-income community," it is being bitterly opposed by public housing residents, community advocate groups, and parts of organized labor.

The reason for the opposition is clear. During the 1980s, the Chicago metropolitan area suffered a net loss of 152,000 living-wage manufacturing jobs. Half of that loss was absorbed by black and Latino workers.[1] That job loss has not been replaced by comparable jobs, particularly for people of color. If we define unemployment to include people who have given up looking for work and those who work part time but prefer to work full time, the estimated unemployment rates for black and Latinos are 33 percent and 29 percent, respectively. The comparable rate for whites is 8 percent.[2] Furthermore, recent research in Chicago has shown that there are simply not enough jobs available.[3] If all unemployed able-bodied people in Chicago who are qualified for entry-level jobs were to seek employment, there would be more than six people for every available job.

39

If we were to stipulate that these jobs would have to pay enough to provide a very basic standard of living in Chicago, there would be forty-four workers looking for every job. If we lowered our standards to insist that the job pay only enough to bring people above the official poverty line, there would still be thirteen people for every available job.

The impact of the decline in employment opportunities has had a profound impact on available housing for the growing ranks of the very poor (most of whom are black and Latino).[4] Without living-wage jobs, people have less for housing. At the same time, the number of units available at rents that people can afford is declining relative to the demand. During the 1980s the city of Chicago lost forty thousand housing units. Most of these were lost to low-income families. Currently, there are more than two lower-income families looking for housing for every affordable unit in the six-county Chicago region. The plan for Cabrini-Green is just the beginning of a process that will eliminate as many as twenty thousand public housing units, while redeveloping the prime land on which they stand into mixed-income communities. Displacement of families from the existing affordable units is slated to occur at a much faster rate than the replacement of those units. Thus, the 2:1 ratio of housing seekers to housing units will increase drastically as more public housing and other affordable units are eliminated.

Given such a dire outlook on both the employment and housing fronts, one might logically ask where the support for the new housing policy and welfare "reform" is coming from and why. At one level, of course, there is the fact that plans like Cabrini-Green are very profitable to politically connected developers. It has been estimated, for example, that the Cabrini-Green development, which is receiving a public subsidy worth $281 million, will provide political allies of the mayor of Chicago with a potential profit margin of $136 million.[5] But the fervor on the part of politicians, public administrators, and policy analysts in the United States for the policy shift behind Cabrini-Green goes deeper.

Academic research has had an important role to play in the present paradigm shift that is demonizing government and glorifying private markets. Nowhere is this shift more significant than in its implications for public policies relating to poverty and its relation to race. There are two major strains in the research behind this shift; one comes from both universities and the think tanks of the far right.[6] But the other, the topic of this essay, comes from those who consider themselves to be liberals or even Social Democrats. In the remainder of this essay I consider the work of two influential and politically progressive U.S. academics: William Julius Wilson[7] and Michael Porter.[8] The basic argument to be developed is that there is an organic connection between the theories of these authors and the demise of the social safety net that is deeper than even their own specific policy conclusions.

I begin with a brief summary of the work of Wilson and Porter. I then critique some underlying themes that have led both liberal and conservative politicians and policy analysts to accept the dissolution of the social safety net and the public housing program in favor of private sector "solutions," including a search for jobs and housing that do not exist and the development of so-called mixed-income communities. Specifically, I explore the authors' treatment of class, race, and gender; their concepts of the importance of work; their views of globalization, technology, and competition; and their substitution of "policy implications" for politics.

Wilson: Declining Significance of Race, the "Underclass," and Joblessness

The ideas of William Julius Wilson, who is a professor of sociology at Harvard University and an adviser to the Clinton administration, are contained in three books that have been published over the past two decades. In his first book, *The Declining Significance of Race* (1978), Wilson argues that social classes in the United States are becoming more racially diverse. He takes that as proof that race is becoming a less significant determinant of economic success than class. In *The Truly Disadvantaged*, published nine years later, Wilson's emphasis is primarily on the concept of "underclass" and its implications for public policies. The fact that blacks are disproportionately members of the underclass is seen as the legacy of past discrimination, which tends to get reinforced through social isolation and the development of a "tangle of pathology in the inner city" that includes violent crime, mother-only households, welfare dependency, out-of-wedlock births, and teenage pregnancy. These same themes are repeated in his 1996 book, *When Work Disappears*. In this book, however, Wilson backs away from the term *underclass* and speaks instead of *widespread poverty* and *joblessness* as surrogates for what he termed the *underclass* in his previous work. In the most recent book, Wilson argues that the root cause of the tangle of pathologies he describes is what he calls *joblessness:* "Many of today's problems in the inner-city ghetto neighborhoods—crime, family dissolution, welfare, low levels of social organization and so on—are fundamentally a consequence of the disappearance of work" (xiii). Work, to Wilson, is not primarily about income. It is a form of behavior. A job is something that provides the worker with "discipline and regularity," qualities that enable one to suffer the adversity of being poor without resorting to behaviors that reinforce that condition.

Porter: The Competitive Advantage of the Inner City

Porter argues that the problems of inner-city neighborhoods stem from a lack of business investment in these communities and that government efforts to alleviate the poverty in the inner city have failed because they are "based on the wrong model." "Relief programs" such as income assistance, housing subsidies, and food stamps, in Porter's view, can only grow larger unless genuine economic development occurs in the inner city. *Genuine economic development* is defined as business activity that produces jobs and income for inner-city residents. Subsidies to business have not worked and will not work, and subsidies for "tangential efforts" such as housing and neighborhood development do not produce sufficient jobs and income.

Applying the principles developed in his studies of international competitiveness, Porter undertook an investigation of inner-city development and came up with the concept of the "competitive advantage of inner cities." He concludes that the answer lies in private-sector initiative and that government and community organizations must limit their activity to acting as facilitators of such private initiatives. Facilitation involves promoting the competitive advantages of inner-city communities, including their strategic location; their potential contribution to "unique clusters of competitive companies" in the metropolitan region; the fact that there is unmet demand for a number of products and services within the inner city; and the unemployed and underemployed human resources. To capitalize on these advantages, it is important to deal with the disadvantages of the inner city. These include the lack of training and education of many inner-city residents, decaying infrastructure, and the high incidence of violent crime.

The Relative "Insignificance" of Race and Gender

Wilson and Porter both contend that, while there is serious discrimination against racial minorities, race-specific policy proposals will not find political acceptance and will not solve the problem. Wilson's work focuses on what he sees as the problem: joblessness that leads to a "tangle of pathological behaviors." There is a distinction to be made between Wilson and more conservative poverty theorists, a distinction made by Wilson himself. Charles Murray, for example, argued in *Losing Ground* that the Great Society programs of the 1960s and the liberal ideology that went with them actually halted progress in the elimination of poverty. The idea that structural problems and discrimination cause poverty was backed up, according to Murray, by federal programs that destroyed the incentive to work. Wilson spends some time in *The Truly Disadvantaged* discrediting the idea that this was the case. Throughout this book and also, more recently, in *When Work Disappears*, he replaces Murray's formulation of federal programs and liberal ideology as the culprit with his own formulation of "joblessness." In doing so, however, Wilson fails to get away entirely from a key aspect of conservation formulations of poverty—that the cause of poverty lies in the behavior of those living in poverty. As I demonstrate later in this essay, joblessness to Wilson is not so much an economic entity as it is a behavioral one. A job is seen primarily as the place where one learns the behavior that will help one get out and keep out of poverty. Despite arguing that structural factors rather than federal programs were initially the cause of joblessness, the problem today, according to this perspective, boils down to behavior, and the solutions thus lie in correcting such behavior.

Both Wilson and Porter argue that having a job, being better educated, being better trained, and ceasing "aberrant behavior" will resolve most problems. These views not only underlie their own "policy implications" but also help to justify the current political consensus about ending poverty. The destruction of public housing in Chicago, for example, is supposed to contribute to ending concentrations of poverty. Welfare "reform" and the decline of housing support are designed to force "welfare-dependent" individuals out of the world of joblessness. Housing vouchers, job training and placement, and even subsidies to the developers of "mixed-income communities" replace race-specific government action that both Wilson and Porter reject.

The Nature of Social Class

The treatment of social class is critical not only to Wilson's and Porter's analyses and policy conclusions concerning the role of race and gender in poverty formation but to much social science concerned with poverty. Often class is not *directly* discussed at all.

But implicitly it is treated as an individual rather than a social concept and is defined in terms of living standards and/or behaviors that are related to living standards.

The construction of mainstream economics (which is a starting point for Porter) eliminates class in favor of "economic man," who strives as an individual to "maximize utility" through rational choices that are mediated by markets. Increasingly, both political science and sociology are adopting the rational-choice model in their respective fields. Wilson, a sociologist, does directly discuss his conception of social class. And that conception, as we shall see, is a key assumption in all of his work. Interestingly, his explicit definition of social class ends up in the same place as Porter's implicit one—with rational individuals making choices in the market: "Classes are defined in terms of their relationship to other classes within the market where different commodities are bought and sold and where people with various resources (goods, services and skills) meet and interact for purposes of exchange."[9]

In this view, "good behavior" (which includes everything from giving a good interview to getting married) constitutes a "resource" that enables individuals to become more competitive in the world of commodity exchange. This is what enables Wilson to place the existence of "mother-only households" and violent crime in the same general "aberrant" category. It also causes him to emphasize that there are strong links among single parenthood, welfare, and poverty. The problem with these behaviors and the reason they are "aberrant" and "pathological" are that they diminish what one brings to the exchange relationship that defines one as lower class or even underclass.

By defining class in terms of exchange relations, Wilson and Porter make social class independent of most social relations. Class becomes an individual matter, and the only association between one's class and one's relationship to others is a competitive one during the act of exchange. It is also in a sense very "Victorian." According to Adolph Reed Jr., "the underclass image proceeds from a view of class in general that strikingly resembles Victorian convention. In that view, class is not so much a category of social position as the reverse; social position flows naturally from the intrinsic qualities of class."[10] Reed goes on to point out that this view easily allows one to use race and class interchangeably. Each is "imbued with a sense of immutability and independence from social relations." It follows that race is of "declining significance" because what is significant in Wilson's Victorian view of class is one's ability to purchase commodities in the market. The only color that really matters is green. Behavior and culture are "good" or "bad" depending on how well they help an individual compete in market exchange relations.

Success in exchange relations, in turn, depends on the qualities of discipline, regularity, and self-sufficiency. These qualities, according to Wilson, are what you learn at a job—even if your job pays below-poverty wages and offers no benefits. These qualities are undermined in Wilson's view in mother-only households and by welfare dependency, which also determines his view of the role of women. The woman can contribute more to disciplined, regular, and self-sufficient family units by being a willing partner in a two-parent household made stable by marriage. Women who have babies out of wedlock and live off welfare undermine discipline, regularity, and self-sufficiency by failing to establish stable families that can function efficiently as "middle-class" consumer units.

I would ask why Wilson fails to see that a woman who is the head of a household and who lives on the minimal stipend of a welfare check without a man needs incredible discipline, regularity, and self-sufficiency to survive. Why can't one gain these same qualities through political organization, a labor union, or a community-based group that is challenging the organization and priorities of the society? Why does neither Wilson nor Porter recognize such organizations in inner-city communities as forms of social organization? The answer lies in another question: discipline, regularity, self-sufficiency, and social organization to what end? For both Wilson and Porter, the point of discipline, regularity, and self-sufficiency is to be a successful consumer, not to change society. Furthermore, the test of the significance of race and gender discrimination ultimately lies in the extent to which they interfere with exchange relations.

An Alternative View of Class

An alternative conception of class is based on the notion that human development is a social process. Individuals develop their capacities to think, create, and develop their abilities through their cooperative relationships and interactions with other individuals. Such creative developmental activity is thus social, and individuals are, through this process, *social individuals*. But under capitalism the developmental activity of social individuals is undermined by the contradictory effect of markets through which human interaction is individualized and directed toward competition. These contradictory aspects of human experience manifest themselves through social classes, which are defined in relation to the production process.

In a capitalist society, most individuals must enter into a labor market and sell their capacity to work (labor power) as a commodity. There are classes of people who control the structure and rules of the exchange of labor power for wages by virtue of their ownership of the means of productions. There are also classes of people whose standard of living depends on serving those who control the terms of exchange. And there are classes of people whose ability to influence the terms of exchange depends on the extent to which they organize themselves as a class and make demands on the upper classes. Class relations in these terms are contradictory for two reasons.

The worker who is forced to sell labor power in a market controlled by others is split into two antagonistic and alienating divisions. On the one hand, he or she has the capacity to create socially useful items. The production process is cooperative and social, and the value of the product depends on its usefulness. Furthermore, the act of creating socially useful items is integrally linked to the self-development of each individual worker. This activity is labor as a creative, self-fulfilling, and socially useful activity. On the other hand, in order to survive and to reproduce, the worker is forced to sell his or her labor power—the capacity to work in general—to the highest bidder. Labor power is a commodity used by those who buy it to produce other commodities that can be exchanged for a profit. Those who control the terms of the sale of labor power have a class interest in getting workers to produce as much of this exchange value as possible in the least amount of time and for the lowest cost possible. The worker has a class interest in league with other workers not only to gain a higher wage but also to maintain a process of self-development through the cooperative labor process. Antagonism between labor and management is based on this contradictory aspect of class.

A second basis for contradictory class relations is that capitalist class control over the terms of the exchange of labor power for wages is critical to the survival of individual companies and of the capitalist system as a whole. Profit depends on that control. Competition among businesses is the driving force that pushes individual capitalists to attempt to gain profits by increasing productivity and cheapening labor power itself. The manner in which control over the terms of the exchange of labor power is manifested has varied during different historical periods.[11] In the earliest period of capitalist history, "primitive accumulation" prevailed. Peasants were forcibly removed from their lands, and humans were sold as slaves. Working conditions were a horror. There followed a period where the mode of accumulation was predominantly based on the lengthening of the working day. That was followed by the domination of efforts to accumulate profits by increasing productivity through speedup and labor-saving machinery. It is my view that we are currently entering a new period, more closely akin to primitive accumulation, in which accumulation is proceeding through the cheapening of labor power globally. (I develop this point later in this essay.) The general point I wish to stress here is that antagonistic class relations stem from the systemic need for capitalists to control the terms of the exchange of labor power toward the end of accumulating profits. Pursuing this motivation results in the cheapening of labor power by making workers work longer, increasing productivity, driving down wages, or some combination of these. Periods of labor upheaval throughout the history of capitalism have been a specific response of workers to the negative impact that the mode of accumulation has on them.

The Role of Technology

One of the motor forces driving the systemic tendency to cheapen labor power is technology. The role of technology in economic development is central to the arguments put forth by Wilson and Porter. But again, their concept of class leads them to see the role that technology plays in social and economic development in a particular way. Both Wilson and Porter treat technological development as independent of all social relations, particularly class relations. Workers lose their jobs or need retraining "because of technological change," as if these changes appeared out of thin air. Treating technology as an independent variable has become fashionable. Analysts representing many different points of view have recently done so.[12] But accepting the specific forms of technological development as immutable and random happenings that are part of human progress eliminates the possibility of contesting their negative effects. Wilson and Porter both argue that inner-city workers have been victimized not because of their race or gender but, rather, because of their failure to adapt to new conditions.

But the treatment of technology as an independent, wealth-producing variable is an analytical assumption that is never critically examined by either author. From the alternative class perspective developed here, technology can be understood as the outcome of a society's class relations. Some recent technological developments have been used to increase productivity and eliminate employment. At the same time, much technological investment has resulted in advanced forms of telecommunications and lower transportation costs. The most direct effect of this investment has been to make capital more mobile, enabling companies to move production geographically and also to move investment into different industries. This mobility enables businesses to lower their costs by moving to cheaper areas. In some instances, living-wage jobs are eliminated in one region and replaced by jobs elsewhere that yield significantly lower living standards. In other instances, profits derived from lower-cost production are used to invest in technology or to implement mergers and acquisitions that actually reduce jobs. In Chicago, the loss of manufacturing jobs in the 1980s that was so devastating to black, Latino, and female workers was the product of the use of technology to shift production to other geographical areas and other product lines in order to cheapen labor power. Assuming that a conscious decision to invest in a particular technology is linked to its proposed use, I conclude that development of technology serves particular class interests in cheapening labor power. Rather than argue, as Wilson and Porter do, that inner-city residents simply adapt to an inevitable set of circumstances, it is important to contest the impacts of these developments and to seek to influence their direction.

The Role of Competition

A second force that drives the systemic tendency to cheapen labor power is competition. But neither Porter nor Wilson sees competition in this light. The focus of Porter's work is on the importance of gaining "competitive advantage." He argues that inner-city economic development that provides employment opportunities to residents can be successful if the community is marketed properly as a place where businesses can have a competitive advantage. A good location, linkages to related economic activity, local unmet demand, and an available labor force are seen as assets attractive to business if the competitive disadvantages of the inner-city location are addressed. These disadvantages include crime, an unprepared workforce, and deficient infrastructure. The interest of business should be the dominant motivation and guide to how to eliminate disadvantages. The key to the economic welfare of inner-city residents, according to Porter, is the competitiveness of business.

While Porter sees the training of inner-city residents to meet the needs of local business as a part of his strategy, it is a key part of the policy implications of Wilson's writing. Wilson's short-term solutions to inner-city problems are focused on behavior modification of the "underclass" members through the discipline and regularity of a legitimate job. Then, in the long run, they can be trained for those jobs that will make them competitive in the new global economy. He also argues for strong business development policies to increase the demand for labor so that employers are less tempted to discriminate against blacks. But what is crucial to Wilson is that black people be competitive as workers.

Many things are being justified these days in the name of competition. If workers ask for decent wages and benefits, they are told that this would diminish their own competitiveness as well as that of the company. Mass layoffs, the rise of temporary and part-time work, and plant closings are all attributed to competition. Behind this construction of competition is the idea that markets themselves—both commodity and labor markets—are competitive. This means that there are enough businesses and workers so that no single business or group of workers is able to affect price or wage; that all parties to the market transaction are informed of all relevant facts; that access to the market is not restricted in any way; that all the products in a particular market are similar. Under these conditions, companies compete on the basis of the quality of the product at a price that reflects the costs of efficient production. Workers compete on the basis of their skill and related productivity. But, in all of the discussion about competitiveness, there is no critique of the role that competition is playing in the real world. The question for me is not only whether the conditions I have described exist but whether competitiveness should be the goal of public policies related to poverty and economic development.

Raising such a question links the concept of competition to class. The dominant view of competition is grounded in the class conception articulated by Wilson. But, coming from my alternative conception of class, I seriously disagree with the widely accepted notion that public policy should be directed toward competitiveness. At a philosophical level, I argue that the goal of development in a society should be human self-development in its broadest sense. Marx called this the human "quest for universality" or "freedom." He interpreted history in terms of social movements of people striving to be whole by opposing obstacles to their self-development. Marx argued that, as this quest unfolds, we move toward a society in which the "full and free development of every human being is its ruling principle."[13] But, if the objective of society is restricted to the realm of exchange relations, a different result occurs. There is an alienating division of the worker into two parts—a creator of useful commodities through concrete labor and a commodity, labor power, that produces abstract exchange values. The individual is left to develop as "an egoistic monad" who is "free to operate in the realm of the market, where each individual's development is a potential barrier to that of every other individual."[14] Marx saw that, in such a social arrangement, *individualism* prevails over the *social individual*, and domination through competition replaces self-development through cooperative human relationships. In the process, human development is distorted and alienated.

One conclusion I draw from this construction is that competition is not class-neutral. It contributes directly to alienation and the truncation of human development as workers are forced to compete with one another. As Cyrus Bina, Laurie Clements, and Chuck Davis note:

> Competition is defined from capital's perspective to sustain long-term profitability. Competition is the *coercive* force of global capital and the accumulation process.... Capitalist competition has continuously pitted worker against worker, attempting to drive wages, conditions of work and the quality of life to the lowest possible level—first locally, then regionally, nationally, and internationally.[15]

Competition, in this view, is not driven by an effort on the part of companies to produce the highest-quality products in the most efficient manner. Rather, when one looks at the capitalist system as a whole rather than at the behavior of individual businesses, the competition is for labor power, the commodity that is the ultimate source of profits. Even when industries become capital intensive, labor power as a whole has been cheapened by being replaced by machines. Workers cannot compete at this level unless they organize as a class. But capitalist-worker competition is not what is being advocated by the likes of Porter and Wilson. They are advocating that workers *compete with one another* for available jobs, which makes it impossible for them to contest the conditions within which they are forced to compete.

Competition and Globalization

Even from the perspective of the upper classes, moreover, the conditions for classic competition—enough businesses and workers, access to markets, information, and markets divided according to comparable products—do not uniformly exist. Earlier I argued that we are entering a new period in terms of how the capitalist system as a whole accumulates profits. This new period has both political-ideological and institutional aspects. Essentially, the accumulation of profits is occurring through the cheapening of production costs—particularly labor power—on a global scale. The vehicle for cheapening costs of production globally is capital mobility. Mobile capital, in turn, requires a political-ideological context and institutions that make cheapening production costs through mobility highly profitable. Politically and ideologically, the global drive to cheapen production costs is supported by monetarist economic policies aimed at keeping inflation and wages low and labor markets slack. It is also supported by fiscal austerity that keeps taxes low by minimizing government social safety nets. Government's role in the regulation of capital is also minimized to enhance capital mobility. The notion of "free trade" has been expanded to include the movement of capital as well as goods.

The political-ideological context of this emerging era of globalization (often termed *neoliberalism*) is being fortified by institutional developments that enforce the regime worldwide. These include the "reinvention" of old Bretton Woods institutions. The primary function of the International Monetary Fund and the World Bank is to impose neoliberalism on the developing world through structural adjustment programs. The General Agreement on Tariffs and Trade (GATT) has been replaced by a more powerful institution, the World Trade Organization (WTO). The WTO has more power than GATT ever did and a much broader agenda that includes basing international economic relations on neoliberal rules. The North American Free Trade Agreement (NAFTA) also enforces neoliberalism in the region defined by Canada, the United States, and Mexico, and it strives to include the entire Western Hemisphere in its orbit. The European Union, not initially built on neoliberal principles, is moving in that direction through the creation of a monetary union with strict entrance requirements that will weaken social safety nets and impose a regime of monetarism throughout Europe.

The other institutional development involves the transformation of the corporations themselves. An increasing share of total global economic activity is being conducted by corporations that have been changed from transnational to supranational. These companies no longer bring wealth extracted offshore back to their home countries. Instead, they have acquired majority-owned affiliates all over the world and have increasingly made use of outsourcing and various other collaborative arrangements with corporations from many different countries. Banks as well as industrial corporations have become supranational. But global finance is no longer totally the preserve of banks. Industrial corporations, mutual fund and pension fund managers, brokerage houses, and individual traders are major players as well.[16] All operate within the context of an era of capital accumulation that aims to cheapen production costs—including, most important, labor.

Globalization, however, is often presented in quite a different light. When competition is used to justify the need for austerity or as the reason for inner-city black and female poverty, the term *global competition* is used with abandon. Both Wilson and Porter argue that such competition has hurt inner-city residents because they are not prepared to compete well. In addition, the description of the new global competition (developed in some detail by Porter) posits a world of *nations* competing with one another through "their" respective corporations on the basis of new technologies and increasingly efficient operations. Porter has expanded his analysis to include competition between inner cities and other parts of the country in the competitive global context.

The fact is, however, that the bulk of the world's economic activity comes from huge oligopolistic corporations whose national headquarters' locations are becoming increasingly less relevant to their distribution of wages, jobs, and investment. Such companies compete not on the basis of efficient, high-quality production but, rather, through the struggle for market shares. Such businesses enjoy considerable market power, which gives them more options in pursuing their drive for profits.[17]

One of these options is to cheapen production costs by externalizing them. When a company shifts its production from one place to another and does not pay workers in the new location a living wage, it is externalizing the cost of production. There are human and economic costs of dislocation; there are human and economic costs for people working in an unsafe environment without adequate compensation. Thus, if corporations move production to avoid paying taxes, to avoid environmental laws, to avoid worker safety standards, to avoid human and worker rights standards, they are externalizing the costs of production.

Furthermore, a struggle for market shares among corporate giants is likely to be achieved by *eliminating* competition rather than by simply competing. Market niches are developed and dominated by giant corporations that buy out their opposition. For example, a major strike occurred in Decatur, Illinois, because a British-based corporate giant that dominated the sweetener industry (Tate and Lyle) bought out a locally owned U.S. corporation (A. E. Staley) and began to implement cost-saving work rules that the labor force felt compromised worker safety.[18] Tate and Lyle was able to implement such an aggressive policy because it dominated the sweetener industry. Prior to the strike it built a pipeline between A. E. Staley and Staley's neighbor Archer Daniels Midland (ADM) so that production could continue during the lockout. ADM was partially owned (7 percent of its stock) by Tate and Lyle. Tate and Lyle's motivation for buying A. E. Staley was that it lacked production capacity in an important and growing market niche (corn sweeteners used in soft drinks). Rather than invest in new production facilities and compete in this market niche, it bought Staley, thereby acquiring greater dominance in the general sweetener market and eliminating an independent producer in the process.

In addition, many of these global giants are outsourcing all or part of their production to other companies. Nike Corporation, for example, is strictly a marketing shell, sourcing virtually all production to small manufacturers. As the giant supranationals struggle for market shares as I have described, many smaller businesses compete fiercely for contracts from the giants. The competition for the sourcing business from the supranationals is not based on high-quality, efficient production but, rather, on low costs. The result is low wages, bad working conditions, and labor and human rights abuses for workers employed by the winning companies.[19] In the process, labor standards throughout the world are compromised in the name of international competition.

None of this has anything to do with competition based on efficient production methods and quality products. It is, rather, the use of market power to cut costs in order to increase profits. These conditions are far from the simplistic view of global competition presented by both Wilson and Porter. The new era of globalization expands the control of the terms for the exchange of labor power to a world scale. Competition among workers is global, amplifying the capability of the capitalist system to cheapen labor power. It also means that the terms for competition over labor power are concentrated in fewer hands as giant supranationals force smaller companies into cutthroat competition for their business.

Class, Race, and Gender Revisited

Under these circumstances, Wilson's and Porter's drive to eliminate poverty by policies that bring inner-city workers and small businesses into this competitive mix will not only fail to meet their objectives but will also undermine efforts of workers to contest the terms of the purchase of labor power worldwide. Furthermore, both race and gender have a great deal to do with setting the terms for the exchange of labor power.

The global drive to cheapen labor power has the most devastating impact on those with the least political power. Of the 150,000 manufacturing jobs eliminated in the Chicago area during the 1980s, half were lost by blacks and Latinos and a third by women.[20] As the system forces workers to compete with one another rather than contest the terms of the sale of labor power, different groups of workers tend to band together to press their advantage over other workers. As the competition among workers moves to a world scale, the tendency to place group over class interests becomes ever more complex, and class interests themselves become difficult to sort out.

Divisions among workers take particular forms in different geographical, political, and cultural contexts. In the United States, race and gender discrimination has a long history, but it takes on new form as the era of globalization develops. Neoliberal policies have generated great income and wealth gains for some but a significant deterioration of living standards for others. A mark of the present period is the growing inequality in the distribution of income. Since 1979 there has been a growing income gap between upper and lower income groups that appears to be accelerating. Between 1992 and 1993 the family income share of total U.S. family income for the top 5 percent grew by 10.3 percent, while the lowest fifth of families lost 1.4 percent of their share.[21] The combination of gains from the civil rights movement that opened up professional and administrative positions to people of color and women and the neoliberal-induced income and wealth gains for those at the top of the economic ladder have given rise to economic disparities within oppressed groups.

Wilson mistakenly takes this as a sign that the significance of race has broken down and that "class" determines economic well-being. He then stretches the argument to contend that because the more well-to-do blacks have left the old neighborhood, the concentration of poverty, rather than racially based economic conditions, is at the root of the problem. Further, negative behavior (such as women with babies and without men who prefer to live on the dole) reinforced by the proximity of others in a similar situation prevents success in the labor market. Wilson's interviews in *When the Work Disappears* offer strong support for the belief that many unemployed black people want to work but cannot find jobs. Interviews with white businesspeople show strong negative images of black workers—especially young black men—that are clearly racially based. Yet he continues to maintain that ultimately it is the lack of discipline and regularity on the part of the unemployed blacks, rather than racism, that is at the root of the problem. His proof is that he has found black businesspeople who support the perceptions of the racist whites.

Earlier I argued that there are classes of people whose interests lie in serving those who control the terms of the exchange of labor power. Indeed, some black people who have been able to share in the fruits of neoliberal policies find their economic interests in line with neoliberalism. But this cannot be offered as evidence that the class contradictions described earlier in this essay and racism are no longer of significance to the group as a whole. And the same can be said when it comes to women or Latinos. The mobility of capital means that the working class as a whole is vulnerable to the competition of workers worldwide. The effect of neoliberalism is to heighten competition among workers. But, as I have discussed, this competition is not based primarily on better skills and education. For unskilled blacks, Latinos, and women in the United States, the competition is based strictly on the cost of labor power. A number of analysts have noted this but avoid the problem of the unskilled as a "long-term" problem and focus their attention on the competitiveness of the upper strata of the working class who may compete on a different basis.

The problem of the unskilled, however, should not be treated as either an anomaly or a problem of "lack of education." As I have argued earlier in this essay, cheapening labor power is at the heart of neoliberalism and is a defining characteristic of the present era of globalized capitalism. The question, then, becomes who is most vulnerable to the drive to cheapen labor power and why.

It is my view that the combination of globalized neoliberalism and the legacy of race and gender relations in the United States means that discrimination is becoming heightened in the present period. The vehicle for discrimination is not solely overt forms of racism (although there is plenty of that). Discrimination is facilitated and intensified by the day-to-day functioning of economic and governmental institutions that operate to facilitate and intensify competition among workers toward the end of cheapening labor power. The reason for increased discrimination in this period is that the expanded basis for competition among workers leaves groups with a legacy of economic vulnerability even more vulnerable. The fact that masses of black people are without living-wage work and are living in poverty is a measure of that vulnerability. The fact that black women must figure out how to raise a family without sufficient resources is also a measure of that vulnerability.

Vulnerability based on class, race, and gender is built into the economic and political system itself. Oppressed groups face the limitations of capitalism as they find again and again that human rights are nothing more than individual rights—the right to compete with others. As Marx noted:

> The right of man to liberty ceases to be a right as soon as it comes into conflict with political life, whereas in theory political life is only the guarantee . . . of the rights of the individual and therefore must be abandoned as soon as it comes into contradiction with its aim, the rights of man.[22]

Any conception of equity or human rights must be abandoned if it comes into conflict with its aim—the prevailing capitalist exchange relations in which bourgeois individual rights are realized. This remains true even though many members of oppressed groups staff the bureaucracies of the state apparatus that enforces these rights. It remains true even if members of oppressed groups are doctors, lawyers, business executives, and stockbrokers. In short, racial and gender-based discrimination is an integral part of the fabric of the economic and political system. And the rights of the group as a whole will always be limited by the right of all to compete without interference in the markets that define exchange relations.

The works of both Wilson and Porter are manifestations of this limitation. Their definition of class itself, widely accepted today in academia, is part of the limits of human emancipation. The conclusion that race-based solutions are ineffective and will not solve the problem is also part of the limits placed on human emancipation. The contention that race is declining in significance relative to "joblessness" also reflects that same limitation. In U.S. society these limits fall most heavily on people of color and on women. Again, as globalization heightens competition among workers and restricts the terms of that competition for the most oppressed groups to the aim of cheapening labor power, the significance of class, race, and gender together is greatly heightened.

Conclusion: Policy Implications or Political Mobilization?

It is common for social scientists to end their contributions with a discussion of *policy implications*. The commonly understood meaning of this term is what government should do and what it should not do. Both Wilson and Porter believe that government should not be involved in race-specific entitlement programs. Porter goes further and argues against all forms of subsidy for inner-city development. They both agree that public funds should be used to strengthen the competitiveness of inner-city residents, as well as workers generally, through high-quality education and job training. They also agree with policies that eliminate the competitive disadvantages of the inner city. This includes the elimination of concentrations of poverty. On the basis of their reasoning (as well as political expediency), public policies are being implemented that eliminate public housing, even when there is not adequate alternative housing. Public policies are also eliminating the social safety net as politicians implore the unemployed to cease their joblessness, despite the absence of jobs that pay a living wage. These are the policy implications of an analysis that sees the solution to poverty in terms of competitive companies and competitive workers.

In this essay I have argued that these policy implications are grounded in a conception of class based on exchange relations. What is important in a world dominated by competition for success in the realm of exchange is not race, gender, or *class*, as I conceive of the term, but individual achievement. I have argued, to the contrary, that class formation is grounded in production relations. Furthermore, the relationship among social classes is antagonistic and contradictory, as individualism prevails over the functioning of the social individual. Furthermore, in the present era of globalized neoliberalism, the significance of racial and gender-based oppression has become heightened.

The implication of this alternative view is that, rather than focus on policy implications for the alleviation of poverty, we need a program geared toward political mobilization. Workers must organize as a class to contest the terms of the exchange of labor power and to seek a society in which the "full and free development of every human being is its ruling principle." In an era of globalization, this organization must cross national boundaries. And it must seek the principled elimination of divisions based on race and gender.

Political mobilization based on class, race, and gender cannot put one or more of these constituencies to the side for a better day or a more opportune time. Both racism and sexism have a historical development independent of class. But class relations shape the form that oppression based on race and gender takes. It must be realized that some people of color and women see their class interests tied to those who control the terms of the exchange of labor power. While this by no means suggests a lessening of the significance of race and gender, as Wilson argues, it does suggest that neither race nor gender is a sufficient basis for principled and unified political mobilization.

The substantive basis for political mobilization needs to be a direct challenge to the notion that markets and competitiveness in those markets are the key to the elimination of poverty as well as racial and gender-based disparities. If workers accept the idea that competitiveness means accepting a work environment of high productivity and low wages, the class basis for political mobilization is lost. Similarly, if workers accept the notion that some workers must work for less than a living wage because they are not competitive, the ground is established for divisive competitiveness among workers, which in many instances will take the form of racism, sexism, and xenophobia.

Declaring the right to a decent life to be a *human right* is a challenge to the limits that capitalism places on that term. It runs head-on into the notion that the limit of a human right is the extent to which it interferes with the individual right to compete in the market. Thus, the current campaign of the U.S. Labor Party for the right to a job that pays a living wage could become the basis for a broad political mobilization that need not (and must not) stop at the U.S. border. Similarly, citizen groups from around the world are launching campaigns that declare housing, food, and a clean and safe environment to be human rights. International campaigns against corporations for the abuse of workers and the rights of workers to organize have this same potential to challenge the limits placed on human rights generally.

While these kinds of campaigns have the potential to make the sort of challenge that my essay has suggested is needed, they can easily fall short if the limits placed on human rights by the larger society are accepted. "Living-wage campaigns" that accept less than a living wage in the spirit of political compromise, for example, lose their potential for political mobilization. That loss is due to the acceptance of limits on human rights, which concedes the basis on which political mobilization must proceed.

Finally, both theoretically and ideologically a challenge must be made to prevailing notions about the nature of poverty. I selected to direct my critique toward the theories of William Julius Wilson and Michael Porter because both these scholars, unlike many of their more conservative colleagues, have a genuine desire to contribute to the improvement of the lives of inner-city people. But because their ideas are gaining wide acceptance among government policymakers and many activists, they are doing more harm to the cause of human liberation than are the more mean-spirited theories of the far right. It is my hope that this essay can be a modest contribution to the debate that will accompany the needed political mobilization.

NOTES

This chapter appeared previously in *Sage Race Relations Abstracts* 23, no. 2 (1998).

1. David C. Ranney, "Transnational Investment and Job Loss: The Case of Chicago," University of Illinois at Chicago Center for Urban Economic Development, #350A (October 1992); David C. Ranney and William Cecil, "Transnational Investment and Job Loss in Chicago: Impacts on Women, Blacks and Latinos," University of Illinois at Chicago Center for Urban Economic Development, #350B (January 1993).

2. Nikolas Theodore and Jodi Pietrowski, "Hidden Unemployment in Chicago: A Look at Worker Discouragement," unpublished paper, March 11, 1997. This study was further developed and published by Danielle Gordon, "Invisible Jobless Ambush Welfare Plan," *Chicago Reporter* 26, no. 2 (March 1997).

3. Virginia L. Carlson and Nikolas C. Theodore, "Are There Enough Jobs? Welfare Reform and Labor Market Reality," Chicago, Illinois Job Gap Project, Woods Fund of Chicago, December 1995.

4. The analysis in the following paragraph is based on the following report: Patricia A. Wright, Yittayih Zelalem, Julie deGraaf, and Linda Roman, "The Plan to Voucher Out Public Housing: An Analysis of the Chicago Experience and a Case Study of the Proposal to Redevelop the Cabrini-Green Public Housing Area," University of Illinois at Chicago, Nathalie P. Voorhees Center for Neighborhood and Community Improvement, May 1997.

5. The extent of city of Chicago land development subsidies and the political connections of the recipients is discussed in a recent issue of *Crain's Chicago Business*: Greg Hinz, "The City That TIFS: Mayor Daley Is Pulling Millions off Local Tax Rolls for an Uncertain Payoff," *Crain's Chicago Business* 20, no. 27 (July 7, 1997): 1, 11-15.

6. Examples include the following: George Gilder, *Wealth and Poverty* (New York: Basic Books, 1981); Lawrence Mead, *Beyond Entitlement: The Social Obligations of Citizenship* (New York: Free Press, 1986); Lawrence Mead, *The New Politics of Poverty: The Working Poor in America* (New York: Basic Books, 1992); Charles Murray, *Losing Ground: American Social Policy 1950-80* (New York: Basic Books, 1984).

7. The analysis that follows is based on the following works: William Julius Wilson, *The Declining Significance of Race: Blacks and Changing American Institutions* (Chicago: University of Chicago Press, 1978); William Julius Wilson, *The Truly Disadvantaged: The Inner City, the Underclass, and Public Policy* (Chicago: University of Chicago Press, 1987); William Julius Wilson, *When the Work Disappears: The World of the New Urban Poor* (New York: Knopf, 1996).

8. Michael E. Porter, *The Competitive Advantage of Nations* (New York: Free Press: 1990; Michael E. Porter, "The Competitive Advantage of the Inner City," *Harvard Business Review* 73 (May-June 1995): 55-71; Michael E. Porter, "New Strategies for Inner-City Development," *Economic Development Quarterly* 11, no. 1 (February 1997): 11-27.

9. Wilson, *Declining Significance of Race,* 156.

10. Adolph Reed Jr., "The Underclass as Myth and Symbol: The Poverty of Discourse about Poverty," *Radical America* 24 (Winter 1991-92): 27.

11. This point is developed in greater detail in David C. Ranney, "Labor and Today's Global Economic Crisis: A Historical View," in *Beyond Survival: Wage Labor in the Late Twentieth Century,* ed. Cyrus Bina, Laurie Clements, and Chuck Davis (New York: M. E. Sharpe, 1996), 49-65.

12. See, for example, Jeremy Rifkin, *The End of Work: The Decline of the Global Labor Force and the Dawn of the Post-Market Era* (New York: Putnam, 1995). Also, in William Greider's most recent work he traces today's technological developments to the chance development of the microchip in someone's garage. The chip in this view becomes a random happening. William Greider, *One World, Ready or Not: The Manic Logic of Global Capitalism* (New York: Simon and Schuster, 1997).

13. Karl Marx, *Capital: A Critical Analysis of Capitalist Production,* vol. 1 (New York: International Publishers, 1972), 592.

14. Karl Marx, "On the Jewish Question," in *Collected Works of Karl Marx and Frederick Engels,* vol. 3 (New York: International Publishers, 1975), 144-74.

15. Cyrus Bina, Laurie Clements, and Chuck Davis, eds., *Beyond Survival: Wage Labor in the Late Twentieth Century* (New York: M. E. Sharpe, 1996), 6, 19.

16. For more in-depth discussions of global capital, see the following: Greider, *One World, Ready or Not,* 227-330; Richard Barnet and John Cavanagh, *Global Dreams: Imperial Corporations and the New World Order* (New York: Simon and Schuster, 1994), 359-418; David Korten, *When Corporations Rule the World* (San Francisco: Berrett-Koehler, 1995), 183-226.

17. This point is developed through a number of case studies in Barnet and Cavanagh, *Global Dreams.*

18. David C. Ranney and Paul Schwalb, "An Analysis of the A. E. Staley/Tate & Lyle Lockout in Decatur, Illinois," Report No. 404, Center for Urban Economic Development, University of Illinois at Chicago, 1995.

19. Korten, *When Corporations Rule the World.*

20. Ranney and Cecil, 1993.

21. Lawrence Mischel and Jared Bernstein, *The State of Working America 1994-95* (Armonk, N.Y.: M. E. Sharpe, 1995, 35-44.

22. Karl Marx, "On the Jewish Question," 165.

DISCUSSION QUESTIONS

1. How is this chapter similar to the earlier one by Jennings?

2. What is the relationship between global and local economic occurrences, and what does this relationship have to do with poverty and race?

3. What does the author mean by a "paradigm shift" on the part of government in terms of the welfare state? What are the major reasons for this kind of development?

4. What are the major points made by Wilson and Porter, and how does the author critique these scholars?

5. According to the author, what are the political and economic reasons for race, gender, and discrimination?

6. What is the significance of class in relationship to race, gender, and poverty?

7. How does the author utilize the concept of competition to ground his arguments?

8. What is the relationship between globalization and racial and gender discrimination, according to the author?

FOR FURTHER READING

Bina, Cyrus, Laurie Clements, and Chuck Davis, eds., *Beyond Survival: Wage Labor in the Late Twentieth Century* (New York: M. E. Sharpe, 1996), 6, 19.

Greider, William, *One World, Ready or Not: The Manic Logic of Global Capitalism* (New York: Simon and Schuster, 1997).

Korten, David, *When Corporations Rule the World* (San Francisco: Berrett-Koehler, 1995).

Porter, Michael E., *The Competitive Advantage of Nations* (New York: Free Press, 1990).

Reed, Adolph, Jr., "The Underclass as Myth and Symbol: The Poverty of Discourse about Poverty," *Radical America* 24 (Winter 1991-92): 27.

Rifkin, Jeremy, *The End of Work: The Decline of the Global Labor Force and the Dawn of the Post-Market Era* (New York: Putnam, 1995).

Wilson, William Julius, *The Declining Significance of Race: Blacks and Changing American Institutions* (Chicago: University of Chicago Press, 1978).

Part II

Researching Race and Poverty
The Absence of History

Chapter Three

Reframing the Underclass Debate

Michael B. Katz

Migration, Marginalization, Exclusion, and Isolation

Throughout modern American history, four great processes have shaped the experience of poverty. These processes are migration, marginalization, exclusion, and isolation. With the urban transformations that gave rise to the postindustrial city, each of them intensified, resulting in the configuration some observers have labeled the "underclass." These processes interconnect so tightly that pulling them apart for discussion threatens to reify them as separable and self-contained. In truth, together they form a great force, for which no adequate label exists, driving urban transformation. The separate presentation of each that follows is, then, only a convenience, a way of trying to understand the same developments by looking at them from slightly different perspectives.

Migration, or the movement of people in space, has always constituted one of the great themes of American history. It is useful to consider three sorts of population movement: the immigration of peoples to America; the short-distance, often seasonal migration of workers within a particular region of the country; and major interregional movements, especially from the rural South to the urban North.

There are two ways to think about the relation of immigration to the underclass story. One is the comparison of group experience, which centers on the familiar but still critical question: why did the descendants of European immigrants move out of both inner cities and poverty more successfully than African Americans have? I will return to this issue. The other question is this: what impact have immigrants had on the rewards, opportunities, and life chances of the poorest Americans? For most of American history the question translates into the impact of European immigrants on African Americans, although, especially in recent years, Latino and Asian immigrants to major cities have made the issue immensely more complicated.

Racism gave European immigrants advantages over African Americans already living in northern and midwestern cities. In the antebellum era, Irish and other immigrants displaced African Americans from trades, such as barbering, in which they had been well represented. At the same time, employers hired white European immigrants for the new jobs in the emergent industrial economy. The same pattern repeated itself in the late nineteenth and early twentieth centuries. In Philadelphia between 1860 and 1890, the proportion of artisans among black males declined from 15 to 1.1 percent. Despite a pool of inexpensive labor among blacks in the South, northern employers recruited huge numbers of semiskilled industrial workers from southern and eastern Europe. Only when World War I and then immigration restriction created a labor shortage and dried up their transatlantic sources did industrial employers seriously begin to recruit southern blacks. The use of African Americans as strikebreakers constitutes the major exception to the pattern. This practice, of course, only heightened hostility between blacks and immigrants.[1]

Within America, frequent, short-distance migration defined the experience of a very high proportion of workers. As one recent social historian after another has shown, the American working class in the nineteenth and early twentieth centuries was transient. In most cities studied by historians, only a minority of workers could be located at intervals a decade apart, and rates of labor force turnover within industry remained staggeringly high at least through the 1920s. This population churning, far from random, had structural sources and an identifiable social structure. Through their labor market practices, industrial employers fostered high turnover, and the irregularity of employment sent workers on the road in search of jobs. With workplaces small and no mass transportation available, workers needed to live within walking distance of their jobs, and finding employment often meant moving to a new town or city. Older workers, especially homeowners, remained the least likely to move. The ability to stay in one place for a long time was in fact a privilege that only a minority of workers enjoyed.[2]

Only in part did the experiences of blacks in the rural South in the late nineteenth century reflect the transience of the American working class. For in one important way the intraregional movement of southern African Americans differed sharply from that of any other group in American history: it was proscribed by the state. After the Civil War, southern legislatures enacted "black codes" that prohibited blacks from traveling for reasons unrelated to the needs of white employers. These laws were enforced unevenly. Although some planters tried desperately to hold onto their labor forces, others, equally desperate for workers, encouraged blacks to move, and some federal officials took seriously their obligation to prevent peonage and involuntary servitude. Later in the century, vagrancy statutes also constrained black mobility. Far more than other workers, blacks often remained unable to use migration to search for better work and to escape poverty. Nonetheless, some blacks managed short-distance or seasonal moves. Regularly cheated and exploited by landlords, sharecroppers often moved every year or so in search of more favorable terms and more equitable treatment. Unable to eke out a living on their own farms, large numbers of men took seasonal work elsewhere in the South (referred to as "shifting"), leaving behind their families. This need to fragment families in order to survive underlay much of what observers saw as marital instability and wrongly attributed to cultural preference.[3]

American history is also a story of great interregional migrations. The westward migration is one of them; another is the forced migration of Native Americans; a third is the movement of African Americans from the South to the urban North. Between World War I and the 1920s, 700,000 to one million moved North; 800,000 migrated during the 1920s. From 1940 to 1970, another five million followed. They moved for various reasons: to escape sharecropping; as a result of the mechanization of southern agriculture; to answer labor demands in northern industries after immigration restrictions closed the supply of European workers; to move out from under the shadow of southern racial violence; to be able to use public facilities; and to find relatively greater access to the ordinary rights of citizens. In the first wave, more men moved to the industrial cities of the Midwest and more women to the older cities of the East, where the demand for domestics was high; later, gender ratios evened out. The result changed America profoundly. In 1940, who would have thought that the majority of African Americans would soon live not in the agricultural South but in the urban North? Some southern states experienced significant population losses, while the composition of northern cities changed rapidly and irrevocably. In Chicago, for instance, blacks were only 8.4 percent of the population in 1940 and 14.1 percent in 1950. By 1960 their share had increased to 23.6 percent, and by 1970 to more than a third, 34.4 percent. Here was the demographic origin of the modern ghetto.[4]

At the same time that southern blacks moved into northern cities, whites increasingly left in search of new opportunities in either the suburbs or the Sun Belt. Despite the immigration of African Americans, the populations of older northern and midwestern cities began to decline, and their population densities decreased. Abandoned housing joined abandoned factories as symbols of formerly industrial cities. Unable to move because they lacked the skills and education required by the new postindustrial economy and because of discrimination, blacks remained locked into increasingly segregated neighborhoods. As a consequence, contemporary inner-city poverty and segregation reflect a partial reversal of the historic relation between migration and income or education. In the past, economic opportunity stimulated migration by both the most and the least educated, by the affluent and the poor. Now, the relation has turned linear, because the least educated and poorest city residents have become the least likely to migrate.[5]

The links between migration and marginalization always have been close. By *marginalization* I mean the process whereby some combination of factors—for instance, technological change, racial competition, or government action—pushes groups to the edges of the labor force, leaving them redundant, unwanted, or confined to the worst jobs. The great changes in Europe unleashed by capitalism in the eighteenth and nineteenth centuries resulted in mass migrations throughout the continent and across oceans as landless workers, newly displaced artisans, and others pessimistic about their futures at home sought to relocate where better opportunities seemed to beckon. Among the variety of factors that brought European immigrants to American shores, marginalization thus ranked very high.[6]

The arrival of European immigrants helped marginalize African Americans in cities. Displaced from skilled trades, denied industrial employment, they clustered in the hardest, most unrewarding work, taking jobs no one else wanted. Men found jobs in hard, unskilled labor and forms of personal service; women found them almost exclusively in the various branches of domestic work. Because employers paid black men so badly, so much less than whites, their wives worked outside their homes far more often than the wives in any other group. When black men did work in heavy industry, such as steel or coal mining, employers relegated them to the most difficult and dangerous jobs. In moments of acute labor shortage, during the two world wars, industrial employers called on black labor and began to move African Americans away from the margins and toward the center of the blue-collar world of work.[7] Otherwise, until the results of affirmative action registered their impact, African Americans remained in the stagnant eddies at the edges of America's industrial economy.

After the 1940s and 1950s, within America as earlier in Europe, marginalization also ranked high among the factors encouraging southern blacks to move north. Until then, planters needed them for cheap labor. Although paid wretchedly, cheated, exploited, terrorized, and killed, blacks remained at the very center of the southern economy until mechanical cotton pickers began to displace them in the post-World War II era. Then, their movement north swelled into a mighty tide.[8]

Marginalized European immigrants by and large had entered American cities at the zenith of America's industrial power during the peak demand for labor. For this reason, they found jobs waiting and real wages growing. Although the Great Depression derailed their progress, the Wagner Act of 1935 and the subsequent development of unions combined with the economic growth of the immediate postwar period to bring them a degree of unprecedented comfort and to open almost undreamed-of opportunities for their children. By contrast, African Americans finally entered the industrial North and Midwest at the start of those regions' decline. As African Americans moved from marginal positions in the southern labor force to the margins of the northern economy as well, they inherited deindustrializing cities. In the 1960s a new black middle class of government workers emerged, primarily through the combined expansion of government jobs and affirmative action, but they did not represent a majority of African Americans, who could see no very bright future for themselves or their children in the dying industrial economies of old cities. Stuck within spreading ghettos that they were too poor to escape, their children trapped in failing schools that they were too poor to leave, a large share of African Americans lacked the skills and the cultural capital to grasp the new opportunities in information processing and related fields that were available in the upper reaches of the dual economies of postindustrial cities.

The marginalization of African Americans in the North and the Midwest resulted from their race as well as their lack of applicable skills, as the case of Appalachian immigrants to the same cities shows clearly. In the decades between 1940 and 1970, when five million blacks migrated from the South to the North, 3.2 million whites left the southern Appalachian region and followed the same route. The two groups shared similar levels of education, skills, and work experience. Indeed, the whites were leaving subsistence farming, commercial tobacco plantations, coal mining, or some combination of these. Yet with easy access to semiskilled work and greater freedom of movement and residence, many more of these southern whites than African Americans prospered. In the largest midwestern cities, employers favored them over blacks for unskilled and semiskilled work; in some areas, they banded together to exclude blacks altogether. The upwardly mobile among the first generation, and many of their children, dropped their accents, dressed in northern fashions, and moved into neighborhoods where no one knew or could identify their geographic origins. The experience of African Americans moved in precisely the opposite directions.[9]

Deindustrialization, of course, has marginalized great numbers of white as well as black workers. Formerly highly paid automobile or steel workers pump gas, if they are lucky. Not only unemployment but the structure of the postindustrial economy, its bifurcation into "symbolic analysts" (to use Robert Reich's phrase) and poorly paid, often part-time routine service workers, permanently relegates huge numbers to the labor market's unrewarding margins. Unhampered by racial stereotypes, racial antagonism, or statistical discrimination, whites fare better than blacks, especially black males, in the competition for even these jobs. Still, the experience of white males illustrates how the forces sustaining black poverty are early, particularly intense, examples of trends that are reshaping America's social structure.[10]

A process that I call *exclusion* combined with technological change to repeatedly push African Americans to the margins of the labor market. Its basis is a combination of racial beliefs, antagonisms, and competition. The story of exclusion is in part a familiar one: employer preference, the concerted actions of white workers, and the policies of unions excluded African Americans from trades, industrial employment, white-collar work, and other economic opportunities. Voter registration procedures excluded them from the normal prerogatives of citizenship. Legal segregation, social customs, and private arrangements excluded them from public facilities and white neighborhoods. However, there is an additional story about this process: the exclusion of African Americans (and now, it appears, Latinos) from the processes that facilitated the economic and social mobility of white ethnics. It shows why neither African Americans nor Latinos in postindustrial cities will recapitulate the experience of white European immigrants of an earlier era.

Because African Americans lacked an ethnic employment niche, they remained excluded from the dominant process of immigrant economic mobility. An *ethnic niche* refers to the overrepresentation of a group in an occupation or industry; that is, the proportion of the ethnic group employed in the industry exceeds the group's share of the population. Ethnic niches developed for different reasons: some groups arrived with special skills; in other instances, early arriving members established a beachhead in an occupation and then recruited their compatriots. The Irish built a niche in politics and government, the Jews in the garment industry, and the Italians in construction. Even post-World War II southern Appalachian migrants built niches in midwestern cities. These niches were important for three reasons: they provided relatively stable work to unskilled and semiskilled immigrants; they facilitated economic mobility; and they exerted social controls by requiring members to conform to standards of behavior set by coworkers, friends, and neighbors.[11]

Neither African Americans nor Latinos were able to create the same sort of ethnic niches that earlier immigrant groups had. Every time African Americans gained a modest presence in a promising trade, discrimination undercut their efforts, and whites replaced them. In New York City, by 1910, immigrants had displaced the black barbers and caterers who had served whites in the nineteenth century. Locked out of entrepreneurial activities, most blacks worked for whites, and then only in the worst jobs. Affirmative action finally provided African Americans with an occupational niche in the 1960s: government employment. Unlike the niches that had facilitated the economic progress of immigrants, government employment required at least modest educational skills. Therefore, it did not facilitate the upward mobility of unskilled African Americans in the way that nineteenth-century public employment, the garment industry, or construction had assisted the Irish, Jews, and Italians. With good blue-collar manufacturing work disappearing, unskilled or poorly educated African Americans and Latinos could hold little hope of building a niche of their own, and cutbacks in government employment narrowed even their new route into the middle class.[12]

Statistics demonstrate the exclusion of African Americans and Latinos from the processes that had fostered the economic progress of white immigrants. The social consequences remain more speculative, but they may have been similar for most of those who remained on the outside, including the many whites not employed within an economic niche. Exclusion from niche employment, that is, may have translated into an absence of important forces that promoted social order and stability in the presence of poverty. This is one way to think about the reasons for differences in crime or indicators of social disorganization among and within groups.[13]

Patterns of migration, marginalization, and exclusion fostered the isolation of the poorest African Americans in inner cities. This isolation has four dimensions: economic, spatial, social, and cultural. I refer to *isolation* as a process because it is ongoing: inner-city African Americans have become more isolated now than at any other point in American history.[14]

Economic isolation refers, first, to the increased detachment from the labor force and, within the labor force, from the rewarding sectors of the new postindustrial economy, which I already have discussed. It also refers to the exclusion of ghetto neighborhoods from the real-estate market. Because the federal government and banks began to "redline" them in the 1930s, inner-city neighborhoods remained starved for capital for housing and business. As the manufacturing base of cities began to erode in the 1960s, financial institutions and private investors not only failed to pump in the capital needed to reverse their deterioration but also began to disinvest in them. Banks and businesses moved or closed; landlords, unwilling to pay taxes and maintenance costs on unprofitable property, simply abandoned housing. Rents nonetheless rose faster than the incomes of the inner-city poor, many of whom found themselves homeless in a sea of abandoned houses. With no prospect of profit, no rational investor would put money into inner cities, where property values often declined. As a consequence, these "redundant" areas moved beyond the boundaries of the market or the reach of market-based policy and remained dependent, instead, on infusions of capital from the government or private philanthropy or on devising their own community-based approaches to economic development.[15]

Spatial isolation is another way of thinking about the expansion of ghettos. Although the homes of African Americans always clustered together in cities, in the nineteenth century they formed pockets, not districts, often filling in behind other housing or in alleyways. The first identifiable ghettos emerged in major cities in the late nineteenth and early twentieth centuries and expanded during the Great Migration of the 1920s. Even these remained relatively small because African Americans did not yet constitute a large share of northern urban populations.

The great era of ghetto expansion began after World War II as a coincidence of two population movements: the migration of African Americans and later Latinos into northern cities and the outmigration of whites to suburbs. Together, these movements reconfigured urban populations. As the areas encompassed by ghettos expanded, measures of segregation within cities rose dramatically, signifying the isolation of their populations. Especially in the 1970s, ghettos also grew poorer. The proportion of their residents living in poverty rose as their geographic boundaries expanded. How much of this impoverishment, this concentration of poverty, reflects the outmigration of middle-class African Americans and how much is the result of greater poverty among existing residents remains unclear. What is clear, however, is that social isolation, the separation of income classes, has accompanied the growing spatial isolation of African Americans in inner cities.[16]

Historians and social scientists disagree about the amount of social interaction between middle-class and poor African Americans when they lived closer to one another in earlier decades. In fact, many scholars remain skeptical about the extent and quality of relations between income classes within ghettos. They stress the poverty of the earlier ghettos, the friction between their classes, and the attempt of the black middle class to distance itself from the poor; they doubt the extensive influence of "old heads" that other writers see in the recent past.[17] Whatever the past and present status of class relations within the ghetto, however, social isolation has influenced culture unmistakably. Linguists find a growing divergence between the speech patterns and language of inner-city African Americans and other versions of American English. Language itself has thereby become another factor that contributes to the isolation of African Americans in inner cities.[18]

The State, Politics, and Reform

Explanations that rely solely on great processes of social transformation often minimize the importance of agency by substituting inexorable, impersonal forces for actions and decisions. However, the situation of contemporary inner cities and the people who live in them cannot be understood without reference to the state, politics, and reform.

The mix of novelty, complexity, and danger within inner cities signified by the underclass did not just happen; its emergence was not inevitable. Like the postindustrial city of which it is a part, it is the product of actions and decisions over a very long span of time. Nonetheless, concentrated and persistent poverty was not, as Charles Murray and other conservatives would argue, the unintended result of well-meaning but misguided social programs.[19] To the contrary, beginning in the 1930s, programs that offered direct aid to poor people often succeeded. Until the mid-1960s, city, state, and federal governments did little to slow or reverse the processes that resulted in the emergence of concentrated and persistent poverty, especially among African Americans in America's inner cities. Instead, many government policies contributed to their marginalization, exclusion, and isolation. One essay cannot even list, let alone explicate, the myriad ways in which governments served these ends. What follows is a very abbreviated listing of some of them, enough to demonstrate that the condition of today's inner cities and their populations result partly from the actions of governments, that they are the product of deliberate decisions as well as of the great impersonal forces of social transformation.

The modern American state's role in the exploitation and poverty of African Americans began, of course, with the Constitution's acceptance of slavery and its subsequent protection at every level of government and by the Supreme Court. Yet it is not only a story of the South. In the antebellum North, local governments and the courts permitted the segregation of schools and did little to protect blacks from other forms of discrimination or racist violence.[20]

After the Civil War, not only did the federal government fail to redistribute land or otherwise compensate former slaves, but the Freedmen's Bureau helped tie freed slaves to plantations in a neoslave relation. Despite constitutional amendments, the federal government did not consistently nor for any duration promote either voting or civil rights, and it even refused repeatedly to pass a law outlawing lynching. State and local governments in the South tried to preserve a cheap labor force by limiting the mobility of blacks through "black codes" and vagrancy statutes. They also legalized segregation, disenfranchised African Americans, and maintained separate and unequal public facilities. Schools for black children suffered especially from the pitiful funding they received.[21]

Southern states attempted to control blacks through violence as well as law. Juries did not convict whites who lynched and murdered blacks. Police treated blacks brutally; blacks lacked access to courts or found in them unequal justice (if the word *justice* can be used at all); later in the twentieth century, not only did state and local governments use police to prevent demonstrations and mobilization, but the FBI also infiltrated and sometimes destroyed groups working for civil rights and related causes.[22] Police brutality, unequal justice, and the infiltration of civil rights movements, of course, all happened in the North as well.

Southern agricultural interests contributed to the impoverishment of African Americans through their influence in Congress, even during President Franklin Delano Roosevelt's New Deal. Federal agricultural policies forced lands out of production, thereby shrinking employment opportunities for blacks, and few farmers adhered to the law requiring them to share their crop subsidies with former black tenants. As a result, blacks began to migrate to cities, where they confronted massive unemployment.[23] Although the Economic Security Act of 1935—the charter of America's federal welfare state—eventually helped African Americans, it initially excluded, at the insistence of southern congressmen, agricultural and domestic workers, the two occupations that employed most black Americans.[24] Despite Social Security and unemployment insurance, most black workers remained for a long time unprotected in times of unemployment and in old age.

One other legacy of the New Deal was America's dual welfare state. The New Deal cemented into the foundation of the welfare state a distinction between social insurance and public assistance. Social insurance is an entitlement for everyone based on fixed criteria such as age, disability, or unemployment. Because its benefits cross class lines, its political support is powerful. The great current example, of course, is Social Security as conceived in the 1930s. By contrast, public assistance is means-tested aid. It is what used to be called relief or what we now usually think of as welfare. Major examples included AFDC (Aid to Families with Dependent Children) and, at the state level, General Assistance.[25]

What we have come to call "welfare" originated as Aid to Dependent Children (ADC, later Aid to Families with Dependent Children), also a component of the Economic Security Act of 1935. Its subsequent history differs in every way from that of Social Security. Aid to Dependent Children did not start as a program for unmarried or separated women with children. Rather, it grew out of state programs that provided mothers' pensions designed to assist widows. Its transmutation, which took place unexpectedly in the post-World War II period, resulted from changing patterns of work, residence, and family. As a program of public assistance directed only toward poor (and increasingly minority) women, AFDC has been able to muster only limited political support. Its benefits, set by state governments, vary dramatically, but in no state do they lift families out of poverty, and they remain much lower than Social Security's. In fact, the gap between the two programs widened as hostility to AFDC provoked both a reaction against welfare and punitive policies intended to control the behavior of its clients. In the 1940s and 1950s, some states introduced "suitable home" clauses into their ADC regulations to control the sexual behavior of black women and to ensure a supply of cheap domestic labor in the South. The result only worsened the poverty of black women and children, as did welfare policies that contributed to family breakup by denying aid to needy families in which a man was present. In the 1980s, the punitive, moralistic component of welfare policy continued in its perverse way by increasing the isolation of poor women with children through "deeming," in effect cutting off aid when women with children lived with working relatives or friends. In this instance, policies failed to recognize that increasing numbers of families were responding to hard times and rising rates of poverty by forming extended households.[26]

The architects who designed the welfare state during the New Deal deliberately excluded relief from the responsibilities of the federal government. Indeed, in 1935, President Roosevelt turned relief back to the states, where he thought it belonged.[27] As a program that applies only to the poorest people, public assistance inherits the stigma always attached to relief, and its funding has remained much lower than Social Security's and more variable across the states. Social Security is but one welfare program that delivers disproportionate benefits to the middle class. Other subsidies add to this inequality of benefits. The largest of these is the income-tax deduction for home mortgage interest. One authority estimated that, in 1990, combined direct and tax expenditures for federal welfare for the poor were $124.6 billion, or 16 percent of the total; for the nonpoor they were $651 billion, or 84 percent.[28]

The New Deal's relief and employment programs, especially the Works Progress Administration (WPA), literally kept many African Americans from starving, even though they received less than their fair share of benefits. With a federal administration providing relief for the first time and First Lady Eleanor Roosevelt campaigning for civil rights, blacks switched their electoral support from the Republicans to the Democrats.[29] Nonetheless, the Democrats did little to promote the welfare of African Americans or to facilitate their civil rights. Not until 1950 did President Harry Truman abolish segregation in the armed forces. John F. Kennedy promised to end discrimination in public housing, but only in 1963 did he sign the necessary order, which applied only to new construction and excluded existing housing. The only federal action came from the judiciary, most notably the *Brown v. Board of Education* decision of 1954, which declared segregation unconstitutional. Kennedy's administration also proved slow to assist the civil rights movement, even when prodded by black leaders and their allies and shocked by the violence directed at civil rights workers in the South.[30] Only in the administration of President Lyndon Johnson, with the Civil Rights Act of 1964 and the Voting Rights Act of 1965, did the legislative and executive branches of the federal government take a major step toward reducing discrimination and the practices that sustained it.

Until the mid-1960s, then, the welfare and civil rights policies of the federal government did little to slow the marginalization, exclusion, and isolation of African Americans and sometimes even facilitated it. The story of federal housing and urban policies in the same years is depressingly similar. In effect, the federal government manipulated market incentives in ways that lured middle-class whites to the suburbs and trapped blacks in inner cities.[31]

In the wake of massive mortgage foreclosures during the Great Depression of the 1930s, the federal government for the first time began to underwrite mortgages. It saved tens of thousands of homes and, by changing the terms of mortgages, helped a great many people to become homeowners. Nonetheless, the Federal Housing Administration (FHA), which administered the mortgage program, redlined areas of cities considered poor risks (that is, it identified areas in which it would not underwrite or recommend mortgages). Redlined areas included virtually all neighborhoods with black residents and many with a sizable proportion of European immigrants as well. In this way, the federal government hastened the decay of inner cities by denying them capital and by encouraging those residents able to purchase homes to leave. The FHA placed racial restrictions on its mortgages until the 1960s.[32]

Other factors—widespread automobile ownership, highway policy, tax exemption for mortgage interest payments, mortgages for veterans, and the development of techniques for producing massive amounts of tract housing quickly and cheaply—also promoted the growth of suburbs. Because suburbs are minigovernments, they exercise a great deal of autonomy, in land use, zoning, and refuted policies, and they used these, along with deed restrictions and covenants, to exclude blacks. As cities filled with poor newcomers requiring expensive services and paying little in taxes, the historic relations between cities and suburbs changed. Whereas, in the nineteenth and early twentieth centuries, cities had annexed their suburbs, offering municipal services as a lever, later suburban governments successfully began to resist incorporation, and annexation largely ended, allowing suburbs to draw their boundaries tighter against blacks, who remained trapped in inner cities. As pressures for integration mounted in the 1960s, suburbs chose to diversify by race rather than class. They retained zoning and other restrictions that allowed only affluent blacks (and in some instances Jews) to enter, thereby intensifying the concentration and isolation of the urban poor.[33]

Urban renewal and highway policies also increased the concentration of poverty and the isolation of poor minorities in inner cities. Urban renewal (chartered by the ironically named Housing Act of 1949) often ripped down viable neighborhoods, displaced their residents, and failed to rehouse them. Between 1950 and 1960, according to one estimate, urban renewal tore down 128,000 units, which rented for an average of $50 or $60 a month, and replaced them with only twenty-eight thousand units, with an average rental of $195. In place of homes, urban renewal and subsequent policy encouraged the redevelopment of central cities with office towers, hospitals, universities, and the facilities that service them. The Highway Act of 1956, which created the interstate highway system, funneled immense sums into cities because it reimbursed them for 90 percent of construction costs. The new highways and expressways not only encouraged more movement away from cities to the suburbs; they also created barriers between the sections of cities, walling off poor and minority neighborhoods from central business districts. Like urban renewal, highway and expressway construction displaced many poor people from their homes.[34]

Public housing reinforced the impact of mortgage policy, urban renewal, and highway construction. Housing is a very old problem in America's cities. New York City suffered the first of its successive housing crises in the early years of the nineteenth century; other cities followed later. Everywhere, urban politicians and elites described housing crises as the unavoidable consequence of market processes. In truth, they resulted at least as much from the transformation of housing and urban land into speculative commodities. In various ways, city governments in the nineteenth century facilitated rising real estate prices; the separation of cities into districts based on function, wealth, and race; and the progressive displacement of the poor into crowded, inferior housing. Early housing reformers, unwilling to intervene in the market by building municipal housing, stressed model housing and regulations to control the sanitary conditions and safety of tenements. Their efforts resulted in marginal improvements in tenement construction, but the larger problem of housing the poor remained unsolved.[35]

The federal government built its first public housing in the 1930s, but only after World War II did the government begin to sponsor the construction of a large number of units. Originally designed for "respectable" working families, public housing turned into shelter for the poor. Resistance to public housing perceived as only for minorities by white neighborhoods and the politicians they supported forced the federal government to agree to build only in areas dominated by minorities and poverty. Influenced by considerations of cost, the need to cram as many units as possible into a small space, and the ideas of architects inspired by visions of high-rise living, authorities designed public housing in the form of large apartment towers, with disastrous results. Because of its location and size, public housing fostered the isolation of African Americans in areas of increasingly concentrated poverty.[36]

In the mid-1960s, federal urban policy began to tilt toward cities in more constructive ways, but it lacked the time for major accomplishments before Richard Nixon, in his second administration, began to disengage the federal government from urban programs. Among other actions, Nixon placed a moratorium on the construction of public housing. In the 1980s President Ronald Reagan accelerated the withdrawal of the federal government from assistance to the cities. The result was a disastrous decade for cities and their poor. As city governments confronted increased poverty, homelessness, crumbling infrastructures, rising drug use, crime, and the spread of AIDS, the federal government virtually stopped building housing, shrank its aid to cities, reduced benefits to individuals, and raised the taxes of the poor at the same time it lowered them for the rich.[37] These are some of the ways that the actions of government fostered the concentration of persistent poverty in inner cities and the isolation of the minority poor.

Organized campaigns to reform the family life of the poor, reduce crime, and ameliorate the worst effects of urban poverty did not begin in the 1960s, or even the 1930s. They date from the late eighteenth and early nineteenth centuries, when the consequences of city growth first seriously alarmed leading citizens. Voluntary associations, often affiliated with Protestant denominations, formed to relieve poverty, suppress vice, and reform morals; public authorities created poorhouses, schools, and penitentiaries; and public funding blended with private sponsorship in the support of hospitals and orphaned children.[38]

The pre-welfare state history of these activities can be characterized, first, by what they did not try to do. They did not intervene in market relations. They did not attempt to relieve poverty by redistributing power or resources, by modifying working conditions or raising wages, or by using public authority to control the cost of housing or the price and use of land. Instead, they translated the conditions and activities that alarmed or disturbed them into questions of behavior, character, and personality, which they approached through educational reform, the regulation of drinking and sexuality, evangelical religion, reinvigorated personal contacts between rich and poor, and institutionally based programs directed at personal transformation. None of these strategies accomplished their goals.[39]

In the early twentieth century, state programs providing workmen's compensation, widows' pensions, and, in a few instances, unemployment and old-age insurance began a cautious modification of earlier traditions.[40] In the same period, however, Prohibition represented a massive victory for the older reform pattern on a national level. The great break with past approaches happened in the 1930s. The New Deal not only sponsored the constitutional amendment that repealed Prohibition; more important for the long run, it set precedents by intervening in economic relations in new ways, affirming labor's right to organize, federalizing (if only temporarily) relief, utilizing massive public-works programs to create employment, and initiating guaranteed economic support to dependent children, the unemployed, and the elderly.

The older tradition lingered, influencing, shaping, even, one of the two main strategies of the War on Poverty of the 1960s. The War on Poverty (I refer here to the programs developed by the Office of Economic Opportunity) defined its target as blocked opportunities. For this reason, it stressed education, job training, the accessibility of legal assistance, and the reform of other services. Despite the pleas of the Department of Labor, those leading this "war" rejected a strategy based on job creation and employment. The major programmatic legacies of the War on Poverty are Operation Headstart, the Job Corps, and the Legal Services Corporation. Important and successful as each of these have proven, they represent oblique assaults on urban poverty and the conditions that sustain it.[41]

Community action, the War on Poverty's other strategy, broke more decisively with reform traditions. The Economic Opportunity Act of 1964—charter of the War on Poverty—required "maximum feasible participation" by communities in the design and administration of programs. In practice, this meant the creation of community action agencies to apply for and receive federal funds. Community action threatened established political arrangements by channeling funds directly to new agencies, bypassing city and state governments, and putting large amounts of money in the hands of people who were often hostile to politicians and social agencies. State and city politicians, not surprisingly, attacked community action from the start and quickly won modifications that seriously compromised its initial intent. Nonetheless, aside from its programmatic accomplishments, community action stimulated and legitimated grass-roots activism, helping to nurture what Harry Boyte has called the "new citizen's movement," which continues to exert a profound influence on American politics and public life. Community action also recruited new leaders, predominantly minority, often women, into politics. Many of them began careers that have led to leadership positions in city governments and social agencies.[42]

The War on Poverty fell victim to the war in Vietnam, which siphoned off the funds it had been promised by President Lyndon Johnson; President Richard Nixon, who despised the War on Poverty, began to wind it down. It therefore lacked a design, the time, and the money necessary for a frontal attack on poverty.[43] Given its small budget, the political hostility it confronted, and its short life, the War on Poverty's legacy emerges as much more impressive than it appears in most assessments based on conventional wisdom, or even in those of historians and social scientists. However, during the same years, programs outside the War on Poverty in fact did the most to reduce poverty and to promote the health of disadvantaged Americans. By increasing and indexing Social Security benefits, the federal government reduced poverty among the elderly by about two-thirds. In fact, improvements in the Social Security system had started in the 1950s under the quiet sponsorship of the program's administration. Those improvements accounted for most of the reduction in poverty during the decade, which, wrongly, is usually attributed to economic growth. In 1972, Supplemental Social Security extended the benefits provided to the blind, disabled, and elderly. Expansion of the food stamp program measurably decreased hunger; nutritional programs improved the health of pregnant women and infants. Medicare and Medicaid (begun in 1965) extended health care to people who previously could not afford it. Visits to physicians by poor people increased, and infant mortality declined. Other programs increased public housing and improved its quality and design. Affirmative action opened educational opportunities and careers to women and minorities, with dramatic results, especially in higher education and government. The common quip that "government fought a war on poverty and poverty won" is ideological slander, not history. To the contrary, the record shows that government has the capacity to reduce poverty; extend health care, access to legal counsel, and housing; improve education and job training; and counter discrimination. The problem is not a lack of precedents or of good program ideas. It is politics and a lack of will.[44]

NOTES

This edited chapter originally appeared as a longer chapter in Michael B. Katz, *The "Underclass" Debate: Views from History* (Princeton, N.J.: Princeton University Press, 1993), 449-78.

1. Joe William Trotter Jr. "Blacks in the Urban North: The 'Underclass Question' in Historical Perspective," in *The "Underclass" Debate: Views from History,* ed. Michael Katz (Princeton, N.J.: Princeton University Press, 1993).

2. For a discussion of the literature of transiency, see Michael Katz, Michael J. Doucet, and Mark J. Stern, *The Social Organization of Early Industrial Capitalism* (Cambridge, Mass.: Harvard University Press, 1982), chap. 3.

3. Jacqueline Jones, "Southern Diaspora: Origins of the Northern 'Underclass,'" in *The "Underclass" Debate: Views from History,* ed. Michael Katz (Princeton, N.J.: Princeton University Press, 1993); the most thorough and definitive study of black mobility in the South after the Civil War is William Cohen, *At Freedom's Edge: Black Mobility and the Southern White Quest for Racial Control, 1861-1915* (Baton Rouge and London: Louisiana State University Press, 1991).

4. Jones, "Southern Diaspora." Also see Trotter, "Blacks in the Urban North."

5. See David W. Bartelt, "Housing the 'Underclass,' " in *The "Underclass" Debate: Views from History*, ed. Michael Katz (Princeton, N.J.: Princeton University Press, 1993).

6. A good overview of the relations between the spread of capitalism and transatlantic migration is John Bodnar, *The Transplanted: A History of Immigrants in Urban America* (Bloomington: Indiana University Press, 1985).

7. See Trotter, "Blacks in the Urban North."

8. Nicholas Lemann, *The Promised Land: The Great Black Migration and How It Changed America* (New York: Knopf, 1991); also see Jones, "Southern Diaspora."

9. See Jones, "Southern Diaspora."

10. Robert B. Reich, *The Work of Nations* (New York: Knopf, 1991), 177-80; on the "convergence" thesis, see June Axinn and Mark Stern, *Dependency and Poverty: Old Problems in a New World* (Lexington, Mass.: Lexington Books, 1988); for an excellent review of the literature on the labor force disadvantages of young black men, see Philip Moss and Chris Tilly, *Why Black Men Are Doing Worse in the Labor Market: A Review of Supply-Side and Demand-Side Explanations* (New York: Social Science Research Council, 1991).

11. Suzanne Model, "The Ethnic Niche and the Structure of Opportunity: Immigrants and Minorities in New York City," in *The "Underclass" Debate: Views from History*, ed. Michael Katz (Princeton, N.J.: Princeton University Press, 1993).

12. Ibid.

13. Ibid.

14. Isolation is a major theme of William J. Wilson's in *The Truly Disadvantaged: The Inner City, the Underclass, and Public Policy* (Chicago: University of Chicago Press, 1987).

15. See Bartelt, "Housing the 'Underclass.' "

16. Wilson, *Truly Disadvantaged*; Paul A. Jargowksy and Mary Jo Bane, "Neighborhood Poverty," Center for Health and Human Resource Policy, Harvard University, Discussion Paper Series No. H-90-3, March 1990; Douglas S. Massey and Mitchell L. Eggers, "The Ecology of Inequality: Minorities and the Concentration of Poverty, 1970-1980" (Chicago: Population Research Center, University of Chicago, 1989); Reynolds Farley, "Residential Segregation of Social and Economic Groups among Blacks, 1970-1980," in Jencks and Peterson, *Urban Underclass*, 274-98; Douglas S. Massey and Nancy A. Denton, *American Apartheid: Segregation and the Making of the Underclass* (Cambridge, Mass.: Harvard University Press, 1995).

17. William J. Wilson stresses the interaction of middle-class and poor ghetto residents in *The Truly Disadvantaged*; "old heads" is the phrase reported by Elijah Anderson in *Streetwise: Race, Class, and Change in an Urban Community* (Chicago: University of Chicago Press, 1990).

18. William Labov, *Language in the Inner City: Studies in the Black English Vernacular* (Philadelphia: University of Pennsylvania Press, 1972).

19. Charles Murray, *Losing Ground: American Social Policy, 1950-1980* (New York: Basic Books, 1984).

20. Leon Litwak, *North of Slavery: The Negro in the Free States, 1790-1860* (Chicago: University of Chicago Press, 1961).

21. See Jones, "Southern Diaspora." There is a large body of literature on the origins of segregation and on the underfunding of education for blacks. See, for instance, John W. Cell, *The Highest Stage of White Supremacy: The Origins of Segregation in South Africa and the American South* (New York: Cambridge University Press, 1982); and Louis Harlan, *Separate and Unequal: Public School Campaigns and Racism in the Southern Seaboard States, 1901-1915* (Chapel Hill: University of North Carolina Press, 1958).

22. See Robin D. G. Kelley, "The Black Poor and the Politics of Opposition in a New South City, 1929-1970," in *The "Underclass" Debate: Views from History*, ed. Michael Katz (Princeton, N.J.: Princeton University Press, 1993).

23. See Jones, "Southern Diaspora."

24. On the influence of southern members of Congress on the Social Security legislation, see especially Jill S. Quadagno, *The Transformation of Old Age Security: Class and Politics in the American Welfare State* (Chicago: University of Chicago Press, 1988).

25. I have written about this distinction in *In the Shadow of the Poorhouse* (New York: Basic Books, 1986).

26. Winifred Bell, *Aid to Dependent Children* (New York: Columbia University Press, 1965); Katz, *Shadow*, chap. 5; James T. Patterson, *America's Struggle against Poverty* (Cambridge, Mass.: Harvard University Press, 1968), 91-112; also see Mark J. Stern, "Poverty and Family Composition since 1940" in *The "Underclass" Debate: Views from History*, ed. Michael Katz (Princeton, N.J.: Princeton University Press, 1993).

27. On this episode see Frances Fox Piven and Richard A. Cloward, *Regulating the Poor: The Functions of Public Welfare* (New York: Vintage Books, 1971); and Katz, *Shadow*.

28. Michael Sherraden, *Assets and the Poor: A New American Welfare Policy* (Armonk, N.Y.: M. E. Sharpe, 1991), 65.

29. See Jones, "Southern Diaspora." On blacks' shift to the Democratic Party, see Nancy J. Weiss, *Farewell to the Party of Lincoln: Black Politics in the Age of FDR* (Princeton, N.J.: Princeton University Press, 1983).

30. The foot dragging of the Kennedy administration emerges vividly in Taylor Branch, *Parting the Waters: America in the King Years, 1954-1963* (New York: Simon and Schuster, 1988).

31. See Bartelt, "Housing the 'Underclass.'"

32. See Bartelt, "Housing the 'Underclass' "; Kelley, "The Black Poor"; and Thomas Sugrue, "The Structures of Urban Poverty: The Reorganization of Space and Work in Three Periods of American History," in *The "Underclass" Debate: Views from History*, ed. Michael Katz (Princeton, N.J.: Princeton University Press, 1993).

33. On the history of suburbs in America, see Kenneth T. Jackson, *Crabgrass Frontier: The Suburbanization of the United States* (New York: Oxford University Press, 1985).

34. See Bartelt, "Housing the 'Underclass' "; Sugrue, "The Structures of Urban Poverty"; and Martin Anderson, *The Federal Bulldozer: A Critical Analysis of Urban Renewal, 1949-1962* (Cambridge, Mass.: MIT Press, 1964).

35. Elizabeth Blackmar, *Manhattan for Rent* (Ithaca, N.Y.: Cornell University Press, 1989); Roy Lubove, *The Progressives and the Slums: Tenement House Reform in New York City, 1890-1917* (Pittsburgh: University of Pittsburgh Press, 1962).

36. See Sugrue, "The Structures of Urban Poverty"; Bartelt, "Housing the 'Underclass' "; and Kelley, "The Black Poor"; Arnold Hirsch, *Making the Second Ghetto: Race and Housing in Chicago, 1940-1960* (Cambridge and New York: Cambridge University Press, 1983); John F. Bauman, Norman P. Hummon, and Edward K. Muller, "Public Housing, Isolation, and the Urban Underclass," *Journal of Urban History* 17, no. 3 (May 1991): 264-92.

37. See, for instance, David R. Goldfield and Blaine A. Brownell, *Urban America: A History*, 2nd ed. (Boston: Houghton Mifflin, 1990), 433-35.

38. For an overview of these activities in the nineteenth century, see Paul Boyer, *Urban Masses and Moral Order in America, 1820-1920* (Cambridge, Mass.: Harvard University Press, 1978), esp. 3-190; and Katz, *Shadow*, chap. 4.

39. An excellent discussion of how reluctance to intervene in market relations handicapped reform is in W. Norton Grubb and Marvin Lazerson, *Broken Promises: How Americans Fail Their Children* (New York: Basic Books, 1982).

40. This story is told in James T. Patterson, *America's Struggle against Poverty, 1900-1985* (Cambridge, Mass.: Harvard University Press, 1986); and Roy Lubove, *Struggle for Social Security, 1900-1935* (Cambridge, Mass.: Harvard University Press, 1968) among others.

41. Katz, *Undeserving Poor* (New York: Pantheon Books, 1989); Margaret Weir, "The Federal Government and Unemployment: The Frustration of Policy Innovation from the New Deal to the

Great Society," in *The Politics of Social Policy in the United States,* ed. Margaret Weir, Ann Shola Orloff, and Theda Skocpol (Princeton, N.J.: Princeton University Press, 1988), 169, 171; see also Thomas F. Jackson, "The State, the Movement, and the Urban Poor: The War on Poverty and Political Mobilization in the 1960s," in *The "Underclass" Debate: Views from History,* ed. Michael Katz (Princeton, N.J.: Princeton University Press, 1993).

42. See Jackson, "The State, the Movement, and the Urban Poor"; and Harry Boyte, *The Backyard Revolution: Understanding the New Citizen Movement* (Philadelphia: Temple University Press, 1980).

43. A useful account of the War on Poverty, the interpretation of which differs in some ways from mine, is in Allen J. Matusow, *The Unraveling of America: A History of Liberalism in the 1960s* (New York: Harper and Row, 1984).

44. See Stern, "Poverty and Family Composition"; Patterson, *America's Struggle*; John E. Schwarz, *America's Hidden Successes: A Reassessment of Twenty Years of Public Policy* (New York: Norton, 1983).

DISCUSSION QUESTIONS

1. What major social and historical factors have molded the experience of poverty in the United States?

2. How did race create privileges for European immigrants but disadvantages for Blacks?

3. What roles did residential segregation have in the maintenance of Black and Latino poverty?

4. How was the presumed sexual behavior of black and Latino women treated as a political issue?

5. Why does the author argue that continuing poverty is a problem of "politics and will"?

FOR FURTHER READING

Anderson, Martin, *The Federal Bulldozer: A Critical Analysis of Urban Renewal, 1949-1962* (Cambridge, Mass.: MIT Press, 1964).

Cohen, William, At *Freedom's Edge: Black Mobility and the Southern White Quest for Racial Control, 1861-1915* (Baton Rouge and London: Louisiana State University Press, 1991).

Jackson, Kenneth, *Crabgrass Frontier: The Suburbanization of the United States* (New York: Oxford University Press, 1985).

Katz, Michael, *In the Shadow of the Poorhouse* (New York: Basic Books, 1986).

Lemann, Nicholas, *The Promised Land: The Great Black Migration and How It Changed America* (New York: Knopf, 1991).

Piven, Frances Fox, and Cloward, Richard A., *Regulating the Poor* (New York: Pantheon, 1971).

Quadagno, Jill S., *The Transformation of Old Age Security: Class and Politics in the American Welfare State* (Chicago: University of Chicago Press, 1988).

Reich, Robert B., *The Work of Nations* (New York: Knopf, 1991), 177-80.

Sherraden, Michael, *Assets and the Poor: A New American Welfare Policy* (Armonk, N.Y.: M. E. Sharpe, 1991), 65.

Chapter Four

Unfinished Democracy

Jill Quadagno

According to the British sociologist T. H. Marshall, democratization has proceeded in three stages, with the granting of civil, political, and, finally, social rights. In Europe the struggle for civil rights emerged out of a feudal heritage where serfdom locked workers to the land. The transition from servile to free labor introduced the notion of citizenship as the right to pursue the occupation of one's choice freely, without compulsion, subject only to requirements for training. By the beginning of the nineteenth century, the principle of individual economic "freedom" was accepted as axiomatic.[1]

Throughout the nineteenth century in most European nations, only monarchs, bureaucrats, and aristocrats could vote, although limited political rights were granted to some men on the basis of property ownership and education. These constitutional monarchies were gradually replaced by representative governments and popular sovereignty. Political democratization in the form of universal suffrage advanced through the dismantling of restrictions on voting based on property ownership or literacy. By 1920 adult men had full voting rights in seventeen nations, while nine nations had given women the vote.[2] Political rights meant not only the right to vote but also the right to a voice in a collective process of decision making.[3]

The third phase of democratization began in the late nineteenth century with the construction of national welfare states. Programs of social protection granted social rights: "The right to a modicum of economic welfare and security, the right to share to the full in the social heritage and to live the life of a civilized being according to the standards prevailing in the society."[4] Much of the industrialized world has instituted three kinds of social rights. Some nations protect the poor against the exigencies of the capitalist marketplace and provide programs that compensate workers against losses caused by injuries on the job, unemployment, and old age. Others, geared to an economy based on mass production, provide not only income security for the working class but also stable product markets for mass-produced goods.[5] Examples include old-age insurance, family allowances, and national health insurance. Social rights also stabilize the labor supply, especially among women workers in the expanding service sector,[6] through job training and employment-referral systems, day-care provisions, paid parental leave, and full-employment policies.

The combination of civil, political, and social rights is the foundation of democracy. While other nations added these rights gradually over centuries, the United States pursued an idiosyncratic path. That path began when the first principles of civil rights—the belief in equality and the right to liberty—were enshrined in the Bill of Rights and the Declaration of Independence. Americans, Thomas Jefferson wrote, had inherent and inalienable rights to "life, liberty and the pursuit of happiness."[7] From the first moments of the nation's existence, however, practice compromised principles. In theory, the concept of inalienable rights meant free labor markets and the absence of servile, or unfree, labor. In practice, lovers of freedom tolerated the total suppression of freedom among slaves, who had no claim on rights and whose masters owned both their labor and their progeny.

Political democracy was an extension of civil liberty, and most Americans enjoyed it early. Even as colonists under British rule, when the franchise was based on property ownership, between 50 and 80 percent of white men qualified to vote.[8] At the end of the revolutionary period, many states extended male suffrage by moving from property qualifications to tax qualifications for voting. By 1840 most white men could vote, and voter turnout ranged from 68 to 98 percent. Government also became more directly representative of the people who participated in the electoral process through the creation of mass political parties, the rotation of political leaders, the practice of local community rule, and the choosing of presidential candidates by party conventions instead of wealthy elites.[9] But democracy remained incomplete. Women could not vote until 1920, and, of course, slaves were denied even the most rudimentary privileges of citizenship.

Though precocious in extending civil and political rights to white men, America lagged behind Europe in developing social rights through a national welfare state. Until 1935 the United States had no national social programs. Instead, it had only scattered, meagerly funded, state-level programs of workers' compensation, old-age pensions, and mothers' pensions that left decisions about eligibility to the discretion of local welfare authorities.[10] Not until the Depression challenged the foundations of this "rugged individualism" did the concept of social rights emerge as a shared ideal. When that finally happened, the presence of a nation within a nation, that is, of the South as a politically and economically distinct entity, imposed limits on what could be done. Instead of a "universal" welfare state that could create solidarity among workers, the New Deal welfare state instituted a regime that reinforced racial inequality.

Creating the Racial Welfare State Regime

Franklin Delano Roosevelt took office in 1932 with a mandate to inaugurate a new era in government intervention. The cornerstone of his New Deal was the Social Security Act of 1935, which provided old-age insurance and unemployment compensation for the industrial labor force. Under the old-age insurance program, workers paid payroll taxes of 1 percent on the first $3,000 earned, an amount matched by their employers, in exchange for a $15 pension a month upon retirement. Under the unemployment insurance program, states levied a payroll tax on employers to protect workers against downturns in the business cycle. Although the unemployment program was technically voluntary, generous tax credits that offset most of the payroll tax provided incentives to employers to participate.[11]

The Social Security Act also included two means-tested social assistance programs, Aid to Dependent Children and Old Age Assistance, in which state expenditures were matched by federal funds. These programs provided minimal support to those outside the wage labor pool. Old-age assistance paid eligible elderly men and women a maximum grant of $30 a month, though most states, especially those in the South, paid less. Aid to Dependent Children was restricted to single-parent families and paid benefits only to children.

The Social Security Act laid the groundwork for a national welfare state and established some benefits as an earned right. Through such measures, the New Deal liberalism of the Democratic party came to mean active, positive intervention for the public good. Public support was high for programs that protected the many against the abuses of the few and taxed the few for the benefit of the many.

Government intervention did not extend to support for civil rights, however, as Roosevelt sought to stabilize his unwieldy coalition of northern workers and white southerners by refusing to back legislation to abolish lynching or poll taxes and by weaving racial inequality into his new welfare state.[12] This was accomplished by excluding agricultural workers and domestic servants from both old-age insurance and unemployment compensation and by failing to provide national standards for unemployment compensation.[13] These omissions were not random. Rather, they reflected a compromise reached with southern Democrats over the structure of the welfare state.

The Repression of Rights

By 1935 the North was industrialized and democratic. It had two active political parties, and its citizenry had full civil and political rights. The South was neither industrialized nor democratic. Its economy was driven by cotton production, which flourished through a sharecropping system that tied tenants, both black and white, to the land. Sharecropping was a system of servitude that denied to African Americans the first civil right, "the right to follow the occupation of one's choice in the place of one's choice."[14] Sharecropping operated without cash. Planters loaned money to croppers for seeds, equipment, food, and rent, in return for a share of the crop grown. Often at year's end, a cropper family owed more than it had earned in the entire year. Debt kept sharecroppers nearly enslaved.

Politically, the South was an oligarchy. Such measures as poll taxes and literacy tests, introduced at the end of the nineteenth century, had disenfranchised not only African Americans but most poor whites, as well. Disenfranchisement reduced opposition to the Democratic party majority and allowed one-party politics to reign. With no competition for elective office, southern Democrats earned seniority in Congress and thus were able to control key committees in the House and the Senate.[15] This power allowed them to exert a negative, controlling influence on national politics.

Although Roosevelt's electoral victory did not hinge on southern support, he needed southern congressmen to move his programs past the key House and Senate committees.

These officials opposed any program that would grant cash directly to black workers, because direct cash could undermine the entire foundation of the plantation economy. In 1935 more than three-quarters of African Americans still lived in the South. Most sharecropped; those not sharecropping worked as day laborers when planters needed extra hands at picking time. The going rate for day laborers was two dollars per one hundred pounds of cotton, a day's labor for a strong worker. Outside the cotton fields black women worked as maids, earning perhaps $2.50 a week.[16] Federal old-age insurance paid directly to retired black men and women, even the meager sum of $15 a month, would provide more cash than a cropper family might see in a year.

Because of southern opposition, agricultural workers and domestic servants—most black men and women—were left out of the core programs of the Social Security Act. Instead, they were relegated to the social-assistance programs, where local welfare authorities could determine benefit levels and set eligibility rules. Even in these programs, southern congressmen vigilantly defended "states' rights." They demanded that two clauses be removed from the old-age assistance legislation, one that would have compelled the states to furnish assistance at "a reasonable subsistence compatible with decency and health" and another that would have required states to designate a single state authority to administer the plan. Southerners simply would not allow the federal government to dictate standards or set benefit levels. They sought control over any social program that might threaten white domination, so precariously balanced on cotton production.

The unemployment insurance program also perpetuated racial inequality by charging Employment Service offices with implementing the legislation. Established in 1933, the U.S. Employment Service was a federal-state organization that provided job placement for the unemployed. In administering unemployment insurance, however, Employment Service offices devoted little attention to job placement. Instead, they spent most of their time figuring benefits. When they did connect workers to jobs, they did so in a highly prejudiced manner, either excluding minority clients entirely or offering them the most menial, low-paying jobs.[17]

Racial inequality was not confined to the South, however. By legitimating discrimination in work and housing, New Deal legislation reinforced racial barriers in other parts of the nation. Skilled craft workers had been organized into unions since the nineteenth century. Most of these workers became members of the American Federation of Labor (AFL) and its affiliates. But unskilled workers in the expanding mass-production industries—iron and steel, autos, rubber, and meat packing—had fought a losing battle with employers over the right to organize. When the National Labor Relations Act, or Wagner Act, of 1935 granted workers the right to organize unions and bargain collectively with employers, unskilled workers clamored to join unions.[18] The issue of race contributed to the already fractious relationship between them and their skilled comrades.

Throughout its history, the AFL had discriminated against black workers. Some affiliates, like the Brotherhood of Railway Carmen, banned black workers by ritual or constitutional provision. Others granted black unions separate charters or established segregated locals as second-class members under the supervision of white workers. Only the United Mine Workers, an AFL affiliate made up mainly of unskilled workers, had integrated unions.[19]

On November 9, 1935, unskilled workers walked out of the AFL convention and founded the Committee for Industrial Organization (CIO). Among their grievances was the refusal of the AFL to address union discrimination. They knew that industrial unionism required interracial cooperation. After all, African Americans made up more than 18 percent of iron and steel workers, 68 percent of tobacco workers, 40 percent of meat packers, and 9 percent of coal miners. Without their participation, any union of the unskilled would fail. From its inception the CIO opened its doors to black workers on an equal basis.[20] Following a massive organizing campaign, by 1940 the CIO had more than 500,000 black members.

Black leaders had little enthusiasm for the Wagner Act, because it legalized closed shops. Since black workers were excluded from most skilled trade unions, blacks feared that the closed shop provision would permanently lock them out of these jobs. The National Association for the Advancement of Colored People (NAACP) tried to have a clause barring discrimination by labor unions written into the Wagner Act, but the AFL refused to support the legislation if the clause was included. The final legislation permitted labor organizations to exclude African Americans, denied the status of "employee" to black workers engaged in strike breaking, and permitted the establishment of separate, racially segregated unions.[21] From 1936 to 1955, when the AFL merged with the CIO, the skilled trade unions maintained policies of racial exclusion and segregation with the tacit approval of the federal government.

The New Deal also preserved and reinforced patterns of racial segregation through its housing policy. The government first intervened in the housing market to restore the confidence of lenders in average homebuyers, thousands of whom had defaulted on loans. The National Housing Act of 1934 sought both to stimulate a depressed economy and to calm the fears of bankers. It authorized low down payments, set up extended loan maturities (as long as forty years), and regulated interest rates so that working-class families could afford mortgage payments. The Act also established the Federal Housing Administration (FHA) to insure lending institutions against loan defaults. The FHA was to behave like a conservative bank, insuring only mortgages that were "economically sound." In practice, economic soundness was translated into "redlining": a red line was literally drawn around areas of cities considered risky for economic *or* racial reasons. Redlining meant that most black families were ineligible for federally insured loans. Until 1949 the FHA also encouraged the use of restrictive covenants that banned African Americans from certain neighborhoods and refused to insure mortgages in integrated neighborhoods.[22] Thanks to FHA, no bank would insure loans in the ghetto, and few African Americans could live outside it.

What housing the federal government did provide to African Americans was racially segregated. The Housing Act of 1937 allowed local housing authorities to use proceeds from tax-free bonds to build public housing projects. Federal subsidies would pay the difference between the housing costs and what tenants could afford to pay in rent.[23] From the start, public housing authorities located new projects in racially segregated neighborhoods and selected tenants by race.[24] Thus, federal housing provided secure loans for the middle class and subsidized rentals in public housing for the poor. The working poor, much of black America but also white families outside the industrial labor force, were left out in the cold.

The New Deal thus united the industrial working class around a party that provided income security against job loss, injury, and old age to working men and their families. At the same time, it left intact, indeed reinforced, the rigid color line. The extension of social rights thus had paradoxical consequences for racial equality. In the words of T. H. Marshall, it granted a modicum of economic welfare and security to whites while denying to others the full perquisites of democracy.[25]

Destabilizing the New Deal

The New Deal also encouraged farmers to replace workers with machines through farm subsidies and other benefits to agriculture. Many farmers used their subsidies to purchase machinery, and increased reliance on machines reduced labor needs. Farm subsidies were thus passed on to black sharecroppers in the form of evictions.[26] Throughout the 1940s evicted sharecroppers migrated in large numbers to northern cities. In 1940, 77 percent of African Americans lived in the South; by 1970, only 53 percent still did.[27] Their departure toppled the political and economic structure that underlay the cotton South and dismantled the system of tenancy that had given southern planters a stranglehold on black labor.

The presence of black migrants in northern cities moved racial inequality from the periphery to the center of national politics. The nation as a whole now confronted the puzzle of incorporating African Americans into the national political economy. At first, political analysts believed that this incorporation would occur naturally. In the past large-scale population shifts had created not only political upheavals but also new opportunities. Perhaps African Americans, like other newly arrived immigrant groups, would use these opportunities to move up the equal-opportunity ladder and out of the inner cities.[28] The problem was that racial segregation had limited the opportunities available to blacks, and, after more than a century of deprivation, they were unwilling to wait longer for their share of the American dream. While elsewhere the extension of democratic rights had proceeded fitfully over centuries, in the United States it took less than a decade to complete the process of democratization for those on the wrong side of the color line. First across the South and then sweeping the North, a social movement arose, demanding that the nation immediately grant to all its citizens the basic perquisites of a democratic society—civil, political, and social rights.

The Search for Rights

The civil rights movement began in the 1950s with an assault on the South's racial order. The first victory came in 1954 when the Supreme Court, in the *Brown v. Topeka Board of Education* decision, struck down the doctrine of "separate but equal" and ordered the schools to integrate. Instead of abiding by the law, however, southern attorneys general advocated that desegregation proceed "with all deliberate speed," and the Supreme Court agreed that local school authorities could determine the pace.[29] Whites mobilized against school desegregation not only officially through legal action but also through a reign of terror that included economic coercion, violence, and murder. But white resistance failed to dampen the ardor of those inspired by the promise of equal opportunity. In December 1955, Rosa Parks, a black woman from Montgomery, Alabama, refused to move to the back of a public bus. Her subsequent arrest was the catalyst in a year-long battle in which the black population took on the entire white power structure and desegregated the public transportation system.[30]

Martin Luther King Jr. emerged from that struggle as the most important black leader in America, and the organization he led, the Southern Christian Leadership Conference (SCLC), became a powerful locus of mobilization for the civil rights movement. The SCLC adopted Mahatma Gandhi's strategy of nonviolent protest, which became an effective political weapon in the struggle for rights. By pitting peaceful demonstrators against often violent opponents, nonviolence turned northern whites against this egregious violation of American values.

College students then formed their own organization, the Student Nonviolent Coordinating Committee (SNCC), which rapidly displaced the SCLC as the most militant civil rights organization.[31] Beginning with a lunch counter protest in the Woolworth's in Greensboro, North Carolina, students mounted a series of sit-in campaigns in 1960 and 1961. The effort to integrate lunch counters expanded to include all public accommodations—restaurants, theaters, department stores, hotels, and hospitals.[32] The SNCC's only rival for the title of most militant civil rights group was the Congress on Racial Equality (CORE), a northern-based civil rights organization. Both SNCC and CORE members willingly exposed themselves to dangers other organizations avoided and were burned, beaten, and murdered for their efforts. From buses to bathrooms, the civil rights movement defied every aspect of the Jim Crow laws that sustained racial inequality and made a mockery of democracy.

The civil rights movement brought to the forefront of national politics not only the brutality of racial oppression but also the instability of the New Deal compromise. The sacrifice of African Americans in order to win the support of southern Democrats had ensnared the party in an unresolvable conflict. In 1935 black voters were irrelevant to Democratic party fortunes; by 1960 the pattern of black settlement had altered the political landscape. The black migration was not so much a general exodus from the South as a selective move out of areas where the political participation of African Americans was most limited. Thus, it was also a move from not voting to voting. From 1940 to 1960, 87 percent of the migrants settled in seven northern industrial states: New York, New Jersey, Pennsylvania, Ohio, California, Illinois, and Michigan. Because of the winner-take-all provision in voting, these states held the key to electoral success in presidential contests.[33] In that year's presidential election, black voters gave John Kennedy the winning margin in New Jersey, Michigan, Illinois, Texas, and South Carolina. Had Kennedy lost these states, Richard Nixon would have won the election.[34] In becoming a powerful electoral force in national elections, the southern migrants posed a political problem for the Democrats. How could the Jim Crow party of the solid South woo black voters without alienating white southerners? In fact, it could not.

President Kennedy could not confront this problem directly, for the Democrats needed the South. So he procrastinated on civil rights even as the movement gained momentum. In 1961 CORE joined with SNCC and the SCLC to organize "freedom rides" into the deep South. The riders would travel together, eat together, and use the whites-only restrooms. As the nightly news brought the sight of freedom riders being beaten and arrested into living rooms across the nation, the federal government sat back and did nothing. Indeed, federal officials attempted to halt one freedom ride. Only when the public, shocked by the attacks on the nonviolent freedom riders, demanded that the government protect them did Kennedy mobilize the National Guard.

What seemed by now the only viable solution was legislation to force the South to do what it refused to do voluntarily. Still, Kennedy vacillated. Instead, he initiated two limited programs for the poor. In 1961 he established the Area Redevelopment Agency to increase employment in depressed areas like Appalachia by providing loans and subsidies to small businesses. The following year he supported the Manpower Development and Training Act to retrain workers displaced by automation.[35] Such measures did not even begin to address the dilemma of incorporating African Americans into the larger American society. In fact, they mostly benefited whites. Then, in 1962, Kennedy asked his Council of Economic Advisors to suggest more comprehensive ways to address the poverty problem.

Scholars have since debated what the attention to poverty signified. Why poverty, Robert Haveman asks, when "there was no organized interest group demanding new programs for the poor...there was no history of party platforms that had assigned this problem particularly high priority, and there was no apparent surge of public opinion designating poverty to be the central domestic problem"?[36] The answer from many social scientists is that Kennedy's concern with poverty was an oblique response to the civil rights movement. Frances Fox Piven and Richard Cloward, for example, argue that the focus on poverty was Kennedy's way out, a means of evading forceful action on civil rights while maintaining the political support of African Americans who had given him his majority in the 1960 election.[37] Further, the civil rights movement had shifted its focus from integration to economic problems just as Kennedy launched his wave of rhetoric about economic injustice.[38]

Margaret Weir disagrees. She argues that the antipoverty programs had no link to the civil rights movement or to the electoral concerns of Democrats over the black vote. She finds no evidence

> that an attack on poverty was conceived as a political strategy for strengthening black loyalty to the Democratic party or that it was even initially intended to focus on African Americans. Instead, the president's vague request...appears to have been motivated by a more general desire to devise some policies that would give his administration a stamp of originality and energy.[39]

This debate about origins, which has dominated much of the literature, matters little. In fact, it obscures the crucial linkages that unquestionably did develop between the War on Poverty and the civil rights movement once the programs began operating. Programs targeted to the poor, and especially the black poor, were rapidly subsumed by the civil rights movement. As a result, the more traditional objectives of social policy—to provide income stability and to guarantee product markets—became secondary to the grander struggle for racial justice. Instead of instituting a new group of social programs to stabilize the labor supply of a service-driven economy and to support a labor force increasingly made up of women, the welfare state became a vehicle of equal opportunity.

The Equal-Opportunity Welfare State

Kennedy's antipoverty program had barely begun when he was assassinated. No one will ever know whether he would have pursued the course he set, a minor program aimed at poor whites, or whether history would have propelled him instead along the path that his successor, Lyndon Baines Johnson, took. What we do know is that when Johnson ascended suddenly to the presidency, he began steering the ship of state toward the familiar liberalism of Roosevelt's New Deal, the liberalism of government intervention to eliminate social ills, but also toward an unknown destination as the federal government sought to end racial discrimination.

In 1964, under Johnson's leadership, Congress passed the Civil Rights Act; then, in 1965, it passed the Voting Rights Act. The Civil Rights Act, which barred discrimination on the basis of race, color, religion, sex, or national origin, destroyed Jim Crow in public accommodations and helped end a decade of paralysis in school desegregation. The Voting Rights Act, which made illegal discriminatory voting regulations, rapidly enfranchised both the mass of southern African Americans and, ironically, a greater number of southern whites—ironically because southern whites would later become an important constituency in the rise of the New Right and the backlash against Johnson's "Great Society."[40]

These victories eliminated barriers to integration and to voting in the South but did little for the African Americans, legally free but unequal, living in squalor in urban ghettos. For those relegated to decrepit housing in the worst sections of cities, forced to send their children to inferior schools, and locked out of opportunities for jobs with upward mobility, the civil rights movement now demanded protection from want and some guarantee of economic security—the social rights of full citizenship. The time had come for the government to provide adequate housing for those displaced by urban renewal; adequate income for mothers raising young children alone; access to jobs in retail establishments, banks, and other businesses; and entry into the white building trades unions, which controlled the good construction jobs. What could dissolve these more intransigent barriers to equality? No one knew. And as this uncertainty became apparent, the cities erupted in explosive upheavals that drove home the message that legal emancipation was an insufficient response to the quest for equality.

Meeting demands for full democratic rights meant confronting the New Deal compromise, which had forsaken racial equality for a stable political coalition between the industrial working class and the South. That coalition was rapidly disintegrating. When the civil rights effort focused on discrimination in the South, the majority of northern whites supported it. In 1964, 68 percent of northern whites supported the administration's effort to integrate the South. When the civil rights movement moved North, support waned. By 1966, 52 percent of northern whites believed that the government was pushing integration too fast.[41]

How could the federal government unify the nation when its major social programs were designed to maintain racial cleavages? President Johnson seemed to have an answer when, on January 8, 1964, in his State of the Union message, he promised to wage an "unconditional war on poverty."[42] Less than eight months later, on August 20, Congress passed the Economic Opportunity Act, an ambitious group of programs for job training, community action, health care, housing, and education. Johnson began preparing his antipoverty programs just months after the 1963 March on Washington in which African Americans dramatically proclaimed the need for freedom (the vote) and jobs. The bill passed during the summer of 1964, as urban riots swept across Harlem, Bedford-Stuyvesant, Rochester, Jersey City, Paterson, Elizabeth, Chicago, and Philadelphia.[43] Perhaps the timing was merely coincidental. However, the structure of the War on Poverty suggests otherwise.

The social institutions created by the New Deal were incapable of incorporating African Americans into the national political economy.[44] Rather, the New Deal legacy could only frustrate the antipoverty effort with its network of local welfare offices, Employment Services, and housing authorities that stretched from governors' offices down into even the most remote rural townships, creating physical and social barriers to efforts to help blacks. An alternative model did exist, however, in two private projects funded by the Ford Foundation: the Grey Areas project and Mobilization for Youth. Both projects emphasized control by local community organizations, and both were founded on the belief that "the first task of community action was to enable [the poor] to assert themselves by placing the means to reform in their own hands."[45] Only by releasing social programs from the old-line agencies could the apathy and resistance generated by existing institutions be transcended.[46]

Johnson's task was not merely to extend the New Deal by expanding social rights but also to eliminate the barriers to equality of opportunity that it had created. Community action could circumvent the entrenched bureaucracies, which were "too preoccupied with day-to-day operations" and consumed by an "inertia dedicated to preserving the status quo."[47] Johnson made community action the centerpiece of his War on Poverty. Directed by a new agency, the Office of Economic Opportunity, community action would bypass old-line agencies and provide services directly to the poor. Its manpower programs operated outside the Department of Labor. Its Head Start program operated outside the established educational system. Johnson also created a new Department of Housing and Urban Development to consolidate the unwieldy hodgepodge of federal housing agencies.

While the New Deal had excluded African Americans, the War on Poverty would favor them. While the New Deal had conspired with southern elites to deny political and social rights to African Americans, the War on Poverty would integrate them into local politics, local job markets, and local housing markets. If the plan was not laid out so succinctly at the start, it was the modus operandi by the time the programs began running. As Kennedy's adviser Adam Yarmolinsky recalled: "We were busy telling people it *wasn't* just racial because we thought it'd be easier to sell that way, and we thought it was less racial than it turned out to be."[48]

While the War on Poverty began as a top-down effort, civil rights activists rapidly seized the opportunity that the local initiatives had created, pushing the Great Society mandate one step further. The War on Poverty would do more than eliminate impediments. It would extend equal opportunity to African Americans and complete the task of fully democratizing American society.

Notes

This chapter was originally published in *The Color of Welfare: How Racism Undermined the War on Poverty* (New York: Oxford University Press, 1994), 17-31.

1. T. H. Marshall, *Class, Citizenship and Social Development* (Chicago: University of Chicago Press, 1964), 82-87.

2. Goran Therborn, "The Rule of Capital and the Rise of Democracy," *New Left Review* 103 (June 1977): 43.

3. Dietrich Rueschemeyer, Evelyne Huber Stephens, and John D. Stephens, *Capitalist Development and Democracy* (Chicago: University of Chicago Press, 1992), 41.

4. Marshall, *Class, Citizenship and Social Development*, 78.

5. John Myles, "States, Labor Markets and Life Cycles," in *Beyond the Marketplace: Rethinking Economy and Society*, ed. Roger Friedland and A. F. Robertson (New York: Aldine de Gruyter, 1990), 280.

6. *Social Security Programs throughout the World, 1983*, Research Report no. 59 (Washington, D.C.: U.S. Department of Health and Human Services, 1984); Peter Flora, *Growth to Limits: The Western European Welfare States since World War II*, vol. 4 (Berlin: Walter de Gruyter, 1987); Jennifer Schirmer, *The Limits of Women, Capital and Welfare* (Cambridge, Mass.: Schenkman, 1982); Dennis Guest, *The Emergence of Social Security in Canada* (Vancouver: University of British Columbia Press, 1985).

7. Quoted in Gunnar Myrdal, *An American Dilemma* (New York: McGraw-Hill, 1944), 9.

8. James Morone, *The Democratic Wish: Popular Participation and the Limits of American Government* (New York: Basic Books, 1990), 36.

9. Ibid., 59.

10. Jane Jenson, "Representations of Gender: Policies to 'Protect' Women Workers and Infants in France and the United States before 1914," in *Women, the State and Welfare*, ed. Barbara Nelson (Madison: University of Wisconsin Press, 1990), 154; Jill Quadagno, *The Transformation of Old-Age Security: Class and Politics in the American Welfare State* (Chicago: University of Chicago Press, 1988), 11; Theda Skocpol, *Protecting Soldiers and Mothers: The Political Origins of Social Policy in the United States* (Cambridge, Mass.: Harvard University Press, 1992), 9.

11. Edward Berkowitz, *America's Welfare State: From Roosevelt to Reagan* (Baltimore: Johns Hopkins University Press, 1991), 13.

12. Edward G. Carmines and James A. Stimson, *Issue Evolution: Race and the Transformation of American Politics* (Princeton, N.J.: Princeton University Press, 1989), 31, 190.

13. James Patterson, *America's Struggle against Poverty* (Cambridge, Mass.: Harvard University Press, 1986), 72; see also Berkowitz, *America's Welfare State*, 37.

14. Marshall, *Class, Citizenship and Social Development*, 82.

15. V. O. Key, *Southern Politics in State and Nation* (New York: Knopf, 1949), 20; C. Vann Woodward, *Origins of the New South, 1877-1913* (New Haven: Yale University Press, 1951), 345; Quadagno, *The Transformation of Old-Age Security*, 15-17.

16. Nicholas Lemann, *The Promised Land: The Great Black Migration and How It Changed America* (New York: Knopf, 1991), 8.

17. Margaret Weir, *Politics and Jobs: The Boundaries of Employment Policy in the United States* (Princeton, N.J.: Princeton University Press, 1992), 81.

18. G. William Domhoff, *The Power Elite and the State: How Policy Is Made in America* (New York: Aldine de Gruyter, 1990), 65.

19. Philip Foner, *Organized Labor and the Black Worker 1619-1981* (New York: International Publishers, 1981), 168-70.

20. Ibid., 213.

21. Charles V. Hamilton and Dona C. Hamilton, "Social Policies, Civil Rights and Poverty," in *Fighting Poverty: What Works and What Doesn't*, ed. Sheldon H. Danziger and Daniel H. Weinberg (Cambridge, Mass.: Harvard University Press, 1986), 291.

22. National Archives, Record Group 207, correspondence files, Robert Weaver, Secretary of Housing and Urban Development, Box 240, File: U.S. Commission on Civil Rights, Race and Education Report, 11.

23. J. Paul Mitchell, "Historical Context for Housing Policy," in *Federal Housing Policy and Programs*, ed. J. Paul Mitchell (New Brunswick, N.J.: Center for Urban Policy Research, 1988), 8.

24. Norman Peel, Garth Pickett, and Stephen Buehl, "Racial Discrimination in Public Housing Site Selection," in *Housing*, ed. George Sternlieb and Lynne Sagalyn (New York: AMS Press, 1972), 322.

25. Marshall, *Class, Citizenship and Social Development*, 78.

26. Quadagno, *The Transformation of Old-Age Security*, 142; Arthur M. Ford, *Political Economies of Rural Poverty in the South* (Cambridge: Ballinger, 1973), 39.

27. Gerald David Jaynes and Robin Williams, eds., *A Common Destiny: Blacks and American Society* (Washington, D.C.: National Academy Press, 1989), 60.

28. Kevin Phillips, *The Emerging Republican Majority* (New York: Doubleday, 1970), 39.

29. Harvard Sitkoff, *The Struggle for Black Equality* (New York: Hill and Wang, 1981), 23-24.

30. Jack Bloom, *Class, Race and the Civil Rights Movement* (Bloomington: Indiana University Press, 1987), 139.

31. Ibid., 155.

32. Doug McAdam, *Political Process and the Development of Black Insurgency: 1930-1970* (Chicago: University of Chicago Press, 1982), 138.

33. Ibid., 79-80; Frances Fox Piven and Richard Cloward, *Poor People's Movements: Why They Succeed, How They Fail* (New York: Vintage, 1979), 272.

34. Steven F. Lawson, *Black Ballots: Voting Rights in the South, 1944-1969* (New York: Columbia University Press, 1976), 256.

35. Allen Matuso, *The Unraveling of America: A History of Liberalism in the 1960s* (New York: Harper and Row, 1984), 105.

36. Robert Haveman, *A Decade of Federal Anti-Poverty Programs* (New York: Academic Press, 1977), 121.

37. Piven and Cloward, *Poor People's Movements*, 27; see also Barbara Ehrenreich, *Fear of Falling: The Inner Life of the Middle Class* (New York: Harper, 1990), 47.

38. Ibid., 270.

39. Margaret Weir, "The Federal Government and Unemployment: The Frustration of Policy Innovation from the New Deal to the Great Society," in *The Politics of Social Policy in the United States*, ed. Margaret Weir, Ann Shola Orloff, and Theda Skocpol (Princeton, N.J.: Princeton University Press, 1988), 68.

40. Hugh Davis Graham, *The Civil Rights Era: Origins and Development of National Policy* (New York: Oxford University Press, 1990), 152.

41. Gary Orfield, "Race and the Federal Agenda: The Loss of the Integrationist Dream, 1965-1974," Working Paper 7, Project on the Federal Social Role (Washington, D.C.: National Conference on Social Welfare, 1965), 19.

42. Quoted in Berkowitz, *America's Welfare State*, 111.

43. Morone, *The Democratic Wish*, 217.

44. Weir, "The Federal Government and Unemployment," 183.

45. Peter Marris and Martin Rein, *Dilemmas of Social Reform* (Chicago: Aldine, 1973), 50.

46. Ibid., 49-52.

47. Lyndon Baines Johnson, *The Vantage Point: Perspectives of the Presidency, 1963-1969* (New York: Popular Library, 1971), 327.

48. Quoted in Lemann, *The Promised Land*, 156.

DISCUSSION QUESTIONS

1. Outline the broad political stages that have been identified as essential for the democratization of modern societies.

2. Describe the essence of political and social rights and how these kinds of rights were or were not reflected in the New Deal period in the United States.

3. How did Southern political power influence the New Deal in terms of race and race relations?

4. How did local and federal governments during the New Deal encourage racism and racial divisions in the United States?

5. What was the racial dilemma and challenge faced by President Lyndon B. Johnson in 1964 and 1965? How was this similar to or different from the racial dilemma faced by President Franklin Roosevelt during the New Deal period?

FOR FURTHER READING

Berkowitz, Edward, *America's Welfare State: From Roosevelt to Reagan* (Baltimore: Johns Hopkins University Press, 1991).

Bloom, Jack, *Class, Race and the Civil Rights Movement* (Bloomington: Indiana University Press, 1987).

Carmines, Edward G., and James A. Stimson, *Issue Evolution: Race and the Transformation of American Politics* (Princeton, N.J.: Princeton University Press, 1989).

Hamilton, Charles V., and Dona C. Hamilton, "Social Policies, Civil Rights and Poverty," in *Fighting Poverty: What Works and What Doesn't*, ed. Sheldon H. Danziger and Daniel H. Weinberg (Cambridge, Mass.: Harvard University Press, 1986), 291.

Jenson, Jane, "Representations of Gender: Policies to 'Protect' Women Workers and Infants in France and the United States before 1914," in *Women, the State and Welfare*, ed. Barbara Nelson (Madison: University of Wisconsin Press, 1990).

Key, V. O., *Southern Politics in State and Nation* (New York: Alfred Knopf, 1949).

McAdam, Doug, *Political Process and the Development of Black Insurgency: 1930-1970* (Chicago: University of Chicago Press, 1982), 138.

Morone, James, *The Democratic Wish: Popular Participation and the Limits of American Government* (New York: Basic Books, 1990).

Patterson, James, *America's Struggle against Poverty* (Cambridge, Mass.: Harvard University Press, 1986).

Phillips, Kevin, *The Emerging Republican Majority* (New York: Doubleday, 1970).

Woodward, C. Vann, *Origins of the New South, 1877-1913* (New Haven: Yale University Press, 1951).

Chapter Five

Missing Links in the Study of Puerto Rican Poverty in the United States

James Jennings

Introduction

The groundwork for studies and analyses of poverty in the Puerto Rican community in the United States during the past two decades was provided by the pioneering work of scholars like Oscar Lewis, Patricia Sexton, and others in the 1950s and 1960s. While a few scholars involved with activism, including Frank Bonilla, Clara Rodriguez, Lloyd Rogler, Antonia Pantoja, Angelo Falcon, Jose Cruz, and Andres Torres, continued to examine the causes of Puerto Rican poverty and related issues in the United States, the topic was until recently generally ignored by many researchers. In fact, a report prepared for the Ford Foundation in 1984 by Frank Bonilla, Harry Pachon, and Marta Tienda and titled *Public Policy Research and the Hispanic Community* pointed out that there existed "a critical shortage of information about Hispanic-origin groups....There still remain substantial gaps limiting the extent to which policy research about specific demographic topics can be conducted."[1]

Recently, more attention has been paid to the problem of poverty in this community, a result of improvements in data collection methods developed since the 1984 report and of the realization that this group is among the most consistently poor in the country. In fact, some have suggested that, while research studies and discourses have identified the problem of poverty in the black community as entrenched, growing, and intensifying, the situation may be far worse for Puerto Rican communities in the United States. While not completely new, this attention to analyzing and understanding Puerto Rican poverty in this country should be encouraged; however, research on this issue should not be confined solely to quantitative tools and approaches, an emerging bias in the germane literature. Despite increased systematization and sophistication in the collection of data, researchers should be aware of the potential limitations of a strictly quantitative analysis of Puerto Rican poverty. While quantitative analyses based on census data or surveys are important, policy discussions and suggestions for resolving the problem of poverty in this community are incomplete if they rely exclusively on quantitative measurements. In fact, quantitative analysis may have quite limited value if implemented without the benefit of other research that provides insights into the causes, nature, and development of poverty among Puerto Ricans in the United States.

Several kinds of research limitations and biases are evident in some of the studies on Puerto Rican poverty in the United States that rely only on quantitative data and analysis. These limitations include the following:

- Surveys and "official" data, such as the census and government agency data, are usually time bound.
- Analysis is driven primarily by "hard" data, presuming that complex social conditions and situations can easily be captured in quantifiable paradigms; language and "counting" are assumed to be neutral within research and evaluative designs.
- Research analysis can be ahistorical, ignoring important and revealing patterns and trends over long periods of time.
- Poverty-related studies may approach a group's culture with the presumptions that pathology exists within it.
- The unit of analysis of much poverty-related research is the individual or the family, rather than the community.
- There is an absence of input from the targets of research studies in determining the conceptualization, design, analysis, and interpretation of research related to poverty.
- Terms that are not defined analytically, such as *underclass* or *inner city*, are used arbitrarily, without precise definition.
- Research is conducted without the benefit of comparative analysis.
- The role of politics and power is minimized or ignored in the analysis of poverty-related issues.

In the following section these criticisms are explained more fully in the context of studying Puerto Rican poverty in the United States.

Data and Numbers Are Time Bound

Perhaps an obvious limitation of some research studies on poverty is that quantitative data collected at one point in time tend to be time bound. This is unavoidable, of course. Some of the literature on poverty raises discussions based on the "latest" census or survey data available, but even the latest can be outdated in terms of recent and even daily developments of people and communities on a broad scale. Official data, such as the census, can be time bound, while living conditions associated with poor communities continually change daily and, at times, rapidly; this kind of limitation is especially evident among the Puerto Rican poor in urban communities due to the continual back-and-forth migration between cities in the United States and Puerto Rico.

Despite this limitation, census and survey data carry much weight in the determination, or justification, of public policies directed at resolving problems related to poverty. But, as observed by the late Sar Levitan in his article "Measurement of Employment, Unemployment and Low Income," "Data needs are not immutable. As reality, application and theory change, measures must be adjusted or added in order for the labor force statistics to remain useful and accurate."[2] Partially for this reason, a major survey of Latino social and civic attitudes, *The Latino National Political Survey,* conducted in the early 1990s, was critiqued by a group of researchers, who pointed out, "Survey research can rarely provide adequate consideration of the historical dynamics that have produced the snapshot it takes; yet such dynamics are essential to the interpretation of survey results. Likewise, the survey snapshot has little ability to predict how historical dynamics will influence the future."[3]

Analysis of Social Conditions Is Based Exclusively on Hard Data

Analysis of poverty should, for the most part, be data driven. But an exclusive reliance on quantification may prevent the discovery of the many facets of social reality among the poor in urban settings. Too many social realities, relationships, and personal and community histories simply cannot be captured by hard data. Yet these kinds of realities may be critical in the formulation of effective and long-lasting antipoverty strategies. Attempts to overly quantify human interaction, as well as the impact of broad social and economic forces, may lead to assumptions that are geared more toward keeping the experiment statistically neat and simple than toward building a theoretical understanding of the history, nature, or causes of poverty and the ways communities can overcome the problems associated with poverty.

Quantification, furthermore, is not an absolute guarantee that the researcher has shed all biases. As we are reminded by Robert Bogdan and Margaret Krander, something as simple, and as "neutral," as mere counting can also reflect bias: "Counting is an attitude to take toward people, objects, and events. Phenomena only appear as rates and measures after an attitude is developed toward them which acknowledges them as existing, important to count, and susceptible to counting procedures."[4]

Poverty Is Not Seen as a Sociohistorical Process

Too many studies that analyze poverty among racial and ethnic groups are ahistorical. This serves to obfuscate certain kinds of queries that should be part of attempts to understand the nature of continuing poverty among some groups. Almost three decades ago, the sociologist Stephen Thernstrom, in his essay "Further Reflections on the Yankee City Series: The Pitfalls of Ahistorical Social Science," issued a warning regarding the use of hard data in the absence of social and historical analysis: "the student of modern society is not free to take his history or leave it alone. Interpretation of the present requires assumptions about the past. The actual choice is between explicit history, based on a careful examination of the sources, and implicit history, rooted in ideological preconceptions and uncritical acceptance of local mythology."[5]

A major issue overlooked by studies that rely exclusively on hard data and fail to consider social history are the persisting gaps in the United States between the living conditions of Puerto Ricans and blacks, on the one hand, and whites, on the other, even when schooling is controlled. Yet continuing racial and ethnic gaps, especially over a long period of time, should be as important a subject for investigation as a group's current social and economic status. Focusing on racial and ethnic gaps may provide insight about the limitations of strategies and policies directed at alleviating living conditions associated with poverty.

As one studies the ongoing debates and discussions regarding the relationship of family structure and poverty in the black community, one can easily get the impression that poverty in the black community emerged only after certain kinds of structural family changes occurred—that is, after the proportion of female-headed households increased. But a disparity in the proportion of poor blacks and whites has remained unchanged for more than fifty years. In other words, blacks were generally three times more likely to be in poverty than whites in the 1940s, and into the 1990s blacks were still generally three times more likely to be in poverty than whites—regardless of changes in black family structure, national administrations, or the national economy.[6] This is also the case for Puerto Ricans in the United States, who have consistently been among the poorest groups in this country for a period of more than fifty years, since World War II.

Lack of sociohistorical analysis has led some researchers on Puerto Rican poverty to repeat the mistake of Daniel P. Moynihan and Nathan Glazer in their study, published in 1963, that viewed the Puerto Rican community in New York City as post-World War II in its origins.[7] In fact, the history of this community shows that a culturally and socially identifiable and growing Puerto Rican community existed in New York City from the late nineteenth century. Works such as *Memorias de Bernado Vega,* Jesus Colon's *A Puerto Rican in New York,* or the writings of Arturo Schomburg all point to a culturally vibrant, albeit relatively small, Puerto Rican community decades before World War II.[8] And this community, while more involved with politics on the island of Puerto Rico before World War II, continued to interact with the city's political establishment. Yet, today, some studies still analyze Puerto Rican poverty within a conceptual framework that depicts Puerto Ricans as having arrived after World War II.

I contend that one should understand the role of the history of groups like Puerto Ricans—and blacks—in the United States, as a critical element in a full and comprehensive discussion of race and poverty in this nation. Is poverty a "new" problem for the Puerto Rican community? How is poverty among Puerto Ricans today similar to or different from white and black poverty forty or fifty years ago? Has this relationship changed over periods of time? If so, how? Unfortunately, studies on Puerto Rican poverty in the United States have generally overlooked this area of inquiry. Yet it might be useful to understand how the nature of Puerto Rican poverty has changed and is changing and whether it has changed at all in relation to other groups and the broader society in different periods of U.S. economic history. This information may shed light on what actually works and what does not in responding to poverty conditions.

Some of the literature over the years has suggested that the strengths and assets of the black community should be utilized as building blocks for effective social welfare policy. Writers have identified the role of the black church, the resiliency of the black family, racial consciousness as a tool for social and economic development, and black protest as some of these strengths. Can we begin similar discussions about the Puerto Rican community in the United States? Are there not important cultural and social resources in the Puerto Rican community that could be tapped by institutions and government as they attempt to reduce poverty in this community? Again, this is an issue that is easily overlooked when researchers become bogged down with the "official" numbers that describe segments of a group's social realities.

Some researchers who are studying Puerto Rican poverty today either have not been exposed to the history of this group, both in the United States and in Puerto Rico, or have decided that it is not relevant in the study of contemporary urban poverty. Both of these positions are problematic in terms of providing an understanding of the causes and resolutions of poverty among Puerto Ricans. Indeed, to conduct studies of poverty in black or Latino communities without attempting to understand the history of these groups is to assume implicitly that the histories and cultural traditions of these groups are insignificant and have nothing to add to the understanding of the researcher.

Culture and Language Are Not Viewed as Assets Rather Than as Pathology

Cultural patterns and behaviors among Puerto Ricans, as well as their use of a different language, are generally approached as pathological by many researchers, who assume that something must be wrong with these people because they do not seem to think or act like white middle-class Americans, nor are they accepted by white middle-class Americans. Many authors of studies on poverty approach a group's culture as, a priori, the major factor explaining the poverty status of that group. This approach reflects a simplistic method to studying the relationship between culture and a group's poverty status; the researcher presumes that culture can be captured in a neat, well-articulated formula. But, as the social anthropologist Lloyd H. Rogler has reminded us, "Culture penetrates human life in multitudinous ways, some of which we are beginning to understand but most of which still remain to be discovered."[9]

A similar criticism has been made by some observers regarding research on the black family in the United States. Robert B. Hill has noted that the media and many social scientists arbitrarily employ a framework for studying the black family that assumes the existence of fundamental cultural deficiencies and uncritically accept "the assumptions of the 'deficit model' which attributes most of the problems of black families to internal deficiencies or pathologies."[10] Despite the complexities and subtleties that are inherent in all cultures, some surveys and questionnaires used in research on poverty are structured in such a way as to impose a "category fallacy"; that is, they employ "categories developed in one culture or another culture without determining the cultural appropriateness of the category."[11]

"Community" Is Not Used as the Unit of Analysis

Another problem with the research on poverty among Puerto Ricans and blacks is that it focuses on the individual or the family as the unit of analysis. Some Puerto Rican scholars and civic activists, like many black intellectuals, have for some time, proposed that "community" be used instead as the unit of analysis, incorporating a presumption of assets and resources rather than pathology. But it seems to me that some researchers assume that community is nonexistent among the poor blacks and Puerto Ricans. Moreover, when poverty researchers do discuss communities in urban areas dominated by people of color, pejorative terms like *slum, ghetto,* or *underclass* frequently show up in their work.

The unit of analysis used can determine which questions are viewed as the important ones. Using only the individual or the family as the reference point for analysis means that questions will typically focus on what has happened to the black individual or the black family rather than on the effect of policies on the community and its institutional, economic, and cultural fabric. An example of this, as pointed out by the housing researcher Sheila Ards, is the debate around housing vouchers.[12] This debate has been confined in some forums and journals to examining whether black individuals or families can be best served by receiving vouchers to seek out housing. But what is the effect of vouchers on the use of land in the black community? This question has been ignored because the unit of analysis in much of the mainstream literature is either the individual or the family, not the community.

Another example of how the particular unit of analysis can mold or influence the kinds of conclusions of even so-called objective studies is commentary on the nature and degree of racial and economic progress in the United States. One might look at this question in terms of the number of black middle-class individuals or families. Using some criterion of "middle-classness" (usually arbitrarily defined), has the number of blacks in this status increased or declined over a period of time? Depending on the answer, the researcher will examine policies that might explain the result.

This same narrow approach has been utilized by scholars examining Latino economic progress in the United States. But another way to examine racial and economic progress is to ask, What has happened to Puerto Rican communities? What has happened to the social, economic, or educational institutions operating in these communities? How have self-help institutions, such as the Sons of Puerto Rico clubs in places like New York City, described by Patricia Cayo Sexton in the 1960s, or community institutions in the 1970s and 1980s fared under various kinds of public policies and national administrations? Changing the unit of analysis may lead to different sets of questions, and a different kind of critique and evaluation of current public policies on poverty.

The Community Is Not Consulted in Designing the Research

Many of the popular perceptions about poor Puerto Ricans and blacks are based on what is presented in the media. Anthony Barker and B. Guy Peters argue that "a great deal of the scholarly literature on public policy is written from the perspective of the decision-maker attempting to make an optimal choice about a policy that will best serve the 'public interest.'...Unfortunately, however, the real world of policy-making is not so neat as that."[13] Because they have relatively little influence in many cities, Puerto Ricans do not have the political or economic clout to counter such images or to present their thinking or collective experiences in a favorable light in the pages of the city's major newspapers.

Perhaps it is the paucity of understanding, knowledge, and appreciation of the culture and history of groups like Puerto Ricans in the United States that permits researchers to rely on the media to influence their own social perceptions of these communities. Thus, as one critic writes, "Journalists have become the publicly recognized ethnographers.... Anyone who talks to or lives among the poor is considered an authority and can describe them and speak on their behalf."[14] Using this kind of "expertise," the media present commentary *about* poor people, seldom on *behalf* of, or *by,* poor people. As one journalist, Dorothy Clark, has pointed out, there may be valid and technical reasons for this.[15] But it is important to note that the methodology of collecting news, and the fact of who collects it and decides what to report and how to report it, not only molds the perceptions the general public has about race, ethnicity, and poverty but contributes to the conceptualizations utilized by researchers on the nature of poverty among Puerto Ricans.[16] Too often, the media-driven conceptualizations are borrowed without question or scrutiny by "objective" researchers to construct their own methodologies for investigating urban poverty, race, and ethnicity.

Pejorative Terms and Arbitrary Definitions Are Used in Research

The research community has defined arbitrarily basic poverty-related terms without the benefit of analytical scrutiny. Researchers assume that language, descriptive terms, and phrases are neutral, if the researchers just treat them as neutral. But this is not the case. The validity of this criticism is evident if one looks at questionnaires and interview instruments that seek information about poverty experiences but are developed by researchers who lack an understanding of or a familiarity with the nuances of everyday life and language usage in various parts of poor communities. Even commonly used names of specific groups should not be approached or treated as research-neutral. As was pointed out by David E. Hayes-Bautista some time ago, the name utilized to identify a racial or ethnic group can have important research implications. Definitional differences (e.g., "Mexican American" versus "of Spanish heritage") may cover major social differences, making it difficult to generate comparisons between groups.[17]

A related problem among researchers in the use of terms that have not been defined analytically or explained in research operational terms. Among the more famous examples of such terms used in poverty research are *middle class, slum, ghetto, broken family,* and what social scientists in the 1950s and 1960s used frequently, referring to the *culturally deprived.* These are imprecise terms, open to a range of definitions and connotations that vary with the user. The definition of the term *middle class,* for instance, depends on who is using it and, in many cases, for what purpose. Both scholars and the media have used this term loosely, sometimes relying on varying measures of income ranges, social attitudes, or occupation. Not specifying the analytical content of such terms leads to major ideological and polemical abuse in political and policy discussions focusing on poverty.

The political scientist Adolph Reed Jr. argues that one term that has been used extensively without the benefit of consistent or analytical rigor is *underclass.*[18] Too often researchers seem to have allowed journalists, in particular, to guide the use of this highly connotative term without insisting on a precise definition. There have been attempts to explain what is meant by the underclass, but invariably the models still include many assumptions about poverty and poor communities. For example, one of the latest attempts is to examine an area with high levels of poverty and unemployment and to assume that the residents of this particular area include the "underclass." This form of social-areas methodology glosses over the many important differences in status, attitudes, and life histories that coexist among the residents of such areas. One needs only to have a few firsthand experiences in such a "high-poverty" area to notice how aggregated census and survey data can hide and arbitrarily oversimplify continually changing social situations.

Poverty Research Lacks a Comparative Basis

Poverty research in the United States tends to be discipline based to an extreme. Developing overarching policy paradigms that allow the perspectives and training of economists, historians, and humanists to integrate their findings and think broadly and dialectically is difficult. The conceptualization of public policy responses to social welfare issues is highly specialized within disciplines and generally lacks comparative frameworks. As suggested by Walter Korpi in his essay "Approaches to the Study of Poverty in the U.S.," poverty research in this country is usually conducted without the benefit of comparative analysis across nations.[19]

This deficit limits our understanding of the nature of poverty among Puerto Ricans in urban America. Though there are many questions about urban poverty that should be raised within a comparative framework, given the social history and current situation of Puerto Ricans and Puerto Rico, the simple one posed decades ago by the sociologist Dardo Cuneo in his introduction to the work by Jesus de Galindez, *Puerto Rico en Nueva York: Sociologia de Una Immigracion,* is still relevant today: "Donde se marcan las fronteras diferenciales entre la America del Norte y la latina; en donde dejan de marcarse?"[20] In this case, the poverty experienced by Puerto Ricans in the United States could perhaps be better understood if we also noted the nature of poverty in Puerto Rico. The work and insights of scholars who have studied poverty in Puerto Rico should not be ignored or summarily excluded from analyses of the poverty experiences of Puerto Ricans in American cities. Thus, I would point to the classic works of Eugenio Fernandez Mendez, as well as the exceptional reader by Rafael L. Ramirez, Carlos Buitrago Ortiz, and Barry B. Levine, *Problemas de Desigualdad en Puerto Rico,* as studies that are still relevant to inquiries about Puerto Rican poverty in the United States today.[21]

The essay by Ramirez, "Marginalidad, Dependencia Participacion Politica en el Arrabal," included in the anthology just mentioned, might suggest models and approaches for studying behavior related to poverty in Puerto Rican communities in the United States other than the pathological and ahistorical approaches popular among many economists in the current period.[22] Another essay in this same reader, "Quienes Son Los Probes en Puerto Rico?" by Celia F. Cintron and Barry B. Levine, reminds us that the Puerto Rican poor may not make up a monolithic category, as has usually been implied in the discussions among poverty researchers in the United States.[23] There are other, more current studies that can assist us in understanding poverty among Puerto Ricans in the United States in a broader context than would be suggested by research that relies exclusively on hard data and surveys. In fact, because of Puerto Ricans' history, culture, and patterns of migration, there is no justification for discussing poverty among Puerto Ricans in the United States as totally separate from the issue of poverty in Puerto Rico.

The Role of Politics and Power in Maintaining Poverty Is Ignored

The role of politics is ignored in many research studies about urban poverty. While everyone acknowledges the importance of politics in driving public policy, when it comes to urban poverty and Puerto Ricans or blacks, research discussions automatically switch to a nonpolitical mode. There seems to be a myopia that exists among some poverty researchers regarding political factors that may lead to and sustain persistent poverty. One widespread presumption among researchers is that the United States has tried everything conceivable to reduce poverty and that, therefore, continuing poverty must be caused by undesirable individual and family characteristics. This "political disclaimer" is interesting in that there is general acknowledgment of the significance of politics and political decision making in driving public policy in other areas. Research studies and findings on poverty are frequently discussed and debated on technical grounds, separated completely from issues of power and wealth. It is suggested, implicitly if not explicitly, in some new research studies on poverty among Puerto Ricans that their lack of political power has virtually nothing to do with the ongoing problem of poverty in their community. This relationship is not even explored for its explanatory possibilities; it is merely assumed that poverty has more to do with pathology or the social welfare planning failures of liberals than with the low level of political power and political respect that Puerto Ricans (or blacks) command.

This weakness is related to the refusal on the part of researchers to acknowledge poor people as participants in research studies and projects. This may be due to the fact that the poverty research community is smug and conceptually incestuous, according to Adolph Reed Jr.[24] This inbred approach is reflected in researchers' bias against the participation of poor people in the conceptualization of public policy and antipoverty efforts. In fact, research is sometimes used to actively discourage such participation. But this is unjustified and should be vigorously challenged. Barker and Peters write that more

"public interaction" even in "scientific issues" is justifiable and more desirable. Indeed the "trans-science" nature of many issues requires that the public be involved and that science to some extent become more responsible to the public. This is by no means a plea to create an "official science" of some sort. Rather, it is a statement of the important public interest issues involved in science and technology.[25]

The importance of the call for this kind of participation on the part of poor people in the formulation of antipoverty efforts has led the Center for Law and Social Welfare Policy in New York City to urge the federal Secretary of Health and Human Services to strengthen and expand rules that would permit poor people to participate in the decision making of federal and state agencies. It has also been suggested that demonstration projects should not be approved unless the opinions of poor persons have been solicited regarding policies and procedures.[26] Researchers should pick up this cause as well.

There is a wide gulf between the policy discussions of researchers who focus on poverty in the United States and the concerns and insights offered by poor people regarding their own status. In some cases, researchers investigating poverty have done so without the benefit of understanding or experiencing how poor people live or appreciating the contributions that poor people can make toward better policies. The political scientist M. E. Hawkesworth has suggested that policy analysis built exclusively on scientism and quantitative technocracy has discouraged people from coming together and deliberating about how to emphasize their common concerns and solve problems that ultimately affect all of society. She adds, furthermore, that the "charge of scientism will continue to haunt the discipline as long as policy science is promoted as a form of objective political problem-solving superior to, and therefore preferable to, democratic deliberation."[27]

Another observer critiques David Ellwood's book *Poor Support*, for the same reason: "He spends 200 pages discussing poor family dynamics without talking to an actual person or reading the work of someone who does. Ellwood seems to believe that one can infer the behavior of all poor people by extrapolating from census data and imagining what their lives might be like."[28] Researchers might take umbrage at the suggestion that they should experience the lives of poor people, or at least allow poor people to explain their experiences for research purposes, arguing that processes to involve the poor would politicize their supposedly objective studies or even give the poor undue influence or veto power over the conduct and findings of their research. But this kind of danger exists to a larger extent with other groups with whom researchers must develop cozy and financial relationships (i.e., sources of research grants), according to Robert Formaini.[29] It is interesting that some researchers take for granted the participation of other sectors in their research that have a much greater capacity than poor persons to control and direct their findings, analysis, and recommendations.

Many people who work for civic and neighborhood organizations and who are involved with antipoverty efforts, like poor people, do not participate in research on the problem of poverty done by academics. This means that researchers may not have the benefit of input from people and organizations who are on the front line in combating urban poverty. It also means that community workers have not been able to utilize applicable findings of the researchers in their own efforts to combat poverty and its effects. Policy processes must be developed to give these workers opportunities to mold the thinking of antipoverty strategies and approaches and to be involved in all aspects of the public policy process in the area of social welfare: setting the civic agenda, conceptualizing and defining the nature of the problem, formulating adequate responses, and determining how such policies should be implemented and evaluated. Amitai Etzioni suggests that only an increase in civic involvement may result in creative and effective social policies regarding the problems facing society. He argues that all citizens, poor and nonpoor, can make a significant improvement in public policies that influence their quality of life by becoming more involved in the political process.[30] Only through the inclusion of more people in the process of formulating policy will the academic and political communities be able to develop new and creative models and concepts that overcome the limitations of current research paradigms.

NOTES

This chapter is based on a presentation to the National Puerto Rican Coalition in Washington, D.C., on June 22, 1992.

1. Frank Bonilla, Harry Pachon, and Marta Tienda, *Public Policy Research and the Hispanic Community: Recommendations from Five Task Forces* (New York: Ford Foundation, 1984), 3.

2. Sar Levitan, "Measurement of Employment, Unemployment and Low Income," *Workforce* (Spring 1994): 19.

3. Luis Frage, Herman Gallegos, Gerald P. Lopez, Mary Louise Pratt, Renato Rosaldo, Jose Saldivar, Ramon Saldivar, and Guadalupe Valdes, *Still Looking for America: Beyond the Latino National Political Survey* (Stanford, Calif.: Public Outreach Project of the Stanford Center for Chicano Research, 1994), 5.

4. Robert Bogdan and Margaret Krander, "Policy Data as a Social Process: A Qualitative Approach to Quantitative Data," *Human Organization* 39, no. 4 (Winter 1980): 303.

5. Stephen Thernstrom, "Further Reflections on the Yankee City Series: The Pitfalls of Ahistorical Social Science," in his book, *Poverty and Progress: Social Mobility in a Nineteenth-Century City* (New York: Atheneum, 1969), 239.

6. See Gerald D. Jaynes and Robin M. Williams Jr., eds., *A Common Destiny: Blacks and American Society* (Washington, D.C.: National Academy Press, 1989); also see Elizabeth Pleck, *Black Migration and Poverty: Boston 1865-1900* (New York: Academic Press, 1979); and W. E. B. Du Bois, *The Philadelphia Negro* (New York: Schocken Books, 1967).

7. Daniel P. Moynihan and Nathan Glazer, *Beyond the Melting Pot: The Negroes, Puerto Ricans, Jews, Italians, and Irish of New York City* (Cambridge, Mass.: MIT Press, 1963).

8. Bernado Vega, *Memorias de Bernado Vega: Contribución a la Historia de la Comunidad Puertorriquena en Nueva York* (Rio Piedras, Puerto Rico: Ediciones Huracan, 1977); also see Jesus Colon, *A Puerto Rican in New York and Other Sketches* (New York: Argo Press, 1975).

9. Lloyd H. Rogler, "The Meaning of Culturally Sensitive Research in Mental Health," *American Journal of Psychiatry* 143, no. 3 (March 1989), 301.

10. Robert B. Hill, "Research on the African American Family: A Holistic Perspective," in Wornie L. Reed, *Assessment of the Status of African-Americans*, vol. 2 (Boston: University of Massachusetts, William Monroe Trotter Institute for the Study of Black Culture, 1989), 2.

11. Lloyd H. Rogler, "Cultural Sensitivity: Research with Hispanics," *Contemporary Psychology* 37, no. 9 (1992): 942.

12. Sheila Ards, "The Theory of Vouchers and Housing Availability in the Black Community," in *Race, Politics, and Economic Development: Community Perspectives*, ed. James Jennings (London: Verso Press, 1992).

13. Anthony Barker and B. Guy Peters, *Science Policy and Government* (Pittsburgh: University of Pittsburgh Press, 1992), 1.

14. Brett Williams, "Poverty among African Americans in the Urban United States," *Human Organization* 51, no. 2 (1992): 166.

15. Dorothy Clark, *Race, Poverty, and the Role of Media: A Review of News Coverage of Boston's Black Community, 1985-1990* (Boston: University of Massachusetts, William Monroe Trotter Institute for the Study of Black Culture, 1994).

16. Ibid.

17. David E. Hayes-Bautista, "Identifying 'Hispanic' Populations: The Influence of Research Methodology upon Public Policy," *American Journal of Public Health* 70, no. 4 (April 1980): 353.

18. Adolph Reed Jr., "The Underclass as Myth and Symbol: The Poverty of Discourse about Poverty," *Radical America* 24, no. 1 (Summer 1991).

19. Walter Korpi, "Approaches to the Study of Poverty in the U.S.: Critical Notes from a European Perspective," in *Poverty and Public Policy: An Evaluation of Social Science Research*, ed. Vincent J. Covello (Cambridge, Mass.: Schenkman, 1980).

20. Dardo Cúneo, "Introduction," in *Puerto Rico en Nueva York: Sociologia de Una Immigracion*, ed. Jesús de Galíndez (Buenos Aires, Argentina: Editorial Tiempo Contemporaneo, 1969), 7.

21. Eugenio Fernandez Mendez, ed., *Portrait of a Society: Readings on Puerto Rican Sociology* (Río Piedras, Puerto Rico: University of Puerto Rico Press, 1972); and Rafael L. Ramírez, Carlos Buitrago Ortiz, and Barry B. Levine, *Problemas de Desigualdad en Puerto Rico* (Río Piedras, Puerto Rico: Ediciones Libreria Internacional, 1972).

22. Rafael L. Ramirez, "Marginalidad, Dependencia y Participacíon Política en el Arrabal," in *Problemas de Desigualdad en Puerto Rico*, ed. Rafael L. Ramirez, Carlos Buitrago Ortiz, and Barry B. Levine (Río Piedras, Puerto Rico: Ediciones Libreria Internacional, 1972).

23. Celia F. Cintron and Barry B. Levine, "Quienes Son Los Probes en Puerto Rico?" in *Problemas de Desigualdad en Puerto Rico*, ed. Rafael L. Ramirez, Carlos Buitrago Ortiz, and Barry B. Levine (Rio Piedras, Puerto Rico: Ediciones Libreria Internacional, 1972).

24. Adolph Reed Jr., "Pimping Poverty, Then and Now," *Progressive* 58, no. 8 (August 1994): 6.

25. Barker and Peters, *Science Policy and Government*, 6.

26. Henry Freedman, "Chronology of HEW/HHS Actions and Recommendations Concerning Participation by Poor Persons and Their Advocates in Agency Policymaking and Decisionmaking," March 1993, no. 645. (Note: This file was obtained from handout computers services.)

27. M. E. Hawkesworth, *Theoretical Issues in Policy Analysis* (Albany: State University of New York Press, 1988), 189.

28. Williams, "Poverty among African Americans in the Urban United States," 164.

29. Robert Formaini, *The Myth of Scientific Public Policy* (New Brunswick, N.J.: Transaction Publishers, 1990).

30. Amitai Etzioni, *Public Policy in a New Key* (New Brunswick, N.J.: Transaction Publishers, 1993).

DISCUSSION QUESTIONS

1. What are the limitations in utilizing purely quantitative measures of poverty among Puerto Ricans?

2. Discuss the implications of viewing poverty within a sociohistorical rather than a behavioral context.

3. Discuss the important cultural and social resources in the Puerto Rican community.

4. Analyze the validity of the "culture of poverty" explanation of Puerto Rican poverty.

5. Discuss the significance of using the community rather than the individual or the family as the unit of analysis for understanding poverty.

6. Discuss the implications of the use by researchers of concepts such as *underclass*.

7. Discuss the consequences of incorporating the experiences and views of the poor themselves in constructing a comprehensive understanding of poverty.

FOR FURTHER READING

Bonilla, Frank, Harry Pachon, and Marta Tienda, *Public Policy Research and the Hispanic Community: Recommendations from Five Task Forces* (New York: Ford Foundation, 1984).

Du Bois, W. E. B., *The Philadelphia Negro* (New York: Schocken Books, 1967).

Hawkesworth, M. E., *Theoretical Issues in Policy Analysis* (Albany: State University of New York Press, 1988), 189.

Hill, Robert B., "Research on the African American Family: A Holistic Perspective," in Wornie L. Reed, *Assessment of the Status of African-Americans,* vol. 2 (Boston: University of Massachusetts, William Monroe Trotter Institute for the Study of Black Culture, 1989).

Levitan, Sar, "Measurement of Employment, Unemployment and Low Income," *Workforce* (Spring 1994): 19.

Moynihan, Daniel P., and Nathan Glazer, *Beyond the Melting Pot: The Negroes, Puerto Ricans, Jews, Italians, and Irish of New York City* (Cambridge, Mass.: MIT Press, 1963).

Reed, Adolph, Jr., "The Underclass as Myth and Symbol: The Poverty of Discourse about Poverty," *Radical America* 24, no. 1 (Summer 1991).

Rogler, Lloyd H., "The Meaning of Culturally Sensitive Research in Mental Health," *American Journal of Psychiatry* 143, no. 3 (March 1989), 301.

Thernstrom, Stephen, "Further Reflections on the Yankee City Series: The Pitfalls of Ahistorical Social Science," in Stephen Thernstrom, *Poverty and Progress: Social Mobility in a Nineteenth-Century City* (New York: Atheneum, 1969).

Vega, Bernado, *Memorias de Bernado Vega: Contribucion a la Historia de la Comunidad Puertorriquena en Nueva York* (Rio Piedras, Puerto Rico: Ediciones Huracan, 1977).

Williams, Brett, "Poverty among African Americans in the Urban United States," *Human Organization* 51, no. 2 (1992): 166.

Part III

Poverty and Race as Functions of Economic and Political Power

Chapter Six

U.S. Urban Policy and Latino Issues

Rebecca Morales

Urban Issues in the 1990s

The Clinton administration and the nation's mayors face an uphill task when it comes to framing a national urban agenda. Urban problems have escalated over the past several decades, and there are no obvious solutions. Cities house the majority of U.S. minorities, immigrants, and those with the most pressing social problems. Among the problems that confront American cities are crime and drugs, failing educational systems, environmental blight, job loss, a dwindling economic base, racial conflict, and the homeless, all of which must be addressed while maintaining fiscal solvency. The intransigence of these problems has become such a political liability that the term *urban policy* has not even been part of this administration's vocabulary.

The ill health of the nation's cities presents troubling prospects for Latinos who are entering the United States at unprecedented rates. For this segment of society, urban areas remain a primary destination. However, the city's traditional function as a reservoir of opportunity seems to have been replaced by an obstacle course, with economic and social parity somehow slipping beyond the reach of the nation's aspiring new entrants. As a result, Latinos have a particular stake in seeing cities returned to their capacity as points of entry for upward mobility.

Despite the critical role of cities to the well-being of the nation, no shared vision of restored urban life has emerged for society as a whole. Instead, what has surfaced is a dichotomy between the interests of urban dwellers and those of a broader society that neither can nor wants to shoulder the burdens of the nation's ailing cities. With a major portion of the population affected by policy choices that will be made over the next few years, reconciliation of these perspectives has taken on a certain urgency. A brief glimpse into the positions adopted by policymakers over the issues captures the divisions at hand.

Alternative Urban Visions

Even though no explicit national urban policy exists, certain preferences are becoming apparent. Since coming into office, Bill Clinton has attempted to forge a new social compact nationwide based on appeal to the majority population. This is essentially a centrist position. President Clinton has not showcased cities or minorities. Rather than proposing policies that explicitly target these groups, this administration has recommended programs that broadly assist regions, individuals, or businesses in need without reference to race or ethnicity or to an urban focus.

The apparent ambivalence toward cities demonstrated by President Clinton was not evident in candidate Clinton. As a candidate, he specified several ways he would support cities in his platform statement, titled *Putting People First: A National Economic Strategy for America*. In this statement, his priorities were to put the United States to work, reward those who work, support lifetime reaming, provide quality yet affordable health care, and revolutionize government. For cities, he promised the following:

> *Investing in communities.* While America's great cities fall into disrepair, the Republicans in Washington continue to ignore their fate. Private enterprise has abandoned our cities, leaving our young people with few job prospects and declining hopes. To restore urban economic vitality and bring back high-paying jobs to our cities, I will:
> - Target funding and Community Development Block Grants to rebuild America's urban roads, bridges, water and sewage treatment plants and low-income housing stock, stressing "ready to go" projects. Require companies that bid on these projects to set up a portion of their operations in low-income neighborhoods and employ local residents.
> - Create a nationwide network of community development banks to provide small loans to low-income entrepreneurs and homeowners in the inner cities...
> - Fight crime by putting 100,000 new police officers on the streets...
> - Create urban enterprise zones in stagnant inner cities...
> - Ease the credit crunch in our inner cities by passing a more progressive Community Reinvestment Act.[1]

The approach was one of job creation through infrastructure development, improved fiscal accounting, capital and labor support of enterprise, and lowered costs of investment in inner cities. Although not revolutionary, this would have gone a long way to assist cities. However, President Clinton got off to a rocky start and began to distance himself from some of these promises. After incurring heavy resistance to his economic stimulus package, especially to items perceived as requiring spending, these ambitious plans for cities began to acquire a more nuanced tone. Funding for infrastructure was drastically reduced. Enterprise zones were recast as empowerment zones and limited in number. Community Development Block Grants were scaled back, and urban programs were recast as assistance for communities—specifically "community empowerment."

The administration's reorientation was captured in a presentation by Housing and Urban Development (HUD) Secretary Henry Cisneros, when he said that in the 1990s HUD stands for five things: respect for community, support for families, creation of a continuum of community supports or services, the balancing of individual rights and responsibilities, and a reduction in the spatial segregation and racial and income separations that exist in America.[2] Rather than stressing economic stimulus, the policy appeared to have shifted toward an emphasis on (using the secretary's own words) "self-sufficiency."[3] Clearly, HUD is only one agency among many that coordinate programs affecting urban areas; nonetheless, its actions can be understood as reflecting the tone of the presidency. At the same time, the president was addressing community groups and telling them that the role of the federal government in urban areas was limited and, further, that local improvement rested on the shoulders of the people who needed assistance.

This "self-sufficiency" position is in stark contrast to that of the nation's mayors, who are calling for more direct support. After twelve years of the Reagan and Bush administrations, federal aid as a percentage of city budgets had fallen nearly 64 percent below 1980 levels, even as city problems had escalated.[4] Approximately 42 percent of the nation's impoverished people lived in the city center in 1992, as opposed to 30 percent in 1968. More than 60 percent of the African American and 59 percent of the Latino poor resided in cities, compared to 34 percent of poor whites.[5] Measures of crime, homelessness, and other indicators of social stress were all concentrated in city centers.

Thus, it is not surprising that in a lengthy set of policy resolutions emanating from the 1993 annual meeting of the U.S. Conference of Mayors, the most prominent item concerned the restoration of federal funds supporting urban programs.[6] Mayors also recognized the need to spread the burden of providing urban services broadly, beyond the federal level. In the proceedings of the 1990 Urban Summit, a meeting of the mayors of the thirty-five largest U.S. cities, the mayors called for a series of new urban partnerships across metropolitan regions, which arbitrarily separate the urban core from the rest of the local economy, and also from businesses.[7] The overriding message coming from urban America is that of fiscal strain coupled with burgeoning demands.

The plight of the mayors was clearly not a concern of former President Reagan when he instituted the "New Federalism." His concept was to shift the responsibility for local needs from Washington to the states and cities—government bodies that were arguably closer to the people. However, this policy was essentially ideologically motivated, since localities never lobbied for the change. As noted in one observation:

> This position rests on two myths: every city and state jurisdiction has enough taxable resources to be afforded a real choice; and the federal government's intervention to fund grants to localities and states and individual benefits for the poor has been a usurpation that took place against the wishes of city and state officials and electorates.[8]

In the late 1990s mayors must confront growing urban problems with fewer resources, yet the concerns they raise are probably less likely to be heard. The reason for this is that during the 1980s they lost not only financial clout in absolute terms but also political power vis-à-vis suburbs and growing areas that reflect the cities' declining economic influence.[9] The newer regions could more effectively effect policies on their own behalf. The result was a power shift that had race and class overtones:

> Reagan's *real* urban policies have remarkably consistent effects....First, changes in the tax laws directly aid firms and taxpayers in growing areas and the suburbs....Second, changes in the composition of the budget reduced social programs that most affect declining areas.[10]

As they lost control over decisions regarding resource allocation, cities were less able to address the underlying causes of their problems. On the one hand, urban areas were becoming increasingly ungovernable because of structural problems. Resources needed to address problems like fiscal crisis and deteriorating physical infrastructure are not readily available to city governments. The lack of resources leads to non-strategic decision making at the local level and an emphasis on attracting investment at any cost, even if harmful to the city's language benefit.[11] Lacking the ability to influence substantive issues, mayors were becoming custodians engaged in reactive policymaking. On the other hand, the loss of federal involvement in urban programs also separated cities from decisions that were causal to their circumstances. As Frances Fox Piven argues:

> The Republican administrations of the 1980s also set about trying to restore the segmented pattern of an earlier federalism, centralizing the policies and politics that shape economic and social development while decentralizing the policies and politics that cope with its effects.[12]

The combined effect of the decade of urban policy reversals was urban fiscal stress, exacerbated social problems, a disconnectedness between the needs of city center residents and those of the broader community, and a diminished ability by cities to address the issues adequately. As a result, Latinos now confront a situation where city mayors are consumed with crisis management at the same time that the federal government is calling for greater self-sufficiency. The situation appears to pose two different sets of challenges for Latinos. One is structural and inherent to all cities: their powers for addressing urban problems are not commensurate with the extent of the need. Serious reexamination of urban powers is required, particularly with a view toward making cities proactive agents in economic development beyond the area of land use control. Even with these changes, there are concerns specific to Latinos.

The second issue is how to meet the needs of Latinos. Identifying an urban agenda that would directly benefit Latinos is difficult because Latinos themselves have yet to articulate an urban policy. One reason for this is that they are clearly not homogeneous, and their mode of incorporation into the economy and into society varies substantially by ethnic subgroup, immigrant status, and gender and by the structure of regional labor markets. Given this enormous diversity, a coherent policy or even the formation of a political constituency appears elusive. Rather than articulating a broad vision, Latino advocacy organizations have tended to focus on particular issues, such as naturalization or voter participation, in the hope of expanding Latinos' political base, or economic inequality and persistent poverty. Even these positions vary by ideology. While some argue that the most lasting approach is to develop the community base from the bottom up,[13] others stress the need to align themselves with the growth potential of businesses and the majority society. The result is a fragmented vision. However, as their numbers increase and as urban issues persist, the focus may begin to sharpen. In spite of a yet to be articulated Latino urban agenda, certain issues remain central.

Latino Urban Issues

Latinos face perhaps two overriding issues: the lack of Latino economic parity and the lack of a political voice that adequately reflects their numbers. For the most part, these are urban issues, though recent studies underscore a significant parallel rural concern.[14] The profile of Latinos reveals that their rate of urbanization (90 percent) far exceeds that of the nation as a whole (75 percent) and that they are clustered in the most dynamic metropolitan areas of the United States, such as Los Angeles and New York, and those most exposed to international influences, such as Miami. As a consequence, their concerns are integrally tied to metropolitan areas.

Within these cities, Latinos have been caught in a national trend toward income inequality and a growing division between the haves and the have-nots.[15] Although current data suggest that some Latinos may be closing the income gap with white Americans, in certain areas, such as California and, within California, Los Angeles, which have the nation's highest concentration of Latinos, the gap continues to widen. Seen as a whole, the prospects confronting those Latinos who are the least well off economically appear to be continued job loss, income and wealth erosion, and a weakened political base.

Economic Dimensions

Poverty and low incomes are not new problems, although in the past they appeared to be surmountable. The history of the incorporation of Latinos into the U.S. economy over the past half century reveals that four major factors explain their economic standing: economic restructuring (the demand for labor), labor migration (the supply of labor), education (human capital characteristics), and discrimination (institutional constraints). From the 1940s on, the economy shifted from an agricultural base to manufacturing and then to services. Whereas the prominence of manufacturing supported the rise of a middle class and growing parity of incomes, the second transformation was characterized by a polarization of services and manufacturing according to wage and skill and by a growing divergence of incomes. During the early part of this fifty-year period, from the 1940s to the 1960s, Latinos improved their economic position. But the period after 1969 was one of marked decline. Aggregate analysis of the gain followed by the reversal shows that, during the post–Second World War economic expansion, Latinos' incomes began to approximate those of whites. This occurred largely because of the growth of urban manufacturing jobs and an increase in the educational level achieved by minorities. However, the post-1973 economic restructuring was felt unevenly and had a greater negative impact on Latinos than on whites. The employment shift most adversely affected those with weak anchorage in the labor force—part-time workers, those who were furthest behind whites educationally, and the foreign born.[16] Among Latinos, the most negatively affected were Puerto Ricans and Mexican Americans, who were unable to navigate a successful transition into higher-paying occupations, and recent immigrants thrust into low-paying jobs.

Along with low wages, unemployment is another major cause of impoverishment among many Latinos. In 1991, when the unemployment rate for the nation as a whole was 6.7 percent, it was 9.4 percent for Hispanics. When separated by subgroups, the rates were 11.8 percent for Puerto Ricans, 9.6 percent for Mexicans, 8.5 percent for Cubans, and 8.2 percent for other Hispanics. For many, poverty is linked with single-parent families. Approximately half of the Hispanic families living below the poverty level are headed by women. This problem is most apparent among Puerto Ricans, who have the highest rate of families headed by women (43 percent).

The result for Latinos has been low average incomes.[17] The average family income among Latinos fell by 12.7 percent from 1978 to 1982 after adjusting for inflation. In the period of economic recovery from 1982 to 1987, the rate of growth in the average family income of Latinos was about half (6.3 percent) that of whites (11.4 percent) or African Americans (13 percent). In 1987, six out of every ten Latino families were among the poorest two-fifths of the total population, while only one in ten were among the wealthiest one-fifth. With each recession, Latinos fell further into poverty. Puerto Ricans displayed the greatest distress, with 40.3 percent classified as poor in 1987, the highest rate for any racial or ethnic group in the United States. They were followed by Mexicans at 28.3 percent.

Latinos' poverty might have been relieved through income transfer payments but instead was reinforced by a decline in social program expenditures. Throughout the 1980s, a 55 percent cut in budgetary allocations to federal social programs sharply reduced the social safety net for low-income people, while deregulation made the remaining available jobs more hazardous and less secure. Since Latinos constitute between 9 and 17 percent of the beneficiaries of low-income programs (or twice their level of representation in the population), they have been about twice as likely to feel the budgetary cutbacks as the population as a whole.[18] The burden of cushioning extreme impoverishment has been increasingly transferred to the local level, despite the fact that cities, as well as states, are ill equipped to handle the heightened demands. Consequently, the rising needs have largely gone unmet.

The structural shifts in the economy have, in some cases, been accompanied by the long-term spatial dislocation of employment within metropolitan regions. New York provides one illustration of this phenomenon. Since 1972, its share of national output, population growth, job generation, and personal income has shown a progressive decline.[19] Here, as in many cities, the suburbanization of both service-oriented and goods-producing industries, the inadequate replacement of entry-level, low-skill, or blue-collar jobs, and an increase in the number of managerial, professional, technical, and administrative jobs in city centers have made it harder for urban-dwelling poor and minorities to find their way into the job market.[20] In this respect, some Latinos are feeling the effect of economic dislocation associated with the "underclass" dynamic. Nationwide, the spatial mismatch of jobs to the skill level of the workforce has meant that poorly educated minorities residing in certain city centers have had less access to employment, which has led to an increase in unemployment rates.[21] The selective outmigration of better-educated minorities from the city center compounds the problem, with the urban population that remains least able to take advantage of the changing job patterns.[22] In New York, the greatest impact has been on blue-collar Puerto Ricans, who have suffered from the lack of low-level replacement jobs. Generations of job loss combined with migratory patterns unrelieved by sufficient economic development in Puerto Rico have contributed to family disruption and disconnection from the formal economy.

In other cities, the issue of Latino poverty is tied more to low salaries associated with the new jobs being created than to the suburbanization of jobs. For example, in Los Angeles the urban core has been revitalized by the garment industry, warehousing, and other immigrant-dependent employment; however, these are highly problematic jobs that offer little security, few benefits, and extremely low wages. Nationwide, the demographics of Latinos changed during the 1970s and 1980s due to a major immigrant wave that coincided with the shift in the sectoral composition of jobs; low-skilled jobs were filled by labor with low levels of educational attainment. Citizen workers unable to survive on low-wage incomes often dropped out of the workforce, thereby opening up whole sectors to poorly paid immigrants. A profile of recent Mexican immigrants in Los Angeles reveals that approximately one-half of men and more than two-thirds of women work in manufacturing;[23] 58 percent of Mexican male and 75 percent of Mexican female immigrants are also part-time workers. Their concentration in highly competitive sectors with unstable employment has led to a downward pressure on wages in these industries. As a result, half of the recent Mexican immigrant population earned poverty-level wages in 1980, in contrast to 20 percent of the total workforce.

Thus, the economic dimensions of Latino concerns focus on a lack of jobs and a proliferation of low-income jobs that offer few ladders for upward mobility or employment security. Cities have the highest rates of unemployment and the greatest amount of economic inequality, yet they are the least able to address these problems. The challenge for cities is to become more responsive to the urban poor while simultaneously becoming more entrepreneurial.

Political Dimensions

Because the problem of economic disenfranchisement is coupled with political powerlessness, Latinos have not been able effectively to voice their concerns. Historical studies of Chicago and Los Angeles, for example, cite repeated instances of disruption of the Latino community caused by forced repatriations or manipulated labor flows that undermined the stability needed to establish a political presence.[24] The problem of political disconnectedness was revealed once again during the Los Angeles riots in April 1992, when half (50.6 percent) of those arrested were Latino. Latino immigrants were disproportionately arrested, often for such minor infractions as curfew violation, yet they failed to find appropriate representation. This was not just an issue of oversight by elected officials, but one that reflected the inability of the Latino community to establish the political presence needed to influence political outcomes. Across the nation, the lack of efficacy has repeatedly been linked to political disconnectedness. Extreme political fragmentation and lack of political voice have made it impossible to identify, much less implement, actions that are responsive to the Latino community.

Attempts to Establish Economic and Political Clout

Where politically guided economic restructuring has been attempted, the outcome has been mixed. For example, in San Antonio, the site of an aggressive effort to redirect the economy toward high-technology development, it was found that poor and Latino residents, for the most part, did not participate in the expansion.[25] They were not appropriately trained to take advantage of the opportunities for advancement and did not have sufficient political power to address the issue head-on. In Miami, where Cuban entrepreneurship and small-business development provide a potential success model for economic development, the ability of other ethnic groups to replicate this experience has proved elusive. To a large degree, capitalization and support for the Cubans' economic development came from government resettlement assistance, job training, job placement, and the like.[26] No other Latino group has had access to such support or has been able to repeat this successful form of economic transition.

The lack of economic and political power has resulted in a complex situation. Although some Latinos are benefiting economically, others are beginning to show signs of social disintegration associated with the "urban underclass" phenomenon. While some have been geographically mobile, others are caught in poor inner-city communities, which are too often the sites of toxic waste dumps, hazardous industries, and polluted air, water, and soil and in which the residents rarely have the resources necessary to effect change. Health statistics document the extent to which residents of inner-city communities suffer disproportionately from diseases believed to be caused by environmental pollutants.[27] The situation is one that some are calling "environmental racism."

Despite some successes, the majority of urban Latinos confront a mixture of displacement from the workforce, job loss due to restructuring, and employment in extremely low-paying jobs—dynamics that reflect the nature of the regional industrial base and the profile of the labor market. Added to this, most Latinos have suffered from a lack of political efficacy necessary to change their circumstances. Furthermore, they have not been the beneficiaries of high-tech growth or ethnic enclave development. Instead, they have been left behind in inner-city wastelands that offer little in the way of social, economic, or physical relief. Neither aggregate statistics nor singular case studies of regions nor studies focused on Latino subgroups alone adequately present an accurate picture of the many dimensions of economic, social, and political disenfranchisement. However, when this picture is seen as a composite, a number of policy implications begin to emerge.

Some Elements in an Urban Policy

A careful examination of the situation reveals several underlying problems. One is that the limited English-language capability and low educational attainment of Latinos, particularly among though not limited to new immigrants, have been major determinants of their low employment status. This is captured in the following research findings:

> The education gap continues to explain about one-half of the total income gap between Latino and white males even as the income gap grows. Much of the educational effect in the 1980s has resulted from the low proportion of Latinos with college education in the face of rapidly rising payoffs to completing college for whites and Latinos, males and females. Since jobs and education are closely related, it is hard to say whether the expansion of low-wage jobs has "enticed" even native-born, young Latinos to leave high school before completion or to end their educational investment at high school graduation, or whether barriers to college attendance (such as the shrinking pool of grants-in-aid for college education) has forced young Latinos to take low-income jobs.[28]

This lack of education is anticipated to have even greater negative consequences in the future. Studies show that in contrast with the 1970s, when the relative earnings of men with some college experience were on average 20 percent higher than those of men with only a high school education, in 1980 this gap had grown to between 40 and 50 percent.[29] According to Sheldon Danziger, college-educated men between the ages of twenty-five and fifty-four realized a 7 percent increase in their incomes between 1979 and 1989, while those with a high school diploma suffered an 11 percent decrease and those without a high school diploma earned a full 23 percent less.[30]

The first and most urgent urban policy must begin at the national level and concerns an improvement in the level of educational attainment of all Latinos, especially Mexicans and Puerto Ricans. The education required is at three levels: basic education for those lacking language and other skills; retraining for those out of work due to restructuring; and higher education for those capable of going further. In each of these instances, however, increased education or vocational training will be of limited value unless jobs are available or if the quality of education is substandard.

A second and related policy area concerns support for the working poor. Workers make a rational calculation about whether to take a job that pays low wages if the costs of child care, transport, and other necessities tied to working will reduce their net income to poverty levels. When employment no longer provides adequate returns, or when individuals are pushed out of life-sustaining employment, they must turn to transfer payments or to working in the informal economy. Given the cutbacks in government programs, the primary strategy for survival may be working off the books. The high number of immigrants arrested in the Los Angeles disturbance is one indicator of economic need among the very poor; another is the apparent rise of activities attributed to trade in the shadow, or informal, economy—activities that are often criminalized yet sometimes necessary for survival. Support for these workers must come in the form of social services, such as child care combined with income supplements and economic development aimed at rebuilding local communities.

New efforts directed at community economic development are also necessary. Lessons can be learned from widely accepted practices in developing countries that emphasize "learning by doing." The core idea is that every community has a reservoir of knowledge and resources that can form the basis of economic development. By drawing on this source, developing and improving it, the community as a whole grows. For example, the idea of starting with the community's resources and knowledge could be applied toward the physical reclamation of blighted inner-city neighborhoods. Inhabitants of these communities have a personal, if not a financial, interest in improving their home environment. However, a critical lesson learned from the experience of the successful Cuban small businesses in Miami is that community development requires significant financial and technical investment. Good will and volunteerism have not been enough to ensure a positive outcome. That said, even policies of community reinvestment are not possible without the political means and authority to engage in these activities.

This leads to a third urban issue: political representation. Latinos not only have to become citizens and vote; they must participate in institutional changes that bring the city policymaking closer to the public. Perhaps some of the most telling evidence of Latinos' political failure was the mayor's appointment, after the Los Angeles riots, of a resident from another county and a member of the private sector (Peter Ueberroth) to head a commission charged with designing a plan for restoring the devastated area. Addressing political isolation was apparently not part of the mayor's agenda. Because of this oversight, political reforms that are being examined include (1) expanding the city council and making the districts smaller or breaking up the city into smaller, more governable units; (2) opening up the political appointment process to include working-class and low-income residents, perhaps through more community-based boards, in order to bring government processes closer to the community; (3) holding commission and council meetings in the neighborhoods and in the evening; and (4) strengthening campaign-finance laws.[31] Clearly, the nature of political reforms required will vary across cities, but the general need appears to be constant.

The Stark Reality

Given the declining political clout of cities and their inherent inability to address the cause of problems rather than their manifestation, is it reasonable to assume that even the rudiments of the urban agenda outlined in this chapter is possible to implement? The reality is that Latinos now confront the same dilemma as African American mayors who may represent the majority of their voting constituents but who control empty purses. Just as the nation's mayors at the 1990 Urban Summit called for new coalitions to overcome their diminishing power, so, too, can Latinos attempt to build coalitions that will strengthen their voice. In some parts of the United States, such coalitions are already emerging and have had some successes, although they have not been sustainable over the long term.

Alternatively, the nation can continue to muddle along the same course, recognizing that growing social and economic divisions may lead to increased violence and protest. In asking whether the 1990s might bring a repeat of history, Piven argues the following:

> It is worth pointing out...that neither in the 1930s nor the 1960s [periods of major urban reform] did the mayors willingly enter national politics on behalf of their constituencies. Rather they were driven to do so by rising demands and escalating tumult in the cities. It remains to be seen whether, in the absence of comparable constituency mobilizations, mayors will take the initiative to try to restore the modest progress made earlier toward the nationalization—and democratization—of American politics.[32]

That is, despite the negative political baggage associated with cities, their continued disintegration may force national action. The following argument, which appeared in an article in the *Los Angeles Times*, seems to have some merit: "I think the Los Angeles riots...are a key reason why Bill Clinton was elected President [by California voters]. The [riots] were a dramatic illustration that we have lost control of our cities in a fundamental way."[33]

Thus, when seen as a whole, the issues important to urban Latinos are being thrust into the midst of a series of contentious national debates. These debates center on the ability of the nation to change a "federal system that separates responsibility for the policies that create urban problems from the policies needed to deal with them";[34] on the ability of cities to overcome the fragmentation that makes them characteristically ungovernable; on the ability of society to absorb its residents; and on the ability of the economy to utilize its resources to the fullest. From this perspective, articulation of a Latino urban policy has become critical to the continued well-being of the nation as a whole.

NOTES

This chapter was previously published in *Sage Race Relations Abstracts* 19, no. 3 (1994). Support for this work has come from the Claremont Graduate School, Center for Politics and Economics, the Tomas Rivera Center, and the Inter-University Program for Latino Research.

1. Bill Clinton, *Putting People First: A National Economic Strategy for America* (Little Rock, Ark.: Clinton for President Campaign, 1992), 6.

2. Henry Cisneros, presentation at HUD meeting, 13 July 1993; transcripts available from Washington, D.C.: Alderson Reporting, 1993.

3. Ibid., 16.

4. Susan B. Garland and Christina Del Valle, "The Economic Crisis of Urban America," *Business Week*, 18 May 1993, 38-46.

5. Ibid.

6. U.S. Conference of Mayors, "Official Policy Resolutions Adopted at the 61st Annual Conference of Mayors, New York City, June 18-22, 1993," Washington, D.C.

7. Ronald Berkman, Joyce F. Brown, Beverly Goldberg, and Tod Mijanovich, eds., *In the National Interest: 1990 Urban Summit with Related Analyses, Transcript, and Papers* (New York: Twentieth Century Fund Press, 1992).

8. Demetrios Caraley, "Washington Abandons the Cities," *Political Science Quarterly* 107, no. 1 (1992): 3-4.

9. William R. Barnes, "Urban Policies and Urban Impacts after Reagan," *Urban Affairs Quarterly* 25, no. 4 (June 1990): 562-73; E. S. Mills, "Non-urban Policies as Urban Policies," *Urban Studies* 24 (1987): 561-69; Committee on the District of Columbia, House of Representatives, Ninety-Ninth Congress, *Changing the Course: Federal Grants-in-Aid Funding, 1964-83: The Effects of the Reagan Administration Budget Cuts on the District of Columbia and Other Urban Centers* (Washington, D.C.: Government Printing Office, 1986).

10. Norman Glickman, "Economic Policy and the Cities," *Journal of the American Planning Association* 50 (Autumn 1984): 476.

11. Douglas Yates, *The Ungovernable City: The Politics of Urban Problems and Policy Making* (Cambridge, Mass.: MIT Press, 1984).

12. Frances Fox Piven, "The Mayors and the Federal System," in *In the National Interest*, ed. R. Berkman et al. (New York: Twentieth Century Fund, 1992), 53.

13. Manuel Pastor Jr., "Latinos and the Los Angeles Uprising," Tomas Rivera Center Working Paper, Claremont, Calif., 1993.

14. Refugio I. Rochin, "Hispanic Americans in the Rural Economy: Conditions, Issues and Probable Future Adjustments," National Rural Studies Committee, report to the Fifth Annual Meeting of the National Rural Studies Committee, Western Rural Development Center, Oregon State University, 1992.

15. Isaac Shapiro and Robert Greenstein, *Selective Prosperity: Increasing Income Disparities Since 1977* (Washington, D.C.: Center on Budget and Policy Priorities, July 1991).

16. Martin Carnoy, Hugh Daley, and Raul Hinojosa, "The Changing Economic Position of Latinos in the U.S. Labor Market Since 1939," in *Latinos in a Changing U.S. Economy: Comparative Perspectives on Growing Inequality*, ed. R. Morales and F. Bonilla (Thousand Oaks, Calif.: Sage, 1993).

17. Rebecca Morales and Frank Bonilla, eds., *Latinos in a Changing U.S. Economy: Comparative Perspectives on Growing Inequality* (Thousand Oaks, Calif.: Sage, 1993).

18. Center on Budget and Policy Priorities (CBPP), *Shortchanged: Recent Developments in Hispanic Poverty, Income and Employment* (Washington, D.C.: CBPP, November 1988).

19. Andres Torres and Frank Bonilla, "Decline within Decline: Latinos in New York," in *Latinos in a Changing U.S. Economy: Comparative Perspectives on Growing Inequality*, ed. R. Morales and F. Bonilla (Thousand Oaks, Calif.: Sage, 1993).

20. John D. Kasarda, "Urban Industrial Transition and the Underclass," *Annals of the American Academy of Political and Social Science* 501 (January 1989): 26-47.

21. Ibid.

22. E. S. Grier and G. Grier, *Minorities in Suburbia: A Mid-1980s Update* (Washington, D.C.: Urban Institute Project on Housing Mobility, 1988).

23. Rebecca Morales and Paul M. Ong, "The Illusion of Progress: Latinos in Los Angeles," in *Latinos in a Changing U.S. Economy: Comparative Perspectives on Growing Inequality*, ed. R. Morales and F. Bonilla (Thousand Oaks, Calif.: Sage, 1993).

24. Ibid.; Teresa Cordova, Maria de los Angeles Torres, and Juan Betancur, "Restructuring and the Reproduction of Inequality in Chicago," in *Latinos in a Changing U.S. Economy: Comparative Perspectives on Growing Inequality*, ed. R. Morales and F. Bonilla (Thousand Oaks, Calif.: Sage, 1993).

25. Gilberto Cardenas, Jorge Capa, and Susan Burek, "The Changing Economic Position of Mexican Americans in San Antonio," in *Latinos in a Changing U.S. Economy: Comparative Perspectives on Growing Inequality*, ed. R. Morales and F. Bonilla (Thousand Oaks, Calif.: Sage, 1993).

26. Marifeli Perez and Miren Uriarte, "Cuban Americans in Miami-1950 to 1990," in *Latinos in a Changing U.S. Economy: Comparative Perspectives on Growing Inequality*, ed. R. Morales and F. Bonilla (Thousand Oaks, Calif.: Sage, 1993).

27. Paul M. Ong and Evelyn Blumenberg, "An Unnatural Trade-off: Latinos and Environmental Justice," in *Latinos in a Changing U.S. Economy: Comparative Perspectives on Growing Inequality*, ed. R. Morales and F. Bonilla (Thousand Oaks, Calif.: Sage, 1993).

28. Carnoy et al., "The Changing Economic Position of Latinos."

29. Kathy M. V. Kristof, "Why Attend College? Start with Earnings," *Los Angeles Times*, 8 August 1992.

30. Quoted in ibid.

31. Frank Clifford, Rich Connell, Stephen Braun, and Andrea Ford, "Leaders Lose Feel for City," *Los Angeles Times*, 30 August 1992.

32. Piven, "The Mayors and the Federal System," 53.

33. Carla Rivera, "Riots Seen as Springboard for New National Urban Strategy," *Los Angeles Times*, 26 March 1993.

34. Piven, "The Mayors and the Federal System," 53.

DISCUSSION QUESTIONS

1. Discuss obstacles to the design of a comprehensive and national urban agenda in the United States.

2. What should be included within a national urban agenda?

3. Explain the factors shaping U.S. President Bill Clinton's administration's urban policy agenda.

4. Discuss major structural forces shaping the ability of city governments to deal with certain social and economic problems. How does ideology play a role in shaping a city's capacity to govern effectively?

5. What are the characteristics associated with and reflected in Latino urban experiences in the United States?

FOR FURTHER READING

Barnes, William R. (1990) "Urban Policies and Urban Impacts after Reagan," *Urban Affairs Quarterly* 25 (4) June: 562-73.

Caraley, Demetrios (1992) "Washington Abandons the Cities," *Political Science Quarterly* 107 (1): 1-30.

Center on Budget and Policy Priorities (1988) *Shortchanged: Recent Developments in Hispanic Poverty, Income and Employment*. Washington, D.C.: CBPP, November.

Glickman, Norman (1984) "Economic Policy and the Cities," *Journal of the American Planning Association* 50 (Autumn): 471-569.

Grier, E. S., and G. Grier (1988) *Minorities in Suburbia: A Mid-1980s Update*. Washington, D.C.: Urban Institute Project on Housing Mobility.

Kasarda, John D. (1989) "Urban Industrial Transition and the Underclass," *Annals of the American Academy of Political and Social Science* 501 (January): 26-47.

Morales, Rebecca, and Frank Bonilla (eds.) (1993) *Latinos in a Changing U.S. Economy: Comparative Perspectives on Growing Inequality*. Thousand Oaks, Calif.: Sage.

Piven, Frances Fox (1992) "The Mayors and the Federal System," in R. Berkman et al. (eds) *In the National Interest*. New York: Twentieth Century Fund.

Shapiro, Isaac, and Robert Greenstein (1991) *Selective Prosperity: Increasing Income Disparities Since 1977*. Washington, D.C.: Center on Budget and Policy Priorities.

U.S. Conference of Mayors (1993) "Official Policy Resolutions Adopted at the 61st Annual Conference of Mayors, New York City, June 18-22, 1993," Washington, D.C.

Yates, Douglas (1984) *The Ungovernable City: The Politics of Urban Problems and Policy Making*. Cambridge, Mass.: MIT Press.

Chapter Seven

White Uses of the Black Underclass

Raymond S. Franklin

Discussion of the black underclass brings out the worst in all of us. In the course of everyday life, white and black leaders, white and black scholars, and, not least, white and black "plain folk" hear references to a black *underclass*, a term that suggests the existence of an evil, threatening cancerous growth in our midst.[1] Perceptions and images are often conjured up to serve a larger agenda that is frequently far removed from the particular conditions that produce a black underclass. The most blatant case in point is the use of Willie Horton, a black convict, in the 1988 presidential campaign. Horton, who raped a woman while on a weekend furlough from a Massachusetts state prison, was intentionally used by conservative politicians to attack the alleged permissiveness of the whole welfare state, to suggest that liberal Democrats were "soft" on blacks, and, finally, to impugn the personal judgment of Governor Michael Dukakis, as if he were responsible for individuals who are furloughed in accordance with a law that was in fact developed during the previous Republican administration.

It is not my intention to suggest that the underclass in American society is exclusively black. Latinos, poor whites, and representatives of other ethnic groups certainly can be identified in various regions of the country as fulfilling the requirements for classification in this degrading category. But this chapter is about blacks, and the black underclass sends messages that reverberate far beyond its own boundaries to affect the status of the whole African American population in ways that do not apply to other ethnic or racial groups.

Almost all discussions by professionals and popular pundits who employ the term *underclass* commence with an apology. As if they were in another world, readers are assured either that the term *underclass* is not pejorative or that the term is misleading because it embraces a large variety of individuals who fall into "bad" ways or hardship for a number of reasons. Generalizations are difficult.[2] Yet, it is said, some term must be used to designate a thematic focus, and the term *underclass* is as good as any.

I make no apology for the term *underclass* or for why I choose to "look" specifically at the black underclass. The reality with which I am concerned does not reflect the debates about the underclass's actual size,[3] composition,[4] origin,[5] behavior,[6] origins,[7] or location in our inner cities.[8] As important as these debates are for social scientists who write for each other and sometimes use their findings to suggest new policy directions, the reality on which I focus is filtered through the myopic perceptions that white minds derive from direct "experience," the mass media, and demagogic rhetoric that plays into legitimate and illegitimate fears. Such perceptions may not be accurate by "scientific" standards, but they are very real in their distortions and consequences. The white lens that is focused on the black underclass sees general images that not only embrace the underclass but link it to the working poor who live in black ghettos, to the middle-income members of the larger black community—indeed, to the whole black population. The underclass is the first step in a process by which whites derive an "understanding" about all black people.

If the "poverty experts" whom Ken Auletta consulted for his highly praised study "generalize about people they barely know," then imagine how large numbers of whites who are miscreant voyeurs of the overexposed and often misrepresented black underclass scene must generalize.[9] Such generalizations constitute racism: they feed into the economic reproduction of the black underclass and promote racial stereotypes and exclusionary practices toward blacks who are far removed from the behavior and statistics that actually define the poorest and most alienated portion of the African American population. Thus, the black underclass stands at the center of the contemporary race-class confusion I have sought to clarify elsewhere. The present entrapment of the black underclass in our major central cities casts shadows that affect the racial judgments of the whole society. But these oversized, racially constructed shadows that are visible to white minds come from sources other than the actual statistical size of the black underclass. If one accepts Christopher Jencks's provocative suggestion that the concept underclass is "an antonym to the terms [white] middle class and working class," then the black underclass must be understood in terms of the economic, moral, and educational categories employed to describe the white middle and working classes.[10] Thus, Jencks seeks to determine the growth or decline of the economic underclass (people without jobs), the moral underclass (people without middle-class values), and the educational underclass (people with little education). Jencks demonstrates that since the mid-fifties, only the economic underclass, both black and white, grew. The size of the moral and educational underclass declined.[11]

If one accepts the more traditional, although severely criticized, measure of the underclass in terms of the number of people living in census tract areas characterized by "high rates of school dropouts, male nonemployment, welfare recipients, and female headed households, [the number rose] more than three-fold between 1970 and 1980."[12] What needs emphasis, for my purposes, is that the underclass, however defined, is a relatively small part of the nation's population; it constitutes 1 percent of the population and is concentrated mainly in our ten major central cities.[13] If one further examines what proportion is black, then we are discussing a fraction of 1 percent.

To this statistically lessened problem, we must add the fact that race as a cause of membership in the underclass "club" is not overemphasized among social scientists.[14] While it is observed that minorities—often a euphemism for blacks—suffer most from the interrelated issues of crime, welfare dependency, family dissolution, and the breakdown of binding moral values, liberal social scientists tend to attribute such conditions to impersonal forces. Thus, from a purely statistical and analytical viewpoint, the race-underclass association seems to be much ado about very little. Yet, the black underclass looms larger than life among the white majority, even in areas and parts of the country where few blacks reside. It is for this reason that the white uses of images of the black underclass warrant special consideration, independent of whether such perceptions are really true.

Emerging Middle-Class Perception

As early as the late sixties, following the passage of the major pieces of civil rights legislation, a white backlash was in motion. Middle- and lower-middle-class concerns were about neighborhoods, schools, parks, and streets. If you let a few "good" kinds of blacks into your territory, they will be followed by a horde of "bad" kinds. Operating in conjunction with, but not caused by, this white preoccupation with blacks entering "their" social spaces was a status anxiety propelled by a slowdown in economic growth and a rise in prices.[15] Increasingly, it took two incomes to remain in the same place.[16] Projections about the future did not automatically assume that the offspring of America's white middle layers would achieve more than their parents had. And the rising tax burden appeared to produce declining benefits, except for the tax revenues that were going to a large, undeserving portion of the black population.[17]

Although welfare liberals and black leaders repressed a serious discussion of a growing black underclass in the seventies, the issue grew beneath the social surface. "After a long eclipse," write two current leading scholars on the black poor, "the ghetto has made a stunning comeback into the collective consciousness of America. Not since the riots of the hot summers of 1966-68 have the black poor received so much attention in academic, activist, and policy making quarters."[18] The reasons for this comeback are complex. It is related, in my judgment, to a sharpening division between the rich and the poor,[19] a growing restlessness among white middle- and working-class voters, and a general rejection of the welfare system, which is viewed as a pillar of support to large portions of the black poor. Central to the concern with the black underclass are the interests and perceptions of the broad white middle class.

By 1970, the white middle class had exhausted its empathy with black causes and the social malaise of our central cities. This became especially true in cities that had a large number of older, less mobile, "God-fearing," affluent, working-class whites who were losing their younger members to the less ethnic suburbs. While the more affluent suburbs sought to protect the value of their homes and the character of their neighborhoods through restrictive covenants such as land-lot size requirements, "preemptive purchase, various petty harassments, implicit or explicit collusion by realtors, banks, mortgage lenders and other lending agencies," lower-middle-class, central-city whites facing a larger black population had fewer options.[20]

Impressions gathered by a reporter in the early seventies who returned to his native Slovak community in Cleveland are worth quoting at some length; they illustrate the reactions of a relatively moderate white ethnic group to African American efforts to find adequate residential space. These observations also illustrate how the Slovaks perceived more militant white ethnic reactions to the black "threat." The writer began with an aging priest, Father Michael Jasko:

We had 2,000 families and 8,000 souls [some years ago]....Now it's 1,000 families and 3,000 souls, and most of them are pensioners. We stopped the Canteen [a weekly dance for teenagers] 10 years ago and hoped to reopen it, but never did. We made $45,000 in a big year at the bazaar; last year we got $24,000. Novenas and other night-time services have been stopped. The old ladies of the church were getting beaten and robbed on their way to early mass, so we stopped those. Now the first mass is at 7 o'clock, except in the summer when we have the 5:30.[21]

The widow of a neighborhood gas station manager who was killed in a robbery lamented:

To many people around here, Joe was a fixture, the honest businessman who made it by hard work. We all knew that the neighborhood was changing, but then this....I think of leaving the neighborhood now, but where would I go? Everything I know is here. I just want those killers found and I want them to get their due.[22]

The editor of the Slovak neighborhood newspaper, a self-described "superhawk and ultra-conservative," concluded after a long conversation:

In everything I've told you, I've not once mentioned race. It isn't race; it's law and order....There was never trouble just because blacks moved in. In Murray Hill, the Italians told the blacks they would kill any who dared to move in. In Sowinski Park, the Polish pointed shotguns at them. This is not our way of life but look at what we are reaping now.[23]

From Bill Blassman, bachelor and owner of a corner grocery:

Things were bad before Mayor Stokes, a black, was elected, but since his election, the situation in the neighborhood has quickly become untenable. Stokes is responsible for encouraging blacks to come up from the South and get on Cleveland's welfare and crime roles. Stokes has allowed a new permissiveness. The blacks are cocky because one of their own is downtown....In Cleveland, in the old neighborhood, it is largely Stokes' fault.[24]

Finally, a neighborhood ethnic militia has arisen in the name of the Buckeye Neighborhood Nationalities Civic Association. One of the organization's founders reported on the planned operations of the group:

This is our battle plan. We want to have each house with a code number so that our police can get to any house in minutes. The city police won't cover us, so we are willing to give ourselves....I know people are calling us vigilantes....Anything blacks say about us is out of ignorance. This neighborhood should be preserved as a national historical monument to mark the contributions of the nationalities. Monuments are WASP or black, nothing for us....And we don't want blacks in our group; we are for the preservation of the national way of life.[25]

What is most relevant about the impressions of this one ethnic group is the range of expressed vindictive feelings and perceptions. In their belief that they were caught between an "uppity" WASP stratum and a pariah black one, this hardworking community of Slovaks, consisting of pensioners, older blue-collar workers, and small-business owners, lashes out in all directions. From events directly observed or experienced at the neighborhood level, they seek concrete revenge or justice for particular black violations. With the election of the black mayor Carl Stokes, they are able to justify the indictment of a large range of black Cleveland residents who have no connection to neighborhood specifics. With considerable ease, they interpret the national economy and concoct reasons for the influx of blacks to Cleveland—not in terms of internal immigrants looking for the jobs, higher living standards, and better way of life that once motivated the whites themselves to come to the United States, but in terms of southern migrants intentionally coming to "their" Cleveland to live on welfare and engage in crime. In a moment of self-pity, they reflect on their "softness" and express envy of the Italians and Polish who "know how" to take care of their "niggers" through the barrel of a gun. And, not least, they move toward a paramilitary solution by organizing armed defense committees and calling for some superchauvinist rituals that would put white ethnics on the social map. Not all reasoning by whites, of course, extends itself to a paramilitary formulation. More commonly, whites wish that blacks had never come to these shores or that the black "problem" would just disappear.

Insofar as blacks worry about violence in their communities, it is less due to paramilitary actions by ethnic whites (who have made their statement with their feet by departing from the central city) and more due to the condition facing black men. In an article by Robert Staples, "Black Male Genocide: A Final Solution to the Race Problem in America," the concern is expressed in statistical terms; it is worth reproducing them:

> While black men account for only six percent of the population of the United States, they make up half of its male prisoners in local, state, and federal jails.
>> The majority of the 20,000 Americans killed in crime-related incidents each year are black.
>> Over thirty-five percent of all black men in American cities are drug and alcohol abusers.
>> Eighteen percent of black males drop out of high school.
>> Twenty-five percent of the victims of AIDS are black men.
>> Over fifty percent of black men under the age of twenty-one are unemployed.
>> Forty-six percent of black men between the ages of sixteen and sixty-two are not in the labor force.
>> About thirty-two percent of black men have incomes below the officially defined poverty level.[26]

While the combination of historic racism and current conditions accounts for the large numbers of black youth at risk, "black parents [naturally] worry that law-abiding young men—their own sons and nephews—will be rounded up with the rest."[27] The evident meaning here is that white police officers do not easily discriminate between "good" ghetto blacks and "bad" ones. It also suggests that most black parents are forever coping with the risks inherent in everyday ghetto life; their offspring need continuous protection against the "bad" black element in their midst.[28] Young black males are destroying themselves, writes Jewelle T. Gibbs, through "their own actions and activities....They are continuing to kill, maim, or narcotize themselves faster than they could be annihilated through wars or natural diseases. They not only destroy themselves, but also jeopardize...family formation for young black women, ... the stability of the black community, and endanger the entire society."[29] Or, as Cornel West suggested in more interpretive terms, there is no need for protection against a vast and growing black underclass, an underclass that embodies a kind of *walking nihilism* of pervasive drug addiction, pervasive alcoholism, pervasive homicide, and an exponential rise in suicide. Now, because of the deindustrialization, we also have a devastated black industrial working class. We are talking here about tremendous hopelessness.[30]

Complementing the quantitative and qualitative portrait of black men is the repeated characterization of black women: unwed teenage mothers, welfare recipients, women who head families because of divorce or because they have never been married. The feminization of poverty, often a euphemism applied to the condition of black women, is a commonly employed category that embraces the general condition.

Drugs, crime, street gangs, muggings, random shootouts, unwed teenagers, welfare dependency, AIDS—these are the code words that enabled a slumlord to defend his actions with a vengeance after being accused of exploiting blacks:

> Who else but me would take care of the whores, pimps, ... addicts, hoodlums, queers—the dregs of humanity that nobody wants. It's a lousy zoo and I take care of some of the animals—but that's more than the federal government.[31]

In suggesting that he is a benign man caring for animals, Mr. Slumlord falls into a pattern that has a long history. While the dominant white majority has intermittently employed nasty epithets to describe the "lower classes" in its midst, categories of "subhumans" have been most often reserved for blacks. As Winthrop D. Jordan noted in his historical explorations of the origin of racism in the United States, "Ever since the days of confrontation in Africa the sexual connection between Negro and ape has served to express the deep-seated feeling that the Negro was more animal—and accordingly more sexual—than the white man."[32]

It was in the late nineteenth century, to continue in the historical vein, when Jim Crow laws throughout the South were instituted, that the imagery of the "Negro as beast" perhaps reached its zenith.[33] In the context of a growing agricultural crisis and the white belief that black sexuality and criminality were on the rise, numerous southern writers lamented the passing of the slave system, in which the "good darkies" knew their place, and focused on the savagery and animality that supposedly characterized the free Negro who had been let out of the cage.[34] Lynchings increased rapidly in this period, and it became less than rare to find vile racist statements about the "Negro as a brute and a savage" or "a fiend, a wild beast, seeking whom he may devour."[35] Lest this image of the "Negro as beast" be thought of as buried in our past, it is worth noting a more current remark by a New York reporter who refused, in a fit of cynical anger, an uptown assignment on the basis that he did not wish to "interview those monkeys."[36]

These crude, public, animal references, although relatively scarce today by past standards, are not without subtle consequences. African Americans are sensitive in unanticipated ways to vulgar, racist rhetoric. This is illustrated by the following classroom experience that took place in the spring of 1980. I was teaching an adult education class that consisted mainly of U.S.-born black women, although there were some who had Caribbean origins. A student brought into class a current newspaper clipping about the creationist perspective on evolution and the Moral Majority's attack on the teaching of scientific evolutionism. The student queried whether I believed in evolution of the Darwinian variety. Suspecting immediately that I was about to clash directly with the class member's religious sentiment, I turned the question around and sought her opinion. The judgment was instantaneous: "It is not possible to think that we are related to monkeys."

The discussion had proceeded aimlessly for about fifteen minutes when another woman cynically commented: "It won't be long before they begin looking for our tail again." Interestingly, the few West Indian blacks refrained from either supporting or rejecting Darwinian evolutionary theory; one merely said that she "lacked sufficient knowledge to make a judgment."[37]

So here we are with the following irony: black working-class women—active unionists in a union-sponsored college program, liberally oriented toward social issues—automatically side with southern white-supremacist religious fundamentalists, despite the fact that the fundamentalists are bringing up the ghost of the Scopes trial and investigating high school textbooks for political reasons that can only foster a social atmosphere detrimental to the interests of blacks. The African American reaction to the evolution issue is not simply a matter of mechanically asserting Sunday-school lessons, as may be the case for grassroots white religious fundamentalists. Blotting out an inquiry into the validity of scientific evolution is a race-specific reaction particular to the history of U.S. blacks. It reflects the ever-present sense of subordination that produces a defensive posture and prevents a genuine opportunity to understand an important area of science.

As the 1980s unfolded, with their attendant change in political climate, the portrait of poor blacks increasingly degenerated to a depiction of the underclass in inner-city neighborhoods. The debate among social scientists about causation aside, the collective portrait that is packaged in one form or another is often beyond vilification.[38] It comes across as a specter haunting us, one that cannot be grasped by normal human feelings or understood by standard cognitive efforts. It puts some portion of the black community outside the human race; this is extended by degrees to measure all blacks, a practice, to repeat, that is common in our racist history. It feeds a deep-seated racialist mind-set, even when it is offset with bracketed explanations that are nonracial or class-based in nature.

Moreover, degrading images of the downtrodden black underclass used by whites are often provided by blacks themselves. The selective use by whites of black statements allows whites to appear less culpable for flaunting stereotypical symbols and expressing racial fears. Mass media reporting is generally not aimed at arousing passion or empathy or at deepening our understanding. Thus, we have testimonies, pictures, movies, and twenty-second TV "interviews" that frequently attribute a willful nature to those who allegedly manifest underclass behavior traits. In the current period, the prevalence of the black underclass is explained by the policies of the welfare state and therefore is used by conservatives against liberals to account for crime, broken homes, the absence of the work ethic, and a host of other phenomena that are assumed to be completely absent from most white families.

Imaging the Black Underclass

A composite profile of the black underclass can begin either at the neighborhood level or through depictions of individuals. Be it one or the other, the details are easy to come by and are often fused into a single image in the white mind from which moral judgments are derived and racially hostile sentiments justified. From the South Bronx to the South Side of Chicago to Watts in Los Angeles, neighborhoods are seen as consisting of

> currency exchanges, bars and liquor stores...stores [that] are boarded up and abandoned. A few buildings have bars across the front and are closed to the public, but they are not empty. They are used, not so secretly, by people involved in illegal activities. Other stretches of the street are simply barren.[39]

Moving from Chicago to Detroit, one writer reports:

> It would be hard to exaggerate the devastation that begins beyond "The Line." It's a scene of weed-choking lots and gutted wooden houses landscaped with shards of glass where teenagers gather aimlessly and children scavenge...from the debris. From their porches, the remaining home owners, mostly black...can point out a half dozen crack houses. In this neighborhood, it is easy to obliterate the present, but hard to think about the future.[40]

A *Time* magazine cover story put it in more graphic terms: "The universe of [the black] underclass is often a junk heap of rotting housing, broken furniture, crummy food, alcohol and drugs."[41] Add graffiti and dimly lit streets littered with garbage and beer cans, and the image that whites have in their minds about black underclass neighborhoods (and, to one degree or another, perhaps all black neighborhoods) is completed.

Black leaders and writers, motivated to bring self-consciousness and self-help schemes into the black community, frequently feed white images, their own intentions, of course, to the contrary. "Among [black] male peers," writes the black sociologist Robert Staples, "demonstrating...masculine prowess in terms of sexual conquests...or fighting is all that is rewarded."[42] Or consider some statements made by the Reverend Jesse Jackson over the past decade. In a fund appeal for PUSH in 1980 he was quoted as saying, with obvious pain, "The door of opportunity is open for our people, but they are too drunk, too unconscious to walk through the door."[43] In a spirit of exhortation for self-development, Jackson continued along the same lines during one of his primary campaign addresses, in 1984, to ghetto high school graduates and their parents: "Don't pickle your brain in liquor—don't you put dope in your veins....[You] must assume responsibility for our children....Assure them they are somebody."[44] And finally, in his commencement address to the graduating class of Medgar Evers College in Brooklyn, in 1986, Jackson dramatically called attention to additional black "sins" that have subsequently received much public attention. In reference to crime, he stated that "more blacks lost their lives from black-on-black murder in 1981 than black men killed in twelve years of war in Vietnam." Turning to the issue of black male-female relations, he chided both: "Brothers, you're not a man because you can make a baby," and, "Sisters, young men do not make babies by themselves."[45] Thus, his homily ends on the sorry state of the poor black family—the unwed mother, the pregnant teenager, the irresponsible black male.

Whether preaching from the public pulpit in a postindustrial "here and now" consumption-addicted society can affect the habits of ghetto-dwelling "sinners" is uncertain; no doubt the self-help motives behind the exhortations of some current black leaders are part of a venerable tradition that was crystallized perhaps most clearly by Booker T. Washington. But when issues like these, discussed by Jackson and other leaders with one set of intentions, are picked up by the same mass media for a sixty-second "show and tell," they are not always understood as intended. When a black woman interviewed on a six o'clock CBS news broadcast says, "I hate to admit this, but for a lot of young women, the only way they can get more money is to have another baby," whites come away with the confirmation that blacks do not want to work.[46] "True confessions" about the realities found in many black communities, and self-declarations about what is to be done, too often feed white stereotypes.

Such images in white minds, whatever the source, have a context. And in our present social climate, the medium of the message and the context in which it is often received provide reasons why whites respond with a resounding nay when the threat of integration knocks on their doors. A citizen of one threatened neighborhood states: "[We have paid in] blood, sweat and tears to keep our neighborhood green; to see low-income [euphemism for blacks] high risers is absolutely a nightmare." Another states, "When we would see the projects go up from our kitchen window, ... I remember my mother saying, that's the end of the neighborhood." Finally, still another concluded, "They call it scattered-site housing....We call it scattered-site cancer."[47]

Cancer, of course, is an uncontrollable human disease; its use as a metaphor applies to more than just the landscape and architecture of a neighborhood. It quickly expands to include the images of black-underclass persons and behaviors that range from welfare mothers and swindlers to "murderers, muggers, stickup men, chain snatchers, pimps, burglars, heroin addicts, drug pushers, and alcoholics."[48] Beyond such criminal categories that spotlight the lazy and the degenerate, there are other, more "scientific" ones like "disorganized," "present-time oriented," and "rarely married." Thus, when whites fight integration, they also need to downgrade African Americans qua persons in one form or another: "All of us have worked for our homes. Our houses are our major investment....Show me some black guys who are working, and I'll go out and get people to sell them houses." "It was no longer working poor, it was welfare poor....It was the way they acted." "You know how I got this house?" Mr. McLaughlin demanded. "We didn't eat out for two years. I hustled at Yankee Stadium. I was a helper on a truck. I was a bartender, a stagehand. I worked my butt off." This attitude of "Why can't 'they' be like 'us'?" culminated in a more general statement by the head of the civic association: "It is not a question of race but of shared values."[49] All these statements tend to be rhetorical, since few whites believed that there were in existence very many hardworking blacks capable of financing entrance into "their" white neighborhoods.

Black Families and Black Criminals

Ultimately, when popular wisdom becomes analytical, the focus turns to the black family. The family is the extent of the environment that most people intuitively grasp in search of explanations. The African American family has been the focus of debate and contention among both blacks and whites for a long time. What was stated by E. Franklin Frazier in 1940 still appears relevant:

Black disorganized families have failed to provide for their emotional needs and have not provided the discipline and habits which are necessary for personality development. Because the disorganized family has failed in its function as a socializing agency, it handicapped the children in their relations to the institutions in the community. Moreover, family disorganization has been partially responsible for a large amount of juvenile delinquency and adult crime among Negroes.[50]

From family breakdowns arise brazen, fearless, unimaginable young toughs. Herb Denton, writing for the *Washington Post*, reports a street conversation with some young black teenagers:

They are small boys, eleven, twelve, and thirteen years old, still blushing, when asked about their girlfriends....But when guns and homemade bombs explode on the street, they stand on the sidewalks with the older boys, hurling rocks and bottles at every passing white motorist. They cheer when they hit a windshield and glass shatters....Alex Moore, 13, ... talks about being on the streets, ... about throwing rocks at whites...as they drove by.

"I hit a cracker cab, then a cracker came down in a van. I hit him, too."

"Why?" He smiles, sighs, gives the visitor a look of mock exasperation. Was he afraid out there with the fires and the police and the older boys exchanging volleys and gunfire? His smooth brown face hardens.

"When they shoot me," he says, "they better had kill me."[51]

Small delinquent boys grow up to be big tough youths, and big tough youths grow up to be the men who constitute the core of the underclass. Black underclass men are pictured in two ways: as unreformable criminals or as irresponsible fathers. "Members" of the black underclass, from brassy teenagers to hardened criminals, terrorize the white imagination that is fed by the mass media, hearsay, or concrete incidents. Judgments are quick to come: "Some of these kids are just...mean human beings," writes the former Urban League president Vernon Jordan.[52] Or compare the relatively benign judgment of a police officer: "I don't blame the kids. I blame the parents. If my kid came home with a watch or a bicycle that I didn't buy him, I'd want to know where he got it. But those parents are delighted. I'd lock up the parents."[53]

Whether young black delinquents are seen as simply mean or as lacking proper adult supervision, they sooner or later get classified as monstrous, as less than human: "They'll kill you for nothing. They'll stare through you. They're cold and callous. They have no remorse."[54] The "less-than-human" category is confirmed by such boastful confessions as "I earned $1,500 to $3,000 a day as a stickup man and I wrote 'sorry notes' to the loved ones of those [I] shot."[55] Pearl Dawson, herself a black ex-convict, reflects: "One thing about Black people, when it comes to crime they don't think. A lot of crime is done without thinking."[56]

Thoughtless, *sadistic*, and *callous* are the words used to describe the black criminal. It follows that violent black crimes are often viewed as random, especially in urban communities, and the "randomness" is often seen as emerging from poor, broken families unable to supply direction to young lives. "As a result, many [big-city] residents feel under a state of siege; they alter their living habits, change their locks, bolt their doors, and nervously glance over their shoulder."[57] Thus, the black-white racial discord between communities becomes a class discord within the African American community, between decent blacks and black criminals, between the black working poor and the nonworking poor. As one old black resident of Tyler House in Washington, D.C., sadly reflected:

> I would like to say I'm black and I'm proud, but I can't say that so easily because I'm not proud of what black people are doing to each other in this building. I'm like most of the other elderly people here. I'm afraid of my own people—not only in Tyler House, but everywhere I go. The men will come up to you and say, "How you doing, sister?" Then they'll snatch your pocketbook.[58]

Downgrading the Black Male

There is one sign of "relief" among whites in this general fear of the black underclass, itself revealing of white racist attitudes. Crime statistics tell us that "95 percent of all victims of crime perpetuated by blacks are blacks. In 1980, more than 2,000 black teenagers were homicide victims, almost all at the hands of other black teenagers."[59] Are whites acting as if they were watching some "weirdo" animals in a zoo, fighting it out in a cage and thereby deriving a sense of racial superiority from the belief that they are not like "them"? It is this white posture that induced Christopher Muldor to title his *Wall Street Journal* op-ed piece with the question "Do Black Crime Victims Matter?" As he reported, the criminal justice system is much more lenient toward blacks who kill other blacks than toward blacks who kill whites.[60] Are not black victims people who should have their victimizers removed from society? Should we not be concerned with all victims of crime equally? The answer in a racist society is no, since black victims are not viewed as completely human or worthy of the same empathy as whites. As one cop commented, "[Blacks] are not ready for society....Civil rights came too fast, too soon." Analyzing why blacks are not ready for society and therefore do not warrant the same civil considerations as whites, the cop continues: "There's no father image....There's no father who runs the family....So you don't have discipline."[61]

Thus, in returning to the state of the black family with its disorganization and weakness as a socializer, we blame the black man. He becomes America's number-one internal enemy. He becomes not only the culprit of black crime, family chaos, juvenile delinquency, and a host of other difficulties within the black community but also the enemy of black women. In the world of one black underclass man, his marriage "did not fail because he failed as a breadwinner and head of a family but because his wife refused to put up with his manly appetite for whiskey and other women"—appetites that rank high in the scale of shadow values on the street corner.[62]

In the words of a black man who was induced to write as if he were making observations characteristic of the whole black professional middle class:

> The truth be known, my friend was a bum whose life was an insult to black people. His death brought to public view some of the dozen or so children he'd fathered by numerous women. Always he'd dillydallied without marriage and without commitment. And once a child was conceived he was off to new conquests. Worse, he managed to glamorize his philandering so that many young blacks envied it.

> We [black men] are, after all, part of the problem....We've indulged our sons so much that they too believe sexual irresponsibility is a rite of manhood. All the while, we have given neither our sons nor our daughters the love, trust and confidence that would make them realize how truly special they are.
>
> As a boy I remember seeing black physicians meeting teenaged girls for tawdry assignations. When the babies came, those doctors adorned their Cadillacs with new girls and never committed even a pittance to the support of the children they fathered.
>
> While the junior-high principal wasn't as sought after as the physicians, he also had a following. He'd leave pregnant teenagers in the lurch—too poorly educated to support themselves and with no hope of getting help from him....By their actions, these men taught us that it was acceptable to use women like whores.[63]

The media technique of inducing black men to testify against themselves, regardless of the testimony's accuracy or merit, enables the white world to observe the black condition in a state of dumb disbelief and scorn. Black men are seen as the cause of the condition in which black women find themselves and, therefore, are blamed for the fact that 56 percent of black births are out of wedlock, compared to 9.4 percent for whites, a difference that identifies the black rate as "pathological."[64] This kind of statistic not infrequently turns the focus to black women and their image in white minds. While some black females, in the name of feminism and the defense of gender, may vent against black males, black women do not escape the victimization process.

Unweds, Babies, and Welfare Dependency

The media during the 1990s have saturated the public with stories and pictures of "black teenager birth rates, black illegitimate birth rates, and black female AIDS rates."[65] Why this state of affairs? The answer conveyed by the media, especially with regard to the unmarried teenager, is glib. It rarely seeks to offer serious insights about what it means to grow up in a socially negating society that projects a dismal future, not only for you specifically but for every acquaintance in the universe of your neighborhood. Frequently, the partial explanation that is teased out of the mouth of the black teenager herself has stereotypical dimensions:

> Their friends were all having babies. Their boyfriends had pressured them into it, because being a father—the fact of it, not the responsibility—is a status symbol for a boy in the ghetto. Welfare does provide an economic underpinning for out-of-wedlock childrearing.[66]
>
> Lots of girls feel that if they get to be eighteen and they don't have a baby, they're not a woman.[67]

To white ears, the statement by a black teenager that having a child is a means of getting on welfare drowns out almost all else one might say. Thus, the more black teenagers talk about having babies, or not knowing who the father was, or why they were shipped off to a foster home, the greater the white belief that black sexual behavior is completely indiscriminate and promiscuous. It is behavior that is inexplicable and outside the normal range of white middle-class moral deliberations. It becomes behavior specifically associated with race, with African Americans, and is assumed to be deeply embedded in black culture in ways that transcend environmental and class considerations. This latter point is often proved by pointing to the fact that less-developed countries have poor masses that manage to keep their families intact and are not sexually permissive.[68]

Out-of-wedlock births are critical to the assumed reasons why so many blacks need welfare assistance. Welfare dependency has become the public policy symbol that both reflects and causes much that ails the black community. It brings together the racist judgments that whites stereotypically employ to describe the black population—ungrateful welfare cheats, laziness, absence of pride—contrasted unfavorably with "them-versus-us" whites who would rather starve than accept welfare. There is no end to the opprobrious phrases cast at the African American population (and frequently accepted as partially true by blacks themselves) that are derived from the underclass-welfare linkage.

The most decisive way to chastise the character of the black welfare population is to use, as I have repeatedly emphasized, black words against blacks as if whites were unrelated to the conditions in which blacks find themselves. The welfare system has become the primary wastepaper basket to collect much of the contempt that whites have for blacks. Whites are profoundly agitated by the belief that their hard-earned taxed incomes go to support black welfare recipients who "stay on the dole most of their lives," believe that there is no point to working "when you can get something for nothing," and have a "baby every year to stay on welfare."[69] The most repeated point is that welfare induces the breakup of the black family, since it "encourages husbands to leave home, knowing that public stipends will provide for their wives."[70] This, moreover, allows black men to live off their wives without working; after all, "there is no law against a lady givin' you all their money."[71] In sum and substance, the welfare system undermines the work ethic and induces the black working poor to ask:

> Why work?...For all practical purposes, the relief check becomes a surrogate for the male breadwinner. The resulting family breakdown and loss of control over the young [are] usually signified by a spread of forms of disorder—for example, school failure, crime and addiction.[72]

The welfare system is indicted beyond its deleterious effects on black women, men, children, work, and learning habits. Blacks are seen as ungrateful cheats who do not care about anything:

> I remember one time my girlfriend and I got drunk and went out and bought drugs.... The next day, we were sick. She said: "Don't worry." She went down to the welfare center, with rags and barged in there yelling. God damn it; look at what my baby has to play in! I didn't get my check....Half an hour later we were sitting at home shooting up with money from the extra check.[73]

Not only, therefore, are children had without thought, but the money acquired from the welfare system is not really used to care properly for them. Thus, the popular mind sees the welfare system as a dumping ground for those blacks who do not wish to work, for having babies in order to stay on the dole, and, not least, for institutionalizing cheating.[74]

In a country in which individuals are judged by their job, by a willingness to work even if the work pays poorly and there is little pride in the job or product itself, the overrepresentation of blacks in the welfare sector induces a profound stigma. It has become a reason that justifies the actions of white blue-collar workers who have left the Democratic party and have rejected the welfare state itself.[75] To such white workers, a "welfare recipient" is synonymous with "black." This welfare-black link, unfortunately, does not end with white misperception. Even black unionized workers, while unlikely to sever their allegiance to the Democratic party, responded enthusiastically to a white conservative speaker who had little rapport with the liberal, unionized audience until the speaker began to attack the welfare system. Thus, regularly employed black workers themselves appear to share views with their white cohorts that many welfare recipients are lazy and irresponsible.[76] In more macrological terms, the welfare system has even been indicted on the wacky belief (assumed to be well known) that it "drains most of the five-hundred-billion-dollar federal budget."[77]

The moral here is complex, although, from my angle of reflection, quite comprehensible. White workers see "race" when they think "welfare"; the link between the two is strong. Employed black workers are a "class" of people with whom they are identified and from whom they wish to be dissociated when they hear the term *welfare* being tossed about in the public arena. Few black employed workers, unlike their white counterparts, are unfamiliar with individual welfare recipients who might fit the publicly held stereotype.

While white workers may acquire a misplaced pride in telling themselves that starvation is preferable to accepting a dole from the state, black employed workers experience something different when welfare recipients and the devalued system are publicly exposed. The overrepresentation of unemployed blacks among those who receive welfare checks calls into question the immediate social status of large numbers of working poor blacks whose income is at or marginally above the threshold of poverty. While middle-class blacks with two incomes also suffer in status from this peculiar "guilt by association," they are not as residentially integrated with high concentrations of welfare recipients and marginally employed blacks. While white workers residing in relatively homogeneous communities view the welfare sector in race terms, black workers residing in black communities necessarily view it in class terms. But this class cleavage within the black community is exacerbated by the stigmatizing white image of black welfare recipients. The black overrepresentation in the welfare sector dramatically impinges on the status of the black stratum immediately above it. In this sense, class tensions within the black population are related to the race-class differences between the populations.

Statistical Myopia

White myopic perceptions are not only confined to popular prejudices, misinformation, and manipulated media images that are devoid of endeavors to deepen the public's understanding and eliminate contemptuous voyeurism. There is also a statistical myopia disguised as value-free research or as the honest effort to find the quantitative magnitudes that underlie popular impressions. An example of this brand of representation appeared in a review of six books by Andrew Hacker, published in 1988 and titled "Black Crime, White Racism."[78] Aside from the fact that three of the six books reviewed had little to do with crime as such, discussion of crime dominated. Without doing full justice to Hacker's quiet and buried one-line critical qualifications, what stands out larger than life is the reproduction of five tables. They constitute a story in themselves and feed the validation of popular impressions, from which academics are not excluded, that are often unsupported by numbers (see Tables 7.1 through 7.5).

Table 7.1 informs us that blacks are disproportionately arrested, a fact that most whites acquire through the habit of watching TV, looking at pictures of the ten most-wanted criminals pinned on post office walls, and reading about arrests in daily tabloids.

TABLE 7.1
Racial Arrest Rates

	Black Share of Arrests (%)	Disproportion of Black Arrests in Population
Robbery	62.0	5.2
Gambling	49.7	4.1
Murder and manslaughter	48.0	4.0
Rape	46.6	3.9
Gambling	46.1	3.9
Prostitution	43.0	3.6
Aggravated assault	39.8	3.3
Receiving stolen property	37.4	3.1
Motor vehicle theft	34.7	2.9
Weapons offenses	34.4	2.9
Forgery and counterfeiting	32.6	2.7
Domestic violence	32.3	2.7
Drug violations	31.8	2.7
Disorderly conduct	30.7	2.6
Burglary	29.5	2.5
Vagrancy	29.4	2.5
Embezzlement	28.8	2.4
Curfew and loitering	21.9	1.8
Vandalism	19.9	1.7
Driving while intoxicated	9.7	0.8

NOTE: Ratios of disproportion assume that blacks make up 12 percent of the population.
SOURCE: Federal Bureau of Investigation (1986).

134   R A Y M O N D   S.   F R A N K L I N

Table 7.2 identifies three criminal behavior patterns, of which whites must worry about only one. We see that blacks murder and rape primarily other blacks; these two categories of facts do not warrant white concern, since white empathy for black victims is minimal. But the third category of criminal information included in Table 7.2 does produce a white concern: the rate of black robberies of whites is higher than black robberies of blacks (37 percent versus 25.8 percent).

TABLE 7.2
Assailants and Victims (in %)

Assailant-Victim	Percentage
	11,099 murders
White-white	46.0
Black-black	46.0
Black-white	5.6
White-black	2.4
	108,826 rapes
White-white	62.1
Black-black	26.9
Black-white	8.8
White-black	2.2
	823,340 robberies
White-white	36.6
Black-black	25.8
Black-white	37.0
White-black	0.6

NOTE: Victims of assailants of other races have been omitted, as have offenses where the assailant's race was not known or recorded.
SOURCES: Federal Bureau of Investigation and Bureau of Justice Statistics (1985-86).

Moving to Table 7.3, we learn that blacks are incarcerated at a much higher rate than whites, with some variation in rates between states. Newsreels of prison riots keep us up-to-date on this kind of demographic data.

TABLE 7.3
Prison Populations

	Rates of Prisoners in the 18-39 Age Group White	Black	Ratio of Blacks to Whites	Racial Income Ratio	Violent Crime Rate
Nebraska	38	584	15.4	662	26.3
Pennsylvania	32	429	13.4	625	35.9
Michigan	41	391	9.5	725	80.4
Maryland	61	528	8.7	704	83.3
Delaware	101	770	7.6	571	42.7
Oklahoma	104	569	5.5	641	43.6
North Carolina	82	366	4.5	633	47.6
Mississippi	59	292	4.9	495	27.4

NOTE: Rates for black and white inmates are per 10,000 men of each race in the 18-39 age group in each state. Income ratios express black earnings for each $1,000 made by whites. State rates for violent crimes include reported rapes, robberies, murders, and aggravated assaults per 10,000 population.
SOURCES: Bureau of Justice Statistics, Bureau of the Census, and Federal Bureau of Investigation.

Table 7.4 is a non sequitur and represents a profound racist injection, intentions to the contrary. Blacks do worse on tests, when income is held constant. Since no evidence about black criminality is provided for those whose income range is between $30,000 and $40,000, what constitutes the relationship among test scores, crime, and middle-income blacks? None is suggested. If we found lower test scores among higher-income blacks compared to whites and, at the same time, found lower crime rates among higher-income blacks relative to whites, what would such a finding mean about inquiries focused on crime? Questions of this nature are not raised. Hacker quotes Arthur Jensen and Thomas Jefferson on their shared belief that African Americans are intellectually inferior and makes reference to the complexity of the issues, but this is inadequate. Given the history of scientific IQism and its misuses, Table 7.4 is simply incomplete information that enables whites to confirm what is assumed to be known as hard fact.

TABLE 7.4
Average SAT Scores (Combined Math and Verbal)
for Students from Families with Incomes in the $30,000-$40,000 Range

Racial Group	Average SAT Scores
Asians	947
Whites	928
Puerto Ricans	844
Mexican-Americans	833
Blacks	742

SOURCES: The College Board (1986).

Finally, Table 7.5 reproduces a standard array of numbers that feed the racist mind-set. It is a common strategy: other nonwhite or ethnic groups "make it"; why not blacks? Why are blacks still so close to the bottom of the income heap? This table asks the same question as the offspring of white working-class ethnics: if my parents or grandparents made it in the old-fashioned way, although poor and discriminated against, why can't blacks make it without special compensation? Is there not something deeply wrong with blacks? In a postindustrial society in which people are assumed to rise as a result of merit, test scores are used to explain why blacks achieve less upward mobility. Since the poor intellectual performance of blacks has long been associated with endowment—with biology or unremitting cultural habits—race preempts class in the final analysis of why blacks are overrepresented in the criminal class. "Hard" data suggest that the "facts" of crime must be caused by the absence of "mental" traits or enduring intergenerational "cultural" transmissions; this, moreover, cannot be changed, even under favorable environmental conditions.

TABLE 7.5
Income Levels of Different Ethnic Groups

	Family Income (in 1987 Dollars)	Foreign Born (in %)
Japanese	43,493	28.4
Asian Indian	39,739	70.4
Filipino	37,662	64.6
Chinese	35,869	63.3
White	33,412	3.9
Korean	32,530	81.9
Hawaiian	30,522	1.6
Cuban	29,010	77.9
Mexican	23,476	26.0
Eskimo	21,988	1.5
American Indian	21,748	2.5
Vietnamese	20,415	90.5
Black	20,077	2.8
Puerto Rican	17,067	3.0

SOURCE: Bureau of the Census (1980 census).

My point is that these are old beliefs dressed in new garb. There are other ways of presenting crime data that enhance our perspectives rather than feed our preexisting racial inclinations.[79]

Getting Tough

The avalanche of concern about black criminality and related issues naturally leads to the question of what must be done. One answer that is emerging from the white backlash perspective is the need to force blacks to "show their mettle" by withdrawing the whole support system that has been constructed over the decades; the imperative now is to come down with severe punishment to straighten out "would-be criminals."[80]

Having tried "everything" and failed, there is the turn to reliance on force. Only a few are willing to make explicit what many more secretly fantasize and wish. We need to undertake the wholesale removal of a large stratum of our black youth from the streets in our major cities. We need to lock them up for a long time, since we are dealing with "black terrorists," and they can be dealt with only in terms they understand.[81]

This urge not only lurks in the minds of whites who now believe or imagine their whole way of life is threatened; it is also held by some elite black intellectuals. Harry Edwards, a former member of the Black Panther party and now a professor of sociology at the University of California and a national sports consultant, gave an account of his views on how to handle young drug peddlers to a San Francisco magazine. His advice, of course, need not apply solely to black youth, as any "imaginative" white might discern. It could easily spill over to include marginal blacks, homeless blacks, and all blacks who look like they might spoil the aesthetic quality of white communities. When asked how to "turn around a 13-year-old [black] kid selling crack in the street," Edwards replied:

> The reality is, you can't. You gotta realize that they're not gonna make it. The cities, the culture and Black people in particular have to begin to move to get that garbage off the street....We have to take a very hard line against them, if we're to preserve our next generation and future generations. Even if they are our children, [we have got to] turn him in, lock him up. Get rid of him. Lock him up for a long time. As long as the law will allow and try to make it as long as possible. I'm for lock 'em up, gettin' 'em off the street, put 'em all behind bars.[82]

The reasons that induce a prestigious black professional to spout off as if he were a redneck southerner with a long tradition of looking at blacks as animals are different from the fears that drive well-intentioned whites, when threatened by integration, to say, "I think people in my community are not concerned about it from a racial point of view, but from an economic one."[83] The difference lies in the way the race-class nexus impinges on individual perceptions. Glenn C. Loury, a conservative black scholar at Harvard University, expressed his concern about the behavior patterns of the black underclass in the following way:

> The criminal behavior of a relatively small number of...black men in big central cities is...a critical factor undermining the quality of life of [all blacks] living in those cities, and also a contributing factor to race relations.[84]

Brent Staples, a black *New York Times* reporter, put the race-class entanglement more incisively:

As a softy who is scarcely able to take a knife to a raw chicken—let alone hold one to a person's throat—I was surprised, embarrassed, and dismayed all at once. Her flight [reference is to a white woman] made me feel like an accomplice in tyranny. It also made it clear that I was indistinguishable from the muggers who occasionally seeped into the area from the surrounding ghetto.[85]

For the white middle class, writes a sensitive suburban resident, to accept blacks into their ranks, they must be safe from street crime. Otherwise, the middle class will continue to identify all blacks with criminal behavior. This is not a just situation. This is not a fair situation; it may be morally despicable, but that is the way it is.[86]

Middle-class blacks suffer from lower-class black life and circumstances. They suffer because whites find it unreasonable in a quasi-segregated society, where resources and social amenities are distributed unequally, to make distinctions along class lines when it applies to African Americans. Thus, even sensitive members of the white middle class are induced to behave along racially guided lines by moving to the suburbs. In the course of this flight, they reflect on the moral injustice of treating middle-class blacks in terms of some kind of mistaken identity, a spillover, so to speak, from the overrepresentation of blacks in the lower class. Finally, our white suburbanite is resigned to the "morally despicable" reality because "that is the way it is."

This white voice represents a profound sensitivity and is genuinely troubled. The actions of such suburbanites are intended to protect their personal well-being; yet the same such voices often become advocates of higher taxes and more state expenditures to help blacks, poor and middle class alike. One's personal, moral, and political interests are not necessarily congruent. There are paradoxical tensions here that need exploration. My main point at present is simply to emphasize that even white racial egalitarians are induced to behave contrary to their convictions. That, as I have argued, is the essence of institutional racism. Most whites, in my judgment, are less morally troubled. While they believe in fairness, they may in fact be morally self-righteous about the present state of the black underclass. They may even believe that the welfare system has been too benign toward the black poor who are not viewed as deserving.[87] For this reason, among others, they are questioning the welfare state itself.

Indicting the Welfare Society

To a growing number of white minds, as well as to some conservative black scholars, the black underclass represents, as I have indicated, a communicable disease that needs to be extirpated, even if it means condoning violence and bypassing the law. Related to this urge to stamp out this disease in our midst is the disillusionment with liberal policies that are currently seen as part of the problem. The evolution of this policy-focused reasoning is described in the following directions:

[Despite] 20 years of civil rights gain and 13 years of anti-poverty programs [involving] tens of billions of dollars...spent every year by the Federal Government, states and cities; [despite] special hiring drives, private job-training programs, university and affirmative-action programs...aimed at aiding [and motivating the black poor], the underclass is still with us and the black poor are hardly better off, and in some cases [are] worse off, than before the War on Poverty.[88]

Thus, so goes the reasoning, not only have liberal policies failed at considerable cost to the taxpayer, but they have abetted the growth of the underclass. Conservatives argue that changes in the "criminal justice system have decreased the sanctions against aberrant behavior and thereby contributed to the rise of serious inner-city crime since 1965."[89] Conservatives point to soft-headed welfare liberal leaders who have added to the incorrigible behavior of the black underclass by pressuring the public to maintain assistance rather than making blacks look for work. Even affirmative action efforts are held responsible for the continued growth of the black underclass, since such efforts allegedly increase the demand for talented blacks and decrease it for less qualified ones.[90]

These critiques converge on the welfare system itself. The claim, initially, was that particular welfare policies undermine self-reliance, promote joblessness, and encourage out-of-wedlock births and female-headed families.[91] Ultimately, however, the whole welfare society falls under suspicion. It leads to "organized altruism" that permits "the State to supplant the family, inadvertently making parents believe they were not responsible—perhaps incapable—of caring for their progress."[92] Thus, in the revisionist history of welfare liberalism, it was the excessive "goodness" of the welfare state that created a growing, unmanageable black underclass. With a very small step, revisionist history can comfortably use images of the black underclass to delegitimize a system that had its origins in another era and that currently has relevance far beyond the particulars of the black images being manipulated to challenge it.

Conclusion

I have shown in this essay how images of the black underclass, representing less than 1 percent of the population and residing primarily in our major central cities, have been magnified to affect not only the status of middle- and working-class blacks but the legitimacy of the liberal welfare society itself. It is unreasonable to expect professional middle-class blacks, as well as working-class families, to accept with equanimity their "inclusion" in the spillover from the core of black underclass neighborhoods. It is this spillover, as well as the underclass itself, that needs to be understood.

African American reactions to the shadows cast by the underclass core are varied: self-denigrating public confessions, programs to fight racism and poverty in poor black neighborhoods, endeavors to establish more social justice for all minorities, and the advocacy of force to eliminate the "disease" in our central cities. While I have suggested that the black underclass problem is an exaggerated social construction that is manipulated for purposes unrelated to the elimination of the conditions that cause the black underclass malaise, I would not wish to suggest that our inner cities do not face difficulties that relate to the existence of an underclass. As Herbert Gans has rightly noted,

An America with a [black] jobless caste would be socially dangerous, for crime addiction, mental illness, as well as various forms of covert and overt protest, some of it violent, would be sure to increase sharply. In the long run,... solution[s] would also be politically dangerous, because...people assigned to an underclass would remain an integral part of the larger society.[93]

Thus, description of any major central city generates a self-evident danger. Take one, for example, where there is

25 percent unemployment. One-third of the residents have moved out. There are many young men [and women] with no jobs collecting welfare checks and on the streets or playing [around] with friends most of the day. There are many young women watching television all day. There are numerous unemployed adult children living with an unemployed parent. Many of these city residents have a problem with alcohol and drugs. Older men who once did heavy labor have been laid off; most have been out of work for years. Many young unmarried women, especially teenagers, in the public housing complexes are pregnant or have already had illegitimate children. Most of the young do not expect to work in the future. They seem resigned, angry, or fatalistic about their lives. They feel no one...cares about them.[94]

Are these problems related to race? I believe that most U.S. whites and blacks would answer yes—even if qualifications about external circumstances like international competition, changes in technology, the occupational mix, the arrival of new immigrants, and other such factors were added to the analysis. But the problems presented in the inner-city description just presented are those of Liverpool, England. The people are white workers and their families.

If this can happen to white workers whose injuries, limited preparedness, and expectations are class determined, why must so much attention be devoted to the behavior of black ghetto dwellers, to their alleged character traits, to their lack of "intelligence," to their drug and crime-ridden patterns, as if such qualities were in the blood or bones of the person or group? If the white skilled workers of Liverpool and their families can be reduced to behavior not unlike that of blacks trapped in American cities in a period of a decade or so, why do we need racially focused descriptions and testimonies? The answer, in my judgment, is that every society needs some categories to shield itself from its deepest shortcomings; it perhaps avoids addressing some intractable contradictions within the society. We employ the racial lens, unique to our history, to explain the special case, to explain why the equality of opportunities (embracing equality in environmental circumstances) available to blacks in principle is not so in fact. We do not escape from racial categories even when they are unnecessary in our analysis. We deny class because we proudly believe that our history demonstrates fluidity in this sphere; therefore, we do not wish to claim that a large group in our society suffers from grossly unequal class or environmental barriers. Thus, both white and black Americans, each for different reasons, use race when they could well use class. We have done this for so long that race has become reified and intermingled with class in a complex but nevertheless coherent way.

NOTES

This chapter originally appeared in Raymond S. Franklin, *Shadows of Race and Class* (Minneapolis: University of Minnesota Press, 1991), 89-116.

1. For a discussion of the origin and uses of the term *underclass,* see Herbert J. Gans, "Deconstructing the Underclass: The Term's Dangers as a Planning Concept," *APA Journal* (Summer 1990): 271-77.

2. William Julius Wilson, who revised the term in his book *The Truly Disadvantaged* in order to break the silence about the poorest of the black poor, is having second thoughts. In a presidential address at the American Sociological Association meetings in August 1990, he suggested that the term has such pejorative connotations that it may not serve to arouse public compassion. On the contrary, it may conjure "an image of people unwilling to help themselves." Jason DeParle, "Underclass Reconsidered: What to Call the Poorest Poor," *New York Times,* 26 August 1990, E4.

3. See Frank Bonilla, "Idle Classes, Underclasses," presented at the Department of Urban Studies and Planning, MIT, April 8, 1988; Ken Auletta, *The Underclass* (New York: Random House, 1982), 20-30.

4. William Julius Wilson, "The Crisis of the Ghetto Underclass and the Liberal Retreat," *Democratic Left* (May-August 1987): 5; Katherine McFate, "Defining the Underclass," *Focus* 15 (June 1987): 8.

5. Nicholas Lemann, "The Origins of the Underclass," parts 1 and 2, *Atlantic* (June 1986): 31-55, and (July 1986): 54-68.

6. Douglas G. Glasgow, *The Black Underclass: Poverty, Unemployment, and Entrapment of Ghetto Youth,* 2nd ed. (New York: Vintage, 1981), 87-104 and chap. 6.

7. Auletta, *The Underclass,* 31-43.

8. Loie J. D. Wacquant and William Julius Wilson, "The Cost of Racial and Class Exclusion in the Inner City," special issue on "The Ghetto Underclass: Social Science Perspectives," *Annals of the American Academy of Political and Social Science* (January 1989); Norman Fainstein, "The Underclass/Mismatch Hypothesis as an Explanation for Black Economic Deprivation," *Politics and Society* 15, no. 4 (1986/1987): 403-52.

9. Auletta, *The Underclass,* xvi.

10. Christopher Jencks, "What Is the Underclass—and Is It Growing?" *Focus* 12, no. 1 (Spring-Summer 1989): 15.

11. Ibid., 19-25. More recently, Jencks has not only demonstrated the decline of the underclass but has even gone so far as to question its very existence. "There Is No Underclass," *Wall Street Journal,* 17 April 1991, 14A.

12. Martha A. Gephart and Robert W. Pearson, "Contemporary Research on the Urban Underclass," *Items,* Social Science Research Council Bulletin 4, nos. 1-2 (June 1988): 2-3.

13. Erol Rickets and Isabel Sawhill, "Defining and Measuring the Underclass," *Journal of Policy Analysis and Management* (Winter 1988): 316-25; Gephart and Pearson, "Urban Underclass," 1-9.

14. In a review of the explanations of the underclass summarized in a publication of the Social Science Research Council, only one of the eleven basic explanations referred to was race: "Continued racial discrimination in jobs and housing." The others were in the direction of impersonal forces: international competition, changes in the nature of jobs, industry location, production methods, composition of commodities, development of the illicit economy, increases in immigration, public policies, culture, and the misfit between "minority" skills and industry skills among inner-city youth. Robert W. Pearson, "Economy, Culture, Public Policy, and the Urban Underclass," *Items* 43, no. 2 (June 1989): 24.

15. Paul Blumberg, *Inequality in an Age of Decline* (New York: Oxford University Press, 1980), 76-83; Jonathan Rieder, *Canarsie: The Jews and Italians of Brooklyn against Liberalism* (Cambridge, Mass.: Harvard University Press, 1985).

16. Lawrence Michelle, *State of Working America* (Armonk, N.Y.: M. E. Sharpe, 1991).

17. "The Squeeze on the Middle Class," *Business Week,* 10 March 1975, 52-60.

18. Wacquant and Wilson, "The Cost of Racial and Class Exclusion," 9.

19. See Kevin Phillips, *The Politics of Rich and Poor* (New York: Random House, 1990).

20. John F. Kain, "Housing Segregation, Negro Employment, and Metropolitan Decentralization," *Quarterly Journal of Economics* 82, no. 2 (February 1968): 176-77.

21. Paul Wilkes, "As the Blacks Move In, the Ethnics Move Out," *New York Times Magazine*, 24 January 1971, 10.

22. Ibid., 10.

23. Ibid., 11.

24. Ibid.

25. Ibid., 57.

26. Robert Staples, "Black Male Genocide: A Final Solution to the Race Problem in America," *Black Scholar* 18, no. 3 (May-June 1987): 3.

27. Andrew Hacker, "Black Crime, White Racism," *New York Review of Books*, 3 March 1988, 36.

28. See Jay MacLeod, *Ain't No Makin' It* (Boulder, Colo.: Westview Press, 1987). It is the slightly hopeful segment of the black poor, struggling against odds, that is the focus of MacLeod's case study.

29. Arthur Kemplon, "Native Sons," *New York Review of Books*, 11 April 1991, 57, quoting Jewelle T. Gibbs, *Young, Black, and Male in America: An Endangered Species* (New York: Auburn House, 1988).

30. Anders Stephanson, "Interview with Cornel West," in *Universal Abandon? The Politics of Postmodernism*, ed. Andrew Ross (Minneapolis: University of Minnesota Press, 1988), 276.

31. Quotes in A. Schucter, *White Power/Black Freedom* (Boston: Beacon Press, 1968), 100.

32. Winthrop D. Jordan, *The White Man's Burden: Historical Origins of Racism in the United States* (New York: Oxford University Press, 1974), 196-97.

33. George M. Fredrickson, *The Black Image in the White Mind* (New York: Harper and Row, 1971), chap. 9.

34. Ibid., 260.

35. Ibid., 274, 276.

36. Sydney H. Schanberg, "Covering the Wrong Wounds," *New York Times*, 10 November 1981, A23.

37. Hofstra University, UAW District 65 Program.

38. Gans, "Deconstructing the Underclass," 274.

39. Arne Duncan, "The Values, Aspirations, and Opportunities of the Urban Underclass" (B.A. honor thesis, Harvard University, 1987), cited in Wacquant and Wilson, "The Cost of Racial and Class Exclusion," 14.

40. C. Krans, "Forty-Two Catholic Churches without a Prayer," *New York Times*, 14 August 1988, A35.

41. "The American Underclass," *Time*, 29 August 1977, 18.

42. Robert Staples, "Bound Manhood in the 1970s: A Critical Look Back," *Black Scholar* 12, no. 3 (May-June 1983): 4.

43. An undated newsletter appealing for funds circulated by PUSH for Excellence, Inc., and addressed, "Dear Fellow Americans." Received by the author in 1980.

44. Quoted in "In Slums, Fields and a Hall of Graduates, Jackson Strives to Turn on Hospitality," *New York Times*, 7 May 1984, B8.

45. "Jackson Advises Class in Brooklyn," *New York Times*, 15 June 1986, 28. This wave of critical self-examination with the intention of generating self-help values is taking place across the political spectrum; see, for example, Glenn C. Loury, "The Moral Quandary of the Black Community," *Public Interest* 79 (Spring 1985): 9-22.

46. CBS, *Six O'clock News*, 14 June 1986.

47. Sar Rimer, "Yonkers Anguish: Family in Two Worlds," *New York Times*, 22 November 1987, B7.

48. Auletta, *The Underclass*, 3.

49. Rimer, "Yonkers Anguish," 7.

50. Quoted in Auletta, *The Underclass*, 40. A major criticism of Assistant Secretary of Labor Daniel Patrick Moynihan's 1965 White House report on the Negro family is that "it did not take into account the emergence, partly as an adaptive response to slavery, of the black extended family—aunts, uncles, grandparents, and friends who never show up in statistics but nevertheless often provide role models and parental guidance." Census Bureau estimates suggest that about 11 percent of black children are members of extended families. Ibid., 41.

51. Ibid., 46.

52. Quoted in ibid., 97.

53. Ibid., 108.

54. Ibid., 96.

55. Ibid., 90.

56. Ibid.

57. Ibid., 97.

58. Christina Milner and Richard Milner, *Black Players* (Boston: Little, Brown, 1972) quoted in Charles E. Silberman, *Criminal Violence, Criminal Justice* (New York: Random House, 1978), 149.

59. Troy Duster, "Social Implications of the 'New' Black Urban Underclass," *Black Scholar* 19, no. 3 (May-June 1988): 5.

60. Christopher Muldor, "Do Black Crime Victims Matter?" *Wall Street Journal*, May 9, 1988, 22.

61. Auletta, *The Underclass*, 109.

62. My paraphrase from Elliot Liebow, *Tally's Corner* (Boston: Little, Brown, 1967) cited in Auletta, *The Underclass*, 47.

63. Sylvester Monroe, "Brothers," *Newsweek*, 23 March 1987, 76.

64. Andrew Hacker, "The Lower Depths," *New York Review of Books*, 12 August 1982, 16.

65. Jacquelyne J. Jackson, "Aging Black Women and Public Policies," *Black Scholar* (May-June 1988): 33.

66. Lemann, "Origins of the Underclass," part 2 (July 1986): 67.

67. Hacker, "The Lower Depths," 16.

68. Lemann, "Origins of the Underclass," part 2 (July 1986): 67.

69. Auletta, *The Underclass*, 52-53.

70. Hacker, "The Lower Depths," 16.

71. Monroe, "Brothers," 76.

72. Piven and Cloward, cited by Auletta, *The Underclass*, 43.

73. Ibid., 73.

74. See Charles Murray, "New Welfare Bill, New Welfare Cheats," *Wall Street Journal*, 29 August 1988, A22.

75. See Thomas Byrne Edsall, *The New Politics of Inequality* (New York: Norton, 1984); William Schneider, "An Insider's View of the Election," *Atlantic* 262, no. 1 (July 1988): 29-57.

76. Michael Harrington, *The New American Poverty* (New York and London: Penguin, 1984), 29-30, 42.

77. Auletta, *The Underclass*, 274.

78. Andrew Hacker, "Black Crime, White Racism," *New York Review of Books*, 3 March 1988, 36-41.

79. See Jencks, "What Is the Underclass?"

80. Hacker, "The Lower Depths," 19. It should be pointed out that this is not Hacker's view; he is underscoring the "solution" provided by the conservative trend.

81. Mike Davis, "Los Angeles: Civil Liberties between the Hammer and the Rock," *New Left Review* (July-August 1988): 47.

82. Quoted in ibid., 46. Interview with Harry Edwards was by Ken Kelly and appeared in the San Francisco *Focus* (March 1984): 100.

83. Rimer, "Yonkers Anguish," 7.

84. "Harvard Teacher Faces Drug Charges in Boston," *New York Times*, 3 December 1987, A20.

85. Brent Staples, "Black Men and Public Spaces," *Harper's*, December 1986, 19-20.

86. Martin Laskin, "The Black Underclass: The Critical Factor in Achieving the Goal of Racial Integration and Equality" (unpublished paper, Graduate Center of City University of New York, Spring 1988): 30. Mr. Laskin is a New Jersey resident and public school teacher.

87. See Michael Katz, *The Undeserving Poor: From the War on Poverty to the War on Welfare* (New York: Pantheon, 1989).

88. "The American Underclass," *Time*, 29 August 1977, 15.

89. Wilson, "The Ghetto Underclass," 7.

90. Ibid.

91. Ibid.

92. Auletta, *The Underclass*, 41; and Alan Wolfe, *Whose Keeper? Social Science and Moral Obligation* (Berkeley and Los Angeles: University of California Press, 1989).

93. Herbert Gans, "Deconstructing the Underclass," 277.

94. Leslie Inniss and Joe R. Feagin, "The Black 'Underclass' Ideology in Race Relations Analysis," *Social Justice* 16, no. 4 (Winter 1989): 13.

DISCUSSION QUESTIONS

1. How does the author define and use the term *underclass*? How is this similar to or different from other contributors in this text?

2. How does the author critique the use of the term *underclass* in the media and in academe?

3. How would you describe social and economic relationships between the white middle class and the black community?

4. How are the interests of the black middle class linked to those of the black poor and working-class sectors?

5. How does the state reflect the utilization of arbitrary power in relation to the problem of poverty? How are media images of race utilized to justify such force?

FOR FURTHER READING

Auletta, Ken, *The Underclass* (New York: Random House, 1982).

Blumberg, Paul, *Inequality in an Age of Decline* (New York: Oxford University Press, 1980).

Duster, Troy, "Social Implications of the 'New' Black Urban Underclass," *Black Scholar* 19, no. 3 (May-June 1988): 5.

Edsall, Thomas Byrne, *The New Politics of Inequality* (New York: Norton, 1984).

Glasgow, Douglas G., *The Black Underclass: Poverty, Unemployment, and Entrapment of Ghetto Youth*, 2nd ed. (New York: Vintage, 1981).

Inniss, Leslie, and Joe R. Feagin, "The Black 'Underclass' Ideology in Race Relations Analysis," *Social Justice* 16, no. 4 (Winter 1989): 13.

Jordan, Winthrop D., *The White Man's Burden: Historical Origins of Racism in the United States* (New York: Oxford University Press, 1974).

Katz, Michael, *The Undeserving Poor: From the War on Poverty to the War on Welfare* (New York: Pantheon, 1989).

Lemann, Nicholas, "The Origins of the Underclass," *Atlantic* (June 1986): 31-55, and (July 1986): 54-68.

Loury, Glenn C., "The Moral Quandary of the Black Community," *Public Interest* 79 (Spring 1985): 9-22.

Michelle, Lawrence, *State of Working America* (Armonk, N.Y.: M. E. Sharpe, 1991).

Staples, Robert, "Black Male Genocide: A Final Solution to the Race Problem in America," *Black Scholar* 18, no. 3 (May-June 1987): 3.

Chapter Eight

Responding to Urban Crisis
Functions of White Racism

Louis Kushnick

The attack on welfare rights and welfare recipients, which has been so central to politics in the United States during the 1980s and 1990s, has served the interests of corporate capital and its political and media allies. The success of the attack depends on the racialization of welfare—and thus on the delegitimization of government programs designed to benefit the poor. This strategy has been so successful because it is based on the historical centrality of white racism in shaping—and distorting—class consciousness among white working-class people. Thus, at precisely the time that corporate capital and its allies began repealing the postwar Keynesian accommodation and increasing income and wealth inequalities, they were able to obtain electoral validation by attacking *big government* as a code word for welfare. This essay analyzes the development of the fundamental structure of the racialized political economy and the use of the attitudes and identities constructed by these processes in the campaign to "end welfare as we knew it."

Origins of White Racism in the United States

Plantation economies based on slavery in the New World provided for the development of manufacturing in the center of the world system. The triangular trade was a stimulus for British manufacturers and for economic development in the British settler colonies in North America. It provided both the raw materials for industry and the capital for investment in new plant and equipment in the South and in New England. It was thus crucial politically and economically[1] for the United States as a whole, not merely for the southern slave states.[2] The development of a racialized system of chattel slavery within Britain's North American colonies was a crucial development in the construction of a hegemonic racist ideology. Britain initially used both indentured white labor and black labor, either indentured or semienslaved. The need for a system that would meet both the demands for a controllable labor system and the continuing political domination of the large landowners was made apparent by Bacon's Rebellion in Virginia in the mid-seventeenth century. Bacon's Rebellion fundamentally threatened the status quo because it was a joint action by both blacks and whites. A way had to be found to maintain stability and order, to increase the supply of cheap, controllable plantation labor, and to avoid adding to the future numbers of yeoman farmers who would contest for political power with the planter elite. The solution involved the enslavement of black labor and the nonenslavement of white labor. This strategy was bolstered by a series of concessions to white labor, which worked to divide the two groups further.

Clearly, if no white could be a slave, and if all slaves were black, the objective conditions for racial separation were well established. This constructed a racial identity for both whites and blacks—an identity of racial superiority for the former, who could never be slaves, and of racial inferiority for the latter, who were racially suited for slavery. In addition, laws were passed that furthered the ideology of white supremacy. For example, it was against the law for a slave to raise her or his hand not only to a master but to any Christian white. Thus, we see the crucial role of state racism in constructing and underpinning popular racism by providing material and psychic rewards for accepting a white identity, that is, a racialized identity in opposition to a more inclusive identity.

The political structure created by the Constitutional Convention of 1787 reflected that importance. Slavery was incorporated into the basic structure of the new political system in a number of ways: the slave trade was protected until 1807, each slave was counted as three-fifths of a human being for purposes of both taxation and representation, and a fugitive slave provision was incorporated. The ideology of racism was incredibly effective, even given the costs to the vast majority of the southern population. So important was this separation of whites from blacks that George Fitzhugh, the slaveholding sociologist, could declare:

> The poor [whites] constitute our militia and our police. They protect men in the possession of property, as in other countries; and they do much more, they secure men in the possession of a kind of property which they could not hold a day but for the supervision and protection of the poor.[3]

Thus, in the United States white supremacy was constructed and reinforced by race-based chattel slavery and a racialized definition of us as opposed to them, which was an integral part of racist ideology.[4] This white supremacy was found not only in the slave South but throughout the society. W. E. B. Du Bois argued that even when white workers "received a low wage [they were] compensated in part by a...public and psychological wage."[5] It is the argument of this essay that this compensation has played a central role in the creation of a white identity, even among workers, farmers, and the poor throughout American history. That identity has retarded the development of an inclusive class identity and has therefore facilitated the reproduction of class inequality in the United States. David Roediger, who has written perceptively on the construction of whiteness has argued that

> whiteness was a way in which white workers responded to a fear of dependency on wage labor and to the necessities of capitalist work discipline. As the U.S. working class matured, principally in the North, within a slaveholding republic, the heritage of the Revolution made independence a powerful masculine personal ideal. But slave labor and "hireling" wage labor proliferated in the new nation. One way to make peace with the latter was to differentiate it sharply from the former.

The effective way this was done was through

the rallying cry of "free labor.".....At the same time, the white working class, disciplined and made anxious by fear of dependency, began during its formation to construct an image of the black population as "other"—as embodying the preindustrial, erotic, careless style of life the white worker hated and longed for.[6]

This differentiation was underscored by the Naturalization Act of 1790, which established the requirements for citizenship, one of which was being white. It was not merely that one had to be white to be an American; obviously, to be white was to be superior. The construction of a white identity provided the basis for incorporation of European immigrants into the society. Thus, the Irish driven out of their own country by the consequences of Anglo-Saxon imperialism arrived in another country largely controlled by Anglo-Saxon elites but were able to avoid permanent suppression and inferiority by virtue of being able to become white rather than remaining Irish and Celtic. Angry Irish miners in Pennsylvania denounced Daniel O'Connell, the Irish Republican leader, for his call for Irish-American opposition to slavery. Despite their own exploitation and the attacks on them from nativist forces, the Irish declared that they would never accept blacks as "brethren," for it was only as whites that they could gain acceptance and opportunity in the United States.

Furthermore, acceptance and opportunity are of crucial importance in the construction of whiteness. Although the Irish suffered discrimination at the hands of the white, Anglo-Saxon Protestant (WASP) elites, they had the basis of gaining acceptance in U.S. society as whites rather than as Catholic Celts.[7] The terms are also conceptually important in challenging the "ethnoracial umbrella" thesis advanced by scholars such as Nathan Glazer,[8] who argue that *ethnicity* was "an umbrella term subsuming all racial, religious and nationality groupings" to form a part of a single family of social identities.[9] E. J. Cornacchia and D. C. Nelson test the validity of this ethnoracial umbrella thesis against the black exceptionalism thesis and conclude that it is the latter that has greater validity: "The findings on the black political experience demonstrate that it would be inappropriate to treat racial minorities as merely ethnic groups competing in the interest group arena for entitlements and preferments. The political system was nearly sealed shut to blacks."[10]

The extension of democracy in the United States, particularly during the Jacksonian era, allowed for the formal incorporation of white men into the Republic as citizens. The outcome was the creation of a "Herrenvolk democracy," or, in Roediger's terms, "Herrenvolk Republicanism." This incorporation of whites regardless of class played a crucial role in ensuring the triumph of racism throughout the United States, in the free states and in the slave states. Before the Civil War, poor whites and the nonslaveholding yeomanry in the South, free soil farmers in the West, and artisans and the emerging working-class immigrant and native in the North were all made citizens in the great white Republic and given an identity that was oppositional to people of color, slave or free. Not only were whites given a psychological wage; state racism provided fundamental objective racialized rewards:

They [whites] were given public deference...because they were white. They were admitted freely, with all classes of white people, to public functions [and] public parks....The police were drawn from their ranks and the courts, dependent on their votes, treated them with leniency....Their votes selected public officials and while this had small effect upon their economic situation, it had great effect upon their personal treatment....White schoolhouses were the best in the community, and conspicuously placed, and cost anywhere from twice to ten times colored schools.[11]

To be white was to be a citizen of the Great Republic. To be white was to be a voter—unheard of for most of the immigrants. The immigrants could become American by successfully asserting their whiteness. Their whiteness and their Americanness were validated when they marched in triumphal parades to vote and then to picnics. Not only were the black slaves excluded from these public events, but, in most states of the antebellum United States, so were free blacks. Free blacks could not protect their employment, political, or civil rights, nor could they protect the rights of their children to a decent education and to a secure and profitable future in the American Dream. Nor could they take part in the great frontier experience, for in most territories on the frontier, free soil meant free soil for free white men. Not surprisingly, wave after wave of European immigrants opted for whiteness, and free blacks were impoverished, undereducated and disproportionately imprisoned.

Because "Herrenvolk" democracy was not and could not be a reality in terms of democracy, despite its state-constructed and -supported "Herrenvolk" character, there remained a class tension within American society. This class tension became central at various points and remained more marginal at others in societal terms; it was more central to the identity of some working people than of others. The point is that it was part of an ongoing set of struggles and that the racially defined identity as whites was not always hegemonic. As Herbert Aptheker, one of the leading antiracist scholars in the United States since the 1930s, has argued, the rank and file of the antislavery and abolitionist movements among whites were made up largely of poor people:

> The hundreds of thousands of people who signed anti-slavery petitions were common people, the poor and the working class. The subscribers to the abolitionist newspapers had to struggle to assemble their pennies....It was also common white people who took risks during this period. Those who saved Garrison from lynching were plain and ordinary people.[12]

There were white people who acted on the basis of values that were in opposition to those based on an identity as whites. The triumph of the white identity, therefore, was not an inevitable consequence of natural or genetic forces but the outcome of unequal struggles. In text we find that opposition to racism could and did go hand in hand in antislavery movements in Britain and the United States with attitudes and politics that opposed slavery without rejecting racism. Thus, the outcomes of the struggle against slavery, including the Civil War in the United States, did not lead to systems of racial justice or of class equality. For example, the ending of slavery in the British West Indies followed the rise of alternative centers of political and economic power. Fears of successful slave uprisings such as Haiti's, the increasing cost of suppressing such uprisings, and diminishing levels of profit overshadowed the moral crusade that had been waged against the evils of the slave trade and of slavery.

In the United States the Civil War was fought by the leaders of the Union less to free the slaves than to extend the sway of the emergent industrial capitalists and to serve the interests of their free-soil allies. Emancipation in neither the Caribbean nor the United States required the overthrow of racialist attitudes or of racist structures, despite the commitment of antiracist whites and free people of color and slaves struggling for freedom. Slavery died so that capitalism could continue to flourish, and, with it, racism.

Slavery Gives Way to Jim Crow

Prejudices, disunion, and distrust were all characteristics of the response of the major part of the working class to the triumph of capitalism. This response involved the acceptance of hierarchy itself and the situating of oneself and one's group into hierarchies based on skill, job status, ethnicity, gender, and race. One owed and was owed respect in relation to one's position along these scales. These divisions were reinforced by the distribution of material resources. State action directly and indirectly maintained this invidious social order and made possible the continued functioning of the system to control the production and distribution of the material resources. Politics based on an inclusive class consciousness had to confront and overcome these ideological and material reinforcements, including state repression, and it was not entirely surprising that such politics had an uphill battle and were successful less frequently than they failed. The development of class consciousness among the rapidly growing working class in the post-Civil War United States was fundamentally shaped and distorted by racism.[13] There was the presence of freed slaves and of other racially distinct colonized peoples within the metropole itself in large numbers. There was a massive immigration of European workers into the United States. Racism provided the ideological and material framework within which the millions of European immigrants who joined the labor force in the half century between 1865 and 1914 became American. Then they and the indigenous white working class were given a racialized identity (or a racialized working-class identity) as an alternative to a working-class identity, and this shaped their responses to being made wage-laborers.

The choice that presented itself throughout this period in U.S. history was between a politics based on an inclusive definition of "us" and one based on an exclusive racial definition. An inclusive definition and political strategy would have necessitated challenging the racialist ideology that had become a dominant characteristic of American identity in the antebellum period.[14] It would have required that workers recognize a common interest and a need to cooperate to achieve common objectives. Although this was not the path chosen by most of the white working class and its organizations, there is evidence that there was consideration of such an option and evidence of attempts to develop such a politics. The Address of the National Labor Congress to the Workingmen of the United States in 1867, for example, declared that "unpalatable as the truth may be to many," Negroes were now in a new position in the United States, and the actions of white working men could "determine whether the freedman becomes an element of strength or an element of weakness" in the labor movement. The solidarity option was not chosen. The exclusive racial definition of "us" was the dominant response. This divisive definition was based both on possession of craft skills and on racial prejudice. As Du Bois put it, [the National Labor Union] began to fight for capital and interest and the right of the upper class of labor to share in the exploitation of common labor. The Negro as a common laborer belonged, therefore, not in but beneath the white American labor movement. Craft and race unions spread. The better-paid skilled and intelligent American labor formed itself into closed guilds and, in combination with capitalist guild-masters, extorted fair wages which could be raised by negotiation.[15]

The craft- and race-based unionization operated to retard the development of mass unionism until the Great Depression. It culminated in the formation of the Congress of Industrial Organizations (CIO) industrial unions of the late 1930s. Exclusiveness ensured the availability of large pools of workers willing to, or having no choice but to, strikebreak and thus to weaken the effectiveness of the craft unions. These factors were reinforced by racial and ethnic divisions in the workplace and in housing, education, and social and political activities. This situation goes a long way toward explaining the present political weakness and the lack of class consciousness of the American working class.[16]

Matters were further complicated because white labor was encouraged to feel superior to nonwhites and thus to become "white." Central Pacific Superintendent Charles Crocker, for example, pointed out the benefits to white labor of Chinese immigration:

I believe that the effect of Chinese labor upon white labor has an elevating instead of degrading tendency. I think that every white man who is intelligent and able to work, who is more than a digger in a ditch...who has the capacity of being something else, can get to be something else by the presence of Chinese labor more than he could without it....There is proof of that in the fact that after we got Chinamen to work, we took the more intelligent of the white laborers and made foremen of them. I know of several of them now who never expected, never had a dream that they were going to be anything but shovellers of dirt, hewers of wood and drawers of water, and they are now respectable farmers, owning farms. They got a start by controlling Chinese labor on our railroad.[17]

Not only could white male workers be elevated by the use of Chinese labor and become "white" men; so could white women become "white" women. Takaki quotes an article by Abby Richardson in *Scribner's Monthly* titled "A Plea for Chinese Labor," in which she argued: "This is the age when much is expected of woman. She must be the ornament of society as well as the mistress of a well-ordered household." Thus, "Chinese labor could become a feature of both the factory and the home." Tensions of class conflict in white society could be resolved if Chinese migrant laborers became the "mudsills" of society, while white men became "capitalists" and their wives "ornaments of society."[18]

These privileges, or, more correctly for many white working-class men and women, these promises of privileges, were only part of the process through which racism remained a dominant characteristic of the American ideology. Repression of those who challenged that response of the working class to their designated position in society also existed. There is a long history in the United States of legal and extralegal repression, ranging from the terrorism directed against blacks and their white allies during reconstruction in the post-Civil War South to the suppression of the Molly McGuires (a militant nineteenth-century working-class organization), the Industrial Workers of the World (IWW, the major class-consciousness of the working class in the pre-World War I period, which was suppressed by the government during the war) to the judicial murders of Sacco and Vanzetti (anarchists convicted and executed for the murder of a payroll guard in what many still regard as a political trial), then the Rosenbergs (the only Americans ever to be executed in peacetime for supposedly supplying atomic secrets to the Soviets) in the twentieth century.

Clearly, the threat posed by class-conscious interracial cooperation was perceived by the ruling class and its agents in control of the state. Repression was accompanied by propaganda campaigns against populist efforts in the final two decades of the nineteenth century. There was a massive campaign that appealed to white supremacist attitudes. The specter of black equality was used to divert poor whites from any incipient class consciousness and toward a renewed racial consciousness. For example, the power of racial identity was tested in Lawrence County, Alabama, which represented Alabama's "strongest and most persistent opposition to the Democratic party" and in which "Free labor ideology and biracial class politics survived...because of the efforts of local black and white radical Republicans, who during congressional Reconstruction refused to be intimidated by Ku Klux Klan terror."[19] Horton identifies the campaign waged by the local Democratic newspaper, the *Advertiser*:

> Because the Democratic party was threatened by the possible emergence of a biracial brotherhood of working men...the Advertiser resorted to a campaign of racial hatred that resembled its earlier pronouncements in support of the Klan....To stir up racial discontent, the Advertiser on election day fell back on its tried and tested formula—race-baiting. The front page of the Advertiser was filled with reports of assaults by blacks on white women. "The Negroes...were getting very troublesome" in Mississippi. "Several Negro women of Tuscumbia" were reported to "have addressed a very insulting letter to several respectable white ladies." Jourd White [the editor] stated that they would "hug a barrel or look up a rope" as a just reward for the insult. The "white men of Lawrence County" were urged by White to "do" their "duty" to "protect the white race from this animalism."[20]

Horton concludes that "A strong tradition of free labor-oriented biracial politics coupled with worsening agricultural depression during the post-Reconstruction period could not overcome the dominance of racial politics even in a county where a legitimate space had been created for class politics."[21]

The southern state governments legitimated the process by establishing the Jim Crow system of de jure segregation, that is, of apartheid. The federal government accepted and legitimated the process through a number of Supreme Court decisions, culminating in the *Plessy v. Ferguson* (1896) decision, which established the "separate but equal" principle. This decision justified segregation in all aspects of life in the South. The federal government's acceptance of the disenfranchisement of the southern black population, of the lynch terror that took hundreds of black lives a year, and of the total denial of blacks' citizenship rights were crucial developments. So was northern capitalist support. This took the form of not recruiting southern black labor into the growing industrial proletariat and largely excluding the northern black population as well. Capitalist reinforcement of racial hatred also meant the recruitment of blacks solely as strikebreakers. This ensured the maintenance of the controlled labor force necessary for the southern share crop system that produced the cotton that was still so crucial to the economy of the United States. This also ensured the exclusion of black labor from the national industrial proletariat, just as it had been excluded from the previous fundamental determinant of American life, the frontier. Now, when blacks entered the labor force, they would be entering turf considered by whites as white.

In addition to the psychological privileges that poor whites obtained from the Jim Crow system (being told that they were superior to all African Americans regardless of their own class position), they received some material privileges. These privileges were unequally distributed within the white working class and were tenuously held. There was the ever-present threat of cheap substitute black labor if whites stepped out of line. The price that white labor paid in the South for its superior position included wages significantly lower than those in other regions, lower levels of public services than in other regions, and the contempt of their ruling-class "white allies" who looked on them in much the same way as they did the blacks. A politics characterized by the absence of issues and the absence of opportunities for poor whites to obtain benefits, even by the standards of the rest of the country, became normal. Poor whites, in effect, gave up their own suffrage through the denial of suffrage to African Americans as part of the price paid to become "white."

Faced with the political culture of racism, the white working class failed to create its own culture to challenge the class-based ethos or to defend and maintain the attempts to do so that were made during this period. Thus, the white working class was unable to meet the growing attacks on its interests that the rise of monopoly capital represented. The growing concentration of capital and centralization of control brought with it increased exploitation of the population through the suppression of wages and benefits. It made possible the process of "de-skilling" and the degradation of labor associated with "scientific management."[22] The skilled-unskilled hierarchy was reinforced in ethnic and racial terms, and the craft-based unions were unable to defeat the power of the monopoly capitalists and their political allies. Rather than reconsider its basic assumptions, the American Federation of Labor (AFL) became more and more exclusionist as it faced the competition of cheaper labor. This pattern was similar to that which characterized British trade unions in the same period. In 1898 an article in the AFL's official organ, the *American Federationist,* declared that blacks were unfit for union membership because they were "of abandoned and reckless disposition," lacking "those peculiarities of temperament such as patriotism, sympathy, sacrifice, etc., which are peculiar to most of the Caucasian race." The AFL therefore recommended deportation of blacks to Liberia or Cuba. Samuel Gompers, the first president of the American Federation of Labor, went further in a speech in 1905 when he declared that "the Caucasians are not going to let their standard of living be destroyed by negroes, Chinamen, Laps, or any others."[23]

White opposition to such attitudes came from movements that posited a class, rather than a sectional or racial, analysis of society. The IWW, for example, took a principled inclusive position and was consequently the target of repressive action by state and capital. The threat that such a position would challenge the common sense popular racism that was being pushed by capital and the state and would offer an alternative identity to that of "White American" for the new immigrants was a serious one. This elicited a mixture of propaganda and repression, with the additional weight of science thrown in for good measure. As science and technology became more central to the economy, scientists and engineers became more important as authority figures.[24]

For example, the expanding field of psychology became an especially important ally of the capitalists, who in their role as philanthropists provided resources for scientists. Edward Thorndike received $325,000 from the Carnegie Foundation from 1918 to 1934 and was the author of one of the basic textbooks used until the 1950s in major American universities. He and his colleagues, Lewis Terman and Henry Goddard, adapted Alfred Binet's intelligence test for American use, propagandized the theories of genetically inherited intelligence, and offered scientific "proof" of the superiority of some races (the Nordic and Teutonic) and the inferiority of others. Coincidentally, the "inferiors" were not only the victims of the "white man's burden" overseas and the nonwhite superexploited races within the United States itself; they were also the recent immigrant employees of the philanthropists, such as the Italians, the Poles, the Slavs, and others. Science simply documented that the class hierarchy was as it should be. If the United States was the land of opportunity, those at the top got there because of their intelligence and hard work. Those at the bottom deserved to be there.

The scientifically objective data produced by such experts as Thorndike were used to justify the racist Immigration Acts of 1921 and 1924, which kept out additional immigrants from southern and Eastern Europe. The demands for such controls on immigration from the AFL and from nativist groups such as the Immigration Restriction League had all failed until after World War I. Why? Although sections of the working class supported such restriction, it was not in response to their wishes that restriction was adopted. World War I had stopped the flow of immigrant workers from Europe. There was a continuing, and indeed increasing, need for workers in the United States, first to supply the British and French war efforts and then its own. This need was met by recruiting black workers from the South. Racialist attitudes and—crucially—the construction of institutional racism by the local state ensured that there would be antagonism between white workers and their new African American colleagues. Racist practices ensured that blacks would be concentrated in particular low-level jobs and in particular ghetto residential areas that were then systematically denied the level of public services to which they were entitled. Thus, the labor force would continue to be divided and controllable.[25]

After the war, fear of the spread of Bolshevism made the prospect of recruiting labor from areas contaminated by its virus particularly unsatisfactory. Segregated reserves of black labor in the South made it unnecessary for capitalists and the state to take that risk. The racist culture provided the guarantee that lower levels of white immigrants and the new black industrial proletariat would be divided. The consequences for the white working class of the adherence of most of its members to a system in which they were exploited as workers and were recipients of privileges, or the promise of privileges, as whites can be seen in their political weakness, low level of unionization, high level of economic insecurity, and low level of state benefits. This situation was challenged by large sections of the working class during the Great Depression. How successful that challenge was to be and to what extent white workers would develop a class, rather than a racial, consciousness is the subject of the next section.

Racism and the Transition from the Keynesian Accommodation
to the Authoritarian State

The development of welfare capitalism in the aftermath of the Great Depression and World War II has been one of the major developments of the contemporary period. It has been argued that capitalism has changed its nature. The state became the protector of the weak and defenseless, the provider of a safety net to catch those who fell, for whatever reason, and the provider of services on the basis of need rather than the ability to pay. The corporations themselves were seen to have become "soulful," in the Harvard economist Carl Kaysen's felicitous phrase. Corporate power evolved into a partnership with government which, in turn, would ensure that national policies supported the economic interests of the former, thus reaching a Republican accommodation. Furthermore, power was seen to have become dispersed because of widespread stock ownership, the separation of ownership and control, and the responsiveness of the new managers in the postindustrial society to interests wider than the hitherto exclusive concern for profit maximization. There were no longer to be struggles over the distribution of scarce sources in an age of plenty and affluence. Class had become an irrelevant concept, and, consequently, there was an end to ideology.

During this same period, there were major changes in race relations. Civil rights legislation, executive action, judicial decisions, and political leadership were all responsive to liberal ideology and to political pressure from the civil rights movement. The state no longer endorsed racism, de jure segregation was overturned, and racial minorities could now compete and rise on the basis of their own worth. Although prejudice might still remain as a residual problem, racism was not—and could not be seen as—a structural characteristic of society in the United States.

Given the reality of capital's most recent counterattacks and revocations of most of these concessions over the past decades, it is, perhaps, hard to remember how taken for granted such fairy tales were in the dominant ideologies of American society from the end of the Great Depression to the present. The soulful corporation has turned out to be a transnational corporation moving production and jobs around the globe in search of ever-greater profits and using its ability to do so to force its remaining workforce in the metropole to accept an escalating series of "take-backs" as a condition of being allowed to continue to work. The state has turned out to be more committed to capitalism than to welfare, which is being eroded as a condition of keeping and attracting jobs. The ending of de jure segregation did not mean the end of racial polarization. But these challenges to the dominant ideology have not led to a reconsideration of the ideological assumptions of mainstream commentators. Far from it. The prevalent belief is that it is either the genetic or the cultural inferiority of the victims that accounts for continuing and increasing inequality; indeed, it is the very welfare system itself that has created a dependency culture in unemployment, homelessness, drug abuse, and so on.[26] Racism, in both its material and its ideological forms, continues to be a central characteristic of American society and has played a crucial role in capital's ability, along with the state's, to overturn what were supposed to have been fundamental changes in the nature of capitalism and in the nature and operations of the liberal democratic state.

The Keynesian Accommodation and Civil Rights

The Great Depression, the New Deal, World War II, and the working-class response to these events played a major role in extracting concessions from capital and in shaping the forms of the state. The federal government came to play the central role in subsidizing capital, in ensuring that a favorable investment climate existed within the United States and abroad, and in ensuring order and stability within the United States. Performing these tasks often brought the federal government into conflict with the states and with local authorities and into conflict with the belief in free enterprise, minimal government, and the inferiority of blacks. For example, in order to ensure that black struggles in the postwar period did not continue the link with the Communist party and with issues of class, it was necessary to combine repression of those wishing to continue that link, W. E. B. Du Bois and Paul Robeson, the political activist, actor, and singer, for example, with sufficient concessions to ensure the triumph of Americanism, despite racism.

Such concessions required changes in the Jim Crow system of the South. De jure segregation was no longer necessary to maintain the southern system of agriculture, which was being rapidly mechanized, in part supported by the policies of the New Deal. These policies served as a lightning rod for black demands and were a force of instability that the newer power centers in the South associated with industry and commerce and wished to defuse. Racial segregation was a contradiction for the United States in its efforts to shape the world order after World War II, a world in which two-thirds of the people were not white and in which U.S. apartheid was available for the Soviets and other nationalist critics to use in challenging U.S. claims to moral leadership. In addition, incorporation of African Americans into the formal democracy channeled the African American middle class into the system, reducing the danger that it would become a counterelite. This reasoning did not mean that the white leaders of the old order in the South would give up their power and privileges without a struggle. Poor whites in the South were not going to give up power either, especially after being assured by word and deed by those with power in the South and in the nation as a whole that they too were superior to blacks because they were white.

The federal government would be in conflict with rural southern elites as it attempted to overturn de jure segregation, with African Americans taking the lead and being beaten and killed as a necessary part of the campaign. The national administration had, at the same time, to deal with overt racial discrimination in the rest of the country, where racial segregation was not legally required. Here, the federal government came into conflict with the principles of private property, which held that individuals could do whatever they wished to with their property and could hire whom they wished and rent to whom they wished. The level of struggle by African Americans and the imperatives of running the world, however, required that overt racial discrimination be outlawed.[27]

The desegregation efforts of the federal government did not mean the end of institutional racism or the end of the role of the state in legitimating popular racism. Racism continued to be part of the normal operations of the state at every level. For example, one of the key engines of state intervention in support of the economy in the postwar years was support for suburbanization, which by 1965 had led to the construction of more than $120 billion worth of owner-occupied housing, 98 percent of which was owned and occupied by whites. This was the result of official government policies administered through the lending decisions of the Veterans Administration and the Federal Housing Agency. State and local governments made similar decisions that led to the construction of what Arnold Hirsch has called Chicago's Second Ghetto.[28] The racialized economic consequences of encouraging and financially subsidizing white flight to the suburbs included the loss of jobs, tax revenues, and affordable housing in the inner cities—which were becoming more black as African Americans were displaced from southern sharecropping and came north looking for work. The decisions of the state at every level constructed the increasingly racialized ghettos with their underresourced education and health systems, appalling housing, and high levels of un- and underemployment. The construction of racialized criminal justice systems ensured the lack of police protection and a massively racialized disparity in rates of imprisonment. These realities of state policy have to be set against statements in favor of tolerance and brotherhood and even against assertions about the decline of racism and the presumption that past civil rights legislation had fundamentally eliminated systematic racism in the United States.

Just as there is a contradiction between the ostensible purposes of the state in the field of race, so there is a similar contradiction in the state's relations with the white working class. An essential part of the construction of "Pax Americana," the period of American economic, military, and political hegemony that followed World War II, was the great or Keynesian accommodation that augmented the new era of welfare capitalism I have discussed. Workers in the primary sector of the economy were allowed to enjoy high pay, job security, and a social wage. But the price they had to pay actually undermined their ability to protect these gains. The purge of the Left from the unions associated with the anti-Communist frenzy of the early 1950s and the requirements of the Taft-Hartley Act (the first postwar limitation of the rights of organized labor) was accompanied by the acceptance of the ideology and practice of the Cold War, of anticommunism, of Military Keynesianism, and by the cessation of serious attempts to unionize the nonunion majority of the working class.[29]

The consequences of these concessions proved devastating over the medium term for those workers who were to be the beneficiaries of this accommodation and devastating for those who were excluded. The purges of the unions drove out those militants and activists who wanted to challenge the structural racism within the workplace and within the unions themselves. It was these workers who wanted to create objective conditions of racial equality. The failure to continue unionizing drives, particularly in the South, created a region where capital could locate future investment and employ labor at a lower social wage. The lack of unionization created the basis upon which capital, the state, and the media could scapegoat organized labor as the cause of inflation and other ills of the society. The ensuing weakness of the working class made it even more difficult for members of that class to resist the transmission of the dominant racist ideology of white supremacy. The acceptance of Pax Americana helped capital and the state to define the national interest in terms most favorable to themselves.

This defining of interest included seeing any foreign government on the periphery that attempts to improve the living conditions of its people by taking control of its economy as an enemy of the United States and as part of the "international communist conspiracy" of the "evil empire." The consequence of such a hegemonic definition of the national interest has been political, military, covert, and economic interventions to overthrow such governments and to put and keep in power regimes that would allow transnational capital a free run in their countries, that would sell their people more cheaply than their neighbors would, thus providing opportunities for the export of jobs from the metropole to the periphery.[30] The limitation of private-sector unionization primarily to the major industrial sectors had another consequence—the expanding sectors of the economy (service, sales, and clerical) were not unionized and consequently were based on cheap labor. The weakening influence of organized labor, a political system that was coming to be more and more under the control of capital, and the lack of meaningful alternatives offered by the Democratic party has left large parts of the white working class alienated from the system and from the Democratic party.

The Repeal of the Keynesian Accommodation and of Civil Rights

Central to the attack on the Keynesian accommodation has been the attack on big government. Big government, of course, did not mean the bloated Military Keynesianism, or Pentagon socialism. Nor did it mean the massive subsidies granted by government to agribusiness or to the rich or the upper middle class. Big government meant welfare, and welfare meant blacks, particularly black women on welfare. The image of the undeserving poor again came center stage. It was brought center stage by the media and the neoconservative intellectuals, supported by right-wing think tanks, and funded by right-wing foundations and by the Republican party in its search to overturn the New Deal coalition. Behind all of these forces was corporate capital and its search for cheaper, more "flexible" labor and a massively cut social wage.

The essence of the Republican strategy since 1964 has been an appeal to the white South and to whites in the rest of the country on the basis that the Democratic party had been captured by blacks and was no longer the white man's party. Race has become the best single predictor of voting behavior. For example, two-thirds of all white voters voted for Reagan in 1984, and 60 percent voted for Bush in 1988. Manning Marable, the director of the Institute of Research in African American Studies at Columbia University, has calculated that overall white support in the South for Republican presidential candidates has been 70 percent and among white evangelical Christians 80 percent: "Since the election of Ronald Reagan in 1980, in presidential contests the Republican Party operates almost like a white united front, dominated by the most racist, reactionary sectors of corporate and finance capital, and the most backward cultural and religious movements."[31]

The essence of the southern strategy was to overcome the disastrous rejection of Barry Goldwater's candidacy for the presidency in 1964 by voters throughout the country— except for the once Solid South and his own state of Arizona. His attack on Social Security was a too obvious attack on the Keynesian accommodation and too much of a threat to the gains of the New Deal. But, by focusing on the undeserving black poor, the Republicans began to fracture the New Deal coalition and to undermine the support for the fundamentals of the Keynesian accommodation among large sections of the white working-class. The deterioration of the living conditions and security of working-class people was laid at the feet of a Democratic party that no longer represented its white supporters, having been taken over by special interests. These ideas were given credence by the daily repetition of misinformation and racialization by the corporate-owned media. In 1969 Peter Drucker made the connection between race and welfare in the influential conservative journal *Public Interest*:

> Our welfare policies were...perfectly rational—and quite effective—as measures for the temporary relief of *competent people* who were unemployed only because of the catastrophe of the Great Depression....And small wonder that these programs did not work, that instead they aggravated the problem and increased the helplessness, the dependence, the despair of the Negro masses.[32]

This linking of African Americans, the undeserving poor, and dependency became a central feature of right-wing ideology and politics and was used to attack big government and the national Democratic party. The undeserving poor were clearly women of color, particularly African American women, who were AFDC recipients and who were immoral and lazy. Among the images identified by Lucy A. Williams are the "growing horde of lazy Negroes" living off the public dole; "the unmarried Negro women who make a business of producing children...for the purpose of securing this easy welfare money"; Barry Goldwater's view that welfare "transforms the individual being into a decadent animal creature."[33] Animal images continued to be used by the nation's legislators. In 1967 Senator Russell Long referred to protesting welfare mothers as "Black Brood Mares, Inc."[34] Almost thirty years later, in the debates in the House of Representatives in 1995 on the welfare reform bill, House Republicans referred to poor mothers who received welfare benefits "as 'breeding mules,' as 'alligators' and as 'monkeys.' " Earlier, House Ways and Means chairman Representative Clay Shaw Jr., who shepherded welfare repeal legislation through the House, stated: "It may be like hitting a mule with a two-by-four, but you've got to get their attention."[35] Not only did these views demean African American women as welfare recipients; they were part of a two-sided attack on women:

> On one hand, a woman's "natural place" is in the home; she finds dignity and security beneath the authority of her husband; and daycare is opposed because it keeps children away from their mothers. On the other hand, a woman without a man [i.e., a single mother welfare recipient] should be in wage work. The implications of these two arguments, as manifested in welfare policy, are racially based.[36]

Welfare destroyed the nuclear family and created a culture of dependency, according to right-wing ideologues such as George Gilder and Charles Murray. According to Gilder, in his book *Wealth and Poverty*, AFDC is the root cause of poverty because it destroys the father's key role and authority within the family; the life of the poor is characterized everywhere by "resignation and rage, escapism and violence, short horizons and promiscuous sexuality."[37] These images became an integral part of Ronald Reagan's successful campaign for the presidency in 1980. He used the image of the black "welfare queen" who supposedly received $150,000 in tax-free income. Clarence Page, writing in the *Chicago Tribune* in 1989, after Reagan's two terms as president, saw the importance of this strategy: "Reagan...put a black and urban face on [poverty] from the time he campaigned against 'welfare queens' in 1980 and the stereotypes are reinforced almost daily by television images of ghetto gang wars and drug busts."[38]

Reagan and the Republicans effectively mobilized the growing dissatisfaction of the white working class with its position in the economy and the society. Obviously, in a racist society that had historically accorded white skin privileges to whites of all classes, even if—or crucially, especially if—those privileges were class differentiated, any advances made by racial minorities after years of struggle could become the basis of racist scapegoating. Blacks—and to a significant extent, white women—were used as scapegoats for structural changes in the position of white working-class men. This strategy had been identified by a number of New Right ideologues in the post-1964 period. For example, Edwin Kuh wrote in *Public Interest* in 1969:

> Much of the white backlash, centered in the ranks of the blue-collar workers, has been of this character. "Why," such workers ask, "should they [the poor blacks] make nearly as much money as I do without working while we have to work?"[39]

The Republicans' successful mobilization of racism has been identified as crucial to Reagan's defeat of Jimmy Carter in 1980. Alphonso Pinkney quoted a *New York Times*/CBS poll and argued that Carter lost in part because "of a perception that he was found by whites to have been 'too concerned with blacks.'"[40]

After almost three decades of such propaganda, it is not surprising that the corporate-financed Democratic party under the "centrist" leadership of its new Democratic Leadership Council would join the Republicans in ending welfare as we knew it. President Clinton provided a view of the history of welfare and its current state remarkably similar to that advanced by the Republicans: "When welfare was created the typical welfare recipient was a miner's widow with no education and small children. Her husband had died in the mine. There were few out-of-wedlock pregnancies."[41]

An example of the ideological offensive against blacks and the poor can be seen in two major articles that appeared in 1981 in the *Los Angeles Times*.[42] They are worth discussing in some detail because they are excellent examples of this ideological assault that continued throughout the 1980s and 1990s.

The articles argue that, while twice as many whites as blacks are part of a new permanent underclass, the black underclass is more worrying because it is concentrated in America's major cities rather than scattered in the Appalachias and other semirural areas. Structural factors in maintaining and creating this underclass are mentioned, but the overriding theme is the underclass's responsibility for its own position. And if statistics will not do to bring the message home to the reader, there is a case study—under the invidious title "The Underclass: How One Family Copes"—of a day in the life of a South Side Chicago black welfare mother, with ten illegitimate children, five of whom are on welfare with her and one of whom has just had an illegitimate child. These blacks are not only living off the rest of us because they cannot or will not work; they also engage, we are told, in widespread criminal activity, which also costs the rest of us. The experts quoted agree that not a great deal can be done; the economy is shrinking, and it's all the fault of the poor, anyhow.

But more dangerous than the familiar blame-the-victim structure of the debate is the way we are encouraged to fear and loathe the victim. The second article, which appeared one week later, drops all pretense at social concern. Luridly titled "Marauders from Inner City Prey on LA's Suburbs," it begins as follows: "One by one and in small bands, young men desperate for money are marauding out of the heart of Los Angeles in a growing wave to prey upon the suburban middle and upper classes, sometimes with senseless savagery."[43] Robbery (with bloodcurdling violence) and the rape of two white women is the stuff, we are informed, of one such "raid." We are then returned to the ghetto with these savage marauders to watch them showing off and spending their ill-gotten gains. We are repeatedly told that the police do not have enough powers or manpower and that the courts are too lenient.

The president of the Los Angeles Urban League, John Mack, sees the solution lying with placing "the major focus on the ones who are still salvageable....We are a race of people who are equal to anyone else, but within that framework we have some winners, and we have some losers. We have to go with the winners." Mayor Tom Bradley has a solution for the "losers":

> I think that there is a concept where you have a controlled environment, where you keep the child not just while he or she is in school but in the hours outside school, you have that child in a controlled environment. The kibbutz in Israel is one such concept....It, of course, would not be a kibbutz, but it would be that kind of concept.[44]

The *Baltimore Evening Sun* offered a similar view two years later when it reported the results of its "three-month" study of black families titled "Homes without Fathers: The Poverty Cycle": "State and local officials describe the breakdown in black family structure as one of the biggest and most perplexing problems confronting the city....The growth in black homes without fathers exacts a high cost in both human and economic terms."[45] Carl Ginsburg points out that, while the series claimed to take the readers into the "tangle of pathology," it failed to contain any discussion of "economic crisis, or corporate policies, or management agendas that promote the very conditions affecting blacks, perpetuating their distress. Nor was there a discussion of the recession's disproportionate effects on blacks."[46]

These views were central to the construction of the "underclass"—which was such a threat to the rest of "us." For example, *Time* magazine published a cover story titled "The American Underclass: Destitute and Desperate in the Land of Plenty" on August 29, 1977. Among the people assigned to the underclass were "juvenile delinquents, school dropouts, drug addicts, and welfare mothers" (also "welfare dependents"), as well as looters, arsonists, violent criminals, unmarried mothers, pimps, pushers, and panhandlers. The New Right theoretician Morton Kondracke wrote in 1989 that "the crisis of the underclass...is so great that probably nothing short of a spiritual renewal of black America would really solve the problem."[47]

Racialized politics has made it possible for capital to use the electoral system to restructure the political economy, as was done in Britain under Prime Minister Margaret Thatcher and her successor, John Major. Policies that have not benefited working-class people, such as those associated with deindustrialization, decertification of trade unions, take-backs by capital from unionized workers, and cuts in the social wage, have been imposed without sustained popular challenge. The explanation for the lack of sustained popular challenge is in large part the manipulation of racial symbolism. During this period there has been an ideological assault on state and collective provision; on the supposed "dependency culture"; and on large sections of the reserve labor force, now called the underclass. The level of state attacks on African American and Latino communities has increased massively during this period, and the level of imprisonment has escalated exponentially, with the United States now the most "imprisoned" nation in the world. A racial order is reflected in this situation: an African American man is more likely to be imprisoned than to be in higher education and is five times more likely to be imprisoned than is a black African in South Africa.[48]

The racial and gender divisions of the working class have weakened its ability to resist the dominant racialized and gendered ideology. This lack of working-class consciousness and autonomous culture severely weakens its ability to respond to these attacks on its living standards and its hopes for the future. The increasing level of scapegoating of African Americans and women is an indication of the determination of those in power to stay in power and to use the system to their maximum advantage. Their ability to buy acquiescence through material concessions to white working-class men is becoming more and more limited, and therefore they are relying more and more on scapegoating and division.

Until the working class creates its own identity and a racially inclusive consciousness and culture, it will continue to be unable to advance its own interests. The European-American working class will have to reject the white part of that identity and the illusory privileges based on racism and sexism. The damage done is not only to people of color: European-Americans are damaged, as well. The dominant ideology of white racial supremacy has served, and continues to serve, the interests of capital and its political allies. Opposition has come from individuals and groups of whites, African Americans, Latinos, and others. This opposition to a racialized identity illustrates that it is possible to choose an alternative identity to that constructed and transmitted by agents of capital. Thus, it is possible for the individual effort and talent used in everyday struggles to survive and to resist class oppression to be used to create a just and truly democratic society.

NOTES

The author would like to acknowledge financial assistance from the University of Manchester and the Nuffield Foundation Small Grants Scheme in the Social Sciences. He would also like to thank Huw Beynon and James Jennings for their assistance.

1. Ronald Bailey, "The Slavery Trade and the Development of Capitalism in the United States: The Textile Industry in New England," *Social Science History* 14, no. 3 (1990): 373-414.

2. See also Eric Williams, *Capitalism and Slavery* (London: Andre Deutsch, 1967).

3. Theodore Allen, "They Would Have Destroyed Me: Slavery and the Origins of Racism," *Radical America* 9, no. 3 (1975): 42-48.

4. Richard Drinnon, *Facing West* (New York: Schocken, 1980); B. B. Ringer, *We the People and Others* (New York: Norton, 1983); David R. Roediger, *The Wages of Whiteness: Race and the Making of the American Working Class* (London: Verso, 1991); Alexander Saxton, *The Rise and Fall of the White Republic: Class Politics and Mass Culture in Nineteenth-Century America* (London:

Verso, 1991); Ronald T. Takaki, *Iron Cages: Race and Culture in Nineteenth-Century America* (London: Athlone, 1980).

5. W. E .B. Du Bois, *Black Reconstruction in America* (London: Frank Cass, 1966), 633-34.

6. Roediger, *The Wages of Whiteness*, 13, 14.

7. Ibid.

8. Nathan Glazer, "Blacks and White Ethnics: The Difference and the Political Difference It Makes," *Social Problems* 18 (1971): 444-61.

9. Eugene J. Cornacchia and Dale C. Nelson, "Historical Differences in the Political Experiences of American Blacks and White Ethnics: Revisiting an Unresolved Controversy," *Ethnic and Racial Studies* 15, no. 1 (1992): 103.

10. Ibid., 120.

11. Du Bois, *Black Reconstruction in America*, 700-701; see also Ira Katznelson and Margaret Weir, *Schooling for All: Class, Race and the Decline of the Democratic Ideal* (New York: Basic Books, 1985).

12. Herbert Aptheker, "Anti-Racism in the U.S.: An Introduction," *Sage Race Relations Abstracts* 12, no. 4 (November 1987): 3-32.

13. Saxton, *The Rise and Fall of the White Republic*.

14. Roediger, *The Wages of Whiteness*.

15. Du Bois, *Black Reconstruction in America*.

16. Mike Davis, *Prisoners of the American Dream* (London: Verso, 1980).

17. Takaki, *Iron Cages*, 238.

18. Ibid., 239.

19. Paul Horton, "Testing the Limits of Class Politics in Postbellum Alabama: Agrarian Radicalism in Lawrence County," *Journal of Southern History* 57, no. 1 (1991): 65.

20. Ibid., 76, 77.

21. Ibid., 83.

22. Harold Braverman, *Labor and Monopoly Capital* (New York: Monthly Review Press, 1974).

23. A. Saxton, "Race and the House of Labor," in *The Great Fear: Race in the Mind of Americans*, ed. G. Nash and R. Weiss (New York: Holt, Rinehart and Winston, 1970), 115.

24. David Noble, *America by Design* (Oxford: Oxford University Press, 1977).

25. William Tuttle, *Race Riot: Chicago in the Red Summer of 1919* (Urbana: University of Illinois Press, 1996). See also Stan Vittoz, "World War I and the Political Accommodation of Transitional Market Forces: The Case of Immigration Restrictions," *Politics and Society* 8 (1978): 49-78.

26. George Gilder, *Wealth and Poverty* (New York: Bantam Books, 1982). See also Charles Murray, *Losing Ground: American Social Policy 1950-1980* (New York: Basic Books, 1986). For a critique of these, see Thomas Boston, *Race, Class and Conservatism* (Boston and London: Unwin Hyman, 1988); Adolph Reed, "The Underclass as Myth and Symbol: The Poverty of Discourse about Poverty," *Radical America* 24, no. 1 (1992): 21-40.

27. Louis Kushnick, "Race, Class and Civil Rights," in *Race, Class and Struggle: Essays on Racism and Inequality in Britain, the United States and Western Europe*, ed. Louis Kushnick (London: Rivers Oram Press, 1997). See also Manning Marable, *Race, Reform and Rebellion*, 2nd ed. (London: Macmillan, 1991).

28. Arnold Hirsch, *Making the Second Ghetto: Race and Housing in Chicago* (Cambridge and New York: Cambridge University Press, 1983).

29. Samuel Bowles, David Gordon, and Herbert Gintis, *Beyond the Waste Land* (New York: Anchor Press/Doubleday, 1984).

30. A. Sivanandan, "Imperialism and Disorganic Development in the Silicon Age," in A. Sivanandan, *A Different Hunger* (London: Pluto Press, 1990), 143-61.

31. Manning Marable, "Race and Class in the U.S. Presidential Election," *Race and Class* 34, no. 3 (January-March 1993): 76.

32. Quoted in Lucy A. Williams, "The Right's Attack on Aid to Families with Dependent Children," *Public Eye* 10, nos. 3/4 (Fall-Winter 1996): 7.

33. Ibid., 5.

34. Ibid., n. 98.

35. Valerie Palace, "The Shredded Net: The End of Welfare as We Knew It," *Sage Race Relations Abstracts* 22, no. 3 (August 1997): 7.

36. Ibid., 6.

37. Quoted in ibid., 11.

38. Quoted in ibid., n. 200.

39. Ibid., 7.

40. Quoted in Carl Ginsburg, *Race and Media: The Enduring Life of the Moynihan Report* (New York: Institute for Media Analysis, 1989), 45-46.

41. Quoted in Onyekachi Wamabu, "Welfare Bill Unleashed Race Row," *Voice*, 13 August 1996.

42. David Treadwell and Gaylord Shaw, "Underclass: How One Family Copes," *Los Angeles Times*, 5 July 1981; Richard E. Meyer and Mike Goodman, "Marauders from Inner City Prey on LA's Suburbs," *Los Angeles Times*, 12 July 1981.

43. Meyer and Goodman, "Marauders from Inner City."

44. Ibid.

45. *Baltimore Evening Sun*, 5 December 1983, 3; quoted in Ginsburg, *Race and Media*, 54.

46. Ginsburg, *Race and Media*, 54.

47. Morton Kondracke, "The Two Black Americas: A Regress Report," *New Republic*, 6 February 1989, 20; quoted in Ginsburg, *Race and Media*, 49.

48. Marc Mauer, *Young Black Men and the Criminal Justice System: A Growing National Problem* (Washington, D.C.: Sentencing Project, 1990). See also C. Shine and M. Mauer, *Does the Punishment Fit the Crime? Drug Users and Drunk Drivers, Questions of Race and Class* (Washington, D.C.: Sentencing Project, 1993); Marc Mauer, *Americans behind Bars: U.S. and International Use of Incarceration, 1995* (Washington, D.C.: Sentencing Project, 1997).

DISCUSSION QUESTIONS

1. Discuss the components of the argument that the United States is an "ideologically racist" nation and was founded as such.

2. Explain the emergence of the idea of "whiteness."

3. What is meant by white working-class consciousness, and how does the author argue that it is supported and maintained?

4. How has the idea of whiteness been resisted by white workers?

5. What does the author mean by the Keynesian accommodation in the post-World War II period? How was it "overthrown"?

6. Discuss the role of racism in the increasing political dominance of the Republican party in the United States. Is this critique about the Republican party applicable to the Democratic party?

7. Discuss the utilization of racialized images of welfare as facilitation in strategies to change or reduce certain kinds of public welfare programs. How does the corporate community utilize and respond to racialized images of welfare, according to the author?

FOR FURTHER READING

Aptheker, Herbert, "Anti-Racism in the U.S.: An Introduction," *Sage Race Relations Abstracts* 12, no. 4 (November 1987): 3-32.

Bailey, Ronald, "The Slavery Trade and the Development of Capitalism in the United States: The Textile Industry in New England," *Social Science History* 14, no. 3 (1990): 373-414.

Braverman, Harold, *Labor and Monopoly Capital* (New York: Monthly Review Press, 1974).

Du Bois, W. E .B., *Black Reconstruction in America* (London: Frank Cass, 1966), 633-34.

Gilder, George, *Wealth and Poverty* (New York: Bantam Books, 1982).

Glazer, Nathan, "Blacks and White Ethnics: The Difference and the Political Difference It Makes," *Social Problems* 18 (1971): 444-61.

Katznelson, Ira, and Margaret Weir, *Schooling for All: Class, Race and the Decline of the Democratic Ideal* (New York: Basic Books, 1985).

Kushnick, Louis, "Race, Class and Civil Rights," in Louis Kushnick (ed.), *Race, Class and Struggle: Essays on Racism and Inequality in Britain, the United States and Western Europe* (London: Rivers Oram Press, 1997).

Marable, Manning, "Race and Class in the U.S. Presidential Election," *Race and Class* 34, no. 3 (January-March 1993): 76.

Mauer, Marc, *Young Black Men and the Criminal Justice System: A Growing National Problem* (Washington, D.C.: Sentencing Project, 1990).

Roediger, David R., *The Wages of Whiteness: Race and the Making of the American Working Class* (London: Verso, 1991).

Williams, Eric, *Capitalism and Slavery* (London: Andre Deutsch, 1967).

Chapter Nine

The Shredded Net
The End of Welfare as We Knew It

Valerie Polakow

When I ran for president four years ago, I pledged to end welfare as we know it. I have worked very hard for four years to do just that....On balance, this bill is a real step forward for our country, our values, and for people who are on welfare.

—President Bill Clinton,
New York Times, 1 August 1996

As a Democratic president and a Republican-controlled House and Senate joined forces to end welfare for the "good of the poor," one of the last remaining vestiges of the federal social safety net—a minimal guarantee of public assistance for poor children—was decisively shredded. In a society where child poverty and family homelessness have become endemic characteristics, the signing of the new welfare legislation and its passage into law on 22 August 1996 was the culmination of a continuing decades-long public policy assault on poor single mothers with dependent children. However, this legislation, which repeals Title IVa of the Social Security Act of 1935, is the most far-reaching and radical of any antiwelfare initiative, which Senator Daniel Patrick Moynihan characterized as "the first step in dismantling a social contract that has been in place in the United States since at least the 1930s. Do not doubt that social security itself...will be next....We would care for the elderly, the unemployed, the dependent children. Drop the latter; watch the others fall."[1]

In a "residual" welfare state such as the United States, market sovereignty is the foundation for the argument that the state should play a minimal role in the distribution of welfare and that individuals are essentially responsible for contracting their own welfare.[2] During the past decade, the boundaries of the public space have contracted, with narrowed public commitments and a discourse that has fostered "self-reliance." Limited public benefits have always been organized in means-tested assistance schemes that target particular segments of the population in stigmatizing ways. In such a residual welfare state, women alone—divorced, separated, or unmarried mothers—are a constituency at risk, disproportionately poor and facing an alarming array of obstacles and impediments to their autonomy.[3]

Furthermore, the impact of global capitalism on domestic infrastructures has been far-reaching; exporting jobs downsizing, outsourcing, and increasing numbers of nonunionized contract workers all represent the face of the meaner, leaner, global economy. The North American Free Trade Agreement (NAFTA), which was implemented in 1994, caused seventy-five thousand U.S. workers to lose jobs and displaced more than a million and a half Mexican workers. In addition, as corporations sell the notion that international competition requires greater "flexibility," more and more part-time workers without benefits are hired, and corporate lobbying of lawmakers promotes government deregulation, the cutting of overtime pay, and the gutting of union shops. In all three NAFTA countries—the United States, Canada, and Mexico—real wages are actually far below increases in productivity. In Mexico real wages in May 1996 were 35 percent below pre-1994 levels, and in Canada and the United States real wages have stagnated and the proportion of full-time workers in poverty continues to grow.[4] While public infrastructures crumble and income inequality soars, powerful global corporations have expanded beyond the boundaries of the nation-state, and, increasingly, beyond the boundaries of governments. Korten points out that between 1980 and 1994 the *Fortune* 500 companies shed 4.4 million jobs, while sales increased 1.4 times and assets increased 2.3 times! Hence, he argues, in an unfettered market economy, "which responds to money, not needs, the rich win this competition every time....The average CEO of a large corporation now receives a compensation package of more than 3.7 million per year. Those same corporations employ 1/20th of 1% of the world's population, but they control 25% of the world's output and 70% of world trade. Of the world's hundred largest economies, fifty are now corporations."[5]

Within the United States, the march toward privatization inexorably continues—schools, prisons, city services, transportation—and, since the passage of the new welfare law, privatized welfare, in which giant corporations vie for contracts to run welfare-to-work programs, is creating what the *New York Times* described as "the business opportunity of a lifetime."[6] The new law permits states to buy both welfare services and gatekeepers who screen eligibility and determine benefits. Lockheed Martin, the formidable $30-billion "giant of the weapons industry" and a major beneficiary of corporate welfare subsidies, plans to close one of its plants in New Jersey; as one congressman put it, "They would be getting a subsidy to lay off these folks and then could be getting additional money from the government to help these people get off welfare."[7]

As such "wealthfare" flourishes and public entitlements are reduced or eliminated, what happens to those who live in the broadening swath of the Other America? What is life like under a shredded net?

Life under the Shredded Net

I lived in public housing in Detroit, I stayed there for two years, and I know the debilitating factors that it takes just to survive. People have tried and tried and tried to find jobs; it's a vicious circle and after you get the door slammed in your face, you don't have the will to go out there and fight anymore....I got a little slip in my son's pocket saying I owed $900 in child care and saying don't bring my children back until that is paid....I couldn't do it so I tried to go back on welfare. It was either pay my rent or pay child care...so I called social services and asked them about getting my benefits again and my worker said I had to wait two months, so I stopped work in November and she said I wouldn't get any benefits until January. I asked my worker, "How'm I supposed to live?" and she said, "It's not for me to tell you!"

—Tanya, a single mother of two young children[8]

At the present time in the United States, 30 percent of all families with children under eighteen are single-parent families, with single-mother families constituting the vast majority, or 82 percent. In addition, more than 40 percent of single-mother families are living in poverty.[9] However, the largest constituency of poor Americans is children: in 1995, 15.3 million children lived in poverty in the United States, and the younger in age, the higher the risk. While 21 percent of children under eighteen are classified as living in poverty, 25 percent of children under six and 27 percent under three live in poverty, the majority of whom reside in poor, single-mother households.[10]

The term *feminization of poverty* has been widely used to describe the particular plight of women in the United States who experience occupational segregation and workplace discrimination, disproportionately occupy part-time service-sector jobs with few or no benefits, perform unpaid domestic work at home and retain primary care of children. As single mothers, they are disproportionately poor and face an alarming array of obstacles that threaten their family stability.[11] By the late 1980s women and their children had become a significant majority of America's poor.[12] Unmet needs in housing, health care, and child care have coalesced to form a triple crisis where single mothers, as both providers for and nurturers of their children, cannot sustain family viability when they are low-wage earners, with no family support provisions in place to act as a buffer against the ravages of the market economy. In 1995, a full-time minimum wage salary was $8,800 a year—$3,000 less than under the federal poverty line for a single-mother family of three. And while the minimum wage was raised by 50 cents to $4.75 an hour in October 1996, full-time minimum wage work still yields a wage well below the poverty line. The child care crisis compounds the situation, with many low-wage mothers unable to afford the high costs of private child care.

Single mothers also make up 70-90 percent of homeless families nationwide,[13] and more than 50 percent of homeless families become homeless because the mother flees domestic violence.[14] One in four homeless persons is now a child younger than eighteen.[15] Furthermore, reports from the Food and Research Action Center indicate that four million children under twelve go hungry during part of each month, and there are now ten million children who have no health insurance coverage.

It is clear that the increasing economic vulnerability of the single-mother family represents a child welfare crisis of growing magnitude that has been further exacerbated by recent welfare repeal legislation. Mothers now struggling to survive on public assistance are being ordered to pay their dues and take up paid or unpaid work—part of the punitive rehabilitation of the "welfare culture" that defines the new "opportunity society," promoted by Newt Gingrich and his fellow Republican supporters, in which the poor are to assume personal responsibility for their family's poverty. Practically speaking, that means that mothers with dependent children are coerced into taking up low-wage jobs, or "voluntary" indentured servitude, as a condition for receiving any benefits, with no guarantee of adequate child care services or subsidies. The blatant failure of the new personal-responsibility legislation to address the daily survival needs of economically vulnerable single mothers clearly threatens their children's basic physical, social, and emotional development.

Unlike other industrialized democracies, the United States, as a residual welfare state, has no national health care system and no universal family support policies such as paid maternity and parental leave, national child/family allowances, or a national subsidized child care system for infants and preschool children.[16] Head Start, the national early childhood intervention program for poor children developed during the "War on Poverty" of the 1960s, was available to only 36 percent of income-eligible children during 1995.[17]

Despite the dismal record of the United States in developing public policies that provide for the basic health, shelter, and daily living needs of its most vulnerable citizens—poor women and their children—female and child poverty is still cast as a "moral" problem, tied to public rhetoric about "family values" and "family breakdown," which in turn is used to rationalize further cuts in public assistance. The structural evidence of poverty wages, contingent no-benefit jobs, corporate downsizing, racial and gender discrimination, and the growing number of job-poor isolated and destitute communities[18] is ignored in favor of "blaming the victim" discourses that reduce poor women to caricatured public parasites or promiscuous sluts, living it up at taxpayer expense. Rarely are their grim survival struggles chronicled, or their children's traumatic lives examined, as part of the consequences of a trickle-down market economy that offers few protections to those who live in the other America.[19]

While Social Security for elderly Americans is still considered an earned entitlement, a Social Security system for children (who in turn must depend on their parents' benefits) forms part of a completely different discourse in the United States, because the parents, specifically poor mothers of dependent children, are viewed as undeserving of government support. The discourse about poor mothers and their children is couched in "moral" and "personal responsibility" frames and, more recently, in terms of "productive work." Taking care of one's own children, however, is not viewed as productive work if one is poor, and having children when poor is perceived as both irresponsible and/or immoral.

It is significant to note that during the House debates in 1995 on the original welfare reform bill, ironically titled the Personal Responsibility Act, which was proposed as part of the Republican's Contract with America, poor mothers receiving public assistance were publicly vilified by Republican lawmakers as "breeding mules," as "alligators," and as "monkeys." Earlier, House Ways and Means chair Representative Clay Shaw Jr., who shepherded welfare repeal legislation through the House, stated, "It may be like hitting a mule with a two-by-four, but you've got to get their attention."[20] When the bill reached the Senate, Senator Phil Gramm demanded, "We've got to get a provision that denies more and more cash benefits to women who have more and more babies while on welfare."[21]

The antiwelfare and "underclass" punitive discourses that have targeted single mothers and pregnant teens have promoted a continuing public perception of poverty as a private and behavioral condition leading to proliferating racialized and sexualized fictions about *them*; the causes of family poverty are seen as rooted in failed and fallen women, failed children, and a failed work ethic—but not in the actual consequence of public policies that produce family poverty by omission and commission. The ravages of a market economy; the lack of affordable, quality child care; the lack of safe and affordable family housing; the absence of universal health care; and the traumas of domestic violence—all coalesce to create a tangled web of obstacles that entrap poor single mothers in poverty, destitution, and homelessness. Hence, a national family policy (or absence thereof) is a potent force in women's lives, either weaving a safety net to support family viability or shredding the net and destabilizing family existence.

In the Scandinavian countries, for example, where family policies are comparatively strong and where universal entitlements such as paid parental leave, health care, child care, absent-parent child support, and housing subsidies are in place, chronic single mother and child poverty has largely been eliminated.[22] Yet, despite the evidence of abysmal life conditions for the poorest Americans, the minimal safety net that formerly existed in the United States has now been dismantled.

The welfare repeal law that passed the House and Senate with bipartisan support in 1996 could hardly be more emblematic of a postmodern market individualism— eliminating "big government" and public responsibility in favor of the surreal privatized self—where to have is to be. In the following sections the practical and existential impact of the new welfare law is discussed.

Dismantling Welfare:
The Impact of Public Law 104-193, the Personal Responsibility and Work Opportunity Reconciliation Act of 1996

The basic federal program that guaranteed government assistance to all poor children, Aid to Families with Dependent Children (AFDC), which was established as Title IVa of the Social Security Act of 1935, has now been eliminated. According to the Center on Budget and Policy Priorities, the impact of the new law is far-reaching, cutting $55 billion of support to low-income programs, and clearly targets single mothers who depend on public assistance.[23] Under the new law, states receive block grants of money, known as TANF (temporary assistance to needy families) grants, based on 1994 public assistance levels without regard to subsequent changes in the level of need in a state. These TANF grants will be disbursed to families in need on a first-come, first-served basis. Being a poor child no longer automatically qualifies you for assistance. If a single-parent family becomes eligible for state assistance, mother and children will be limited to two years of support if the mother does not comply with stringent work requirements. After a maximum of two years (and states may choose to provide less), all benefits may be cut, and the mother will be forced to find employment. If no jobs are available and the two-year limit is up, mother and children may be left with no safety net other than private charity. And there is a lifetime limit of five years on public assistance, with states given the option of choosing to set stricter limits. While hardship exemptions will be available to 20 percent of families, it is anticipated that during periods of high unemployment or during a recession, larger and larger pools of destitute families will emerge and become homeless.

The Urban Institute estimates that the immediate effect of the new law will be to throw 1.1 million more children into poverty and predicts the further destituting of those already impoverished. Between 1996 and 2002, it is anticipated that approximately three million more children will fall into poverty. In addition, the bill includes sweeping cuts in services to children, and their aging parents, as well as cuts in benefits to thousands of disabled poor children who will lose their SSI (Supplemental Security Income) payments due to far more stringent eligibility requirements. And food stamps will be cut $27.7 billion over the same period; stamps will be denied to single, unemployed adults, limited to a maximum of three months during any thirty-six-month period.[24] The Center on Budget and Policy Priorities estimates that in an average month one million jobless individuals unable to find work will be denied food stamps under this provision. While there are *no* funds for job creation in the new welfare law, there are not sufficient jobs available in poor urban and rural communities. As William Julius Wilson has pointed out, the problem issue has never been welfare but, rather, the disappearance of work in isolated poor communities—and the problem has now reached catastrophic proportions for unskilled and uneducated poor Americans.[25]

During the House debates about the new welfare law, the state of Michigan was consistently cited as a model of how states can implement so-called welfare reform. Michigan's Republican governor, John Engler, was credited with reducing welfare dependency during his two terms in office. He did. In 1991 he threw eighty-three thousand single adults off general assistance and cut AFDC benefits—the main federal welfare program for single-parent families—to mothers and children by 11 percent. He also decreased taxes and authorized spending $23 million to operate four new prisons.[26] An analysis of Engler's recent welfare experiments and welfare waivers raises additional concerns about shifting responsibility for welfare to the states. While the Engler administration has been praised as one of the leading lights of welfare reform because of the emphasis on work requirements as a condition for receiving aid, there is no plan in place to provide educational and vocational job training for unskilled and uneducated recipients so that they may qualify for jobs that pay viable family wages. Moreover, "Work First" requirements, which mandate that all parents receiving public assistance work for a minimum of twenty hours per week, place further obstacles in the path of single mothers who wish to pursue higher education or job training as their one route out of poverty.

Prior to the passage of the new welfare law, Michigan had already allowed its public assistance grants to drop to a level 55 percent below the federal poverty line and had drastically reduced state emergency assistance funding and shifted one-quarter of the state's AFDC funds to other areas of the budget. The Michigan League for Human Services, a Lansing-based public advocacy group, warns that this dismantled social welfare safety net will "leave in its wake a legacy of increased poverty and deprivation which may take decades to reverse."[27]

The New Welfare Law and the Child Care Crisis

The new legislation eliminates three current child care programs—child care assistance for AFDC families in work or training programs; child care assistance for families making the transition from welfare to work; and the at-risk child care program for low-income families—and replaces them with a single child care block grant. The new law repeals the entitlements of families to such assistance. While many claims have been made about the increase in child care funds under the new law, an analysis by the Center on Budget and Policy Priorities indicates that these claims are, in fact, misleading, given the vast increase ·of funds needed to meet the expanded work requirements imposed on mothers of young children. The center cites projections by the Congressional Budget Office that indicate that, by 1999, the child care funding will fall far short of what would be needed to fulfill the law's work requirements and to maintain current levels of child care assistance, which at present are vastly inadequate. The center's researchers point out that "transforming open-ended entitlement programs to a block grant that caps the level of resources that states can draw upon for child care assistance does not represent a liberalization of child care funding."[28] In fact, the law actually contains $1.4 billion less than what will be needed between 1996 and 2002 to provide child care for all the families whose parents must meet the new stringent work requirements.[29] Currently, thirty-eight states and the District of Columbia have long waiting lists for families in need of child care. The work requirements of the new welfare law and the five-year lifetime limit on welfare increase the demand for child care, while at the same time the provisions of the new law have eliminated guaranteed funding for families receiving welfare and transitioning off welfare. In addition, the bill imposes severe cuts of $2.3 billion during the six-year-period to the child- and adult-care food program, a major form of support for family day care homes and child care centers.[30]

At present, there is an acute national shortage of quality, affordable child care for all American children whose parents are low-wage earners. Recent national reports have documented widespread problems in many states: unsafe, unsanitary centers; poor quality care; lack of regulation; chronic unavailability of infant care; and closed access to low-income families.[31] Nancy Ebb's report on child care options for low-income families also raised urgent concerns about the quality and availability of federally subsidized child care for AFDC families and working poor families.[32] The level of care is particularly poor for toddlers and infants. Findings from the national *Cost, Quality and Child Outcomes Study* indicate that child care at most centers was rated as poor to mediocre, and only 8 percent of the infant/toddler rooms received a rating of "good" quality, with 40 percent receiving a rating of less than minimal quality.[33]

Furthermore, in the absence of a nationally subsidized public child care system, private child care costs are prohibitive, not only for poor parents but for middle-income families as well. The average cost of full-time care in 1995 was $4,940 per year;[34] yet in many cities across the nation, costs may exceed $800 to $900 a month for high-quality infant care. Given the current shortage of affordable child care and the alarming quality of cheap child care, who will care for the infants and children of poor mothers who are being forced to work for their benefits? While the new welfare law creates work exemptions for mothers with children under one year old, states are permitted to choose even stricter requirements.

In Michigan, for example, under Governor Engler's Work First Plan, work exemptions are granted only for mothers with infants under twelve weeks old. Sanctions for failure to participate in work programs range from grant reductions of 25 percent to a complete cutoff of all benefits after one year. And these severe repercussions become even more alarming as we consider the large numbers of infants born to adolescents.

The New Welfare Law and the Impact on Pregnant Adolescents

During the 1990s there has been an onslaught of media and public policy rhetoric about teenage pregnancy, in which poor adolescent girls are depicted as promiscuous, having more and more babies "at taxpayer expense" and thereby contributing to the "breakdown of family values." One of the outcomes of this scapegoating of young girls has been a series of legislative attempts to deny aid to the babies of teen mothers. This denial of aid was mandated in the original Personal Responsibility Act of 1995 as part of the Republican Contract with America and was followed by a public debate about the notorious orphanage proposals of Newt Gingrich. The new welfare law, while not as extreme as the original 1995 version, still has devastating consequences for teen mothers. States may now *choose* to deny or provide state assistance to teen parents and their babies, and mothers under eighteen must stay in school and live at home (or with a guardian) in order to receive any aid. In cases of demonstrated violence or abuse, exemptions may be granted. But what about situations that are not demonstrable? Or documented?

Consider the following stories of the desperate lives of teen mothers in Michigan.[35] One eighteen-year-old (mother of a one-year-old) has been deserted by her twenty-five-year-old boyfriend, and she describes her situation thus: "I'm scared....I got no place to go now that he left and I'm sleeping at a friend's place...who's going to help me and the baby with my family living down south....I can't find a place to rent and the waiting list for Section 8 [subsidized housing vouchers] is two years....We got no place to go." She struggles to survive on her meager public assistance allotment, now slated for possible elimination unless she complies with the new welfare-to-work requirements.

Or consider the situation of sixteen-year-old Jamie, raped by her stepfather and terrorized by threats of retaliation if she told anyone; unable to obtain a Medicaid abortion; thrown out of her parents' house, in which her mother is a battered spouse. Where will she turn in her isolated rural county as she now faces the specter of destitution and homelessness and of foster care for her baby? Seventeen-year-old Debbie, who fled an abusive parental home, tells another harrowing story. The father of her child has threatened to kill her and the baby if she reveals his paternity, and she will be unable to obtain public assistance and Medicaid unless she does so. "And now I got nowhere to turn, and nowhere to go. And how will I graduate with all this stuff 'gainst me, and nobody there no more to help with the baby. And he keeps threatening to kill us." Debbie has also lost child care and her only support system at the teen parent center, which has now closed due to funding cuts. She too will be denied all aid under the new welfare law as she has failed to document family violence and is afraid to report it.

Furthermore, there is a glaring lack of contraceptive education in many of our public schools (due in large measure to the successful "just-say-no" abstinence campaigns of the Religious Right lobby), and severe restrictions on access to abortions for poor women and girls remain in place. As a result, many poor teens become adolescent mothers. According to the Children's Defense Fund, 83 percent of teens who give birth are from economically disadvantaged households, only three-fifths of teen mothers receive early prenatal care, and one in ten receives late or no prenatal care.[36] Many of these adolescents face harsh and frightening futures. To be a pregnant teenager in the late 1990s is to face an increasingly diminished future in which a victim-blaming discourse spikes the airwaves and the legislative chambers. However, the most startling piece of this vindictive discourse is left unsaid: the molestation, the rapes, and the predatory acts by adult men, twenty to fifty years old. According to the National Center for Health Statistics, 67 percent of all pregnant teens have been impregnated by adult men twenty years and older (where the identity of the fathers is actually known).[37] It is also adult men who are responsible for more than 202,000 births to teenage mothers every year, and, as the Alan Guttmacher Institute reports, 74 percent of all girls under fourteen who have had sex were actual rape victims.[38] Frequently rejected by their own families, often fleeing abusive home situations, they face increasing isolation and punitive sanctions if they fail to comply with the stay-in-school and live-at-home requirements of the new welfare law.

Domestic Violence and the Welfare Law

All women, irrespective of their social class, are at risk when living in a relationship where domestic violence exists. Domestic violence is the largest cause of injury to women in the United States, where between two and four million women are assaulted annually by their partners.[39] One of the primary reasons that women fail to leave abusive relationships is their economic dependence on their batterers and their fears about how their family will survive without economic support.[40] These fears translate into a particularly acute reality for poor women, and for women who have few outside networks and resources to draw on. In 1990, during hearings on the Violence against Women Act, the Senate Judiciary Committee noted that 50 percent of all homeless women and children in the United States had become homeless because of domestic violence.[41] Bassuk and colleagues's recent study of a community in Massachusetts suggests that the real figure may in fact be even higher. Two-thirds of the homeless mothers in Bassuk's sample had experienced severe physical violence by adult intimate partners.[42]

When women and their children flee violence, their family viability is always threatened physically and psychologically. However, when domestic violence precipitates a fall into destitution and homelessness, the need for strong public assistance measures becomes even more urgent. In considering the impact of the new welfare law on domestic violence victims,[43] it is clear that several disturbing consequences may ensue. Reduced welfare assistance and restrictive eligibility requirements may mean that more mothers will be forced to stay with their batterers—or to return to them because public assistance is terminated. In the case of immigrant women, there will no longer be any form of public assistance available, unless states choose to continue their benefits. Furthermore, if women participate in mandatory workfare programs, as they are already required to do in Michigan, the abusive partner may continue to stalk and terrorize them, making many women unable to comply with job or work requirements. The requirement that women disclose the paternity of their child in order to receive time-limited benefits also places at risk mothers who are threatened by the fathers if they name names. Punitive sanctions that reduce monthly welfare payments if the mother does not participate in a work program are already in force in Michigan, where recipients are punished by a 25 percent grant reduction for each month of noncompliance. Although "good cause" exceptions exist, they are extremely difficult to prove and document; hence, many women continue to fall through the gaping cracks, and their children become the discards of a punitive politics of retribution.

Homelessness, the New Welfare Law, and the Legacy of the 104th Congress

I hate this life. It's not fair. I won't have no friends no more at school. It's the worst thing in the world when you don't got no home. I never never want to go in that shelter. Why can't we have a regular home like other kids. I can't go to school no more 'cause my friends will find out I'm in a shelter. I'm gonna run away from here.[44]

Michael is eight years old; during the time he spent alternating between the dreaded shelter and a "welfare" motel with his mother and his older brother and sister, he experienced terrible nightmares, became very fearful, and aggressively lashed out at classmates in school. Due to his homelessness, he was forced to change schools, and he repeatedly encountered hostility from teachers and children alike. Twice he ran away from school in the middle of the day and was punished by suspension. Until Michael became suicidal and was hospitalized, there had been no psychological or educational interventions available to support him, even though he had exhibited clear signs of posttraumatic stress disorder. Instead, he was considered a burden, one of "them," a kid who did not fit, whose destitution and continuing family upheaval disrupted the classroom. In many ways, Michael serves as a poster child for the Other America—one of many discards trampled along the way to the wasteland spawned by deregulated markets, gentrified housing developments, and soaring condo/Cadillac neighborhoods.

The severe crisis of homeless children is directly linked to the chronic shortage of affordable housing for families. Nationally, the U.S. Department of Education estimates that there are 750,000 school-age children who are homeless.[45] Children are now the fastest-growing constituency among the homeless population, and approximately 23 percent of homeless children do not attend school during their periods of homelessness.

The passage of the Stewart B. McKinney Act in 1987 was designed to provide emergency assistance, programs, and benefits to homeless people. Title VII(b) of the McKinney Act—Education for Homeless Children and Youth—and the McKinney amendments passed in 1990 and 1994 require states to remove barriers that impede the education of homeless children and to provide protections for their educational needs.[46] However, while the Act and the 1990 and 1994 amendments strengthened the legal and educational rights of homeless children in many states McKinney remains a chronically unfunded mandate, subject to congressional funding cuts and to noncompliance by school districts, leaving many homeless children and their families floundering amid transportation barriers, missing school and immunization records, and facing residency requirements that they cannot meet.[47]

Family homelessness has been made even more acute by congressional funding cuts during the past several years—all part of the legacy of the 104th Congress. Cuts totaling

$297 million to the HUD Homeless Assistance programs, $30 million to the Emergency Food and Shelter Program, and $5.8 million to the Education for Homeless Children and Youth Program were all made in fiscal year 1996. Although $2 million was restored to the latter program in fiscal year 1997, all other programs were frozen at fiscal year 1996 levels. In addition, the Emergency Community Services Grant, which during fiscal year 1995 was funded at $19.7 million, was eliminated. When all homeless assistance programs are considered, the funding cuts from fiscal year 1995 to fiscal year 1997 involve a 26 percent loss of overall funding. And these cuts merely exacerbate what was already a critical situation nationwide, leaving millions of families with children unable to find permanent shelter.[48] At present only one-third of households eligible for federal housing assistance actually receive it;[49] 3.8 million households with children spend more than 50 percent of their income on rent, while more than 2.2 million households with children spend more than 70 percent of their income on rent.[50] In forty-five states and the District of Columbia, it is estimated that families would need to earn at least double the minimum wage in order to afford a two-bedroom apartment at fair market rent.[51]

The National Coalition for the Homeless also warns that the relationship between state block TANF grants and the new work requirements for women on welfare will provide states with a further incentive to reduce the number of recipients on welfare by redefining eligibility criteria. Rather than actually paying for work programs, "the likely result will simply be rules that eliminate people from the welfare rolls, denying them needed resources and pushing them into homelessness....in many cases needy families will have to choose between housing and food."[52]

As the United States blazes a trail of Dickensian workfare, punitive welfare cuts, and a "five-years-and-you're-on-the-grates" scenario, welfare caseloads are being drastically reduced and the welfare repeal law continues to be seen by liberals and conservatives alike as an interesting, perhaps necessary, "tough-love" experiment to reduce the "culture of dependency." Recent headlines in the *New York Times* proclaim "A Sharp Decrease in Welfare Cases Is Gathering Speed: Windfall for the States" and "Tougher Policies Have Helped Cut Rolls by 18% since 1994," thereby giving a further seal of approval to this grotesque caricature of welfare "reform."[53] And as the echoes of the personal responsibility discourse and welfare-to-work tough-love reforms resound across the Atlantic, is the policy-induced destitution of the United States that unlikely a scenario for Britain?

Some Disturbing U.S./U.K. Parallels: Impoverishment, "Illegitimacy," and "Personal Responsibility"

Illegitimacy is the single most important social problem of our time—more important than crime, drugs, poverty, illiteracy, welfare, or homelessness because it drives everything else.
—Charles Murray, "The Coming White Underclass"

Charles Murray, the right-wing American policy analyst and coauthor of the infamous *The Bell Curve*, appears to have gained even more prominence in Britain—in both Conservative and New Labor circles—as he dresses up Mr. Darwin in postmodern garb and bemoans the infestation of the disintegrating social order by those who have chosen to be destitute and to propagate morally (and financially) weaker genes. Frequently cited in *The Sunday Times*, he has also been adopted by the right-wing Institute of Economic Affairs. Murray's moral panic exhortations and prescriptions for patriarchal nuclear families, marriage, and the return to a family-values idyll have found a splendid niche not only among Thatcher hardliners and Tory traditionalists but apparently among many liberals as well.[54] Once again the social costs of lone motherhood and the support for such "promiscuity" not only lead to moral disintegration but can be directly attributed to the benefits of the welfare state. While Murray's policy mantra—"end all economic support for single mothers"—has now come to pass in the United States, is Britain far behind?[55]

The cross-national discourse parallels are startling, not only among right-wing ideologues who echo across the Atlantic but among New Democrats and New Labor, as well. Yvette Cooper, writing a provocative piece in the *New Statesman* titled "Me Blair, You Clinton," is correct that "a single mother whose benefit runs out in the U.S. will have plenty of responsibilities but very few rights," but she doubts whether "the U.S. welfare bill really could be a precursor to a Labour-led assault on the welfare state here."[56] Yet when entitlements are steadily eroded and means-tested benefits replace the universal, dependency and personal responsibility rhetoric increasingly rationalizes the dismantling of social citizenship rights.

Twenty percent of families are now headed by a lone mother in Britain—the highest rate in the European Union (EU)—and most of these are economically marginal, with almost 70 percent dependent on social assistance.[57] Women as workers predominantly occupy low-wage clerical and service-sector jobs, concentrated in a narrow economic band where pension rights and other benefits are reduced or nonexistent. Women suffer employment discrimination in terms of wages, promotion, and security, and two-thirds of women with dependent children who work part-time do so for fewer than thirty-one hours a week; hence, they experience further discrimination in terms of employment rights, pensions, and training.[58] Reductions in benefits when taking up paid work (despite the deduction permitted under Family Credit) leave lone mothers substantially worse off if they are employed in part-time work.

While Britain has the highest number of lone-parent families in the EU, the parents are far less likely to be in full-time employment, because Britain has the second lowest number of child care places in the EU and, more significant, the lowest public provision—90 percent of child care is unsubsidized. For infants and toddlers under three it is even worse, dropping to a dismal 2 percent. Hence, substantial numbers of lone mothers with young children are unable to take up paid employment, because lack of access to child care constitutes a major barrier.[59] Child care costs are prohibitively high for working-class or middle-class women; and quality care raises the cost of this service beyond reach for many workers.[60]

Britain's lack of commitment to universal day care for the children of working parents has been characterized as demonstrating a lack of commitment to equality as outlined by the European Community (EC). Britain's equality legislation, in contrast to that of the EC, has been criticized as passive and negative, since it is guided by the principle of nondiscrimination, whereas the guiding principle of EC law is equal treatment. Public child care provisions are clearly critical to equal opportunity for women in the labor market, particularly lone mothers. While Britain ratified the UN Convention of the

Rights of the Child in 1989, it has ignored Article 18, which gives children of working parents the right to day care.[61] Britain is also one of only three EU countries that has no universal system of parental leave, and it has been criticized by the Equal Opportunities Commission for the continued exclusion of 2.25 million women from the new arrangements for eighteen weeks of paid maternity leave because they earn less than the national insurance threshold.[62]

The controversial Child Support Act of 1993, which received a great deal of "feckless fathers" moralistic hype, similar to the "deadbeat dad" rhetoric in the United States, has actually been of little help to low-income lone mothers, as "in most cases it is not mothers and children who will benefit from the increase in maintenance payments, but the Treasury."[63] And as Ruth Lister points out, the impact on middle-class men, an unanticipated target of the act, has dominated the media, but there has been minimal beneficial impact on poor mothers; in cases where the "benefit penalty" is imposed, the act will actually exacerbate the poverty of lone-mother families.[64] In addition, Glendinning reports on interviews with lone mothers that she and colleagues conducted two years after the introduction of the act; not one of the fifty-three mothers interviewed, who had been on means-tested benefits, was now better off as a result of receiving child maintenance payments through the Child Support Agency.[65] Furthermore, as a result of a backlash, primarily among middle-class men, several amendments to the act were introduced during 1995-1996; these further weaken the act, and the benefit penalty was doubled to further sanction lone mothers who refuse to cooperate without "good cause." This, coupled with the elimination of extra payments for all new lone parents coming on to benefits after April 1998, places lone mothers in an increasingly vulnerable situation.[66] As in the United States, it appears that family policy initiatives are designed to "discipline and punish," with Foucauldian overtones, predictably resulting in a further marginalization of lone mothers and their children.[67]

As poverty in Britain becomes increasingly feminized and racialized, "dependency" rhetoric has increased, and *privatization* and *individual responsibility* have become code words for shutting down the welfare state. Beginning in the 1980s during the Reagan-Thatcher "wealthfare" axis, Margaret Thatcher's New Right agenda claimed that "there is no such thing as society; there are only individuals and families";[68] and Social Security Secretary Peter Lilly's strident declaration, at the 1992 Conservative Party Conference, that he intended to "close down the something-for-nothing society," was followed by an attack on teen girls for becoming pregnant "just to jump the housing list."[69] In 1993 *The Sunday Times* had a special pullout section titled "Wedded to Welfare; Do They Want to Marry a Man or the State?" in which Charles Murray was again lavishly quoted.[70] Hence, the "underclass-immorality-illegitimacy" triage so common in the United States has become well entrenched in Britain as the image of the lone mother preying on the generosity of taxpayers is promoted as a social threat; for it is her irresponsible and promiscuous lifestyle that presages the ruin of the moral empire with dire economic consequences.

Such discourse has ominous echoes. The United States has become a powerful and successful model of privatization and welfare state termination, assuming Kafkaesque proportions as poor mothers—in a postmodern and gendered version of "K"—are increasingly placed under state surveillance and the trial of public interrogation.

The shredded net in the United States stands as a grim emblem of the existential havoc wrought by a set of pernicious public policies that target the most vulnerable. The end of an entitlement to social assistance for families has constructed a life world of daily fear and instability, a desperate existence for impoverished lone mothers and their children who have been reduced to paupers, grubbing for food amid unprecedented affluence. Neither housing, nor health care, nor public assistance, nor vulnerable youth protection is part of the civil rights of the poor in the United States. There is a terror in that realization, where not to have—to be completely without resources—is to live in peril.

Poverty, constructed and expanded by legislative complicity and corporate pillaging, has eroded the public space and denied millions their social citizenship rights and their capacity to participate in a democratic life. To be destitute is to be fundamentally disenfranchised, an economic migrant with no geography of rights. The slowly unraveling social safety net in the United Kingdom bears many disturbing imprints of the United States; how to confront and avert this direction is the question, for the human rights of poor mothers and their children are at stake. Toni Morrison's words are disquieting:

> The genius of fascism is that any political structure can host the virus and virtually any developed country can become a suitable home....It is recognizable by its need to purge, by the strategies it uses to purge and by its terror of truly democratic agendas...so individuals become angry at even the notion of the public good...so the measure of our value as humans is not our humanity or our compassion or our generosity but what we own.[71]

To have is to be in a dollar democracy.

NOTES

This chapter was originally published in *Sage Race Relations Abstracts* 22, no. 3 (1997).

1. *New York Times*, 2 August 1996.

2. Gösta Esping-Anderson and Walter Korpi, "From Poor Relief to Institutional Welfare States: The Development of Scandinavian Social Policy," in *The Scandinavian Model: Welfare States and Welfare Research*, ed. R. Erikson, E. J. Hansen, S. Ringen, and H. Uusitalo (Armonk, N.Y.: M. E. Sharpe, 1987), 39-74.

3. Valerie Polakow, "Savage Distributions: Welfare Myths and Daily Lives," *Sage Race Relations Abstracts* 19, no. 4 (1994): 3-29.

4. Sarah Anderson, John Cavanagh, and David Ranney, "NAFTA: Trinational Fiasco," *Nation*, 15/22 July 1996, 26-28.

5. David C. Korten, "The Limits of the Earth," *Nation*, 15/22 July 1996, 16, 18.

6. *New York Times*, 15 September 1996.

7. Ibid., A14.

8. Excerpt from an interview conducted by the author and published in *Nation*, 1 May 1995.

9. U.S. Bureau of the Census, "Poverty in the United States," *Current Population Reports.* Series P60-194 (Washington, D.C.: Government Printing Office, 1995).

10. Children's Defense Fund, *The State of America's Children: Yearbook*. Washington, D.C.: Children's Defense Fund, 1996).

11. Barbara Ehrenreich and Frances Fox Piven, "The Feminization of Poverty: When the Family Wage System Breaks Down," *Dissent* 31 (Summer 1984): 162-68; Gertrude S. Goldberg and Eleanor Kremen, *The Feminization of Poverty: Only in America?* (New York: Greenwood Press, 1990); Linda Gordon, ed., *Women, the State and Welfare* (Madison: University of Wisconsin Press, 1990); Diana Pearce, "The Feminization of Poverty: Women, Work and Welfare," *Urban and Social Change Review* 11, nos. 1-2 (1978): 28-36; Valerie Polakow, *Lives on the Edge: Single Mothers and their Children in the Other America* (Chicago: University of Chicago Press, 1993); Valerie Polakow, "On a Tightrope without a Net," *Nation*, May 1995, 590-92.

12. U.S. Bureau of the Census, "Poverty in the United States," *Current Population Reports.* Series P60-163 (Washington, D.C.: Government Printing Office, 1989).

13. Ellen L. Bassuk, "Who Are the Homeless Families? Characteristics of Sheltered Mothers and Children," *Community Mental Health Journal* 26 (1990): 425-34; Marcia Steinbock, "Homeless Female-headed Families: Relationships at Risk," *Marriage and Family Review* 20 (1995): 143-59.

14. National Clearinghouse for the Defense of Battered Women, *Statistics Packet,* 3rd ed. (Philadelphia: National Clearinghouse for the Defense of Battered Women, 1994).

15. National Law Center on Homelessness and Poverty, *A Foot in the Schoolhouse Door* (Washington, D.C.: National Law Center on Homelessness and Poverty, 1995).

16. Sheila B. Kamerman and Alfred J. Kahn, eds., *Child Care, Parental Leave, and the Under 3's: Policy Innovation in Europe* (New York: Auburn House, 1991); Sheila B. Kamerman and Alfred J. Kahn, *Starting Right: How America Neglects Its Youngest Children and What We Can Do about It* (New York: Oxford University Press, 1995); Polakow, *Lives on the Edge.*

17. Children's Defense Fund, *The State of America's Children: Yearbook* (1996).

18. James Jennings, "Persistent Poverty in the United States: Review of Theories and Explanations," *Sage Race Relations Abstracts* 19, no. 1 (1994): 5-34; William J. Wilson, "Work," *New York Times Magazine*, 18 August 1996.

19. Polakow, "Savage Distributions."

20. Quoted in Jason DeParle, "Momentum Builds for Cutting Back Welfare System," *New York Times*, 13 November 1994.

21. Quoted in Robin Toner, "Senate Passes Bill to Abolish Guarantees of Aid for the Poor," *New York Times*, 20 September 1995.

22. Sheila Kamerman and Alfred Kahn, *Child Care, Parental Leave, and the Under 3's*; Kamerman and Kahn, *Starting Right*; Valerie Polakow, "Family Policy in the United States and Denmark: A Cross-national Study of Discourse and Practice," *Early Education and Development* 8, no. 3 (1997): 242-60.

23. David A. Super et al., *The New Welfare Law* (Washington, D.C.: Center on Budget and Policy Priorities, 1996).

24. Ibid.

25. Wilson, "Work."

26. Richard L. Berke, "Conservative Hero from the Rust Belt," *New York Times*, 12 February 1995; Polakow, "On a Tightrope."

27. Michigan League for Human Services, *Memo to Members* 1, no. 2 (September 1996): 1.

28. Super et al., *The New Welfare Law*, 13.

29. Helen Blank, *Helping Parents Work and Children Succeed: A Guide to Child Care and the 1990 Welfare Act* (Washington, D.C.: Children's Defense Fund, 1997).

30. Ibid.

31. U.S. General Accounting Office, *Review of Health and Safety Standards at Child Care Facilities* (Washington, D.C.: Department of Health and Human Services, 1993); Children's Defense Fund, *The State of America's Children: Yearbook* (1996).

32. Nancy Ebb, *Child Care Tradeoffs: States Make Painful Choices* (Washington, D.C.: Children's Defense Fund, 1994).

33. Suzanne Helburn, ed., *Cost Quality and Child Outcomes in Child Care Centers* (ERIC Documentation Reproduction Service No. ED 386 297), 1995.

34. Children's Defense Fund, *The State of America's Children: Yearbook* (1996).

35. Excerpts from interviews conducted by the author in Michigan, 1993-96.

36. Children's Defense Fund, *The State of America's Children: Yearbook* (1996).

37. National Center for Health Statistics, personal communication with Stephanie Ventura, senior demographer, February 1995.

38. Alan Guttmacher Institute, *Sex and America's Teenagers* (New York: Alan Guttmacher Institute, 1994).

39. Bonnie McClure, "Domestic Violence: The Role of the Health Care Professional," *Michigan Family Review* 2, no. 1 (1996): 63-75; Murray A. Strauss and R. J. Gelles, *Physical Violence in American Families: Risk Factors and Adaptations to Violence in 8,145 Families* (New Brunswick, N.J.: Transaction Publishers, 1990).

40. National Clearinghouse for the Defense of Battered Women, *Statistics Packet*.

41. U.S. Senate Judiciary Committee, *Women and Violence Hearings*, 29 August, 11 December 1990. Senate Hearing 101-939, pt. 2, 79.

42. Ellen Bassuk, et al. "The Characteristics and Needs of Sheltered Homeless and Low-Income Housed Mothers," *Journal of the American Medical Association* 276, no. 8 (1986).

43. Jill Davies, "The New Welfare Law: Implications for Battered Women—Introduction to the Law," *Welfare and Domestic Violence Information Series: Paper 1* (Washington, D.C.: National Resource Center on Domestic Violence, 1996).

44. Excerpts from an interview with Michael, conducted by the author in 1995 in Michigan.

45. National Law Center on Homelessness and Poverty, *A Foot in the Schoolhouse Door*.

46. Ibid.; Yvonne Rafferty, "The Legal Rights and Educational Problems of Homeless Children and Youth," *Educational Foundations and Policy Analysis* 17, no. 1 (1995): 39-61.

47. National Law Center on Homelessness and Poverty, *A Foot in the Schoolhouse Door*.

48. National Coalition for the Homeless, *FY 95-FY 97 Funding for Homeless Assistance Programs* (Washington, D.C.: National Coalition for the Homeless, 1996).

49. Edward B. Lazere, *In Short Supply: The Growing Affordable Housing Gap* (Washington, D.C.: Center on Budget and Policy Priorities, 1995).

50. Tracy Kaufman, *Housing America's Future: Children at Risk* (Washington, D.C.: National Low Income Housing Coalition, 1996).

51. National Low Income Housing Coalition, *Out of Reach: Can America Pay the Rent?* (Washington, D.C.: National Low Income Housing Coalition, 1996).

52. National Coalition for the Homeless, *Welfare Repeal: Moving Americans off Welfare into Homelessness* (Washington, D.C.: National Coalition for the Homeless, 1996), 1.

53. *New York Times,* 2 February 1997.

54. Sasha Roseneil and Kirk Mann, "Unpalatable Choices and Inadequate Families: Lone Mothers and the Underclass Debate," in *Good Enough Mothering? Feminist Perspectives on Lone Mothering,* ed. Elizabeth B. Silva (London: Routledge, 1996).

55. Charles Murray, "The Coming White Underclass," *Wall Street Journal,* 29 October 1993.

56. Yvette Cooper, "Me Blair, You Clinton," *New Statesman,* 9 August 1996.

57. Simon Duncan and Rosalind Edwards, "Lone Mothers and Paid Work: Neighborhoods, Local Labor Markets, and Welfare State Regimes," *Social Politics* (Summer-Fall 1996): 195-222.

58. Proceedings of the House of Commons Employment Committee, *Mothers in Employment,* Vol. 1, 15 February 1995, London: Her Majesty Stationary Office, HC-227-1.

59. J. Bradshaw and J. Millar, *Lone Parent Families in the UK* (London: Her Majesty Stationary Office, 1991).

60. Proceedings of the House of Commons Employment Committee, *Mothers in Employment*.

61. Julia Edwards and Linda Mckie, "The European Economic Community—A Vehicle for Promoting Equal Opportunities in Britain," *Critical Social Policy* 13, no. 3 (1993-1994): 51-65.

62. Proceedings of the House of Commons Employment Committee, *Mothers in Employment.*

63. Ruth Lister, "The Child Support Act: Shifting Family Obligations in the United Kingdom," *Social Politics* (Summer 1994): 218.

64. Ibid., 220.

65. Caroline Glendinning et al., "Implementing the Child Support Act," *Journal of Social Welfare and Family Law* 18, no. 3 (1996): 273-89.

66. This information was kindly supplied to the author by Ruth Lister, Loughborough University, 4 January 1997, by e-mail.

67. Michel Foucault, *Discipline and Punish: The Birth of the Prison* (New York: Vintage, 1979).

68. Fiona Williams, "Gender, 'Race' and Class in British Welfare Policy," in *Comparing Welfare States: Britain in International Context*, ed. A. Cochrane and J. Clarke (London: Sage/Open University, 1993), 91.

69. Quoted in A. Sinfield, "The Latest Trends in Social Security in the United Kingdom," in *Recent Trends in Cash Benefits in Europe*, ed. N. Ploug and J. Kvist (Copenhagen: Danish National Institute of Social Research, 1994), 130-31.

70. Roseneil and Mann, "Unpalatable Choices."

71. Toni Morrison, "Racism and Fascism," *Nation*, 29 May 1995, 760.

DISCUSSION QUESTIONS

1. How does the author approach the concept of "welfare"? Is there justification for her approach?

2. Why was the U.S. welfare state in terms of benefits for poor people curtailed in the 1990s?

3. Describe the process and facets of "the feminization of poverty." What are the causes of this kind of development?

4. What are the political and economic implications of welfare reform in the United States, according to the author?

5. On the basis of the author's presentation, what might be essential elements of effective antipoverty strategies, in your opinion?

FOR FURTHER READING

Children's Defense Fund (1996) *The State of America's Children: Yearbook*. Washington, D.C.

DeParle, Jason (1994, November 13) "Momentum Builds for Cutting Back Welfare System." *New York Times.*

Ehrenreich, Barbara, and Frances Fox Piven (1984, Summer) "The Feminization of Poverty; When the Family Wage System Breaks Down." *Dissent* 31:162-68.

Goldberg, Gertrude S., and Eleanor Kremen (1990) *The Feminization of Poverty: Only in America?* New York: Greenwood Press.

Kamerman, Sheila B., and Alfred J. Kahn (1995) *Starting Right: How America Neglects Its Youngest Children and What We Can Do about It*. New York: Oxford University Press.

Lazere, Edward B. (1995) *In Short Supply: The Growing Affordable Housing Gap.* Washington, D.C.: Center on Budget and Policy Priorities.

Morrison, Toni (1995, May 29) "Racism and Fascism." *Nation* 260(21): 760.

Murray, Charles (1993, October 29) "The Coming White Underclass." *Wall Street Journal.*

Polakow, Valerie (1993) *Lives on the Edge: Single Mothers and Their Children in the Other America.* Chicago: University of Chicago Press.

U.S. Bureau of the Census (1996) "Income, Poverty, and Valuation of Non-cash Benefits: 1995." *Current Population Reports.* Consumer Income Series P60-193, P60-194.

Wilson, William J. (1996, August 18) "Work." *New York Times Magazine.*

Chapter Ten

Racism and Poverty in Britain

Peter Alcock

Any understanding of the distribution of poverty and inequality in society must pay attention to the impact of this distribution on significant social divisions and cultural differences. In modern British society, such an analysis involves recognizing and analyzing the impact of racism within the social structure. In broad terms, modern Britain is a racist society in that there is significant evidence that black and other minority ethnic communities experience discrimination and disadvantage on a disproportionate basis, and this discrimination cannot be explained merely as a result of chance or misfortune.

This does not make British society unique, nor in a sense is it all that surprising. Discrimination and disadvantage for ethnic minority groups is common in many if not most social structures, and certainly there is overt evidence of racism similar to, and in some cases more exaggerated than, that found in Britain in most other European and Western capitalist countries. However, widespread evidence of racism elsewhere should not lead us to overlook the particular features and particular causes of racism in British society, which have produced a unique pattern of discrimination and disadvantage that has resulted in significant inequality and levels of poverty for certain groups within society. Nor, of course, should the widespread experience of racism be interpreted as suggesting that its consequences are not a problem, or that they do not constitute a problem amenable to analysis and policy response. Indeed, it is because race is such an important feature of the structure of poverty and inequality that its impact must be included in understanding, and tackled by, policy development.

What is meant by *race* in this context, however, has been the subject of some debate, both on terminology and on the use of terms adopted. It is probably not a debate that can be entirely satisfactorily resolved, because—as, to some extent, with the debates on the definition of poverty—meaning is inextricably linked to broader theoretical and political questions about the nature of the problem and the appropriate response to it. In the case of modern Britain, this debate is founded in the country's imperial past, its subjugation of colonial populations, and the assumption of "white supremacy" that arose from this past.

In Britain, "race" is often taken to mean skin color, and in particular the difference between white skin and black skin. This has been accentuated by the entry into Britain of a significant number of black residents of former British colonies, especially after the Second World War. These immigrants and their offspring often vary in cultural backgrounds and in skin color. However, they are all potential victims of discrimination or disadvantage based on skin color, and thus they are often generically referred to as "black" when compared with the indigenous "white" populations.

Within Britain's black population there are a range of different communities, with different cultural and religious traditions. These are sometimes referred to as "ethnic minority communities," although they also include nonblack communities such as Jews, Arabs, and Eastern Europeans, all of whom may experience discrimination or disadvantage because of their culture, language, or religion. Despite this, however, in modern Britain, the racism experienced by the black population overlays their situation as minority ethnic communities. It is this racism, of course, and not skin color or cultural differences, that is the problem for black people in Britain, and it is this problem that is generally the focus of research on and analysis of race and inequality in Britain. Thus, it is racism and its consequences for poverty and inequality that we discuss here.

The racism faced by Britain's black population has a history as long as that of the population itself, certainly extending back to the early days of overseas trade and Britain's involvement in the slave trade during the growth of colonization. Early black immigrants to Britain were generally associated with trading and seafaring activities and tended to be concentrated in ports such as Cardiff, Liverpool, and London. This geographical concentration was a trend that was followed by later groups of black immigrants to Britain, primarily as a result of discrimination in housing and employment markets, which forced the new residents into poor inner-city areas that were less popular among the indigenous population. However, this concentration may have compounded the problem of racism by appearing to limit the wider integration of black people into other parts of British society, and, as we shall see, it has certainly contributed to the problems of poverty that have flowed from this lack of social and economic integration.

In the early part of the twentieth century, immigration by Jews and Eastern Europeans introduced new ethnic minority communities into Britain, and many of these new immigrants faced discrimination and hostility from sections of the indigenous population. After the Second World War, however, and following the conversion of the British Empire into a commonwealth of independent countries with close links with Britain, large numbers of black immigrants from the former colonies were encouraged to come to Britain, mainly in order to fill menial and poorly paid jobs that an indigenous population enjoying "full employment" did not find attractive.

It was these immigrants in particular who experienced the discrimination and hostility that forced them into the poorer areas of London and of the large cities in the Midlands, Lancashire, and Yorkshire. It was also they, because of their black skins and their former colonial status, who became the focus of a new racism among the white community, which began to surface in the form of hostility, abuse, harassment, and even violence in the late 1950s. By the 1960s this racism, allied to the weaker economic and geographical situation of the new black populations, was beginning to coalesce into a broader structure of discrimination and disadvantage based on race.

The hostility and racism faced by Britain's ethnic minority communities had not, however, been a feature of the academic and political debate that surrounded the introduction of the welfare state reforms of the postwar period.[1] The welfare state was intended to challenge the "evils"of prewar Britain, identified by Sir William Beveridge, through the development of universal state welfare services. Racism was not recognized as an evil requiring state action, however, although, when black immigration began to increase during the early years after the war, racist reactions meant that black people did not experience equal access to universal welfare services such as council, or publicly funded, housing.

In fact, the major period of black immigration into Britain was relatively short. By the 1960s, fears about unemployment and economic growth had resulted in the imposition of immigration controls. These controls applied to all potential immigrants into Britain (although not, after 1973, citizens of EU countries), but they were enforced with particular severity against black migrants.[2] The effect of this dual system of enforcement was to compound the hostility and suspicion experienced by the resident black population, all of whom could thus be labeled as potentially unwanted or illegal immigrants.

The pattern of immigration also means that the black population in Britain shows some demographic differences from the indigenous population, as revealed in research surveys carried out by the Policy Studies Institute (PSI), the most recent of which was carried out by Trevor Jones.[3] The most significant feature of the black population in Britain is the fact that most blacks are not immigrants at all but were born in Britain and have lived there all their lives. As already mentioned, Britain's black population is not evenly dispersed throughout the country. Access to (largely poorly paid) employment, discrimination in housing and education, and general racism have all resulted in black people's being concentrated in poor neighborhoods in a number of British cities. The geographical concentration of poverty can compound the deprivation experienced by those living in these areas. In the United States, inner-city areas with large black populations are referred to as ghettos; this ghetto existence is a particular feature of the poverty and social exclusion experienced by many black people in Britain, which may be compounded by racist assumptions that identify even their presence as a cause of local deprivation.

In addition to geographical polarization, black people in Britain also experience isolation and exclusion from the indigenous white population as a result of linguistic and cultural differences. Formal communication in Britain, both written and verbal, relies on the use of English. Those who do not speak or read English fluently are thus unable to communicate adequately with formal agencies, if they can communicate at all. This is a significant problem for many black people, especially with regard to the benefit system, as we shall see later. Linguistic exclusion can be compounded by cultural differences and misunderstandings between black people and British institutions; for instance, the assumptions that large Asian families will provide financial support for unemployed elderly or young relatives and that West Indian families are unstable and prone to separation are both unfounded but prevalent.

Cultural exclusion extends to a failure to take account of the particular, and different, needs of ethnic minority community members in the provision of universal services that have been geared to the needs of an indigenous culture, a problem that is sometimes unfortunately referred to as color-blindness. This includes, for instance, the national health service's inability to respond to conditions to which black people are particularly or exclusively prone, such as the disease sickle cell anemia, and the provision of standard services that do not recognize the religious or cultural preferences of some communities, such as school meals that do not include halal meat or school clothing stores that do not stock traditional dress for Muslim girls.

It is now increasingly widely recognized that there is a link between racism and poverty and exclusion in modern British society; for example, the Child Poverty Action Group (CPAG)'s pamphlet on poverty in Britain contains a chapter on race and poverty.[4] However, it has not always been easy to establish a clear empirical link between poverty and race in Britain because most of the research on poverty and many of the statistical surveys, both government and independent, have not traditionally identified the skin color or ethnic origin of respondents. This is not simply an oversight, a case of color-blindness; it is in some cases also a response to a real, and reasonable, fear among the black population that identifying race in official statistics may pose a real or potential threat to the immigrant status of respondents or may be the basis for further racism against blacks.

It was partly as a result of such fears, for instance, that questions about ethnic origin were not included in the decennial census taken in 1981 and in those conducted earlier, although a question on ethnicity was included in the 1991 version. Nor do the government's "Households Below Average Income" figures include an ethnic breakdown, although the Department of Social Security (DSS) Family Resources Survey does now provide data on income and benefits grouped according to ethnic origin. In the United States, in contrast, where debate and data on poverty and race are much more widespread, such categorization is common.[5] However, some of the gaps have been filled in Britain by the publication of the CPAG's pamphlet on poverty and race, which discusses the greater risk of poverty for ethnic minorities in Britain that is associated with employment and unemployment, housing and health, social security, and immigration policy.[6]

Employment, Unemployment, and Race

In the employment field, evidence of the disadvantaged position of black people comes in particular from the Labor Force Survey by Ethnic Origin and the PSI research, together with a range of other independent or local sources.[7] In general, these reveal that the occupational segregation that many black people experienced when they came to Britain in the 1950s has continued into more recent times. Black people coming to Britain were initially concentrated in low-paid shift work in the labor-intensive manufacturing process such as textiles and hosiery. The PSI survey shows that black people were still disproportionately employed in distribution and particular sectors of manufacturing at the end of the 1980s.[8] The CPAG pamphlet also reveals that black employees are more likely to be working shifts, Asian men are more likely than men from other ethnic minorities to be self-employed, West Indian women are more likely than white or Asian women to be employed full time, and Asian women are more likely than others to be engaged in low-paid domestic labor.[9]

The result of this distribution is that average earnings are lower for black people than for white people. For instance, the average hourly pay for all ethnic minority workers in

1993-1994 was lower than that for whites (£6.82 compared with £7.44).[10] The only significant exception here was the position of West Indian women, whose average rate was higher, although, as Irene Bruegel discusses, this may be because their average earnings were boosted by their greater likelihood of full-time employment.[11] There are other differences within the black and ethnic minority populations, however—Chinese and Indian workers often enjoy higher status and pay than West Indians, Pakistanis, and Bangladeshis—but these do not outweigh the overall impact of inequality.[12]

Lower wages obviously create a greater risk of poverty for black workers. This can be compounded by the larger average family size for some, especially Asian, workers to support, and the likelihood that wages will also be needed to support family members outside the household. An earlier PSI survey found that 40 percent of West Indian households and 30 percent of Asian households sent money to dependents.[13] Low wages for families may be supplemented by means-tested benefits, but, as we discuss later, there is evidence that black people are less likely than white people to claim these.

Black people's disadvantaged position in the labor market is mirrored by their position outside it. Many of the low-status, labor-intensive jobs in manufacturing and public services into which black immigrant workers were recruited were those that were disproportionately affected by the impact of recession and public expenditure cuts in the 1970s and 1980s. This has led to higher levels of unemployment among black people throughout Britain, accentuated by the discrimination in recruitment experienced by black people seeking jobs, especially young, British-born blacks who are leaving education and who are unable to find any employment.

The unemployment rates are higher for black people in Britain than for whites. In 1994 the unemployment rate for all ethnic minority men was 25 percent, compared with 11 percent for white men. The difference was exaggerated for young men under twenty-four years of age and was much more serious for some ethnic groups, such as West Indian and African blacks (33 percent) and Pakistanis and Bangladeshis (29 percent). Similar patterns were revealed for women within women's lower overall figures (16 percent ethnic minority versus 7 percent white).[14] There is also evidence that black people experience longer periods of unemployment than whites, and again that this disparity is more severe for the young unemployed.[15]

Thus, the labor market position of black people in Britain has remained significantly inferior to that of the indigenous white population, and, as Amin and Oppenheim conclude, the restructuring of employment patterns that has taken place in recent times has affected ethnic minority communities particularly harshly.[16] This is a consequence of both direct discrimination and structural disadvantage in the labor market, and it has affected young British-born black people as well as their immigrant parents. It has exposed black people to a greater risk of poverty, and it has also resulted in higher levels of benefit dependency among black people. As is discussed in the next section, however, black people also experience discrimination and disadvantage within the benefits system.

Racism and the Benefits System

Because of their relative exclusion from the labor market, black people in Britain experience disproportionate levels of dependency on the benefits system; because of low levels of benefit, dependency is closely related to poverty and deprivation. Direct evidence of the number of black people dependent on the benefits has in the past been difficult to obtain; however, the DSS Family Resources Survey now provides information on benefit receipt and ethnic origin.[17] It also confirms previous evidence that, within the state benefit system, black claimants are likely to be disproportionately dependent on less generous and lower-status means-tested benefits.

The reason for this segregation within benefits is that, as with much of the postwelfare state setup in Britain, the Beveridge social security system failed to recognize the ways in which its structures could operate to exclude certain groups of people.[18] This is particularly true of retirement benefits, which are paid in return for contributions made during employment. Black people's relative exclusion from secure and well-paid employment is also likely to exclude them from insurance benefits, especially pensions (and especially earnings-related pensions), which are based on contributions made throughout a working life that for blacks may have been broken by periods of absence abroad as well as by unemployment.

Other apparently neutral qualifications for benefit entitlement may also operate against black people because of their immigrant status. This applies in particular to the residence tests that are applied to some of the noncontributory disability benefits. As a result of these factors, black households are much more likely than white households to be in receipt of means-tested benefits such as Income Support and Housing Benefit, and much less likely to be in receipt of the National Insurance retirement pension provided by the government.[19] These means-tested benefits are generally lower than those within the insurance scheme, and they are also subject to other restrictions that have a disproportionately disadvantageous impact on black claimants.

Means-tested benefits are available only to those ordinarily resident in Britain, and claimants are thus technically required to establish residency when they make a claim. Normally, this is a formality, but, since some recent immigrants are excluded from the entitlement, evidence of resident status may be required. This has resulted on some occasions in the practice of checking the passports of all "suspicious" black claimants in social security offices. Passport checking operates as an invidious disincentive to any black claimants to seek benefit support, whatever their residence status and can lead to problems if passports are not readily obtainable. Benefits officers are instructed not to request passports routinely as proof of entitlement, but, as Paul Gordon and Anne Newnham found, the practice had become so widespread that "many black claimants volunteer their passports believing it is only a matter of time before they are asked to produce them."[20] They quote one case where "L, a 22-year-old student, born in Britain, was asked for his passport four times in twelve months when he was claiming benefit in Manchester and Huddersfield."[21]

The requirement to produce passports as evidence of entitlement acts as a particular disincentive for many black claimants because of its apparent links with immigration control. Immigrants who do not have a right to remain in the country may expose their status if they claim benefits in order to relieve poverty, because information provided to benefits offices may well be passed on to Home Office immigration control. Much more serious, however, fear of the Home Office connection may dissuade many perfectly legitimate black claimants from ever approaching the Benefits Agency because of misplaced uncertainty about their status in the country.[22] Even for some of those who do have the right to reside in Britain, however, immigration status may affect potential benefit entitlement.

Most important here is the so-called no-resource-to-public-funds rule. Under this provision in the immigrant rules, all dependents coming to join their families in Britain are prevented from claiming support from public funds. Public funds include all the major means-tested benefits, including Income Support, and housing for homeless families under housing law. The intention of the rule is to prevent immigrants from coming to Britain in order to claim state support, but its effect is to exclude from even minimum benefit protection a significant number of new entrants who may have no other practical source of support if the arrangements made on their entry fall through. Once again, however, the more disconcerting wider impact of the rule is its role as an indirect disincentive, growing out of a mistaken belief about exclusion from entitlement, for any black claimants, especially family dependents, to claim benefits, even insurance benefits to which they do have independent rights.

This problem is likely to be further compounded by the rules governing sponsorship, which require spouses, children, or elderly dependents coming to Britain to be sponsored by someone who is willing to give a written undertaking to provide for them in circumstances of need. This is a particularly draconian requirement, although it is legally enforceable in only a minority of cases; it effectively excludes people who already receive benefits from acting as sponsors and thus prevents their families from joining them. It also contributes to the problem of passport checking in benefit administration to identify potential sponsors for certain claimants, even when divorced or separated single parents may be seeking support many years after becoming legally resident in the country.

There are other groups of claimants who are excluded, in full or in part, from benefit entitlement because of their immigrant status. These include "overstayers," people whose right to remain in Britain has technically expired and who may be threatened with deportation if they have to recourse to benefit, and those who are appealing against deportation or refusal of entry, who at best can get only urgent payments.[23] Refugees and asylum seekers are also entitled only to reduced levels of benefit support and in the late 1990s will be excluded entirely from protection; yet, as the National Association of Citizens Advice Bureau (NACAB) has pointed out, this is a group that frequently experiences acute deprivation.[24]

All the rules on immigrant status and benefit entitlement, of course, apply equally to all immigrants, except those from EU countries, who are free to travel within member states and to claim benefit support. However, the effect of the rules within a racist social structure in which immigrant status is associated closely with skin color is to exclude, either directly or indirectly, black people in Britain from free and equal access to the benefit system and thus to increase significantly their risk of poverty.

There are other factors related to immigration status that may further disadvantage black claimants. Those who have dependents or relatives abroad may experience difficulty in providing for or maintaining them within the British benefits system, resulting in potential hardship for claimants in Britain and for their relatives overseas. Children or other dependents abroad cannot be classed as part of a family for benefit purposes; there is no benefit entitlement to cover them, even if payment is being made to support them in another country. The same is true for absences abroad to visit dependents; benefits are generally payable only to those resident in Britain, and this exclusion can result in unwarranted hardships for dependents who remain in Britain during a visit abroad by a head of household, for they may fail to recognize the need to claim independently in their own right during the absence, especially when language barriers mean that leaflets and forms on entitlement, even if provided, are not understood. Conversely, resources held abroad may be treated as available to claimants in Britain, thus reducing or removing a family's entitlement to support, even when these assets are not readily available.

In addition to the formal exclusion of black claimants from full benefit entitlement as a result of rules with discriminatory impact, there are also a number of informal ways in which black people can be excluded from receipt of full benefit support. A survey of black clients using the Citizens' Advice Bureau revealed many such practices, described by the National Association of Citizens Advisory Bureau (NACAB) as "barriers to benefit."[25] These included delays in processing benefit claims while unnecessary checks were carried out to determine entitlement and intrusive questioning to establish certain personal details, such as marital status when marriages had been contracted abroad. They could also include direct racist discrimination against black claimants, as revealed in a PSI study of the Administration of Supplementary Benefit in 1982. Part of the PSI study involved observation of officers, one of whom was quoted as saying, "We get quite a few Pakis like that wandering in like lost sheep."[26]

Even when treatment is formally equal, however, black people may in practice be denied equal access to support because of the failure of the benefits system to address the particular problems they experience. Most important is the language barrier. Social security benefits are administrated in English. English is spoken in all offices, all forms are printed in English and must be completed in English, and, with one or two minor exceptions, all leaflets and publicity material on benefit entitlement are also printed in English. For those who do not speak or write English fluently, which is still quite common in some Asian communities, this can be a major barrier to receipt of support, as the NACAB survey revealed.[27] It is quite rare for benefits offices to be able to provide interpreter services for non-English speakers, and thus those making claims may not be able to pursue their entitlement adequately. However, it is equally likely that the absence of publicity and other literature in ethnic-minority languages means that, for many potential claimants, even this point of contact is never reached. Cultural differences stemming from socialization in different social structures may also lead people to fail to identify a right to state benefits as a potential source of support during times of need.[28]

Thus, although the problem of "take-up" benefits is a significant one throughout the social security system, culture and language problems may make it a more serious one for black (non)claimants.[29] A survey of claimants by National Opinion Polls for the National Audit Office revealed lower levels of take-up of means-tested education and health benefits among non-British and non-Irish respondents and research in Leeds in 1993 revealed problems of "take-up" among Chinese and Bangladeshi communities.[30] These differences are likely to represent a significant accentuation of benefit-related poverty for Britain's black population.

Racism and Social Exclusion

The problem of poverty is not just a problem of insecure or inadequate cash incomes. Deprivation and social exclusion include a broader range of disadvantages, denials, and powerlessness that can result in a reduced quality of life for some. For black people in Britain, the existence of racism at all levels of the social structure means that many of these broader features of deprivation are also likely to affect them disproportionately, and racism itself adds a further burden to the problems with which they have to cope.

Housing is a significant source of inequality and deprivation, and housing conditions differ widely. After their entry into this country as immigrants in the 1950s and 1960s it was in trying to secure housing that many black people first encountered racism and exclusion. This included both the direct racism of private landlords and vendors who refused to rent or to sell to them and the indirect racism of local authorities who put conditions on the allocation of council, or public, houses, such as residence tests, which black immigrants could not meet.[31] For those buying their own houses, a practice that is more common among some sections of the Asian community, restrictions in lending by building societies have also meant that purchasers have had to seek poorer properties in particular areas. As a result, many black people have been forced to live in deprived inner-city areas that are considered less desirable by the indigenous population and where the housing conditions are worst. For instance, ethnic minority households are more likely than whites to be living in overcrowded accommodation, with 10 percent having less than one room per person compared with only 1 percent of white households; among Pakistani and Bangladeshi households the proportion is one-third.[32]

Inequalities in health can also be associated with severe deprivation, and, as recognized in the Black Report on health inequalities, racial differences can be detected here too.[33] Richard Skellington and Paulette Morris reveal evidence of higher rates of mortality, including prenatal and infant mortality, among sections of the black community.[34] This is generally associated with poorer health, although black people also suffer specifically from some debilitating diseases that do not affect the indigenous population, such as sickle cell anemia among people of black African descent. Inequalities in health can further be compounded by unequal use of health care and social services by black people; there is evidence that major services such as community care do not serve many ethnic minority communities as well as they do other communities.[35]

Another state service within which black people do not receive equal treatment is education. As well as being a form of deprivation in itself, failure or underachievement in education is closely linked to poverty and inequality later in life. Poorer education is initially linked to the generally poorer services to be found in the inner-city areas where large numbers of black people live. It is compounded both by direct discrimination within the education system, such as stereotyping black pupils as troublemakers or low achievers, and by the indirect exclusion that results from the ethnocentrism of the school curriculum. The Swann Report on the education of children from ethnic minority groups laid much of the blame for inequalities within education on racism within the wider community,[36] but Skellington and Morris provide evidence that black people's experience of education is structured by racism within the service and not just outside it.[37]

Deprivation in housing, health, and education add significantly to the financial inequality of black people in Britain, and they have remained important factors despite the introduction in the 1960s of race relations legislation designed to prevent direct and indirect discrimination and promote equality of opportunity. However, these indirect consequences may be compounded by some of the more direct scars of racism in ways that may severely deplete the quality of life enjoyed, or endured, by those who suffer under them. Racial harassment is part of a daily burden borne by most, if not all, black people in Britain. It is a burden that white people can never fully understand and many do not even recognize, although they may be contributing to it. Harassment ranges from being made to feel different and excluded to being a victim of violence and disturbance in public or at home. This can discourage black people from sharing public spaces and can bring enduring fear and insecurity to the heart of their daily lives.

The experience of racial harassment is not, of course, confined to the poor inner-city areas where large numbers of black people still live, and, indeed, the support and strength of black neighbors and friends in such areas may in part make such experiences a little easier to bear. Nevertheless, the concentration of disadvantage and deprivation that black people experience throughout British society, especially when it is compounded by the fear and isolation produced by racial harassment, can contribute to an experience of poverty for Britain's black population that is overlain by a feeling of exclusion and entrapment.

NOTES

This chapter was originally published in Peter Alcock, *Understanding Poverty*, 2nd ed. (London: Macmillan, 1997), 151-164.

1. Fiona Williams, *Social Policy: A Critical Introduction* (Polity, 1989).
2. Robert Moore and Tina Wallace, *Slamming the Door* (Martin Robertson, 1975).
3. Trevor Jones, *Britain's Ethnic Minorities: An Analysis of the Labor Force Survey* (Policy Studies Institute, 1993).
4. Carey Oppenheim and Lisa Harker, *Poverty: The Facts*, 3rd ed. (Child Poverty Action Group, 1996).
5. James Jennings, *Understanding the Nature of Poverty* (Praeger, 1994).
6. K. Amin and C. Oppenheim, *Poverty in Black and White: Deprivation and Ethnic Minorities* (CPAG/Runnymede Trust, 1992).
7. Jones.
8. Ibid.
9. Amin and Oppenheim, chapter 2.
10. Oppenheim and Harker, 118.
11. Irene Bruegel, "Sex and Race in the Labor Market," *Feminist Review* 32 (1989).
12. Oppenheim and Harker, 124.
13. Colin Brown, *Black and White in Britain: The Third PSI Survey* (Heinermann EB, 1984), 302.
14. Oppenheim and Harker, 116.
15. Amin and Oppenheim, 4.
16. Ibid., 41.
17. Department of Social Security, Family Resource Survey, Great Britain (1993).
18. The "Beveridge social security system" refers to the UK social security reforms of the late 1940s which were based on the recommendations of the Beveridge Report of 1942. This was the most thorough review of social security policy (before and since) and contained a "blueprint" for

a reformed system, which was (more or less) followed by the postwar Labour government. That benefit structure remains the formal basis of social security provision to this day. There have been many reforms and changes, but the overall structure has not (thus far) been significantly challenged or changed. The main features are social insurance protection based on flat-rate benefits for unemployment, sickness and retirement, means-tested support and supplements for those (now a large number) outside the insurance scheme, and a universal child support (Child Benefit).

19. Oppenheim and Harker, 120.

20. Paul Gordon and Anne Newnham, *Passport to Benefits: Racism in Social Security* (CPAG/Runnymede Trust, 1985), 24.

21. Ibid., 25.

22. Ibid., 29.

23. Ibid., chapter 1.

24. National Association of Citizens Advisory Bureau, *Barriers to Benefit: Black Claimants and Social Security* (NACAB, 1991), 63 and 64.

25. CABs are local "Third Sector" bodies which provide free advice and assistance to citizens in a local neighborhood. Advice can cover any problem, but the work is mainly focused upon rights to social and welfare services, and particularly rights to social security benefits. CAB workers thus become experts in providing independent advice to welfare benefit claimants, and helping them pursue their rights. They are funded by voluntary effort and by grants from central and local government.

26. Stephen Cooper, *Observations in Supplementary Offices: The Reform of Supplementary Benefits, Working Paper C* (PSI, 1985), 53.

27. National Association of Citizens Advisory Bureau.

28. Ruth Cohen and Maryrose Tarpey, "Are We Up on Take-Up?" *Poverty* 63 (1986); also see Ian Law et al., "The Effect of Ethnicity on Claiming Benefits: Evidence from Chinese and Bangladeshi Communities," *Benefits* (1994).

29. Those "taking-up" their social security benefits are the claimants who are entitled to receive them and are currently in receipt of such benefits. It is recognized by government and independent commentators that there are many (only, of course, a guesstimate) who may be entitled, but (for some reason) are not currently in receipt of benefits because they have not initiated a claim. The scale of such "non-take-up" varies between different types of benefit and between different claimant groups (black people being generally accepted as a group with relatively low levels of take-up—i.e., many not getting their entitlement). The new UK government has recently acknowledged some responsibility for responding to this problem and is now piloting an initiative to improve take-up of Income Support among pensioner claimants in the country.

30. Amin and Oppenheim, 54; and Law et al.

31. Norman Ginsburg, "Race and Housing: Concepts and Reality," in Peter Brahmin, Ali Rattansi, and Richard Skellington, eds., *Racism and Antiracism: Inequalities, Opportunities, and Policies* (Sage, 1992).

32. Amin and Oppenheim, 32.

33. Peter Townsend, Nick Davidson, and Margaret Whitehead, eds., *Inequalities in Health: The Black Report and the Health Divide* (Penguin, 1992).

34. Richard Skellington and Paulette Morris, *"Race" in Britain Today* (Sage, 1992).

35. Wagar Ahmad and Karl Atkin, eds., *Race and Community Core* (Open University Press, 1996).

36. Swann Report, *Education for All: The Report of the Committee of Enquiry into the Education of Children from Ethnic Minority Groups*, Cmnd. 9453 (HMSO, 1985).

37. Skellington and Morris, chapter 9.

DISCUSSION QUESTIONS

1. Discuss the role of race and poverty and the relationship of these two dynamics in British society.

2. On the basis of other chapters, how is the relationship between race and poverty in Britain similar to or different from that in the United States?

3. How is the problem of poverty compounded by racism?

4. Discuss how immigrants from the Commonwealth nations were received and treated within the context of the British welfare state in the post-World War II period. How did this framework emerge, and what explains its particular evolution?

5. Discuss how presumably race-neutral welfare rules and regulations can have an impact on race relations and social inequality. Can you cite examples of this situation in the history of the United States?

6. How has race been utilized in relation to class-based politics in British society?

FOR FURTHER READING

Braham, Peter, Ali Rattansi, and Richard Skelllington, eds., *Racism and Antiracism: Inequalities, Opportunities and Policies* (Sage, 1992).

Brown, Colin, *Black and White Britain: The Third PSI Survey* (Heinemann, 1984).

Gordon, Paul, and Anne Newnham, *Passport to Benefits: Racism in Social Security* (CPAG/Runnymede Trust, 1985).

Moore, Robert, and Tina Wallace, *Slamming the Door* (Martin Robertson, 1975).

Rex, John, and Sally Tomlinson, *Colonial Immigrants in a British City* (Routledge and Kegan Paul, 1979).

Skellington, Richard, and Paulette Morris, *"Race" in Britain Today* (Sage, 1992).

Chapter Eleven

Black America, the "Underclass," and the Subordination Process

Hermon George Jr.

In 1980 Douglas Glasgow offered a vision of "the black underclass," which found its lack of socioeconomic mobility, "survival culture," social preference for the ghetto as a reference point, and maintenance by welfare, law enforcement, and health agencies to be its defining characteristics.[1] Two years later, Ken Auletta weighed in with a tome that did not profess to settle any debate about the size of the "underclass" or the causes of its existence but that nevertheless maintained "that neither the political right nor the political left fully comprehends the changing nature of poverty."[2]

Auletta's remark is perhaps more revealing than he intended, since it is precisely *the ideological nature* of the discussion of recent poverty in the United States that is its most important aspect. In the pages of *Society*, the liberal Sar A. Levitan defends "the American welfare system" as he contradictorily notes, "Millions of people work but remain poor. In 1984, 9.1 million poor Americans were in the labor force, including 2.1 million who worked full-time year-round and 1.2 million who were heads of households."[3]

Meanwhile, Levitan's seven conservative critics, dutifully "outraged" by the "disincentives" that the welfare system imposes on the working poor and the rest of the poverty stricken (presumably, the underclass as well), offer palliatives ranging from "workfare" and decreased governmental and increased private charitable funding to decreased governmental intervention in labor markets, thus allowing union busting and the elimination of the minimum wage.[4]

Condition of the Black Poor

Charles Murray and William J. Wilson discuss the condition of the black poor in *U.S. News and World Report*, agreeing on its description, in part, as a "black underclass" but disagreeing as to the nature of its joblessness and on the need for massive governmental full-employment programs. Murray, in fact, announces that he is ready to abandon a sizable portion of this group to its unpleasant fate.[5]

Finally, *Fortune* magazine publishes a special report whose author also announces his willingness to abandon some members of the underclass, "the adult underclass," while trumpeting the virtues of low-wage work as an enforcer of social obligation. The author never makes clear:

- Why the situation of this estimated five million poor—the underclass—should be detached from the twenty-eight million others (1987 figures)
- Why the black underclass and the black middle-income group have grown simultaneously in the last twenty years
- Why the term *respectable poor* is preferable to the older, more transparent distinction between the *deserving* and the *undeserving* poor
- Why agnosticism about the causes of American poverty is more desirable than a cogent explanation.[6]

Some time ago, Paul Baran and Paul Sweezy offered a cogent explanation of American poverty. Specifically discussing the prospects for eliminating black poverty through liberal social engineering and incrementalism, they argued that

> there is really no mystery about why reforms which remain within the confines of the system hold out no prospect of meaningful improvement to the Negro masses. *The system has two poles: wealth, privilege, power at one, poverty, deprivation, powerlessness at the other....*Today, Negroes are at the bottom, and there is neither room above nor anyone ready to take their place. Thus, only individuals can move up, not the group as such: reforms help the few, not the many. For the many nothing short of a complete change in the system—the abolition of both poles and the substitution of a society in which wealth and power are shared by all can transform their condition.[7]

Changing System of Class Relations

More recently, Mike Davis has maintained that there is a new regime of capital accumulation in the United States. This accumulation, fueled by high energy prices, strained tax resources for infrastructure maintenance, a reorganized international division of labor and capital, and debt-led expansion into the periphery (for example, the Philippines, Taiwan, South Korea, Brazil), has weakened the mass consumerist working class and increased income polarization and, consequently, impoverishment.[8] The views of Baran, Sweezy, and Davis suggest that the real issue is not "the black underclass" but the system of class relations in which the existence of the black proletariat and lumpen proletariat is embedded. Understanding the nature of capitalism's changing impact on American classes becomes important.

For black America, this need to understand is urgent. As we face a new century, the role in U.S. society to be played by the vast majority of its black members seems open to question. This question arises, in part, because many of the indicators of socioeconomic conditions in black America have shown an alarming deterioration in material circumstances since the 1980s. Whether one measures unemployment rates, families below the poverty level, the median family income ratio, enrollment in institutions of higher education, or health care standards, it is clear that a significant decline in living standards for many African Americans has taken place.[9] In fact, one of the oldest controversies surrounding African American socioeconomic status—the debate generated by the condition of the black family—has resurfaced with the usual clouding of issues.[10]

Framework of the Debate

The debate over the condition of the black family may be taken as representing a microcosm of the issues needing analysis as one examines the situation of African Americans. The academic mainstream and the complementary cultural apparatus have worked hard to frame the debate as one shaped by "ethnicity." A popular variant of this position espouses "pluralism," suitably modified as being "cultural" or "structural."

Dissenting voices, to whose critique of mainstream theories this chapter seeks to add, have usually centered their analysis on racism and the process of subordination. The remainder of this chapter attempts to provide critical analysis of these two schools of thought.

Daniel P. Moynihan and Nathan Glazer offer an interpretation of ethnicity that may be taken as representative of mainstream scholarship.[11] For them, ethnicity has become a focal point of modern life because of the emergence of the welfare state, the resultant tension between egalitarianism and inequality, the heterogeneity of modern states, and the efficacy of the international system of communication in disseminating ethnic imagery throughout the world.[12] Most important, they state that "our hypothesis is that ethnic groups bring different norms to bear on common circumstances with consequent different levels of success—hence *group* differences in status."[13]

From this perspective, the subject of racism cannot be incorporated meaningfully into one's analysis. Moreover, in an earlier work the authors regarded residential segregation as an "aspect of ethnicity" and declared that "massive, institutionalized racism" did not exist as a major obstacle to black assimilation.[14]

The Ethnicity Argument

A perceptive rebuttal to this position may be constructed, in part, from an essay by Leith Mullings.[15] Mullings argues that ethnicity is actually composed of two dimensions, the cognitive, or "symbolic-ideological," and the social structural.[16] The first of these refers to "shared cultural norms, values, symbols" and is common to all ethnic groups in the United States.[17] However, it is only on examination of the second dimension of ethnicity, the social structural, that it becomes possible to explain the hierarchical stratification of American ethnic groups.

Mullings maintains that an examination of eastern U.S. urban history reveals that African Americans, in distinction to Euro-Americans, were always confined to menial jobs marked by wage discrimination, or excluded from occupational fields entirely.[18] Thus, it is the "division of labor" and the "allocation of resources" that determine a group's position in the hierarchy. Because racism benefits Euro-American groups, they have been preserved essentially as culturally symbolic "cultural minorities," while the subordinate place of African Americans ratifies their existence as an "oppressed minority."[19]

In conclusion, Mullings postulates that U.S. ethnic groups are secondary, not primary or given, social entities, since their very existence has been "precipitated" by the interaction between the existing political economy and "an incoming congery of people."[20] Elsewhere, I have indicated the problems of obscurantism, failure to examine the interaction of groups and the political economy, and the conceptual vapidity that mars the work of Moynihan and Glazer and other mainstream ethnic group analysis.[21]

The Pluralism Argument

The concept of pluralism has recently enjoyed a widespread popularity in American social discourse. In large measure, it was the revolt of the urban African American masses in the 1960s against their subordinate position in U.S. society that is responsible for this conceptual reaction.[22] The manner in which the proponents of pluralism argue for this concept illuminates the point being made.

For example, Michael Novak is unable to bring any clarity to his efforts at distilling a "humanistic perspective" on pluralism, other than to suggest that "individuals in our society tend to develop a plurality of cultural roots." Traditions from Anglo-American and Jewish sources are elaborated. Significantly, those from black and Native American cultures are only mentioned, not elaborated.[23] Novak maintains that America's "common culture" does not belong to a single ethnic group, "although much of it has an Anglo-American origin."[24] Pluralism in the United States, then, seems to be composed of the Judeo-Christian tradition, with ancillary, minor, and relatively unimportant cultural elements from other traditions.

Similarly, Michael Walzer confronts an equally unmanageable task in trying to define pluralism politically without incorporating the historical experience of people of color.[25] In fact, he asserts that "the minority races were politically impotent and socially invisible during much of the time when American pluralism was taking shape—and the shape it took was not determined by their presence or by their repression."[26]

Pluralism versus Racism

In order to explain U.S. political life, we are left with a formulation much like that of Moynihan and Glazer's quoted earlier regarding "different norms" leading to "different levels of success." For Walzer, "historically specific cultures necessarily produce histori-cally specific patterns of interest and work."[27] Ultimately, pluralism is defined by Walzer as a political system that "recognizes each citizen as the equal of every other, without regard to ethnicity, [and that] fosters a unity of individuals alongside the diversity of groups."[28] Within this system, Euro-American ethnic groups display a low level of social cohesion and organization, since

> America's immigrant communities...[have] a center of active participants some of them men and women who have been "born again," and a much larger periphery of individuals and families who are little more than occasional recipients of services generated at the center.

They are communities without boundaries shading off into a residual mass of people who think of themselves simply as Americans.[29]

Such a description may be regarded as an accurate statement of white American identity, but it bears no relation whatsoever to the historical experience of African Americans or other Third World communities of color. Even Walzer is constrained to admit that "racism is the great barrier to a fully developed pluralism" in America.[30] Hence, this admission relieves Walzer's opinions of any pretense of providing a reliable analysis of U.S. pluralism. It is patently obvious what both Novak and Walzer are describing is *not* pluralism, despite their labored, arid disquisitions. An alternative theoretical formulation must be sought.

A greater degree of theoretical sophistication is demonstrated by Milton M. Gordon. Gordon is frank to admit that his early work on pluralism, published in 1964, must be reexamined in view of the black revolts of the 1960s and 1970s.[31] The concepts of power and conflict must be added to assimilationist theory, he concedes.[32] But Gordon's treatment of pluralism is no more satisfying than that of his colleagues. When Gordon contemplates pluralism, it is clear that he is merely proposing a theoretical fig leaf to cover the "embarrassing" (to liberals like him) fact of racial subordination in the United States. Or, as he puts it:

> Within this context (i.e., the bourgeois reformist struggle for civil rights), the prediction of indefinitely continuing structural separation, or structural pluralism, was seen as a concession to the realities of both existing (though hopefully lessening) attitudes of prejudice and avoidance, and the factual presence of an already built-up institutional structure within the communities of racial minorities.[33]

Gordon's advocacy of "cultural pluralism" is really an elaborate apologetics, since the basis for pluralism is not genuine cultural democracy legitimating and supporting all distinctive American cultures but, rather, a "massive...acculturation to Anglo-Saxon norms and patterns."[34]

Moreover, Gordon's attempt to incorporate power and conflict into his theoretical schema must be deemed inadequate, since he takes account of neither the former's latency aspect nor the latter's disjunctive aspect.[35] Hence, he is unable to account for the black revolt of the 1960s and early 1970s other than by relying on discredited postulates such as "rising expectations," "relative deprivation," "status inconsistency," and so forth.[36]

Rationalization of Racism

Gordon's theorizing on this point is guided by his adherence to a classically reactionary view of human nature as "basically motivated by self-interest, irresistibly narcissistic and protective of the self, ready to defend the self by aggressive behavior...and possessed of not unlimited intellectual capacity."[37] Since ethnic groups, like individuals, tend to be aggressive and self-centered (that is, "ethnocentric") and conflicts between them "naturally" escalate, Gordon even shrinks from the idea of equal power for all groups, since this would produce instability. Better that they should settle for "an intermediate degree of power."[38] This is nothing but a rationalization for the unequal actual power relations that characterize racial subordination.

Gordon, in sum, cannot account for the culture of struggle that has propelled black resistance to racial oppression in America for more than 360 years.[39] He makes no connection between capitalist political economy and the relations of ethnic and racial groups.[40] No theoretical advances in treating pluralism have been registered by this author, even though almost a decade separates two of his works on the subject.[41]

We are now prepared to render a judgment of pluralism. Its theoretical utility is compromised by the numerous and unclear or contradictory meanings that are often attached to the word. Oliver C. Cox notes that three common social science uses of pluralism prevail—political, legalistic, and societal. Treatments of the latter two, including one author's plea for respected national cultures (legalistic) and another's assertion that pluralism is basically the grafting of a dominant culture onto an indigenous one in a conflict-ridden setting (societal), are often at odds.[42]

When we combine these conceptual difficulties with the negligible and stereotypical treatment given to African American culture and experience as seen in the works of the orthodox pluralist analysts reviewed earlier, we can readily accept Cox's judgment that "It is...obvious that pluralism cannot...be accepted as a scientific concept....the value of the term...for the study of race relations is quite limited. It has been given no consistent meaning or interpretation."[43]

More to the point, pluralism is essentially an ideology of the status quo. As Herman Schwendinger and Julia Schwendinger argue, the domain assumptions of pluralism are that

> capitalism [is] gradually evolving toward a full democracy based on cooperation between such conflicting interests as capital and labor....[Capitalist democracy is] self-regulating; ... the state forever seeks to maintain a homeostatic "balance of power" between the units within the framework of capitalism...[and] diffusion of power among interest groups and an attitude of tolerance [are] regarded as necessary pre-conditions for behavior in the political arena.[44]

Racial Subordination

The conceptual imprecision of the term *pluralism*, its diminution, distortion, or dismissal of the significance of African American culture and history, and its reliance on politically conservative domain assumptions mark this approach as inadequate to the task of describing the African American experience. As I have argued elsewhere, this experience has been a "subordination process" within the American social order.[45]

The subordination process is essentially a set of political-economic relationships, which, dictated by U.S. capitalism, have determined the specific forms of inclusive exclusion that have characterized the histories of groups incorporated into the social order, in particular, people of African, Latin American, and Asian descent.[46] By *inclusive exclusion* I mean the manner in which working people are incorporated into social production and consumption, but always so as to minimize or prohibit their access to vital decision-making and power-holding institutions. There are four distinct features of the subordination process: economic exploitation, racism, cultural hegemony, and political exclusion. Each will be commented on in turn.

History of Economic Exploitation of Blacks

Mullings's work, referred to earlier, offers a useful historical overview of the subordination process as it affected African Americans, with special attention to economic exploitation. Reviewing "eastern U.S. urban history," Mullings notes that in the earliest phase of American urbanization, 1607-1865, the great majority of Africans were southern agricultural workers, slaves on plantations. Their free black counterparts were prohibited from forming or joining trade unions and subjected to special taxes. The ideology of white supremacy was elaborated and given scientific credibility.[47] As this period drew to a close, African American artisans, domestics, and common laborers were being displaced by Europeans, especially Irish immigrants. African Americans were excluded from public schools and effectively disfranchised.[48]

In the second phase, 1865-1914, industrialization in the South (textiles, steel, iron) relegated African Americans to menial, segregated tasks at the lowest pay. The process of displacement by European immigrants (for example, Swedes, Poles, Italians, and Greeks) from jobs such as barber, bootblack, cook, waiter, and janitor, continued.[49]

The third phase, 1914 to the present, was characterized by northern migration by African Americans in response to the labor demand caused by World Wars I and II. Discriminatory wage differentials and segregation by company or department also appeared, together with continued trade union discrimination and the emergence of disproportionate rates of unemployment.[50]

Mullings provides a lucid, exemplary summation of her sketch as follows:

> For the Euro-American "ethnics," the product of, for the most part, voluntary migration into an expanding capitalist system as unskilled workers, economic leveling with the host population of earlier immigrants from the British Isles and northern Germany has occurred....The situation of Afro-Americans presents a significantly different picture. While Africans arrived on this continent at an earlier date than most Europeans, their presence was a result, not of voluntary migration and entry into a labor market, as free laborers, but of capture and enslavement. After slavery, they have been confined, by racism, to the least desirable and lowest-paying occupations.[51]

Black Wage Labor

Lloyd Hogan has provided another cogent analysis of the subordination process and its central dynamic, exploitation:

> The dominant factor in their [African Americans'] history to date has been the exploitation of their labors by an alien people under three distinct historical modes of social-economic organization—slavery, sharecropping, and wage laboring.[52]

Hogan reports that African Americans entered the capitalist wage labor system between 1910 and 1965 but were consigned to jobs "heavily weighted on the side of great physical exertion, high degree of danger, deadening monotony, minimal opportunity for arbitrary decision-making, [and] significant distance from the levers of power and control over the work of others."[53] These are precisely the types of positions most subject to automation, thus rendering black workers more susceptible to unemployment.[54]

Similarly, Jay R. Mandle finds that African American economic mobility after slavery was hampered by entrapment in a nonbourgeois, neither wholly feudal nor wholly capitalist, third type of political-economic social order, "the plantation economy," whose stigmata negatively prejudiced African Americans' entry into the free-wage labor market of the North.[55] The plantation economy tended to stifle technological innovation by reason of the immobility that it forced on black labor through "nonmarket labor force control" (for example, lynchings, antilabor recruiter laws).

When this impediment is combined with the propertylessness and the relative lack of educational opportunity that the post-Civil War southern economy forced on black workers, their subsequent low-status incorporation into "the occupational structure of the North" is explained.[56]

History of Black Workers

On the basis of the work of Mullings, Hogan, and Mandle, we can argue that the exploitation of African American labor as part of the subordination process was accomplished first in the South, through means of the plantation economy, and subsequently in the North through limited productive space accorded free black persons during slavery. Later, after slavery and the Great Migration (1890-1920, 1940-1960), as European immigration is slowed by the world wars, the subordination process continues in the form of differential proletarianization, with the South industrializing tardily, in pursuit of its more economically developed regional competitor.

It is important to maintain a national framework (that is, North and South, with the broad category of the West conventionally subsumed under the former) for this process because, as Mandle argues, labor market demand and, we would add, political struggle in the North have always intimately affected the fate of black workers in both regions.[57] What remains to be accomplished is the examination of racism as a part of the subordination process, something that neither Mullings, Hogan, nor Mandle attempts. In fact, their analyses of this issue tend toward economism.[58]

Clearly, racism is a central feature of the subordination process. Roxanne Mitchell and Frank Weiss have offered an explanation of racism, or "white supremacy" as they prefer to call it, that is both profound and polemical.[59] They argue that the persistence, pervasiveness, and power of white supremacist ideas in the United States are anchored in a system of

> *relative advantages* that the bourgeoisie dispenses to white people. The *actual substance* of white-skin privileges varies . . . depending on factors such as the strength of U.S. imperialism, the health...of the U.S. economy, the amount of spontaneous militancy among the workforce, and, most importantly, the strength of organized resistance to white supremacist practices.[60]

White Supremacy

Mitchell and Weiss contend that the ideology of white supremacy and the practices that sustain it are a form of political and ideological domination imposed by the bourgeoisie over the entire working class in order to guarantee bourgeois rule.[61] It is not the economic component of these relative advantages but, rather, their *political significance* that is most important. It is through differential access to social institutions and political power that the bourgeoisie binds white workers to it in "whiteness." The class being (proletariat) of white workers is overshadowed by their class position (that is, bourgeois class policy of favoritism for whites).[62]

Reducing white racism to a purely economic question is characteristic of economism, Mitchell and Weiss charge—as in labor aristocracy, superprofits, and bribery theories of white supremacy—and usually ends up advocating some form of "radish socialism" (whites only), or a parallel struggles approach, leaving intact the material basis of racism or denigrating struggle against it as reformist.[63]

Privileges of White Workers

Historically, according to Mitchell and Weiss, the emergence of racism in the United States has evolved through two periods, preimperialist and imperialist. In the former, defined as including the colonial and early capitalist development of the American political economy, racism appeared as an expression of economic competition among workers. This period was also characterized by the national ideology of "Manifest Destiny" and religiously and pseudoscientifically grounded racial superiority, both forms of opportunism.

In the imperialist period, these earlier tendencies were combined with a system of material benefits for the labor aristocracy and material preferences for the masses of white workers to create the present form of U.S. racism.[64] This ideology and its social consequences are the "secret" power of American capital over the working class, claim the authors. Capital has never pursued a consistently economic policy with regard to racial competition; rather, it has pursued a political policy of favoring white labor in order to bind it to capital's interests.[65]

Thus, Mitchell and Weiss contend, to the extent that white workers identify with "whiteness," "a central component of *Anglo-American bourgeois consciousness*," and not with their proletarian status as workers, they will remain supporters and defenders of relative privileges for whites as extended by capital.[66] Racism and black subordination will be perpetuated.

Several critical issues concerning the analysis of Mitchell and Weiss may be raised. The authors do not convincingly portray the difference between "material benefits" and "material preferences," nor is their reluctance to admit the real, demonstrable gains that accrue to whites comprehensible.[67] The admission that such advantages are real under capitalism does not mean, as the authors seem to fear, that an American socialist society would be powerless against them.

Cultural Hegemony

When Mitchell and Weiss deny that race exists, they do not recognize the difference between objective and subjective reality that their own work suggests. Though not a *scientific* category, race is a *social* category whose power in the modern world is incontestable.[68] Ideas become social forces once they grip the masses of people in a society. Polemics aside, the most important aspect of the analysis of racism by Mitchell and Weiss is their insistence that it is not simply, or purely, an economic matter. Other radical social scientists have seemingly understood that "politics and ideology...are not merely 'superstructural' in the sense of being derivative phenomena. Rather, they constitute necessary conditions for reproduction of capital and the capitalist relations of production."[69] Racism, as a political and ideological phenomenon, must be cast in the wide sphere of culture.

In this connection we may posit, with Antonio Gramsci, that cultural hegemony expresses both the "spontaneous" and the coerced consent of the masses in a capitalist society to the worldview of the ruling class as expressed by its intellectuals.[70] That this U.S. worldview has been, and is, saturated with racist ideology has been amply and repeatedly demonstrated.[71] For black America, subjection to the cultural hegemony of the U.S. capitalist class and its intellectuals has meant degradation and oppression at the hands of a racist tradition.

African American Culture of Struggles

With respect to African Americans, the historical and continuing experience of white racism has called into being its opposite, a culture of struggle. An oppression/resistance dialectic forms the core of this culture of struggle; or, as Manning Marable has averred, at "every stage of Western capitalist underdevelopment the African population (and its descendants) resisted."[72] This resistance to dehumanization and exploitation can be seen in the traditions of black religion. Gayraud S. Wilmore asserts that the "radical thrust of blacks for human liberation expressed in theological terms and religious institutions...is the defining characteristic of black Christianity and black religion in the United States."[73]

More generally, Lawrence W. Levine has presented evidence that the aesthetic products of black culture—folk beliefs and tales and, in particular, slave songs, sacred and secular, and, later, gospel—were conceived through a process of "improvisational communal consciousness" with elements of individualism subsequently more visibly accreted.[74] When an appreciation of the political-economic context of this process is infused into this analysis, a task that Levine unfortunately, does not undertake, a sound basis for comprehending the African American culture of struggle will emerge.[75]

Herbert Gutman's contention that a specifically African American culture evolved during the first three and one-half generations in slavery must also be incorporated. This culture grew out of the interplay of high importation rates, African heritage, the construction and dispersal of a symbolic kin network, and the field labor gang system of the plantations.[76] It is this African American culture of struggle, elaborated against and within the context of white racism and subordination, that stubbornly rejects the concepts of "ethnicity" and "pluralism" as suitable explanatory frameworks.

Political Exclusion

Political exclusion provides the final complement to our view of the subordination process. Following Michael Parenti, we may define politics as

> the process of struggle over conflicting interests carried out in the public arena; it may also involve the process of muting and suppressing conflicting interests. Politics involves the activation and mediation of conflict, the setting of public priorities, and goals and the denial of others....Politics involves not only the competition among groups within the present system but also the struggle to change the entire system....Politics...covers every kind of issue...*but the bulk of public policy is concerned with economic matters.*[77]

For African Americans, politics has usually meant trying to place issues on the public agenda, but with little success. Without the opportunity to participate in public debate and to hold office in decision-making institutions, black people have most often had to circumvent these institutions through means of informal, noninstitutional participation or to see themselves and their concerns unrepresented.

In the colonial and antebellum periods, only free black persons were sometimes allowed the right of suffrage. In fact, from 1787 to 1865, only five states consistently allowed free black persons to vote: Maine, New Hampshire, Vermont, Rhode Island, and Massachusetts. Slaves often petitioned unresponsive legislatures for their freedom, in Massachusetts in 1777 and Connecticut in 1779.[78]

Effectiveness of Political Representation

African Americans did not begin to hold office regularly or to vote until the Reconstruction era, whose gains were nearly completely obliterated by the political, white supremacist reaction that followed.[79] The damage inflicted on black political aspirations by this reaction in the late nineteenth and early twentieth centuries has only started to be reversed since the 1960s. Despite a relatively small, but increasing number of elected officials in the current period, black America must still travel a long road before adequate political representation in U.S. institutions is reached.[80]

Moreover, the issue is the effectiveness of representation, not simply representation in itself. Edwin Dorn points out that even proportional racial representation would not necessarily produce policy outcomes favorable to African Americans, because their votes alone would be insufficient to effect change. On such issues as welfare, open housing, and affirmative action, black America cannot expect, by itself, to vote in substantive reforms.[81]

In matters of foreign policy, as a lawsuit brought by 257 African American foreign officers in the State Department demonstrates, underrepresentation, discriminatory evaluation, promotion, assignments, and exclusion from posting to certain areas of the world (for example, the Middle East) act to exclude or hamper black opinion and decision making.[82]

Denial of Political Power

The effect of the exclusion or minimization of black opinion on U.S. political life is the denial of access to levers of political power. This political exclusion mirrors the similar exclusion of black people from the centers of economic and corporate power in America. Hogan has calculated that the African American capitalist class numbers perhaps fifteen thousand. The total U.S. capitalist class numbers between approximately 1.13 to 3.6 million people.[83]

Economic exploitation, racism, cultural hegemony, and political exclusion are the central expressions of the subordination process that U.S. capitalism has imposed on African Americans. Racism is the most visible term in this equation. Caused and exacerbated by capitalism, it has created a system of relative privileges for persons of European ancestry, the most important of which, for the bulk of the white population, is access to political power.[84]

U.S. capitalist cultural hegemony over black people is suffused with racist omissions, stereotypes, lies, and fantasies that limit social vision and justify unequal racial statuses.[85] In opposition to this treatment, a culture of struggle among African Americans has arisen, both to nurture their sociocultural heritage and to provide solace against an exploitative social order.[86] The entire ideological and social edifice of black subordination rests on capitalist exploitation, as it has from the slave period on, and is buttressed in crucial ways by political exclusion.

Resistance to Racial Oppression

The tradition of black social inquiry in the United States has long contained a focus on the need to understand and resist racial oppression.[87] The view of racism presented in this chapter forms a part of this tradition. Studies of race relations and racism in the United States are highly fragmented, reflecting no overarching consensus. This has been true at least since the time that W. E. B. Du Bois forthrightly challenged the "magnolia-and-mint-juleps" scholarship on slavery of Ulrich Bonnell Phillips and others.[88] Mainstream scholarship continues to propagate misleading and unsatisfying interpretations, as evidenced by those reviewed here. Nevertheless, a critical alternative does exist, with the subordination process that we have outlined being a part of it. The struggle continues.

NOTES

This chapter was originally published in the journal *Black Scholar* 19, no. 3 (1994).

1. Douglas C. Glasgow, *The Black Underclass: Poverty, Unemployment and Entrapment of Ghetto Youth* (New York: Random House, 1980), 8, 12 13, 25, 63, 65, 123.

2. Ken Auletta, *The Underclass* (New York: Random House, 1982), 318.

3. Sar A. Levitan, "The Evolving Welfare System," *Society* 23, no. 2 (January-February 1986): 4-10; and Sar A. Levitan, "An Affirmation of Faith," *Society* 23, no. 2 (January February 1986): 26 27; the quotation is from p. 27.

4. The following critiques are from the same issue of *Society* that featured Levitan's commentary (see note 3): Blanche Bernstein, "Some Things Are Wrong with the System," 10-11; Lawrence M. Mead, "The Real Crisis," 12-15; John Pencavel, "Believing What We Cannot Prove," 17-18; Simon Rottenberg, "The Enemy of Society," 22-23; and Walter E. Williams, "Work, Wealth and Welfare," 23-25.

5. Charles Murray and William J. Wilson, "Debating Plight of the Urban Poor," *U.S. News and World Report*, March 3, 1986, 21-22.

6. Myron Magent, "America's Underclass: What to Do?" *Fortune*, May 11, 1987, 130-50.

7. Paul A. Baran and Paul M. Sweezy, *Monopoly Capital: An Essay on the American Economic and Social Order* (New York: Monthly Review Press, 1966), 279 (emphasis added).

8. Mike Davis, *Prisoners of the American Dream: Politics and Economy in the History of the U.S. Working Class* (London: Verso-New Left Books, 1986), 197-98, 214-15, 217-18.

9. Two general statements about these worsening conditions are contained in the annual reports issued by the National Urban League. See Alvin F. Poussaint, "The Mental Health Status of Blacks" in *The State of Black America: 1983*, ed. James D. Williams (New York: National Urban League, 1983), 187-239; and David Swinton, "Economic Status of Blacks—1985," in *The State of Black America: 1986*, ed. James D. Williams (New York: National Urban League, 1986), 1-22.

10. See Robert J. Samuelson, "The New Candor on Race," *Newsweek*, February 10, 1986, 64, an article written in favorable response to the January 25, 1986, airing of a CBS television documentary, "The Vanishing Family-Crisis in Black America," hosted by Bill Moyers. Also reacting favorably is Ellen Goodman, "Black Families Seek 'Old' Values," *Greeley Tribune*, January 27, 1986. For a critical perspective on the current discussion of the black family, see Manning Marable, "Black Families: What's in 'Crisis'—and What's Not," *Guardian*, May 30, 1984, 19.

11. Nathan Glazer and Daniel P. Moynihan, "Introduction," in *Ethnicity: Theory and Experience*, ed. Glazer and Moynihan (Cambridge, Mass.: Harvard University Press, 1975), 1-26.

12. Ibid., 25.

13. Ibid., 17.

14. Nathan Glazer and Daniel Patrick Moynihan, *Beyond the Melting Pot: The Negroes, Puerto Ricans, Jews, Italians, and Irish of New York City*, 2nd ed. (Cambridge, Mass.: MIT Press, 1970), x-xi, xxix.

15. Leith Mullings, "Ethnicity and Stratification in the Urban United States," in *Racism and the Denial of Human Rights: Beyond Ethnicity*, ed. Marvin J. Berlowitz and Ronald S. Edari (Minneapolis: MEP Publications, 1984), 21-38.

16. Ibid., 23.

17. Ibid., 23, 32.

18. Ibid., 24-29.

19. Ibid., 32-34. A further distinction is added when Mullings proposes that African Americans, mainland Puerto Ricans, Chicanos, and Asian Americans form "oppressed minorities," while island Puerto Ricans and Native Americans are "oppressed nationalities." Ibid., 33-34.

20. Ibid., 34.

21. See Hermon George Jr., *American Race Relations Theory: A Review of Four Models* (Lanham, Md.: University Press of America, 1984), esp. 26-31, 181-82, 201-3.

22. Ibid., 178. The same point is made in Martin Kilson, "Blacks and Neo-Ethnicity in American Political Life," in *Ethnicity: Theory and Experience*, ed. Glazer and Moynihan, 236.

23. Michael Novak, "Pluralism: A Humanistic Perspective," in *Harvard Encyclopedia of American Ethnic Groups*, ed. Stephan Thernstrom et al. (Cambridge, Mass.: Harvard University Press, 1980), 772-81, esp. 777.

24. Ibid., 778.

25. Michael Walzer, "Pluralism: A Political Perspective," in *Harvard Encyclopedia of American Ethnic Groups*, ed. Stephan Thernstrom et al., 781-87.

26. Ibid., 782.

27. Ibid., 786.

28. Ibid., 785.

29. Ibid., 786.

30. Ibid., 787.

31. Milton M. Gordon, "Toward a General Theory of Racial and Ethnic Group Relations," in *Ethnicity: Theory and Experience,* ed. Glazer and Moynihan, 84, 110. See also 85-86.

32. Ibid., 86-88.

33. Ibid., 88.

34. Ibid., 85.

35. The hydraulic/generative (or latent) aspects of power and the homeostatic/disjunctive aspects of conflict are treated in my *American Race Relations Theory,* xiv-xv and passim.

36. Gordon, "Toward a General Theory of Racial and Ethnic Group Relations," 97-98. A classic rebuttal to these notions is found in Charles A. Valentine, *Culture and Poverty: Critique and Counter-Proposals* (Chicago: University of Chicago Press, 1968).

37. Gordon, "Toward a General Theory of Racial and Ethnic Group Relations," 97.

38. Ibid., 109; see also 91-92, 101.

39. I use this phrase in *American Race Relations Theory,* 161, 186. Two historical works that begin to delineate African Americans' culture of struggle are Vincent Harding, *There Is A River* (New York: Harcourt, Brace, Jovanovich, 1981); and Manning Marable, *Race, Reform, and Rebellion: The Second Reconstruction in Black America, 1945-1982* (Jackson: University Press of Mississippi, 1984).

40. Urbanization and industrialization appear as afterthoughts in the article; Gordon, "Toward a General Theory of Racial and Ethnic Group Relations," 106.

41. The earlier work by Gordon referred to here and earlier is *Assimilation in American Life: The Role of Race, Religion, and National Origins* (New York: Oxford University Press, 1964).

42. Oliver C. Cox, "The Question of Pluralism," *Race* 12, no. 4 (April 1971): 385-400; esp. 385-89.

43. Ibid., 392, 398.

44. Herman Schwendinger and Julia Schwendinger, *The Sociologists of the Chair: A Radical Analysis of the Formative Years of North America Sociology (1883-1922)* (New York: Basic Books, 1974), 274-75, cited in Marvin J. Berlowitz, "Multicultural Education: Fallacies and Alternatives," in *Racism and the Denial of Human Rights: Beyond Ethnicity,* ed. Berlowitz and Edari, 131.

45. George, *American Race Relations Theory,* 2, 22, 31, 87.

46. The subordination process applies, differentially, to the entire U.S. proletariat, even its European component. It is, however, beyond the scope of this essay to trace its exact workings with regard to white workers.

47. Mullings, "Ethnicity and Stratification," 24.

48. Ibid., 25.

49. Ibid., 25-26.

50. Ibid., 26-28.

51. Ibid., 28.

52. Lloyd Hogan, *Principles of Black Political Economy* (Boston: Routledge and Kegan Paul, 1984), 1.

53. Ibid., 135; see also 11, 113, 114.

54. Ibid., 135-36, 161.

55. Jay R. Mandle, *The Roots of Black Poverty: The Southern Plantation Economy after the Civil War* (Durham, N.C.: Duke University Press, 1978), 10-11, 53, 68-69, 99-100.

56. Ibid., 17, 60, 99-100, 104, 119-20.

57. Ibid., 98-99.

58. Mullings is content to merely point out that racism is not simply economic, while emphasizing its economic roots without specifying the connection between the two (30-31). Hogan attempts the unenviable task of explaining black political economy *without* accounting for racism except to note that race is a concept "contaminated with the filth of deceitful scholarship" and that it is manipulated by the ruling class as it enlists the support of working-class whites in defense of the status quo (68, 97, 103). And Mandle places an investigation of "the sources of racism in the United States" outside the scope of his work, while simultaneously speculating that "on theoretical grounds: racism need not be endemic to capitalism since racial discrimination tends to create shortages of skilled labor" (37, 120).

59. Roxanne Mitchell and Frank Weiss, *A House Divided: Labor and White Supremacy* (New York: United Labor Press, 1981).

60. Ibid., 41.

61. Ibid., 55, 61.

62. Ibid., 82-84.

63. Ibid., 78, 95, 99; chapters 2, 3, 4, and 5 contain provocative critiques of labor aristocracy, superprofits, and bribery theories of white supremacy, In *American Race Relations Theory*, chapter 4, "The Marxist Model," I have criticized "mechanical" (or economist) treatments of racism.

64. Mitchell and Weiss, *A House Divided*, 27, 28, 30, 39, 44.

65. Ibid., 32, 114.

66. Ibid., 84.

67. Ibid., 62.

68. Ibid., 84. On the power of racism in the modern world, see Rod Bush, "Racism and the Rise of the Right," in *World Capitalist Crisis and the Rise of the Right,* ed. Marlene Dixon et al. (San Francisco: Synthesis Publications, 1982), 40-47.

69. Ronald Edari, "Introduction: Racial Minorities and Forms of Ideological Mystification," in *Racism and the Denial of Human Rights: Beyond Ethnicity,* ed. Berlowitz and Edari, 9. Edari, however, fails to sustain this insight and concludes by perpetuating the economist analysis that Mitchell and Weiss so cogently criticize.

70. Antonio Gramsci, *The Modern Prince and Other Writings*, trans. Louis Marks (New York: International Publishers, 1972; orig. 1957), 124.

71. For recent discussion of the depths of racism in American popular culture, see Robert Chrisman, "Subjective Factors in the Re-election of Ronald Reagan," *Black Scholar* 16, no. 1 (January-February, 1985): 9-19.

72. Manning Marable, *How Capitalism Underdeveloped Black America: Problems in Race, Political Economy and Society* (Boston: South End Press, 1983), 121.

73. Gayraud S. Wilmore, "Black Religion and Black Radicalism," *Monthly Review* 36, no. 3 (July-August 1984): 121.

74. Lawrence W. Levine, *Black Culture and Black Consciousness: Afro-American Folk Thought from Slavery to Freedom* (New York: Oxford University Press, 1977), 29 and passim.

75. In passing, it is appropriate to note that this task will *not* be accomplished by constructing a priori subjectivist, metaphysical categories of cultural analysis that tend to disconnect African and African American history from the broad sweep of human history, in the name of "phenomenology."

76. Herbert Gutman, *The Black Family in Slavery and Freedom, 1750-1925* (New York: Random House, 1976).

77. Michael Parenti, *Democracy for the Few*, 4th ed. (New York: St. Martin's Press, 1983), 4.

78. G. James Fleming, "The Black Role in American Politics: Part II, The Past," in *The Black American Reference Book*, ed. Mabel M. Smythe (Englewood Cliffs, N.J.: Prentice-Hall, 1976), 625; Lerone Bennett Jr., *Before the Mayflower: A History of the Negro in America, 1619-1964*, rev. ed. (Baltimore: Penguin Books, 1966), 62-63; Earl E. Thorpe, *The Mind of the Negro: An Intellectual*

History of Afro-Americans (Westport, Conn.: Greenwood Press, 1970; orig. 1961), 65; Vincent Harding, *There Is a River*, 43.

79. Fleming, "The Black Role in American Politics," 627, 629-30.

80. U.S. Census Bureau, *Statistical Abstract of the United States, 1986*, 106th ed. (Washington, D.C.: Government Printing Office, 1985), 252.

81. Edwin Dorn, *Rules and Racial Equality* (New Haven, Conn.: Yale University Press, 1979), 101.

82. Abe Weisburd, "Blacks Sue State Dept. on Bias," *Guardian*, November 5, 1986, 7.

83. Hogan, *Principles of Black Political Economy*, 158. Calculations of the size of the American capitalist class vary from 1.6 percent (Parenti's "owning class") to 0.5 percent (G. William Domhoff's "upper class") of the American population in 1980, 226 million. See Parenti, *Democracy for the Few*, 11, and G. William Domhoff, *Who Rules America Now? A View for the 80s* (New York: Simon and Schuster, 1983), 49.

84. On the causal relationship between capitalism and racism, see Bernard Magubane, *The Political Economy of Race and Class in South Africa* (New York: Monthly Review Press, 1979), 3.

85. For a revealing critique of Hollywood's long history of stereotypical portrayal of black people, see Donald Bogle, *Toms, Coons, Mulattoes, Mammies and Bucks: An Interpretive History of Blacks in American Films* (New York: Bantam Books, 1974).

86. An excellent illustration of the African American culture of struggle is given by Harry Haywood when he explains the ability of black Southern sharecroppers to organize in the 1930s by reason of their "tradition of underground organization." See Harry Haywood, *Black Bolshevik: Autobiography of an Afro-American Communist* (Chicago: Liberator Press, 1978), esp. chapter 15, "Sharecroppers with Guns: Organizing the Black Belt," 391-415. The quoted phrase appears on 401.

87. Thorpe, *The Mind of the Negro*, 441-42.

88. See Ulrich B. Phillips, *American Negro Slavery* (New York: Appleton, 1918), and the very different portrait of slavery in W. E. B. Du Bois, *Black Reconstruction in America* (New York: Atheneum, 1969; orig. 1935).

DISCUSSION QUESTIONS

1. How does the author define and describe the concept of a black underclass? How is the author's approach similar to or different from those of other contributors to the book?

2. What are the major explanations for black poverty discussed by the author?

3. What is "pluralism"? How is it defined and utilized to support the continuing significance of racism?

4. What is racial subordination, and what is the relationship of this idea to certain national and international economic developments?

FOR FURTHER READING

Auletta, Ken, *The Underclass* (New York: Random House, 1982).
Baran, Paul A., and Paul M. Sweezy, *Monopoly Capital: An Essay on the American Economic and Social Order* (New York: Monthly Review Press, 1966).

Davis, Mike, *Prisoners of the American Dream: Politics and Economy in the History of the U.S. Working Class* (London: Verso-New Left Books, 1986).

George, Hermon, Jr., *American Race Relations Theory: A Review of Four Models* (Lanham, Md.: University Press of America, 1984).

Glasgow, Douglas C., *The Black Underclass: Poverty, Unemployment and Entrapment of Ghetto Youth* (New York: Random House, 1980).

Gutman, Herbert, *The Black Family in Slavery and Freedom, 1750-1925* (New York: Random House, 1976).

Harding, Vincent, *There Is A River* (New York: Harcourt, Brace, Jovanovich, 1981).

Hogan, Lloyd, *Principles of Black Political Economy* (Boston: Routledge and Kegan Paul, 1984).

Jennings, James, *Race, Politics and Economic Development: Community Perspectives* (London: Verso, 1994).

Mandle, Jay R., *The Roots of Black Poverty: The Southern Plantation Economy after the Civil War* (Durham, N.C.: Duke University Press, 1978).

Marable, Manning, *Race, Reform, and Rebellion: The Second Reconstruction in Black America, 1945-1982* (Jackson: University Press of Mississippi, 1984).

Novak, Michael, "Pluralism: A Humanistic Perspective," in *Harvard Encyclopedia of American Ethnic Groups*, ed. Stephan Thernstrom et al. (Cambridge, Mass.: Harvard University Press, 1980).

Part IV

Poverty and Race
Gender as Fundamental

Chapter Twelve

Fighting Back
From the Legislature to the Academy to the Streets

Mimi Abramovitz

When you hear the words *organizer, leader, rebel,* or *participant,* what type of person comes to mind? These words typically evoke images of white men, because for centuries most people believed that women did not, and should not, fill these activist roles.[1] It was not that women were not activists, however, but that their activism was hidden. Traditional, liberal, social citizenship, and Marxist theories all addressed social conflict and, despite their different interpretations, consistently located political struggle within established organizations, movements, and institutions, all of which excluded women. Having failed to look for, much less locate, women's activism where it in fact took place, they found few women activists; they then decided that this must mean that women are conservative, politically unmotivated, and thus unworthy of study. This exclusion of women from the traditional scholarship on activism not only distorts the historical record but disempowers women by denying them knowledge of an important part of their heritage.

The liberal political theorists dealt with the role of social conflict by minimizing it. They argued that industrialization eliminated the most basic sources of tension between workers and employers and generated the political mechanisms needed to resolve the new conflicts that emerged.[2] It was not that discord disappeared but that technology narrowed the economic gap between the haves and the have-nots and generated a set of political institutions and a shared body of ideas, beliefs, and values that effectively replaced class conflict. The welfare state emerged naturally from a process of mediating conflict, the result of agreement among diverse social groups that social welfare provision was necessary to protect and compensate individuals and families for the risks they incurred while living and working in a market economy.

The social citizenship theorists agreed that welfare state benefits were won politically. Less interested than their liberal counterparts in showing that democratic societies have no need for class conflict and more willing to acknowledge the role of "pressure from below," they suggested that political conflict was in fact critical to the development of the welfare state.[3] Their analysis held that social rights (e.g., social welfare programs) emerged from political struggles that were in turn predicated on earlier successful battles for legal and political rights. Having fought for and won these democratic rights of citizenship, male workers insisted on economic security, which included a government-protected, minimal standard of living. Governments responded to the pressure by smoothing out the rough edges of capitalism and ensuring that market inequality did not undermine economic stability, political harmony, and social solidarity. To the extent that these hard-won social welfare benefits had the potential to insulate workers against market forces and provide them with leverage in their struggles with employers, they became a power resource that could embolden workers individually and collectively to take the risks involved in fighting economic exploitation.

The traditional Marxist theorists focused more directly on conflict as class struggle, which they argued arose from the contradictions of capitalism. One of these contradictions—the contradiction between the private nature of profitable production and the "social" character of work—made collective action possible[4] as the continued accumulation of capital moved economic production to ever larger factories, thereby bringing workers together in one place and exposing them to their shared exploitation and a common enemy. A second contradiction—that between production for profit and production for need—also created the potential for collective action. Profitable capital accumulation requires certain levels of unemployment to keep profits up and labor costs down. Because this leads to an unequal distribution of income and wealth and deprives workers of an adequate standard of living, it periodically stimulates demands for higher wages, government regulation of the market, and greater access to political power. To forestall such turmoil, business and government may try to repress striking workers and popular movements, or they may try to diffuse the unrest by meeting at least some of the workers' needs. The resulting reforms become the building blocks of the welfare state. But the outcome of this struggle is neither inevitable nor predetermined; it is the result of a contest between the demands of capital and those of popular movements, as mediated by the state.

The Feminist Corrective

The discussion of social conflict in all three traditional theories focused on established political institutions—primarily trade unions, electoral parties, social movements, and the state—and therefore missed the activism of women, which often took place in other arenas. It was only when feminists began to investigate the "spaces" that women inhabit—their clubs, auxiliaries, workplaces, unions, and social networks—that they discovered a long and inspiring history of activism. White middle-class women's activism surfaced first because most scholars expected these women to be the most important and because privileged women left behind the kinds of materials— letters, diaries, and organizational files—that historians depend on to piece the past together. Gradually, however, feminists began to capture the collective activism of working women,[5] community-based homemakers,[6] and welfare state clients,[7] as well as that of the middle-class reformers who worked in women's organizations and large-scale women's movements.

As they uncovered women's activism, feminist scholars began to see how the gender division of labor structures the activism of men and women differently. Although both men and women become active when the contradictions between economic production and social reproduction prevent them from carrying out their gendered obligations, the locus of their activism is different. The standard male-oriented theories presumed that all political struggle took place at the point of production and therefore focused on workplace issues. Workers typically took action through their unions—for instance, when low wages and unsafe working conditions prevented them from performing their breadwinning responsibilities. But feminists found that women also engaged in struggle at the point of consumption.[8] Women, especially working-class women, became active when they were not able to secure the food, clothing, shelter, or other resources they needed to carry out their homemaking and caretaking responsibilities. To carry out their socially assigned tasks, women engaged in collective protest at local grocery stores, housing agencies, and welfare offices. Because this activism was often sporadic, sometimes spontaneous, not always highly organized, and rarely sustained, many scholars and political pundits dismissed it as politically insignificant. However, as the French historian George Rude reminds us, under certain conditions small everyday collective actions can have far-reaching effects and can create unanticipated possibilities for social change.[9]

The following account of middle- and working-class women's activism "at the point of consumption" is far from complete. Nevertheless, it provides us with an important glimpse of the collective actions taken by women of different classes and races and the relationship between their concerns and the expanding welfare state. Even before the advent of substantial government aid, women were active when their families needed food, clothing, and shelter, or economic and racial justice. As the state increasingly underwrote the costs of social reproduction in the home, women began to target the welfare state. The gender division of labor, the tasks of social reproduction, and, in some cases, the shared status of being "on welfare" encouraged women to unite to enforce their rights. Thus, women turned both their communities and the welfare state into arenas of political struggle.

Middle-Class Women Take Action

The gender division of labor that sent men into the labor market and isolated women in their homes led directly to the exclusion of women from the male sphere of formal politics. The social networks and the female "culture" that then developed among women were highly supportive of social activism and social reform.[10] In the years before the Civil War, women could not vote or join political parties, but religious and "moral reform" activities were considered suitable for them. Evangelist revivals swept the nation beginning in the 1820s, becoming one of the earliest "movements" to draw women out of the home. Although the revivals were led by men, women filled the churches, published the religious tracts, and founded the Sunday schools. Women also created roles for themselves in the moral reform movement that evangelism encouraged. For example, driven by notions of female moral superiority, the New England American Female Moral Reform Society (which claimed 445 auxiliaries) and other such organizations worked to rehabilitate prostitutes and eliminate sin. Women also played leading roles in the abolition and temperance movements, as well as in organizations that assisted the poor and the mentally ill.

After the Civil War, white middle-class women became active in charity associations, government boards, and the suffrage movement. From 1870 to 1900, they joined the National Women's Suffrage Association and the more conservative American Women Suffrage Association and conducted 480 campaigns in thirty-three states. The Women's Christian Temperance Union (WCTU) drew even more women into the militant fight against alcohol and saloons, arguing that male drinking depleted household funds. By 1900 the WCTU had more than 168,000 dues-paying members in seven thousand locals in forty-eight states.

In addition, scores of women attended the art and literature discussions organized by the women's clubs that proliferated beginning in the late 1860s.[11] By the 1890s, these clubs had coalesced into a national organization, the General Federation of Women's Clubs (GFWC). By 1911, GFWC-affiliated clubs had involved women in cultural, civic, and social welfare activities in towns and cities in all forty-eight states. Women also founded the National Consumers' League (1890s), the Congress of Mothers (1897), the Women's Trade Union League (1903), new suffrage organizations, neighborhood settlement houses, and many other social welfare and civic organizations.

With its ties to the grass roots, this network of women and organizations suggested the direction that activism would take among white middle-class women. Barred from careers in academia, business, and the professions, many educated women carved out an area of expertise as social reformers.[12] By the early 1900s, these women had expanded their arena of responsibility from the home to the larger community. Some groups, led by the National American Women's Suffrage Association (NAWSA) and the National Women's party (NWP), believed that women should be treated as equal to men and therefore focused nearly exclusively on women's rights, especially the vote (finally won in 1919). Other groups believed that working women and mothers of young children needed special protection because they differed from men[13] and led small and large battles against slums, dirty milk, and child labor, and for clean cities, decent housing, health insurance, shorter work days, and the minimum wage. These women justified their own activism with the argument that their socialization left them better equipped than men to look out for the welfare of humanity and especially suited for *municipal housekeeping*—a phrase they often used for social reform. Referred to today as "maternalists," members of this network staffed the settlement houses, supported trade unions, and engaged in a wide range of research, lobbying, and community work. Some, such as Julia Lathrop, the first director of the Children's Bureau, moved into important public posts. Many of these white women and their spiritual descendants carried the reform tradition forward when they worked for Franklin Roosevelt and the New Deal in the 1930s.

African American women were also active reformers.[14] If gender segregation fostered female social reform organizations among white women, racial segregation forced African Americans to form their own networks. The mobilization of black women had deep roots in the church and drew on the tradition of slave women's networks, free black women's associations, and antislavery work. Driven by "duty" and "obligation to the race," black women organized on behalf of what they referred to as "racial uplift," that is, charity, self-improvement through social service, education, and progress. Before the Civil War, black church women raised funds, organized voluntary missionary societies, and taught Sunday school. Free African American women also participated in black-led antislavery, suffrage, and temperance organizations and, occasionally, those organized by whites, although they frequently encountered hostility and outright exclusion. After the Civil War, middle-class African American women worked to bring resources to the thousands of emancipated but impoverished former slaves, most of whom lived in the rural South. Almost every black women's organization worked to alleviate one or more of the many social problems afflicting an increasingly urban, impoverished, politically powerless, and segregated black population.

By the turn of the century, black people were suffering rampant racial repression: lynching, white primaries, race riots, and urban poverty. In response to the deteriorating condition of "the race," black women established at least as many voluntary associations as their white counterparts, and possibly even more, although they lacked similar resources or political connections. Nonetheless, this network of women's clubs, church organizations, and mutual-aid societies provided the foundation for powerful national organizations, including the National Association of Colored Women (NACW), founded in 1896. By 1914, the NACW represented fifty thousand middle-class, educated black women in twenty-eight federations and more than one thousand clubs. NACW activities ranged from running antilynching campaigns to refuting negative stereotypes of black women as sexually loose to fighting for women's suffrage and other social reforms. Its members helped their communities establish separate educational and health care facilities, settlement houses, and social service organizations. The women in the NACW were also instrumental in the formation of the National Association for the Advancement of Colored People (NAACP) in 1910 and the National Urban League in 1911. Others joined the women's arm of the more separatist Universal Negro Improvement Association (UNIA), headed by Amy Jacques Garvey, Marcus Garvey's wife. Like their white counterparts, black women later worked in the New Deal: for instance, the National Council of Negro Women, formed by Mary McLeod Bethune in 1935, became the most important black women's lobby in Washington, D.C., and Roosevelt appointed Bethune head of the Office of Minority Affairs in the National Youth Administration at a time when few blacks of either gender held high political office.

There was a potential for cooperation between the white and the black women's networks because both espoused maternalist values, endorsed a strict work ethic, and promoted services for the poor. But these shared values could not overcome the racial divide. While white women's organizations ignored the issue of race, it was the central issue for the African American women reformers, who believed that race, poverty, and gender were inextricably intertwined. The black women espoused a maternalism that to a certain extent mirrored that of whites, but they were more accepting of single motherhood and of women's having to work outside the home, and they therefore opposed making income tests or moralistic behavioral standards prerequisites for government help. They upheld the family ethic not as a behavioral prescription but because it was a means by which women could claim respect and justice in white America.

Black women's groups occasionally made overtures to white women's organizations, only to be ignored or slighted. For instance, when the white women's organizations prepared an exhibit for the Colombian Exposition at the 1893 Chicago World's Fair, they turned down a request from the black women's clubs to be represented on the board. The next year, the General Federation of Women's Clubs refused to let a well-known black woman—who was representing an established black women's group from Boston—into their convention. Some white suffragists pandered to southern segregationists, arguing that the votes of native-born, educated white women could be used to outweigh those of uneducated blacks in the South and immigrants in the North. Others supported the use of literacy or educational qualifications to reduce the number of such voters. A controversy arose over the participation of black women in a suffrage parade in 1913, and in the early 1920s a major suffrage organization, the National Women's Party, excluded blacks. Even those white women who privately deplored discrimination tacitly accepted the exclusion of African Americans, and African American women reformers came to regard their white counterparts with considerable distrust.

What impact did these women, white and black, have on the welfare state? Feminist scholars have answered this question differently. Some have suggested that they institutionalized government intervention on behalf of women and children and therefore helped pave the way for a broader welfare state.[15] Others contend that, although well intentioned, they left a harmful legacy: for instance, Mothers' Pensions stigmatized single mothers, while employers used protective labor laws to exclude women from better paying jobs.[16] Still others argue that, by alleviating the worst miseries of the poor, the reformers stood in the path of more militant demands.[17] In terms of the maternalist strategy itself, some scholars have argued that it idealized motherhood and reinforced women's traditional roles, while others maintain that the women reformers knowingly extolled the virtues of private domesticity in order to legitimize their own activism, which violated prevailing gender norms, and to disarm resistance to their proposals, which called for a greater role for the state.[18] Regardless of the reformers' intent, however, it is generally agreed that they helped create highly gendered notions of women's citizenship, on the one hand, and deepened the state's involvement in the private lives of less privileged women, on the other.

Poor and Working-Class Women Rise Up Angry

Working-class women had their own social welfare agenda in the late nineteenth and early twentieth centuries, one that arose directly from the conditions of their lives. For instance, many employed women joined unions and demanded better wages and working conditions. In 1909, in one of the more dramatic actions, twenty thousand New York City shirtwaist-makers, almost all women (many young and immigrant), staged a militant thirteen-week strike. The "uprising of twenty thousand," as it became known, forced employers to deal with the newly formed International Ladies' Garment Workers' Union.

In the early twentieth century, as younger single women were becoming militant on the job, mothers and wives—mostly but not entirely immigrants—engaged in collective action in their communities when economic conditions prevented them from carrying out their family responsibilities.[19] For example, they organized food boycotts and rent strikes that were aimed at local merchants and landlords.[20] One of the earliest, the food boycott of 1902, lasted for almost a month. Inside one day, thousands of women streamed through the streets of New York's Lower East Side, breaking into kosher butcher shops, flinging meat into the streets, and refusing to buy their goods until the prices came down. The protest quickly spread to neighborhoods in Brooklyn and the Bronx. To keep the boycott going, the women called mass meetings, canvassed their neighborhoods, set up picket lines, and raised funds. When, during the protests, twenty thousand people gathered for a demonstration, the *New York Times* called for speedy police action against this "dangerous class"—the women, according to the *Times*, "were very ignorant" and "mostly speak a foreign language." The police arrested seventy women and fifteen men.

The meat boycott of 1902 was not an isolated event but the forerunner of many other price-driven protests. In 1904, 1907, and 1908, housewives organized rent strikes in New York, Philadelphia, Boston, and Providence, Rhode Island. In 1910, Jewish women in Providence declared war on the kosher butchers, and in August 1914 more than one thousand Italians in Providence took to the streets and brought pasta prices down after shattering a wholesaler's shop windows and throwing his stock of macaroni into the street. Price increases during World War I sparked militant neighborhood boycotts and mass demonstrations by women in Boston, Chicago, Philadelphia, and many other cities. The high cost of living drew local women into the Mother's Anti-High Price League, organized by the Socialist party, which among other things demanded a government response—in this case, food assistance. The NACW and NAACP helped lead similar protests in black communities.[21]

The women who took part in these boycotts and strikes turned their status as housewives and their neighborhood networks to good advantage. Although the housewives were not necessarily sympathetic to either trade unions or left politics, they nevertheless felt compelled to take action against the high prices that had eroded their buying power, forced them to work outside the home, and otherwise interfered with their ability to perform their domestic responsibilities. The communities accepted, and even expected, these militant actions because the merchants and landlords were members of the same ethnic groups and as such were expected not to take advantage of their customers. In other words, the assumptions of a "moral economy" in which mutual obligations governed consumption effectively legitimized the boycotts.

The "consumer economy" that replaced this "moral economy" after World War I created a new set of social expectations for women. Electrification, refrigeration, indoor plumbing, and the telephone transformed housework. To sell new goods and services to a public still wedded to habits of thrift or too poor to buy much, business and industry built supermarkets, began to extend credit, and advertised.[22] Advertisers portrayed the American standard of living as the model for all families and targeted women because they were the family shoppers. A "feminine mystique" was created, one that defined housework as an expression of a woman's personality and love of her family and linked identity, status, and fulfillment to material acquisition. Convinced by Madison Avenue of the benefits of consumption, women of all classes began to demand more goods and services for their families.[23]

The cost-of-living protests that resumed immediately after the end of World War I were thus driven less by retribution for merchants who had violated the rules of the moral economy than by the discrepancy between the promises of consumerism and the realities of rising prices. The wives of the more skilled and therefore better paid workers were especially frustrated, and some turned to the trade union's women's auxiliaries for help. These auxiliaries, which had begun to support male workers, became a way for women to become involved in the central political, economic, and social questions of the day.

One of the more visible women's auxiliaries was organized in the 1920s by the wives of railroad workers who belonged to the Machinist Union. With chapters in thirty-five states, the District of Columbia, and several Canadian provinces, the machinists' wives demanded a "saving wage," rather than a "living wage," so that they could take advantage of buying on credit to purchase appliances and other products that would enhance their families' standard of living. The wives of the men in the Brotherhood of Sleeping Car Porters, the only black-led union in the country at the time, also wanted to participate in the new consumer culture. The Sleeping Car Porters' auxiliary, which was known as the Women's Economic Council, also assisted families that were having problems with employers, formed alliances with elite black women, and addressed the black community's concerns about race.

By the mid-1920s, all the more socially conscious women's auxiliaries had begun to call for government-sponsored maternal and health care programs for children, for local health departments, and for children's bureaus. In 1928 there were enough active groups for the National Women's Trade Union League (NWTUL), an alliance of working women and middle-class reformers linked to the labor movement, to call the first national conference of trade union auxiliaries.[24]

But the major protest against rising prices and unfulfilled dreams took place in tenant and consumer organizations. These, like the auxiliaries, increasingly targeted the welfare state.[25] Large numbers of women were recruited from the Community Councils for National Defense, originally created by the federal government to support the war effort, as well as from religious groups and the trade union auxiliaries. By May 1919, the Brooklyn Tenant Union (BTU), one of the first tenant advocacy groups, had many of its four thousand members ready to withhold their rents until increases were rolled back. To make their case, they barricaded themselves into apartments, made speeches from tenement windows, and threatened to pour boiling water on anyone who tried to evict them.

In 1922 the New York Women's Trade Union League (NYWTUL) founded the Housewives' Industrial League, which called for a public investigation into the health, housing, and other conditions of nonwage-earning women in the home. Mothers in the Communist party created the United Council of Working-Class Wives to support workplace strikes but soon focused on the cost of food, fuel, housing, education, and other social welfare issues. Their activities attracted large numbers of nonparty women. That same year, the New England Conference of Working-Class Women, representing forty-eight organizations, pledged to fight not only for lower food prices but also for maternity insurance and an end to child labor.

The collapse of the economy in 1929 led to a new round of community activism. Working-class women found various ways to protect their families from the ravages of the Depression. In rural communities they exchanged skills, services, clothing, and food, while in urban areas they began to demand state action. Building on existing networks, housewives in Jewish, Polish, Finnish, Swedish, Irish, Slavic, and African American communities once again supported strikes, organized consumer boycotts, and blocked evictions. One of the largest consumer actions took place in 1935, when housewives boycotted butcher shops in many large cities, closing some 4,500 in New York City alone. Black working-class women formed their own Housewives' Leagues, launched "Don't Buy Where You Can't Work" campaigns in Baltimore, Chicago, Cleveland, Detroit, New York City, and Washington, D.C., and demanded seventy-five thousand jobs for blacks who had lost theirs during the Depression. In the South, black women joined the ten-thousand-member interracial Southern Tenant Farmers' Union, which was founded in Arkansas to resist the evictions that began when the Agricultural Adjustment Act paid farmers to destroy crops in order to increase prices. In the end, these cost-of-living protests galvanized women in Chicago, Cleveland, Detroit, Los Angeles, Milwaukee, Minneapolis, Newark, Philadelphia, Paterson, New Jersey, St. Louis, Missouri, and Seattle—to name just a few of the places they rose up angry.

In some cities, the uprisings were short-lived. In others, they led to sophisticated organizations—most notably, the Detroit Women's League against the High Cost of Living, the Chicago United Council against the High Cost of Living, and the Women's Work Committee of the Washington Commonwealth Federation. The United Council of Working-Class Wives was formed in June 1929 and by 1931 had forty-eight branches in New York City alone. In 1937, as the Depression deepened, its successor, the Progressive Women's Council, led three thousand women in sit-ins at New York City's twenty-nine largest relief centers, demanding a 40 percent increase in benefits, a cash allowance for clothing, and twenty-four-hour service for emergency cases. This housewife activism peaked in an explosion of protests in the early 1940s after Roosevelt cut social spending in response to conservative critics.[26] The advent of World War II led to a suspension of protest, but huge price increases in 1946-1947 and in 1951 sparked two of the largest consumer strikes in U.S. history.

The housewives' movement was a national phenomenon in which women politicized the home, the family, and motherhood in unprecedented ways. They increasingly put pressure on the government to regulate the meat and milk industries, to provide decent and affordable housing, and to give them the health, education, and welfare services they felt they needed to fulfill their gendered obligations. On the one hand, this activism perpetuated women's traditional roles. On the other hand, however, by holding both the system of production and the state responsible for meeting basic human needs, it implicitly endorsed a more radical vision of how society should work.

A Woman's Work Is Never Done: Activism after World War II

Contrary to popular wisdom, middle- and working-class women remained active after World War II. By this time, however, the "welfare state economy" had begun to shape their efforts. Although virulently antigovernment, anticommunist, and antifeminist attitudes limited what they could accomplish, between 1945 and 1960 many women worked in peace, civil rights, religious, and other organizations. They increasingly held the government responsible for correcting social conditions.[27] One group of women's organizations clustered around the National Women's party (NWP), which had been founded during the suffrage battle and was the only national women's rights group that remained active in this period. Although the organization shrank dramatically and became marginalized because it harbored racist, anti-Semitic, and right-wing leanings, it nonetheless continued to press Congress to support an Equal Rights Amendment (ERA), which it had first introduced in 1921.

The second, and much larger, postwar group of women's organizations was allied to the Women's Bureau of the Department of Labor. From the Business and Professional Women to the United Auto Workers' Women's Bureau, these reform-oriented women considered feminism too narrowly focused on women's rights at the expense of working-class women's concerns. They actively opposed the ERA during the 1940s and 1950s, fearing that it would undercut labor laws that protected employed women. Instead, they continued to argue for pay equity, improved working conditions, and special protection for women on the job.

A third group, closely connected to the second, included women who became active in the Democratic and Republican parties, each of which had a women's division. By the 1950s, women were the backbone of both local and national electoral activity, but they were still locked out of major decision-making roles. Among many other activities, therefore, the women's divisions and their supporters fought to place women in top policy-making posts. They hoped that by presenting lists of qualified women to party leaders, supporting women who were running for elected office, and organizing women into a political constituency, they would improve the status of all women and help transform society.

A fourth group was made up of African American women. Often unrecognized outside their own communities because the women's movement remained effectively segregated, these women continued to work on issues of central concern to them. They also played key leadership roles in the civil rights movement. They worked with the National Council of Negro Women, the National Association of Colored Women, and black sororities to protest racial discrimination, although, like white women, they were divided over the ERA, with the National Association of Colored Women in favor and the National Council of Negro Women opposed. They played a major behind-the-scenes role in the Southern Christian Leadership Conference, the church-based organization formed by Martin Luther King Jr. in 1957, and, although they received little credit at the time, it was the Women's Political Council of Montgomery, Alabama, a group of professional black women, that organized the historic Montgomery bus boycott. The 381-day protest—triggered when Rosa Parks, a department store seamstress and the secretary of the Alabama NAACP, was arrested for refusing to move to the back of bus—became a critical event in the postwar civil rights struggle.[28]

Many black women who later became nationally known leaders started out as local civil rights activists in the late 1950s and early 1960s.[29] They assisted the Freedom Riders, were central to the movement to desegregate public accommodations,[30] and organized voter registration drives, including the one in Mississippi that led to the formation of the Mississippi Freedom Democratic party (MFDP). Headed by Fannie Lou Hamer, the MFDP delegation to the 1964 Democratic National Convention not only successfully challenged the party but elected the first black legislator in a southern state. Black women students joined the first sit-ins in the 1960s—a strategy that became the guiding philosophy of the Student Nonviolent Coordinating Committee (SNCC)—and later, in 1964, they created the Black Women's Liberation Committee within SNCC.[31]

In the mid-1960s, white women broke away from the gradualism that characterized the major political parties and the mainstream women's groups to form new feminist organizations, including the National Organization for Women (1967), the Women's Equity Action League (1968), and the National Women's Political Caucus (1971).[32] These "second-wave" feminists demanded that the government outlaw sex discrimination and enforce equal rights in employment, education, and health care. They also targeted welfare state benefits and won a minimum wage for domestic workers, greater access to education, admission to most military academies, job protection for pregnant workers, and a woman's right to receive credit on the basis of her own record. It was winning the right to abortion, however, that gave the greatest impetus to the new feminist movement.

In addition, younger, more militant, and mostly white women in SNCC and Students for a Democratic Society (SDS) began to resist male domination in their organizations and personal lives and to call for women's *liberation,* not just women's *rights.*[33] This insurgency, which crossed race, class, and age lines, led to the creation of the National Conference of Puerto Rican Women (1972), the National Black Feminist Organization (1973), the National Alliance of Black Feminists (1973), the Mexican American Women's Association (1974), the Coalition of Labor Union Women (1974), and the Older Women's League (1980). Each organization targeted its own constituency, however, and the women's movement has continued to be plagued by race, class, and other tensions.

The tumultuous climate of the late 1960s and early 1970s also sparked activism among working-class housewives and single mothers on welfare. In city after city, community-based women began to revive the effort to improve their standard of living. Black, Latina, and white housewives fought against bank redlining practices and toxic waste dumps and for rent control, social services, better schools, and safe streets. In the mid-1970s, when fiscal cutbacks threatened neighborhood services, working-class women mobilized against clinic and hospital closings and demanded better funding for schools. The Congress of Neighborhood Women, founded in 1974 and one of the better-known groups of working-class women, has continued its work.

Early Welfare Rights Organizing: The National Welfare Rights Organization

In the 1960s, women on welfare also began to organize in their own interests.[34] Drawing on the long tradition of informal support networks, especially in the black community, these women redefined welfare as a right rather than a privilege and fought to obtain the benefits to which they were entitled by law. Just as workers employed in factories had discovered their common plight and formed unions to gain strength in numbers, so being "on welfare" provided a basis for women to join forces to protest their meager benefits and the system's controlling rules. While client protest against the welfare system was not new, the welfare rights movement that grew out of these local efforts turned out to be the most significant social protest by poor people since World War II.

The conditions of the mid-1960s—economic prosperity, a liberal political climate, active social movements, political uprisings, and a national war on poverty—created a space in which women on welfare could organize.[35] By this time, the southern civil rights movement had all but ended, and many activists had turned their efforts northward, drawn by incipient political stirrings among the black urban masses. The March on Washington in 1963 and the War on Poverty in 1964 focused national attention on economic as well as civil rights issues, as did the twenty-one major riots and civil disorders in 1966 and the eighty-three in 1967. The War on Poverty's Community Action Program provided legal and counseling services that helped poor women assert their rights, and, with the help of VISTA volunteers, nuns, priests, ministers, and social workers, it facilitated the formation of local welfare rights groups.

The convergence of these forces led George Wiley, a black chemistry professor from Syracuse University and a former associate director of the Congress of Racial Equality (CORE), along with other mostly male veterans of the civil rights movement, to form a national welfare rights organization. Its program was based on "A Strategy to End Poverty," a paper written by two academically based social activists, Frances Fox Piven and Richard A. Cloward, that proposed flooding the welfare system with applicants and demands for benefits. Piven and Cloward argued that at least half the families entitled to Aid to Families with Dependent Children (AFDC) never applied, while many others were turned away. They pointed out that welfare departments kept women on welfare uninformed of the range of benefits to which they were entitled, including special grants for clothing and household items, and that if women insisted on what was theirs by law, many more would receive needed financial aid. The resulting surge of applications would also create a fiscal crisis for welfare departments and a political crisis for the Democratic party. The demand for more welfare dollars would lead big-city Democratic coalitions to split over how to use urban resources and would force the national Democratic party to put forward a federal solution to poverty that involved the redistribution of income toward the poor.

The formation of a national movement was preceded by growing activity at the local level. In 1963 Johnnie Tillmon, a welfare mother of five, organized Mothers Anonymous in Watts, California; other women formed the Alameda County, California, Welfare Rights organization. The Minneapolis AFDC League, founded in 1964, grew out of a single parents' group at the local YWCA. In 1965 agitation by poor women against welfare cuts led to the Ohio Steering Committee for Adequate Welfare, and in 1966 the Brooklyn Welfare Action Council (B-WAC) was organized after some women attended a welfare rights planning meeting in Washington, D.C. Within a year after the conference, storefront welfare rights centers existed in almost every low-income Brooklyn community. In June 1966 welfare rights groups in Ohio staged a 155-mile "Walk for Adequate Welfare" from Cleveland to the state capital in Columbus. National welfare rights planners, led by Wiley, turned this local march into a national media event. They mobilized support for the forty people who set out from Cleveland and for the five thousand or so others who joined them for some part of the ten-day march. On the last day, simultaneous demonstrations were held in twenty-four cities nationwide, giving official birth to the national welfare rights movement.

In August 1967 the National Welfare Rights Organization (NWRO) held its first national convention, attended by 175 people from forty-five cities in twenty-one states. An organizational structure was set up, and Johnnie Tillmon was elected chair. George Wiley, who had earlier been chosen as national director, had already opened the first field office in Washington, D.C. By the time of the convention, the NWRO had five thousand dues-paying members, concentrated in New York, California, Pennsylvania, Michigan, Virginia, Massachusetts, Ohio, New Jersey, and Illinois. Using a grass-roots organizing strategy, it expanded its membership to twenty-two thousand by 1969. The number of local WROs grew as well, from 130 in twenty-three states in 1966 to nine hundred in fifty states in 1971.

The NWRO had two main aims: to improve public assistance and to establish a federally guaranteed income. Its organizing strategies ranged from solving individual grievances to collective agitation at welfare offices. Its strategy contributed to the welfare "explosion" of the late 1960s, and it mounted a militant counteroffensive to welfare cuts in cities in California, New York, Massachusetts, Minnesota, Nevada, New Jersey, and Wisconsin, many of which drew the police and led to arrests. In addition, it lobbied against forced work programs, suitable-home policies, and man-in-the-house rules. Its work transferred millions of dollars to the poor and attracted thousands of women to the welfare rights movement.

Despite positive media coverage and success in mobilizing women across the nation, the NWRO was forced to shift from a street strategy to a political strategy as the times changed. Funding became harder to come by, liberal support diminished, the leadership was co-opted by both politicians and welfare agencies, and the general political climate became more conservative. The organization turned to lobbying against the Family Assistance Plan (1969-1971) proposed by the Nixon administration, working with local welfare departments to bring about change, and applying for government grants. None of this worked, and in 1975 it declared bankruptcy and closed its doors.

Welfare Becomes a Women's Issue

The welfare rights movement did not disappear, however, for it had created a sense of entitlement and a cadre of politicized and battle-tested women who were willing to work to keep the cause alive. Moreover, in the mid-1970s a new generation of welfare rights groups arose. Unlike the first wave, which was composed mainly of black women and which pursued the politics of class, the second wave included increasing numbers of white women, whose standard of living had fallen due to rising divorce rates and low wages.[36] Influenced by the women's liberation movement, women on welfare—both white women and women of color—began to see welfare as a matter of gender as well as economics.

The first sign of this new wave of activity came in 1972, when the NWRO's women leaders wrested control of the organization from Wiley, forcing him to resign, and made Johnnie Tillmon the executive director. In 1974 white feminists organized the Downtown Welfare Rights Action Center (D-WRAC) in New York City. Influenced by feminism, its members (along with groups in New Jersey and elsewhere) argued that welfare was a women's issue because so few jobs with decent pay were available to women and because there was so little affordable child care. More and more white women, including young feminists identified with the feminist *and* the welfare rights movements, attended the NWRO's conventions in 1974 and 1977.

The more established feminist groups had played a very minor role in the earlier welfare rights movement, but in the early 1970s the National Organization for Women (NOW), the Women's Equity Action League (WEAL), and the Women's Lobby began to take note of poverty. While the majority of women in NOW remained indifferent or resistant, NOW chapters in New Mexico, California, Minnesota, and Maryland made limited overtures to the NWRO as part of an effort to address poor women's issues.[37] A few black feminist groups, such as the National Black Feminist Organization and the Coalition of One Hundred Black Women, also established loose ties with the NWRO. In 1976 some mainstream women's groups, as well as the Coalition of Labor Union Women, the National Congress of Neighborhood Women, and Housewives for the ERA, took a stand against the welfare reform bill proposed by President Jimmy Carter because it failed to value women's work at home and because it did not provide for child care so that a woman could choose to work in or outside the home without penalty. In 1977 the National Council of Women, Work, and Welfare—a coalition that came out of the welfare rights movement—also attempted to mobilize political support for welfare as a women's issue.

These efforts on the part of middle-class feminist groups came too late to significantly influence the welfare reform debate, however, especially since a backlash against the War on Poverty and the social movements of the 1960s was under way. The effort was in any case difficult because feminists and the NWRO disagreed on some basic issues. First, many feminists supported government work programs as a way to help women move out of the home. In contrast, the NWRO saw this as forced labor that prevented women from choosing where—home or market—they wanted to work. On another front, most feminist groups of the 1970s were devoting considerable resources to the ERA, which ranked low on the NWRO's priority list because it would do away with protective labor laws. On the other hand, the NWRO male leadership believed that poor women needed husbands rather than economic independence through work; this not only alienated nearly all feminists but was eventually disavowed by the women leaders of NWRO as well.

The attack on social programs by President Ronald Reagan's administration in the 1980s spawned another round of welfare rights activism, this time shaped by the "austerity economy." On June 30, 1987, the twenty-first anniversary of the NWRO's founding, welfare mothers and organizers formed the National Welfare Rights Union (NWRU). With leadership from the earlier movement, as well as ties to other poor people's groups, the NWRU dedicated itself "to the pursuit of social justice for all members of our society, particularly those who have been excluded from the benefits of this nation."[38] Its first annual convention, in September 1988, drew more than one hundred people from eighteen states. In July 1989, more than 350 people attended a National Survival Summit in Philadelphia organized by the NWRU, the National Union of the Homeless, and the National Anti-Hunger Coalition. The participants agreed to organize state survival summits and a national "Up and Out of Poverty, Now!" campaign, to be led by people who themselves lived in poverty. Subsequent survival summits have targeted youth, hunger, homelessness, poor women, media blackouts of poor people's activism, and, of course, the renewed drive to reform welfare.

Like their predecessors, the NWRU and its allies took on the practices of local welfare offices, on the one hand, and national policy, on the other. NWRU members frequently "turned up the street heat" by staging militant actions, including civil disobedience. They organized "No Heat, No Peace" sit-ins at a Michigan welfare office, a lengthy "No Housing, No Peace" takeover of empty houses owned by the Department of Housing and Urban Development in New York City and Salt Lake City, Utah, and tent cities in Michigan and New York. The Philadelphia-based Kensington Welfare Rights Union appropriated an abandoned building and turned it into a community center in a neighborhood that had none, while the NWRU chapter in Oakland, California, agitated long and hard against that state's punitive welfare policies.

Nationally, the NWRU regularly holds conferences where women (and men) on welfare from around the country are trained as activists. The NWRU opposed the Family Support Act of 1988, the welfare reform bill proposed by Bill Clinton in 1994, the Republican Contract with America of January 1995, and the House and Senate welfare reform bills passed in 1996. At its "Who Speaks for the Poor?" conference, in July 1994, it announced a four-part organizing, legislative, public relations, and legal strategy to combat these welfare reform efforts.[39] That same year, the "Up and Out of Poverty, Now!" campaign mobilized poor women and their supporters for a tax-day protest in fifteen cities across the United States and Canada. In 1995 the NWRU, along with the rest of the welfare advocacy community, demanded that President Clinton veto any welfare reform legislation that came out of Congress.

The growing welfare rights network includes long-standing welfare rights groups, such as the Coalition for Basic Human Needs in Massachusetts; Parents for Justice in New Hampshire; the Welfare Warriors in Milwaukee; Empower in Rochester, New York; the Reform Organization of Welfare in St. Louis; Women for Economic Security in Chicago; the Women's Union in Vermont; and Arise in Springfield, Massachusetts. It also includes groups formed in the late 1980s and early 1990s, such as the Welfare Warriors in Long Island, New York; JEDI Women (Justice, Economic Dignity and Independence for Women) in Salt Lake City, Utah; and the Women's Economic Agenda Project (WEAP) in Oakland, California. Welfare reform activism has cropped up on many college campuses, as local, state, and national welfare cutbacks and stricter mandatory-work programs make it nearly impossible for welfare recipients to complete their college education. News of all these efforts rarely makes it into the mainstream press, but it is regularly reported in *Survival News* (published in Boston) and the *Welfare Mothers' Voice* (published in Milwaukee), both of which are written by and for welfare mothers, as well as in many smaller organizational newsletters. Although federal priorities have certainly not been turned around, women on welfare are on the move and, in some states, have managed to limit some of the worst welfare reforms.

Following the lead of the groups that formed in the 1970s, some of newer groups are organizing women on welfare self-consciously as *women*. The names of their organizations—Women for Economic Security; the Women's Union; Justice, Independence, and Dignity for Women; and Women's Economic Agenda—reflect this. Although they worked at first at the local level, they have recently begun to connect nationally. For instance, the Oakland-based WEAP convened more than four hundred poor women in 1992 for the first-ever Poor Women's Convention; their theme was "Under Attack but Fighting Back" (which inspired the title of the book from which this chapter was reprinted). The meeting was the first chance many of the women had to leave their communities and discover that other women lived exactly as they did. The following week, a group of women who had attended the convention joined two hundred other poor women at the San Francisco Hilton to let Governor Pete Wilson, who was holding a fund-raiser, know what they thought of his welfare ideas. After the governor refused to meet with them, eleven of the women sat down in the hotel lobby. The arrest of the "Hilton 11" hit the network news, and viewers heard one women cry out, "I'm getting arrested for wanting to feed my kids."[40] On Valentine's Day 1995, under JEDI leadership, welfare rights groups in seventy-seven cities in thirty-eight states mounted local actions and sent thousands of postcards to local and state legislators, reminding them that "Our children's hearts are in your hands." This network was also mobilized to join the campaign to get President Clinton to veto all punitive welfare legislation.

The NWRU and other welfare rights groups have also made overtures to middle-class women's organizations, recognizing that it is important for poor women to build bridges across class and race lines. While this is only a beginning, women's groups in and outside of the feminist community have caught up with Johnnie Tillmon, who back in 1972 pointed out how welfare is a women's issue:

> There's one good thing about welfare. It kills your illusions about yourself, and about where this society is really at. It's laid out for you straight. You have to learn to fight, to be aggressive, or you just don't make it. If you can survive long enough on welfare, you can survive anything. It gives you a kind of freedom, a sense of your own power and togetherness with other women.[41]

NOW responded positively when the NWRU invited it to become a member of its "Up and Out of Poverty, Now!" campaign. In 1992 NOW invited NWRU president Marion Kramer to address its annual convention and went on to recommend that all local branches find ways to support the poor women's organizations in their areas. NOW also voted not to endorse any political candidate who called for harsh welfare reforms. Patricia Ireland, president of NOW, went on record against welfare reform and, along with Marion Kramer, was arrested trying to gain entry to a congressional hearing on the issue. NOW intensified its commitment to welfare rights at its 1994 convention, where it launched an emergency national campaign, called "As If Women Matter," to generate opposition to the welfare reforms that were then emanating from both state legislatures and Congress and to promote nonpunitive solutions for "ending poverty as we know it."[42] NOW's "One Hundred Days of Action" campaign against the Contract with America culminated in a mass rally in Washington, D.C., in April 1995, where NOW expanded the definition of violence against women—the theme of the rally—to include poverty and punitive welfare reform.

In varying degrees, other feminist groups have also joined the welfare rights movement. The NOW Legal Defense and Education Fund (which is not part of NOW) was one of the first feminist organizations to do the hard work of bringing welfare mothers, antipoverty advocates, and feminists into the same room. It also helped organize eighty groups into the Child Exclusion Coalition, which included leading feminist, reproductive rights, religious, and right-to-life organizations. For very different reasons, each of these groups strongly opposed any welfare reform that denied aid to children born while their mothers were on AFDC. The Institute for Women's Policy Research, Wider Opportunities for Women, the Center for Reproductive Law and Policy, the National Black Women's Health Project, and the American Civil Liberties Union's Reproductive Rights Project, among other groups, have put opposition to punitive welfare reform on their agendas.

Some organizations with large female memberships but not necessarily feminist programs have also begun to see that welfare reform affects women (and children). In spring 1995, the *Women's Initiative Network* newsletter, published by the American

Association of Retired Persons (AARP), warned that welfare reform was a testing ground for changes in entitlement programs that "would be a disaster for mid-life and older women" who depend heavily on Medicaid, Medicare, Supplemental Security Income, and public housing or who raise grandchildren with the help of AFDC.[43] It added that the stereotypes used to justify cutting senior citizen programs—that the elderly are "greedy geezers" who do not need government aid or "undeserving" people who use public benefits instead of saving for their old age—are not unlike the myths used to demonize welfare mothers and that such threats ultimately harm everyone.

In 1994 and 1995, as Congress considered various welfare reform bills, many women academics and professionals lent their names and expertise to efforts to refute the myths behind welfare reform. In 1994 a group of seventy-six scholars (male and female) issued a press release that stated that the existing research contained little or no evidence of a relationship between receipt of welfare and a woman's childbearing decisions. Individual women have also conducted research, appeared on radio and TV, written op-ed pieces, and made themselves available to local groups fighting welfare reform. On several occasions when Congress seemed on the brink of passing a reform bill, women's groups mobilized nationwide opposition. In fall 1994, for instance, more than 750 women academics issued a statement—printed in the *New York Review of Books* and the *New Republic*—that opposed Bill Clinton's plan. On August 8, 1995, the Committee of One Hundred Women, joined by many other women's, labor, and professional groups, ran a full-page ad in the *New York Times* that explained "Why Every Woman in America Should Beware of Welfare Cuts" and declared that "A War against Poor Women Is a War against All Women!" Drawing on its roster of well-established artists, authors, politicians, professionals, academics, and activists, the Committee of One Hundred Women has lobbied intensively against congressional welfare bills, organized press conferences, and conducted vigils outside the White House. In December 1995 the National Association of Social Workers, the majority of whose members are women, collected several thousand signatures for still another *New York Times* ad directed at President Clinton. Supporting the national Veto Campaign, it stated, "Don't Sign Any Welfare Bill That Abandons the Nation's Children." The Council of Presidents (of national women's organizations), which represents six million women and ninety women's organizations, developed a "Women's Pledge on Welfare Reform" to organize opposition to welfare reform among feminist professional and advocacy groups. If they can be sustained and developed, these efforts at solidarity among women of different classes and races holds some promise for building a base for a more progressive social welfare policy in the future.

What Can the Future Hold?

The current welfare reform has brought us full circle, back to the social welfare structures that existed before the Social Security Act of 1935. The first order of business, therefore, is to continue to organize against poverty by providing women with child and health care services, and eliminating punitive measures designed to control their work and family behavior.

But in addition to defending AFDC against the current assault, welfare rights advocates have tried to envision better alternatives. While some of the proposals hope to improve welfare in the short run, others are more far-reaching plans to secure economic independence for women. For instance, Barbara Bergmann and Heidi Hartmann, two nationally known economists and the cochairs of the Economists' Policy Group for Women's Issues, have developed a plan to help women within the framework of what they believe might be tolerated in today's conservative political climate. Called Help for Working Parents (HWP), it stresses work as the means to economic independence and argues for moving poor parents out of poverty by providing child care, health care, and housing assistance—all regardless of a woman's marital status. HWP would reward work by supplementing minimum-wage jobs with noncash benefits and by expanding the Earned Income Tax Credit. For instance, a single mother with two children who worked full-time at the minimum wage would receive about $24,500 a year, double the 1994 poverty level of income for a family of three. Single parents not in paid jobs would receive a series of vouchers each month, including Food Stamps and $100 in cash. The HWP program would cost much more than the $25 billion currently spent on AFDC, but it would provide a far better way to help women who work.[44]

Nancy Fraser, a professor of philosophy and research fellow at the Center for Urban Affairs and Policy at Northwestern University, has a less immediately pragmatic vision that emphasizes the importance of women's caretaking work and allows women to choose between home and market. Fraser would make the labor market more woman-friendly through the provision of better child care, elder care, and other services; an end to sex discrimination, sexual harassment, and other obstacles to equal employment; and the creation of permanent, full-time, well-paid jobs. She would also upgrade existing social insurance plans to take women's labor market needs into account. In recognition of caretaking as socially valuable work, she proposes "caregiver parity"—that is, a caregiver allowance to compensate women for the work of bearing and raising children, for housework, and for other socially necessary domestic labor. The caregiver allowance would support a family at the same level as a breadwinner's wage and be combined with flextime, family leave, and other policies to make the workplace more accessible to caretakers. Fraser also would integrate breadwinner and caregiver benefits into a single system so that, for example, a woman finishing a spell of supported caregiving but unable to find market work and a laid-off factory worker in the same situation would both become eligible for Unemployment Insurance. She adds another need-based, means-tested benefit for those unable to do either waged or caregiving work.[45]

Ann Orloff, a professor of sociology at the University of Wisconsin, has developed a plan that specifically targets the gender relations of power.[46] This more radical reform is based on the belief that women need programs that will enhance their autonomy and permit them to escape both market exploitation and male domination. It argues that, if social policy is to help women, it must go beyond promoting women's work, covering the costs of social reproduction, and easing caretaking burdens to freeing women from the need to enter into potentially oppressive relationships of any kind. The programs that Orloff proposes would provide women with access to independent incomes in order to insulate them from exploitation in the labor market and free them from depending on marriage for economic support. To be woman-friendly, such programs would make it possible for women to form and maintain households without having to marry and would increase the standard of living in such women-maintained homes.

Martha Fineman, a professor at the Columbia University School of Law, goes one step further and calls for an end to the legal basis of marriage (but not necessarily the relationship itself), the elimination of all government subsidies and protection designed to uphold this institution, *and* the recognition that nurturing units—that is, caregiving families, whatever their shape or structure—are inevitably dependent and may require some type of government support.[47]

Speaking for welfare mothers themselves, the National Welfare Rights Union has called for replacing welfare with a guaranteed annual income, echoing various components of other feminist plans. Their manifesto states:

> All people should have an adequate income whether from benefits or from jobs that pay enough to live on, a guaranteed annual income so that no one in this nation need live in poverty. All people should be able to live a life of dignity with full freedom and respect for human rights.... All women who want to work outside the home should have the opportunity to earn a wage that will allow them to meet all the needs of their families. We also respect the right of all women who chose to stay in the home and nurture their children. They should be fully supported in their task for the important contribution that they are making to society.[48]

In these harsh times, we need to dream while we struggle to protect poor women. It is imperative that we question existing programs and invent alternatives, even if these at first seem outrageous. In the end, this will help us come to terms with a future in which there may not be enough paid work or adequate incomes for everyone but in which people will still need a decent standard of living and caregiving work will still need to be done. Faced with these realities, instead of debating the relative merits of income support versus employment policies, as often happens today, we need to develop the best policies we can on *both* fronts. Fraser has five gender-sensitive objectives that could be used to assess such future reforms. She suggests that social welfare programs should (1) prevent poverty, (2) prohibit the exploitation of vulnerable people, (3) reduce gender, race, and class inequalities, (4) promote women's full participation in society on par with men and that of persons of color on par with whites, and (5) restructure government programs, along with other social institutions designed primarily for white men, so that women can fully benefit from them.[49] If these guidelines were to be followed, welfare "as we know it" would be replaced by a responsive welfare state in a society based on justice and equality for all.

As this chapter has tried to show, achieving these changes will require pressure from below. In the words of Frederick Douglass, abolitionist and supporter of women's rights, "Power concedes nothing without a demand." And as women activists have always known, we must dare to struggle if we expect to win!

NOTES

This chapter was originally published in Mimi Abramovitz, *Under Attack, Fighting Back: Women and Welfare in the U.S.* (New York: Monthly Review Press, 1996), 109-141.

1. Guida West and Rhoda Lois Blumberg, *Women and Social Protest* (New York: Oxford University Press, 1990), 7.

2. See Walter Korpi, *The Working Class and Welfare Capitalism: Work, Unions and Politics in Sweden* (London: Routledge and Kegan Paul, 1978), chap. 1; Ramesh Mishra, *Society and Social Policy: Theories and Practice of Welfare*, 2nd ed. (London: Macmillan, 1981), chaps. 1 and 2.

3. Gosta Epsing-Anderson, *Three Worlds of Welfare Capitalism* (Princeton, N.J.: Princeton University Press, 1990); Gosta Epsing-Anderson, *Politics against Markets: The Social Democratic Road to Power* (Princeton, N.J.: Princeton University Press, 1985); Korpi, *The Working Class and Welfare Capitalism*.

4. Korpi, *The Working Class and Welfare Capitalism*, 5-10; Mishra, *Society and Social Policy*, 68-87; Paul M. Sweezy, *The Theory of Capitalist Development* (New York: Monthly Review Press, 1968), 244-50.

5. Diane Balser, *Sisterhood and Solidarity: Feminism and Labor in Modern Times* (Boston: South End Press, 1987); Philip Foner, *Women and the American Labor Movement from World War I to the Present* (New York: Free Press, 1980); Barbara Kingsolver, *Women in the Great Arizona Mine Strike of 1983* (Ithaca, N.Y.: ILR Press, 1989); Ruth Milkman, ed., *Women, Work, and Protest: A Century of U.S. Women's Labor History* (Boston: Routledge and Kegan Paul, 1985).

6. Ann Bookman and Sandra Morgen, eds., *Women and the Politics of Empowerment* (Philadelphia: Temple University Press, 1988); Nancy Hewitt and Suzanne Lebsock, *Visible Women: New Essays on American Activism* (Urbana: University of Illinois Press, 1991); Ida Susser, *Norman Street: Poverty and Politics in an Urban Neighborhood* (New York: Oxford University Press, 1982); Ann Gibson Robinson, *The Montgomery Bus Boycott and the Women Who Started It* (Knoxville: University of Tennessee Press, 1987); Nancy Naples, "Contradictions in the Gender Subtext of the War on Poverty: The Community Work and Resistance of Women from Low-Income Communities," *Social Problems* 38, no. 3 (1991): 316-32.

7. Linda Gordon, *Heroes of Their Own Lives: The Politics and History of Family Violence* (New York: Penguin Books, 1988); Susan Handley Hertz, *The Welfare Mothers Movement: A Decade of Change for Poor Women* (Washington, D.C.: University Press of America, 1981); Megan H. Morrissey, "The Downtown Welfare Advocate Center: A Case Study of a Welfare Rights Organization," *Social Service Review* 64, no. 2 (June 1990): 189-20; Frances Fox Piven and Richard A. Cloward, *Poor People's Movements: Why They Succeed, How They Fail* (New York: Vintage Books, 1979), 264-362; Jackie Pope, "Women in the Welfare Rights Struggle: The Brooklyn Welfare Action Council," in *Women and Social Protest*, ed. West and Blumberg, 57-74; Guida West, *The National Welfare Rights Movement: The Social Protest of Poor Women* (New York: Praeger, 1981).

8. Kathleen Thee, "Family Patterns and the Politicization of Consumption Relations," *Sociological Spectrum* 5, no. 4 (1985): 295-316; Dana Frank, "Housewives, Socialists, and the Politics of Food: The 1917 Cost-of-Living Protests," *Feminist Studies* 11, no. 2 (1985): 265-85; Paula Hyman, "Immigrant Women and Consumer Protest: The New York City Kosher Meat Boycott of 1902," *American Jewish History* 70 (Summer 1980): 91-105; Tamar Kaplan, "Female Consciousness and Collective Action: Barcelona, 1910-1918," *Signs: Journal of Women in Culture and Society* 7 (1982): 545-65; Barbara Laslett and Johanna Brenner, "Gender and Social Reproduction: Historical Perspectives," *Annual Review of Sociology* 15 (1989): 381-404; Batya Weinbaum and Amy Bridges, "The Other Side of the Paycheck: Monopoly Capital and the Structure of Consumption," in *Capitalist Patriarchy and the Case for Socialist Feminism*, ed. Zillah Eisenstein (New York: Monthly Review Press, 1979), 90-205.

9. George Rude, *The Crowd in History* (New York: Wiley, 1964).

10. The discussion of nineteenth-century reform draws on Eleanor Flexner, *Century of Struggle: The Women's Rights Movement in the United States* (New York: Atheneum, 1968); Nancy E. McGlen and Karen O'Conner, *Women's Rights: The Struggle for Equality in the Nineteenth and*

Twentieth Centuries (New York: Praeger, 1983); Mary Ryan, *Womanhood in America: From Colonial Times to the Present* (New York: New Viewpoints, 1975), 137-92; Theda Skocpol, *Protecting Soldiers and Mothers: The Political Origins of Social Policy in the United States* (Cambridge, Mass.: Harvard University Press, 1992).

11. The discussion of Progressive Era and New Deal activism by white women draws on Johanna Brenner and Barbara Laslett, "Gender, Social Reproduction, and Women's Self-Organization: Considering the U.S. Welfare State," *Gender and Society* 5, no. 3 (September 1991): 311-33; Linda Gordon, *Pitied but Not Entitled: Single Mothers and the History of Welfare* (New York: Free Press, 1994); Robyn Muncy, *Creating a Female Dominion in American Reform, 1890-1935* (New York: Oxford University Press, 1991), chaps. 2 and 3; Skocpol, *Protecting Soldiers and Mothers*; Susan Ware, *Beyond Suffrage: Women in the New Deal* (Cambridge, Mass.: Harvard University Press, 1981).

12. The phenomenon of female social reform was not unique to the United States. During the same period, intense activism by European women helped to forge the modern welfare state in France and Britain. See Beth Koven and Sonya Michel, "Womanly Duties: Maternalist Politics and the Origins of Welfare States in France, Germany, Great Britain, and the United States," unpublished manuscript.

13. The debate about whether social policy that treats women as equals of men is better for women than social policy that treats women and men differently based on their differences has continued to rage.

14. The discussion of Progressive Era and New Deal activism among African American women draws on Eileen Boris, "The Power of Motherhood: Black and White Activist Women Redefine the Political," in *Mothers of a New World: Maternalist Politics and the Origins of the Welfare State,* ed. Beth Koven and Sonya Michel (New York: Routledge, 1993), 213-46; Angela Davis, *Women, Race, and Class* (New York: Vintage, 1983); Paula Giddings, *When and Where I Enter: The Impact of Black Women on Race and Sex in America* (Toronto: Bantam Books, 1984); Gordon, *Pitied but Not Entitled,* chap. 5; Darlene Clark Hine, "Lifting the Veil, Shattering the Silence: Black Women's History in Slavery and Freedom," in *The State of Afro-American History: Past, Present and Future,* ed. D. C. Hine (Baton Rouge: Louisiana State University Press, 1986), 223-52; Gerda Lerner, *Black Women in White America: A Documentary History* (New York: Vintage Books, 1973); Gwendolyn Mink, *The Wages of Motherhood: Inequality in the Welfare State, 1917-1942* (Ithaca, N.Y.: Cornell University Press, 1995); Ann Firor Scott, "On Seeing and Not Seeing: A Case of Historical Invisibility," *Journal of American History* 7 (June 1984): 7-21; Deborah Gray White, "The Cost of Club Work, the Price of Black Feminism," in *Visible Women: New Essays on American Activism* (Urbana: University of Illinois Press, 1993), 247-69.

15. Laslett and Brenner, "Gender and Social Reproduction," 381-404.

16. Gordon, *Pitied but Not Entitled;* Alice Kessler Harris, "Women and Welfare: Public Interventions in Private Lives," *Radical History Review* 56 (1993): 127-36.

17. Dorothy Gallagher, review of *Florence Kelly and the Nation's Work* by Kathryn Kish Sklar, *New York Times Book Review,* 9 July 1995, 9.

18. Gordon, *Pitied but Not Entitled,* 55-56; Koven and Michel, "Womanly Duties"; Aileen Kraditor, *Ideas of the Women's Suffrage Movement, 1880-1920* (New York: W. W. Norton, 1981), 67; Muncy, *Creating a Female Dominion in American Reform.*

19. Dana Frank, "Food Wins All Struggles: Seattle Labor and the Politicization of Consumption," *Radical History Review* 51 (1991): 65-89.

20. For a detailed discussion of these events, see Frank, "Housewives, Socialists, and the Politics of Food," 265-85; William Frieburger, "War, Prosperity, and Hunger: The New York Food Riots," *Labor History* 25 (Spring 1984): 217-39; Hyman, "Immigrant Women and Consumer Protest," 91-105; Annelise Orleck, "Common Sense and a Little Fire: Working-Class Women's Activism in the Twentieth Century United States," Ph.D. diss., New York University, 1989, 540-42; Judith

Smith, "Our Own Kind: Family and Networks in Providence," in *A Heritage of Her Own: Toward a New Social History of American Women,* ed. Nancy Cott and Elizabeth H. Pleck (New York: Simon and Schuster, 1979), 393-411.

21. Lerner, *Black Women in White America,* 211-12.

22. John Ehrenreich, *The Altruistic Imagination: A History of Social Work and Social Policy in the United States* (Ithaca, N.Y.: Cornell University Press, 1985), 49; William Graebner, *The Engineering of Consent: Democracy and Authority in Twentieth-Century America* (Madison: University of Wisconsin Press, 1987), 58-59.

23. Ruth Schwartz Cowan, "Two Washes in the Morning and a Bridge Party at Night: The American Housewife between the Wars," *Women's Studies* 3 (1976): 147-72; Heidi Hartmann, "Capitalism and Women's Work in the Home, 1900-1950," Ph.D. diss., Yale University, 1984, 68-69.

24. Orleck, "Common Sense and a Little Fire," 556-58.

25. Unless otherwise noted, the discussion of the community-based cost of living protests during the 1920s, 1930s, and 1940s draws on Orleck, "Common Sense and a Little Fire," chap. 8, "We Are That Mythic Thing Called the Public—Militant Housewives during the Great Depression," 534-609.

26. Anne Stein, "Postwar Consumer Boycotts," *Radical America* 9 (July-August 1975): 156-61.

27. The discussion of these groups is based largely on Verta Taylor, "Social Movement Continuity: The Women's Movement in Abeyance," *American Sociological Review* 54, no. 5 (October 1989): 761-76; Leila Rupp and Verta Taylor, *Survival in the Doldrums: The American Women's Rights Movement, 1945 to the 1960s* (New York: Oxford University Press, 1987).

28. Ann Gibson Robinson, *The Montgomery Bus Boycott*; Janelle Scott, "Local Leadership in the Woman Suffrage Movement: Houston's Campaign for the Vote, 1917-1918," *Houston Review* 12, no. 1 (1990): 3-22.

29. For example, the NAACP leadership included Ruby Hurley (youth director), Daisy Bates (president, Little Rock, Arkansas, chapter), Rosa Parks (secretary, Montgomery, Alabama, chapter), and Ella Baker (president, New York City chapter, and national director of branch work). Women were also active in the Urban League (formed in 1911); the Congress of Racial Equality (1943); the National Negro Labor Council (1951); the Southern Christian Leadership Conference (1957); and the Student Non-Violent Coordinating Committee (1960).

30. Giddings, *When and Where I Enter,* 291-92.

31. Shulamit Reinharz, "Women as Competent Community Builders: The Other Side of the Coin," in *Social and Psychological Problems of Women: Prevention and Crisis,* ed. Annette U. Rickel, Meg Gerrard, and Ira Iscoe (Washington, D.C.: Hemisphere Publishing Corporation, 1984), 19-43; Jacqueline Jones, *Labor of Love, Labor of Sorrow: Black Women, Work, and the Family from Slavery to the Present* (New York: Basic Books, 1985), 310-21.

32. Susan Lynn, *Progressive Women in Conservative Times: Racial Justice, Peace, and Feminism, 1945-1960* (New Brunswick, N.J.: Rutgers University Press, 1992); Myra Marx Ferree and Beth B. Hess, *Controversy and Coalition: The New Feminist Movement* (Boston: Twayne, 1985).

33. William Henry Chafe, *The American Woman: Her Changing Social, Economic and Political Roles, 1920-1970* (London: Oxford University Press, 1974); Sara Evans, *Born for Liberty: A History of Women in America* (New York: Free Press, 1989).

34. The discussion of welfare rights before the formation of the National Welfare Rights Organization relies on Hertz, *The Welfare Mothers' Movement*; Morrissey, "The Downtown Welfare Advocate Center," 189-207; Piven and Cloward, *Poor People's Movements,* 264-362; Pope, "Women in the Welfare Rights Struggle," 57-74.

35. Unless otherwise noted, this discussion of the National Welfare Rights Organization relies on Martha Davis, "Welfare Rights and Women's Rights in the 1960s," presented at the Integrating

the Sixties Conference, Washington, D.C., 30 May 1995; Piven and Cloward, *Poor People's Movements,* 264-362; West, *The National Welfare Rights Movement.*

36. The percentage of white women on welfare rose from 46.9 percent in 1973 to 50.2 percent in 1977, while the percentage of black women fell off. See West, *The National Welfare Rights Movement,* 262.

37. Davis, "Welfare Rights and Women's Rights in the 1960s," 21-22.

38. Testimony of Marian Kramer, president, National Welfare Rights Union, before the Subcommittee on Human Resources, Government Operations Committee, Washington, D.C., 10 March 1994, 1.

39. Up and Out of Poverty, Now! Coalition, The Grassroots Organizing Campaign to Redefine Welfare Reform, grant proposal, October 1994.

40. Nina Schuyler, "Under Attack but Fighting Back: The Birth of the Poor Women's Movement," *On the Issues* (Winter 1992): 22-28.

41. Johnnie Tillmon, "Welfare Is a Women's Issue," in *American Working Women: A Documentary History from 1600 to the Present,* ed. Rosalyn Baxandall, Linda Gordon, and Susan Reverby (New York: Vintage Books, 1976), 358.

42. *Survival News* (Fall/Winter 1994): 29.

43. AARP *Women's Initiative Network* newsletter, Spring 1995.

44. Barbara Bergmann and Heidi Hartmann, "A Welfare Reform Based on Help for Working Parents," *Feminist Economics* 1, no. 2 (1995): 85-89.

45. Nancy Fraser, "After the Family Wage: What Do Women Want in Social Welfare?" in "Women and Welfare Reform: A Policy Conference," proceedings of conference sponsored by the Institute for Women's Policy Research, Washington, D.C., 23 October 1993.

46. Ann S. Orloff, "Gender and the Social Rights of Citizenship: A Comparative Analysis of Gender Relations and Welfare States," *American Sociological Review* 58, no. 3 (June 1993): 303-28.

47. Martha Albertson Fineman, *The Neutered Mother, the Sexual Family, and Other Twentieth-Century Tragedies* (New York: Routledge, 1995).

48. Testimony of Marian Kramer, before the Subcommittee on Human Resources, 2.

49. Nancy Fraser, "After the Family Wage."

DISCUSSION QUESTIONS

1. Describe the activist tradition led and sustained by women as explained by the author.

2. How has women's activism, especially among women of color, been obscured by scholarship and the media? And, what are the reasons for this?

3. What does the author mean by "the feminist corrective"? How can this concept be utilized in the contemporary period to discuss race, gender, and the welfare state?

4. What are the similarities and differences between the activist tradition of black and white women? Do you believe that Latina or Asian women would reflect similar experiences?

5. How have women influenced and molded the welfare state in the United States?

FOR FURTHER READING

Balser, Diane, *Sisterhood and Solidarity: Feminism and Labor in Modern Times* (Boston: South End Press, 1987).

Bookman, Ann, and Sandra Morgen, eds., *Women and the Politics of Empowerment* (Philadelphia: Temple University Press, 1988).

Davis, Angela, *Women, Race, and Class* (New York: Vintage, 1983).

Flexner, Eleanor, *Century of Struggle: The Women's Rights Movement in the United States* (New York: Atheneum, 1968).

Giddings, Paula, *When and Where I Enter: The Impact of Black Women on Race and Sex in America* (Toronto: Bantam Books, 1984).

Hertz, Susan Handley, *The Welfare Mothers Movement: A Decade of Change for Poor Women* (Washington, D.C.: University Press of America, 1981).

Jones, Jacqueline, *Labor of Love, Labor of Sorrow: Black Women, Work, and the Family from Slavery to the Present* (New York: Basic Books, 1985).

Korpi, Walter, *The Working Class and Welfare Capitalism: Work, Unions and Politics in Sweden* (London: Routledge and Kegan Paul, 1978).

Lerner, Gerda, *Black Women in White America: A Documentary History* (New York: Vintage Books, 1973).

Milkman, Ruth, ed., *Women, Work, and Protest: A Century of U.S. Women's Labor History* (Boston: Routledge and Kegan Paul, 1985).

Mink, Gwendolyn, *The Wages of Motherhood: Inequality in the Welfare State, 1917-1942* (Ithaca, N.Y.: Cornell University Press, 1995).

Piven, Frances Fox, and Richard A. Cloward, *Poor People's Movements: Why They Succeed, How They Fail* (New York: Vintage Books, 1979).

Robinson, Ann Gibson, *The Montgomery Bus Boycott and the Women Who Started It* (Knoxville: University of Tennessee Press, 1987).

Skocpol, Theda, *Protecting Soldiers and Mothers: The Political Origins of Social Policy in the United States* (Cambridge, Mass.: Harvard University Press, 1992).

Chapter Thirteen

Savage Distributions
Welfare Myths and Daily Lives

Valerie Polakow

Let me repeat it, the causes of poverty are looked for, and found, in him or her who suffers it.
> —W. Channing, "An Address on the Prevention of Pauperism" (1843)

Born out of wedlock, her first ten years spent with an immoral mother who lived in a wretched tenement in a poor district...Jane proved to be untruthful, restless, never happy. Several times she ran away to her [mother], and to the vicious old neighborhood which she seemed to love....We believe the chief factors in our failure were the bad home background [and the] strong affection for a mother she knew to be immoral.
> —Children's Aid Association Records (1927-1928)

Throughout human history, a single woman with a small child has not been a viable economic unit. Not being a viable economic unit, neither have the single woman and child been a legitimate social unit... Restoring economic penalties translates into the first and central policy prescription: to end all economic support for single mothers....From society's perspective to have a baby that you cannot care for yourself is profoundly irresponsible, and the government will no longer subsidize it.
> —Charles Murray, "The Coming White Underclass" (1993)

Not much has changed in the discourse about poverty or single parenthood during the past century. Historically, it was single parents' vices and immorality that led to moral decay and urban dissolution; now it is their bad choices, their misconduct, and their failure to rear their children successfully in the land of opportunity that cause the current disintegration of the American family. The perception of poverty as a private affair—its causes rooted in failed individuals, family dysfunction, and female pathology—has led to proliferating social science fictions of the "underclass" that rest on "very disturbing assumptions about poor people, poverty and the world in which both are reproduced."[1] It is the "welfare culture" that cradles crime, drugs, fraud, sloth, and urban decay; President Ronald Reagan's State of the Union address in 1986, in which he blamed welfare for "the breakdown of the family, female and child poverty, child abandonment, horrible crimes and deteriorating schools," set the race—and the gender-coded tone—for a new and invigorated bipartisan assault on single-parent families in poverty. But what do childhood and motherhood mean to poor women and their children, who are the dispossessed citizens of the other America?

Historically, in the West, single mothers have always been made "incomplete" mothers when they failed to fulfill the obligations of marriage, normalized motherhood, and a proper family life. Evaluated against the enduring myth of a stable, nuclear, two-parent, traditional family, single mothers were judged and condemned within the patriarchal power structure of both religion and the state.[2] As children's lives have always been inextricably entwined with their mothers' lives, both women and children have shared the space of the voiceless: their contingent lives under surveillance and characterized by submission. It is clear that, as we examine forms of family life lived amid destitution and homelessness, mothering emerges as a set of practices shaped by economic conditions and state policies.[3] The treatment of the family as an isolated private unit that sinks or swims by its own resources and moral fitness—a family that represents Darwinism writ large—has also placed mothers and domestic ideology at center stage so that when the family fails, women fail, thereby justifying the indifference of the state to those who "are not fulfilling their end of the bargain," by virtue of their class, their race, and their life choices.[4]

The contemporary discourse on women and children in poverty is a discourse of otherness securely embedded in the nest of democracy, where choice, responsibility, and freedom are fettered. This soothing language of concealment has succeeded in muffling the voices of poor women and their children who, as citizens of the United States, are now living in one of the most dangerous democracies in the West, where destitution is no longer an aberration but has become a lifeworld. In this article I explore the meaning of that lifeworld: the existential tissue of daily life, the nuts and bolts of suffering and survival.

The Landscape of Poverty

In 1993, 14.6 million children lived in poverty in the United States—nearly 9 million white children, 4.9 million black children, and 3.1 million Latino children, according to the Children's Defense Fund.[5] Although there are more white children actually living in poverty, the child poverty rates are far higher for children of color (46.6 percent for black children, 39.9 percent for Latino children, who may be of any race, and 16.9 percent for white children). The Children's Defense Fund also reported that 59 percent of poor children live in female-headed families, and many of these families subsist on "incomes" less than one-half that defined by the federal government as poverty-level; that every fifty-three minutes an American child dies from poverty-related causes; that the United States has a higher infant mortality rate than nineteen other nations; that the United States has a death rate among preschool children worse than nineteen other nations, and a nonimmunization rate for preventable childhood diseases that approaches 50 percent in the largest cities; that the United States is not one of seventy nations worldwide that provide medical care and financial assistance to all pregnant women.[6] Neither universal health care, nor paid maternity/parental leave, nor child allowances, nor national subsidized child care is a guaranteed entitlement. In addition, according to the National Law Center on Homelessness and Poverty, fifty-two thousand families (roughly 210,000 people, of whom the majority are children) are homeless on any given night.[7]

Despite the overwhelming structural evidence of low wages, declining and contingent jobs, racism, racial segregation, gender discrimination, and the growing isolation of poor communities as plausible theories to explain the persistence of poverty, family structure and "breakdown" are the favored trump card for the popular press and for the social science theorists who obscure the politics of distribution behind the facade of family values and individual responsibility.[8] In his attack on the "freeze frames" of poverty theorists (both liberal and conservative) that are used to construct the "underclass," Adolph Reed points out that direct investigation of poor people's lives is generally absent; what is substituted are impressionistic journalistic generalities legitimated "in an authenticating mist of quantification."[9]

However, behind the cold contours of statistics lies the landscape of everyday life. What is it like to live a life of destitution, surrounded by images of wealthy consumerism? How does it feel to become easy prey and cheap decoy for the welfare hunters—the legislators and policymakers, the health care professionals, the educators, the get-tough-on-them American family advocates, the hysterical talk-show hosts? How does a mother cope when she is dependent on punitive state policies for her survival as a person, when her young children look to her for care and nurture, for a sense of home and safety, although she has come to know that her life and their lives are disposable and contingent? In the following section, several stories of single mothers in poverty are chronicled.

Mothers' Stories

Jenny O'Connor is white and in her late twenties.[10] She has lived alone with her son since he was six months old. Dan has been diagnosed as hyperactive with ADD (attention-deficit disorder) and suffers from severe asthma. Jenny's life has been a series of traumas, from childhood in an abusive alcoholic family to marriage with an abusive husband; she now encounters a constant struggle to make a life for herself and her son. Jenny describes her choice to leave the marriage and become a single parent:

When Danny was six months old, we left. It was very secretive. I left because I needed to avoid being pursued and followed. It was an awful wife-beating kind of relationship. When I realized that was what it was, I knew I had to leave, and when I figured how to do it secretly, I did. It was very difficult and depressing. Danny had never been abused, and I had to get out before he got hurt. I never thought this would happen to me, but now I see there were many things in my past which predisposed me to this kind of abuse. I came from a rigid Catholic background; my parents were wealthy. They threw me out when I started experimenting with drugs and sex in school, and other people in my family were physically abused. My brother was a healthy, beautiful child who was battered, totally battered, and he went to drug abuse, now he's a very dangerous man to be around.... So when Dan was born, I never left him with his father, because I was afraid that he could not handle the pressure and soon after, I fled.

After Jenny escapes from her husband, she lives with her sister, but when her sister moves to New York, Jenny and Dan relocate to another city in Michigan, where Jenny hopes to find an apartment, child care, and work. But Jenny's welfare payment goes astray, and things start to fall apart:

As soon as I got my summer apartment, my welfare check was lost, and they were ready to evict me. Then my health began to suffer; Dan still needed me and wasn't ready for day care—it was a task to keep myself and my baby alive! I had stopped doing drugs, but now I had no one to lean on and I felt as if I was in a trap.... Even with cheap rent you can't believe how little money there is after expenses. There were days when I didn't have money for sanitary napkins—there was just nothing—there was no way anymore for me to take care of us. My summer lease was up and we had nowhere to go. So I take all of my things and store them in someone's garage who I'd only known for three months, and they let us sleep on their floor.... All this time my health is bad: I would get my period for three weeks in a row, I would get headaches and spells of dizziness. Dan was constantly irritable; he would only sleep when he was totally exhausted.... I had no money saved and I don't understand how to get ahead with the welfare system. I had nowhere to go. My life was in crisis.

While Jenny's life and that of her child approach desperation, Christy Fantan's domestic world has already unraveled. She, too, fled an abusive spouse who had sexually molested their two younger children. Christy, a white mother of three, is forced to go on welfare, and, because her welfare allowance does not cover the high cost of her apartment, she is soon evicted. As Christy puts it:

We had no place to go—it was summer, school was out, and DSS [Department of Social Services] gave us this voucher for a motel, and you're only meant to stay there for thirty days, but there was no housing for us so they extended it. So we lived for sixty-nine days in that motel: DSS put us there; they said there was nothing else....There were rats and roaches. I called the health department and told them but they never came....Outside they were dealing drugs and there were prostitutes walking up and down....My children just lost their personalities. My eight-year-old stopped eating.

During this period Christy must show proof that she is actively searching for housing. So after she and her children negotiate the immediate dangers outside their welfare motel, where all four of them are holed up in one room with no cooking facilities and no refrigerator, they search for housing:

So all this time I tried to search for an apartment with the $310 limit from DSS. I could find a two-bedroom that fit that but not a three-bedroom, and with three kids, they said, I couldn't live there. They said if you can do something about one of your kids....Well what do you want me to do? Get rid of one of my kids? And the wait for public housing is three or four years in some places.

After more than two months of futile searching, while staying at a roach-infested motel for which DSS paid more than $500 per month although it will not raise the housing allowance to comparable market rates, the family finds itself back on the streets. A friend of a friend offers his trailer; Christy and her children move in temporarily:

We stayed in the trailer for September and October. There was no electricity and no heat, but it did have running water. We got a space heater—it was okay; at least we were together and we had a place.

Christy's sense of place is short-lived, however, because the owner reclaims the trailer, and Christy returns to the streets with her young family.

Both she and Jenny and their respective children, like thousands of other families across the country, are in crisis with nowhere to go and nowhere to turn. For them, "social suffering" is continuous and chronic, and poverty has become, in Victor Hugo's words, a sustained "social asphyxia."[11] While both Jenny and Christy fell from conventional marriages into the gendered pit of physical and sexual abuse and the terrors of homelessness and destitution, they now have joined the faceless statistics at the bottom of the well: single mothers who are poor and who, by virtue of their status, are active contributors to the so-called breakdown of the American family. They are the silent members of what Charles Murray terms "the coming white underclass."[12] Indeed, marriage and its often violent rewards are consistently touted as the answer to single mothers—whether unwed, abused, deserted, or active agents of their divorce, no matter; the sacred covenant will save them and their children from poverty, even if their bodies and their human dignity are scorned and violated. If not, economic penalties that stop subsidized single mothers will do the job.

In the situation of Justine Wilson, a black mother of three, marriage certainly did not protect her from gang violence and daily life-threatening risks. She decided to flee public housing twice for the same reason: physical danger to herself and her children:

I knew when I start seeing a lot of traffic, that's when I knew...and it's dangerous if you even know they doing drugs. So we just got up and left and went to my aunt, but living with your folks, like that is not a good matter. Your kids are there, other people's kids—it was just a terrible hassle. I was just falling apart....we left there and we had nowhere to go. My brother lives in the area, but he's got four kids in a trailer and he couldn't take us. I never been in this situation before where I don't have no place for me and my kids to stay, where I been living off other people and now we got no place to go....So I said Lord, you gotta find us a place to stay.

Justine, pregnant with her third child, receives no support from her husband, who has now abandoned the family, and they are given emergency shelter through a crisis center. Soon after the baby is born, she and the three children are allocated an apartment in a housing project in another area, with a better reputation, but the safety and drug problems prove to be even worse. Justine describes the terror of those five months:

> Lord, what a place that was. I mean you couldn't go outside; even the little kids was cursing you—the parents over there, they didn't help or do nothing. It's white people and it's black people—they all mixed in, but they was all selling stuff right there in front of the kids. There was shooting and it was dealers coming in from all over. There was no respect for the women. I mean I've seen them beat up people. I mean men beating the women—black and white—how they just actually beat them and always the police took their time coming. The people be halfway dead before the police come. It was sickening to live in a place like that. We were there five months, and then, when Jesse almost got shot, that was it!

After ten-year-old Jesse is caught in cross-fire between two dealers behind his apartment, Justine takes her children and flees the daily dangers and deadly assaults, becoming another of the fifty-two thousand families homeless on any given night.

It is clear that "in America being poor is deadly,"[13] and if you are female and a mother of color with young children concentrated in one of the projects designed for the underclass, there is no sense of place or daily stability; rather, there is a pervasive sense of powerlessness that mirrors the experience of living in a war zone. Nancy Dubrow and James Garbarino's study of families living in the Chicago public housing projects points to shootings, gangs, elevators, and darkness as the most serious daily dangers that single mothers and their children confront, where "100 percent of the children five years old and under had direct contact with shooting."[14] In another report, Garbarino and colleagues argue that the costs to children are immense: children living in the projects, like children living in a war zone, experience sustained chronic danger that often produces posttraumatic stress disorder, where hopelessness and despair may translate into within-group violence, depression, and self-hatred.[15]

Welfare Myths and Contingent Lives

As we learn about the daily life experiences of Jenny, Christy, and Justine, and those of countless other single mothers across the nation, their stories tell us of abuse and terror, of daily grinding struggles, and of their courage and coping strategies. Behind these stories of recurring unmet needs lie gaping public policy holes that actually structure family poverty, destitution, and homelessness. How does a single mother survive in public housing when she and her children are prey to sexual violence and physical assaults as drug dealers and gangs stake out territory? How does she hold down a full-time or part-time job when there is no available, accessible, or affordable child care?

The National Law Center on Homelessness and Poverty reports that, in 63 percent of the nineteen cities they surveyed, the market cost of two children in child care actually exceeds the total earnings from a full-time minimum wage job and that the fair market rent for a two-bedroom apartment exceeds the maximum Aid to Families with Dependent Children (AFDC) allowance for a family of three in all nineteen of the cities.[16] How does one take care of a family on welfare when in 1992, in the median state, the AFDC grant for a family of three with no other income was $372 a month, or 41 percent of the poverty line? If food stamps were included, the combined benefits in the median state made up only 72 percent of the poverty line.[17] How does a single mother get immunizations for her baby when the free clinic is open only twice a week and the bus fails to run and her older child is ill? If she fails, she risks another cut in her monthly welfare payment. How does she ever escape poverty, even when she attends job training and miraculously finds a job among the few available, when the job itself pays the minimum wage or just above, offers no benefits, and when she has two young children? Working full-time, a single parent at minimum wage earns $740 per month, or just over $8,800 per year. The 1993 federal poverty line for a family of three was $11,800. It is clear that in such cases the minimum wage itself is a constructed inequity that continues to perpetuate child and family poverty, when affordable safe housing and child care needs cannot be met.[18] How does a single mother, who must serve as both nurturer and provider, cope in the face of all these state-constructed obstacles?

The obstacles and daily struggles facing single mothers in poverty that are documented here are not unusual. What is unusual is the persistence of the myths that surround their lives. The political rhetoric of "stop favoring unwed mothers" and "stop subsidizing the parents who made them victims"[19] casts the single mother as a moral deviant—the sexually irresponsible actress in the theater of the procreating poor, the unfit mother/addict, conjuring up nineteenth-century French images of the "dangerous classes."[20] The pro-family commentators call for "the restoration of the moral environment in which the poor live," which fuels the popular public discourse that advocates turning sluts into married women, parasites into able-bodied workers, single mothers into homemakers baking apple pie even if homes are war zones and shelters and apple pie has been lost amid the dry crackle of food stamp allotments.[21] But the calls continue not only from former vice president Dan Quayle, Republican House Speaker Newt Gingrich, and the right-wing coalitions, but also from Bill Clinton's administration and the Democratic legislators whose media sound bite is the constant refrain "to end welfare as we know it." The "we" clearly refers to the definers, not the defined, and is yet another coded attack on poor women.

The reality is that most women on welfare have worked part time, and many are cyclical part-time workers forced out of the labor market by lack of jobs, layoffs, and/or ever-pressing needs for health care and child care. A recent study from the Institute for Women's Policy Research indicates that more than 40 percent of mothers on AFDC work approximately nine hundred hours a year, which closely mirrors the labor force participation rates of all working mothers in the country, and that these workers often combine AFDC payments with earnings from part-time jobs.[22] Yet, despite the evidence that most mothers on welfare work as much as their middle-class counterparts and that they have the same number of children as other women (1.9 on average), pernicious assumptions continue to prevail: that they have more and more babies to get more welfare (at $2.25 per day, that is hardly an incentive!); that they need to be put to work; that they need to be made accountable to "us," the taxpayers; that they must be forced to take responsibility for their nonlegitimacy as mothers; that placing their lives under increasing state surveillance will deter them from their social and individual female pathologies. These myths persist, they are sustained by policymakers, and they reverberate through middle America, while the patterned inequalities that are created by the politics of distribution are ignored. So, too, are the deep legacies of racism, of continuing gender discrimination in the workplace, and of punitive public policies that neither value women as workers nor support them as both providers for and nurturers of their children. Clearly, for women, particularly single mothers, a job is no way out of poverty, earning approximately 69 cents to the male dollar, predominantly occupying the pink-collar ghetto of low-wage, part-time, no-benefits, service-sector work. Paradoxically, single-mother families are made responsible for state-constructed poverty; yet there is little state accountability in current welfare workfare policies, which coerce women to work or require them to do community service. Perhaps even more ironic is the bitter fact that even as welfare budgets are targeted for further cuts, economic analysis by the Center on Budget and Policy Priorities reveal that the combined state and federal revenues for AFDC amounted to approximately 3.4 percent of the average state's budget![23]

Michigan, home state of the women whose stories are profiled here, has often been cited by the current federal administration for its innovative "welfare reform," specifically, the social contract, the provisions of which are currently under consideration as part of national welfare reform. At present in Michigan, public assistance recipients must participate in the social contract, which means twenty hours of job training, community service, or work per week. Yet no child care and no transportation are provided under the social contract for community service, and no exemptions are granted for mothers of young children. If one works, or attends a community college, or participates in the MOST (Michigan Opportunity and Skills Training) program, child care is subsidized by the Department of Social Services—but at minimal and inadequate rates. Who pays the deficit? Average child care costs in the state in 1992 were $4,423, which as a percentage of mean family income was 8.9 percent for married couples, 28.7 percent for single-parent families, and 50 percent for a single parent working at minimum wage.[24]

The situation in Michigan is mirrored across the United States, where lack of available, accessible, affordable, quality child care continues to present a severe obstacle for working parents and an overwhelming crisis for single parents. In the areas of infant and toddler care, special-needs children, and after-hours shifts, the crisis is even more acute. The Children's Defense Fund highlighted this crisis in 1991, reporting that child care costs were prohibitive, not only for poor single mothers but for middle-income single parents as well. Costs varied from $4,836 in Oakland, California, to $3,380 in Dallas, Texas; a single parent working full-time at minimum wage in Oakland, California, would pay up to 56.9 percent of her income on child care, and in Dallas, 39.8 percent. In 1993, the National Law Center on Homelessness and Poverty merely confirmed the alarming implications of the child care crisis, reporting that, in New York City, the cost of one child in child care exceeds 100 percent of minimum wage earnings, and in 63 percent of the nineteen cities they surveyed the cost of two children in child care exceeded earnings from a full-time minimum wage job![25] As demand for child care far exceeds availability and affordability across the nation, it is poor young children who are consigned to unregulated, poor-quality child care and to makeshift unreliable arrangements, and it is their mothers who become trapped in cycles of desperation.

In the case of teenage mothers who are alone and whose adolescent lives are suddenly shadowed by both baby and ominous public policy threats, the child care crisis becomes hazardous to their survival and that of their babies. However, it is their "politics of conduct" that becomes the focus (and the racial coinage of newspaper columnists and social commentators), lending credibility to some politicians' calls for orphanages to house the children of the unwed and the unfit, even while they deny reproductive choice to poor young mothers in order to "protect life."[26]

Teenage Mother Stories

Sara Thomas is young and poor. She is a black high school graduate who has lived on her own since she was sixteen. She gave birth to Des when she was seventeen. She has suffered enormously from the chronic scarcity of available subsidized quality child care. Her baby's father, who was on drugs, abandoned her when the baby was born but returned temporarily several months later. Like many other young single mothers, Sara has continued working full time but faces enormous struggles in finding good child care for her son:

> At that time my baby's father was home, who was on drugs. So it was like he would watch my baby, our baby, some of the time, but then he left again and the baby went to his great-aunt's house. It was not a safe environment. I mean it was like in poverty on that side. The self-esteem, the motivation was not there. Things that may have kept Des from being at the point he's at now maybe could have been prevented if I could afford proper child care...I mean it's a drug area, where dope is sold. His great-aunt drinks beer, she smokes weed. There's people running in and out all the time. I mean, the area is just a criminal area—it's poverty—and that's where Des had to go because I could not afford the child care I would want him in. I could not afford it. No, there was no way. I was paying her about $35 a week, but she just couldn't keep him rotating shifts. And I'm talking about this great-aunt is like about thirty or forty years old, so that was like $35 a week that I had to give her. And say I wanted to work overtime—just to make a little more money. I would give her at least $45 for him staying that time and that's somebody feeding him, changing his diapers, spending time with him. And I worked anywhere from nine to ten hours a day.... It wasn't a good environment for him, but it was the safest environment I could get him in. I know that he wouldn't have been hurt, but I know at the same time it was not a positive role model in his life—but that's the best I could have him in.
>
> Then I had like a friend that I thought would be a really good babysitter for my son, but I come to find they were neglecting my son. They would like put him in a crib and just leave him in there—they never held him, they never cuddled him. And you know he's very affectionate, he loves you, but I felt that he felt like he was in jail, you know, and this is a $35-a-week babysitter, and I'm not making that much money at this time. So she would watch him, plus I began to float-shift—I would work days, I would work afternoons, midnights—so it was really hard...and a lot of stuff later could have been avoided if I could have put him in proper child care but I couldn't afford it.

Anna Adams is also a teenage mother who graduated pregnant from high school. She is black and poor and was unable to obtain an abortion due to the Medicaid ban. After her daughter was born, she described her growing disillusionment when her boyfriend deserted her and their newborn baby. She is also one of the many resilient teenage mothers who have continued to work, despite low wages that fail to make her economically self-sufficient, as she tries desperately to meet her growing baby's needs. She is heavily dependent on child care support from her family, yet her relationship with her mother is fraught with conflict. As Anna's work schedule increases, neither her sister nor her mother is able to meet her child care needs. She leads a grim and harsh life, one that she wishes fervently to escape:

> I hate being poor and a single mom, but there's nothing I can do about it. I hate this life! I hate it! I hate it from day to day. I can't stand it, and everyday I'm thinking what can I do to get away from this? How can I better myself to get away from this?

But each effort that Anna makes, and she has attempted many, is met with obstacles from an intransigent welfare bureaucracy that punishes single mothers for initiative and partial economic self-sufficiency:

> All the time I don't think this system's here to help me; it's just to keep you right where you're at—to be poor—to make you psychologically dependent. It just doesn't work for you at all. It's like you're working—well, they want you to work—but then they take away what you make and they cut you off just as you get going, so it's like you're never on top. But I gotta find a way out of this—it's just too crazy.

Anna experienced enormous frustration in trying to move ahead. After the baby was born, she found a job working forty hours a week at a department store, earning just over $5 an hour. In addition, because her earnings exceeded the Department of Social Services (DSS) cutoff amount, she lost most of her food stamp allotment and Medicaid and is now several months behind in her rent payment:

> I don't want to be on AFDC [Aid to Families with Dependent Children], but I had to get back so I could get caught up on my rent and get Medicaid for my baby, so I was working forty hours and since I got back on AFDC, I had to cut back to fifteen to twenty hours a week. I hate it—I hate being on AFDC. They make you feel so belittled, I hate that! I hate going to the office and I hate dealing with the social worker and dealing with every worker that has something to say about my life....Sometimes they make you think that they're the one giving you this money and they're not—it's the government and they make me pay taxes, so I'm the one giving the money back to myself....
>
> And then I was asking what if I wanted to go back to school, and the worker said, "You didn't graduate," and I said, "I graduated! And I want to go to college." I don't want to be on AFDC the rest of my life and if I keep doing what I'm doing now, I'm never going to get off. I got my high hopes for me and I don't want [my daughter] to go through the same things I have—it's terrible.

Anna's anger at the welfare system illustrates the common double bind that so many single mothers are caught in. Her pink-collar job keeps her at just above minimum wage, but still in poverty; there are few opportunities for advancement, particularly as she has to reduce her hours in order to protect her health coverage through Medicaid. She is thus condemned to being a low-wage permanent part-time worker with few alternatives, other than succumbing to "the statistics" that make her "a nothing":

> I feel so much better about myself when I'm working 'cause I'm also doing something for myself, and all the time I'm trying to better myself. I'm not just one of those statistics that they say just gets on AFDC and sits there—especially about your being black—that's how they

think you are, anyway, having baby after baby as if you want to just sit all your life on AFDC...and when you go to the supermarket I get that different treatment when I pull out the food stamps and people look at you and say you're on AFDC and you're not trying to better yourself. And then I feel bad, I want to cry, I want to tell them, "Don't look like that! You don't know what's going on in our life!" Those people who look at you in the line and say, "She's one of those," and I want to tell them, "You just don't know. If you have a kid like this and you got no way out, see what you'd go through."

Anna feels trapped in a never-ending cycle of hurdles, where daily life is a constant battle through a minefield of obstacles. She wants to go back to school while working part-time, but the college child care center is unaffordable, her family can no longer help her with child care, and the DSS child care subsidies pay only 75 percent of the costs of child care in her area. She is a trapped young mother who cannot find an exit: "If you're on AFDC, you can't put your kid in a good all-day preschool 'cause of your low income, and it just costs too much and AFDC only pays for the real cheap places."

For both Anna and Sara, chronic and insurmountable child care problems compound their stressed and vulnerable lives. Both have high aspirations that defy the statistics structuring the public accounting of their lives, yet both are held captive by the child care needs of their children and their low-wage labor. As with so many other young single-parent families in poverty, there is little hope for change in their immediate futures. Meanwhile, stresses compound, children grow from babyhood to preschool age, housing and safety issues are ever present—and all it takes is a case of the chicken pox for one of these young mothers to lose her job, be evicted, become homeless, or move to another, more dangerous housing project.

Consider the situation of Tara Mays, who became pregnant when she was sixteen and a junior in high school. A young black teenager with neither family support nor adequate welfare in her southern state, she and her baby moved to be with relatives in Michigan:

At first everybody was all supportive. You know: Okay, you made a mistake. We're gonna help you, we're gonna do this, we're gonna do this and that and this and this. But it's like the calls got shorter and letters less and less. I couldn't find a shoulder to cry on. At first I kind of resented it, and then I kind of felt like, well, you put yourself in this situation, and I'm also thinking, well, they got their lives. But I felt like they set me up—they told me they'd help me and then when it came time, it's like, where are you guys? So I moved up here, I had to drop out of school, and one of the reasons is because of the welfare system—this is paradise here in Michigan compared to Mississippi! So I came up here, and I moved in with my cousin and her husband. And I was seventeen, and I still had another year of high school to go after I had my baby, and they had legal guardianship of me to go back to public school 'cause I'm still a minor. At first, it was, they was like, you can go back to school, and we'll take you to this place to get this done and this done, and, okay, we'll help you. And it's like as a senior you have all these expectations, like prom and a ring and graduation, but on welfare you can forget it. And they said we gonna have an open house, and then the plans got fewer and fewer and they lied to me. They got evicted, so they decide they'll move to another city, but I just got started back in school and I didn't want to move there. So I ended up moving—me and the baby—into this apartment. I have a baby bed, a bed, a cooler, and that's it. I didn't have a stove or a refrigerator. And they left me and I'm here alone—no family, no care, no job, no nothing—me and the baby.

Alone at seventeen with her new baby, Tara is desperate. Fortunately, through her new public school, she is referred to a teen-parent center and is assisted in finding child care for her baby so that she can continue to attend school and graduate. The center, however, has since been scheduled to close as part of a cost-cutting budget move, which means both the babies in care and the teenage mothers risk further desertion by both the education system and the state. For young mothers such as Tara, afraid and alone as so many poor teenagers are, these centers become lifelines and temporarily sustain both mothers and their babies. The future of many other young women and their babies are severely threatened, as punitive budget cuts aimed at cutting assistance to unmarried teenage mothers threaten to push them further over the edge.

It is in the reality of young women's daily lives that the current media and public policy rhetoric about teenage pregnancy should be concentrated. Clearly, having a baby alone as an adolescent is a traumatic event. But in the absence of effective contraception education in the public schools, now virtually eliminated by the hysteria of pro-family abstinence advocates and the religious right, as well as the severe restrictions on access to abortion by poor women, it is not surprising that sexually active teenagers become pregnant and give birth. It is instructive to note that findings by the Alan Guttmacher Institute indicate that the United States is the only one of six industrialized countries studied (with Canada, Britain, France, the Netherlands, and Sweden) in which the incidence of teenage pregnancy has increased over time and by a considerable margin. The Netherlands, described as the perfect contraceptive population, has the lowest rates of pregnancy, births, and abortions—achieved in a little more than three decades through intensive public education and widely available public health reproductive services for teenagers.[27] While national statistics in the United States indicate the dangerous links between low- birth-weight babies and teenage pregnancies, it is apparent that abstinence is no public health panacea; rather, it should be the responsibility of the state to ensure that all pregnant females receive adequate and early prenatal care. The fact that girls under fifteen frequently receive no care at all is a testimony to the way in which children in need of public health care and intensive counseling become throwaway casualties in a society that, in the words of Joycelyn Elders, the former U.S. surgeon general, "has a love affair with the fetus." Teenage pregnancy is a complex ideological issue, with the political right urging punishment and orphanages and some on the left ignoring the emotional and real-life constraints that a newborn child can put on an adolescent mother. So that while Reed is right that the focus on teenage pregnancy is really a focus on unmarried mothers and perceived sexual promiscuity, it is too easy to dismiss teenage pregnancy as a nonissue.[28] The existential consequences for mother and child are traumatic in a society that lacks a safety net of family support policies to help single mothers survive as a group and, in particular, to support teenage parents.

In 1990, in the absence of national contraceptive support services and abysmal public health services for adolescents, more than 92 percent of the births to black teenagers, 59 percent of births to Latina teenagers, and 56 percent of births to white teenagers were to unmarried mothers.[29] Many of these adolescents face harsh and frightening futures, isolated and disempowered by their vulnerable status. Black youngsters experience a disproportionate share of social isolation and are often further marginalized as a result. Joycelyn Elders put it bluntly: "If you're poor and ignorant, you're a slave. Meaning that you're never going to get out of it....You can't control your life."[30] And control and power are what all poor women lack, and the younger in age and the darker in color, the more regulated and oppressed their futures become. To be a poor young mother is to face daily assaults from a punitive public and a retaliatory legislature. To be all that and more, a poor young mother of color lives at the intersecting points of a racist and gendered society—a double burden.

In the stories of all the single mothers portrayed in this article, we see that daily life is contingent and family survival constantly under siege. But what is life like for their children? If their children are among the fortunate few who actually gain access to public preschool services, what are their early childhood experiences like? And when their children begin elementary school, how are they perceived and treated in public school classrooms? How do poor young children negotiate daily life in their classroom worlds? A detailed look inside the windows of their classrooms is illuminating.

The Classroom Worlds of Poor Children

In the classroom described in the following excerpt, four-year-old Greg is observed in a state-funded preschool at-risk program, which runs for part of the day.[31] The children in this program come from destitute black, Latino, and white families who have experienced persistent episodes of homelessness. Greg is black, the child of a single teenage mother, who is alone and struggling to survive on her meager AFDC payments while she works at completing her high school diploma:

> As I enter the room teacher Peggy (who is the white headteacher) tells me: "These kids are real problems. I don't know if I can work here much longer." The children receive breakfast, snack, and lunch at the program, which runs four mornings a week. I notice that several of the children have insatiable appetites and constantly ask for seconds and thirds. Snack is served at midmorning and teacher Dee (the black teacher aide) prepares crackers with peanut butter with two child helpers. The remaining sixteen four-year-olds are required to sit with their arms folded in silence as snack is passed around. Teacher Peggy twice reprimands Greg for comments that the snack "looks real yummy." As Greg has talked out of turn, he is passed over and has to wait for his snack until the children at the table behind him receive theirs. Greg begins to protest. "Gimme mine. No fair. Gimme," and he grabs at the tray. Teacher Peggy grabs Greg and wipes his runny nose with a look of distaste and takes him to the "time-out" chair. At this point Greg is sobbing and yelling "No fair!" and is forced to sit on the chair for fifteen minutes as he looks hungrily at the others eating. Teacher Peggy comes over to tell me this is part of her classroom management plan with Greg, as "food is what he really cares about."

In this incident Greg is stripped of his child dignity and reduced to the mechanistic behavior-modification schedules reminiscent of John Broadus Watson's notorious experiments with Albert and the white rat. This becomes even more problematic when we realize that Greg has very little choice; he either complies or he goes hungry. Meted out to any child, this is clearly unethical practice; however, this becomes a particularly disturbing incident when we realize its impact on the life of a hungry child. While this form of discipline is unethical and clearly in violation of early childhood education guidelines, it happened. It happened because children like Greg are condemned before they enter such classrooms. Teachers like Peggy and many others in the educational profession share the general public's negative perceptions of the poor, and the fact that one teaches in a preschool program for poor, so-called at-risk children is no guarantee that one is free of prejudice toward the poor or free of racism.

Later that day, teacher Peggy is overheard telling Greg's mother, "You people better do something about your kids."

On another occasion, four-year-old Casey came in crying, and the bus driver told teacher Dee that Casey's father literally threw him screaming on the bus this morning and that a neighbor had told her his mother had been beaten last night by Casey's father. Casey has bruises over his back, which teacher Dee shows to teacher Peggy, while holding Casey. Teacher Peggy sighs and says, "These migrant workers really shouldn't have children," and she tells teacher Dee to go to the office and have the director call Protective Services. She directs the children into a circle and begins with a song-and-finger play. Kelly lies down on the floor and sucks her thumb. "Kelly, sit on your bottom," says teacher Peggy sternly, and Kelly obediently sits. A few minutes later as the choices for the day are being reviewed, blocks, housekeeping, or pasting at the art table, Kelly goes to the library corner and quietly lies down with a book in her hands. "Kelly, get over here right now," shouts teacher Peggy. "The book corner is closed today and circle time is not over." Kelly walks back sucking her thumb and sits in the circle, playing with her velcro sneaker. The velcro tie comes off in her hand, and she begins to cry. "Kelly, you'll have to go and sit outside the door until you can quiet down," orders teacher Peggy. Kelly sits crying outside the door, still holding the broken velcro snapper in her hand.

The visits made to this public preschool revealed a continuing pattern of harsh and punitive practice by the headteacher, whose contempt for the children and their families was evident on many disturbing occasions. The abused child, Casey, a migrant child, was not treated with any compassion or concern but, rather, confirmed teacher Peggy's stereotypes of Latino children, who were part of migrant families in the area. Teacher Dee somewhat ameliorated the harsh classroom world by treating the children with gentleness, but she, too, was intimidated by her supervisor. Kelly, a white homeless child, was often dirty and smelly when she came to class, and she became the frequent target of teacher Peggy's wrath. There was little that Kelly could do right in that classroom. She found it difficult to respond to the rigid classroom routines and would try and curl up unnoticed in the reading area, where there were cozy cushions to sleep on. At the time, Kelly was living in an overcrowded shelter with her single mother and two siblings; the family had recently been evicted for unpaid rent.

Greg, Casey, and Kelly were part of the undeserving poor, the children of "welfare" mothers who were perceived as immoral and unable to care for their children adequately. As W. N. Grubb and M. Lazerson have pointed out, "we so desperately distrust and dislike lower-class adults that we are willing to let their children suffer as well."[32]

While the preceding observations were drawn from public preschools, the following description portrays the elementary classroom world of Tim, the white child of a young single mother. Tim has attended four schools in the past year, since the family is homeless and he, his mother, and younger sister have moved from truck to shelter to trailer to welfare hotel. In his third grade class, Tim has been described by his teacher as "socially maladjusted with real learning problems":

During social studies, Mrs. Devon tells the children to select a partner and to begin working on their maps. There are twenty-six children in the class, but Tim is left without a partner as a threesome forms amid whispering. I overhear one of the three saying, "Yuck, he's an asshole. Can I be partners with you guys?" Mrs. Devon calls Tim over and says, "Well, I guess they want to work in a threesome, so you'll have to do it by yourself after you come back from reading." At that point a reading aide comes to call Tim out of class and he goes to remedial reading. I follow him and find a certified remedial education teacher assisted by several aides, one of whom can barely read. However, it does not matter, as no reading takes place. Tim is given worksheets to complete. Later, during lunch, I follow Tim to the lunchroom. No child sits with him and he goes to sit at the other end of a large table, hungrily eating his free lunch and looking at the wasted leftovers on other plates. When no one is looking during cleanup, he quickly takes an apple, from which a small bite has been taken, and slips it into his pocket, which makes a noticeable bulge. On the way back to afternoon class, Tim slips the apple into his locker without being caught.

After school, Tim is particularly upset because two children called him names during gym and made fun of his socks, which are holey. He says, "They think 'cause I haven't got no home that I haven't got nothing inside of me. They won't play with me. They won't be a buddy when we go on trips either, and no kids will be my friends....Also, they all think I'm so dumb, and I hate this school, and Mrs. Devon keeps saying she got no time when I ask her things." A week later, on another visit to the classroom, Tim's name is up on the board; he is being punished and cannot go to recess because he did not complete or return his homework assignments. Mrs. Devon describes Tim as "lacking motivation—he's always staring out the window and he has not completed any of his assignments this week." Tim says,

> "She hates everything I do. She made red checks on all my worksheets, and anyhow, I can't do homework and stuff in the shelter. There's always noise and stuff going on." I notice that Tim seems to drop off to sleep several times in the afternoon and is jerked back to attention by Mrs. Devon's voice loudly calling his name.

Tim's teacher is stressed by a large class of children, many of whom have special and pressing needs. Because Tim is chronically tired and hungry, he is often inattentive in school. Because he has changed schools four times, his academic skills are understandably lacking. But I notice he is also a bright child who learns quickly, is a fluent reader, and shows remarkable persistence in coping with daily obstacles. However, for his teacher he is a nuisance factor, who disrupts the class. "I just don't have time for these kids on top of my teaching....It's just too much of a burden, and their mothers move them from place to place. They don't have proper records, and Tim's the third one of them I've had in the past two years." Tim as "one of them," like Greg, Casey, and Kelly, has little entitlement to an education. In their fragile lives, as with millions of other destitute children, school becomes a landscape of condemnation.

In the following situation, we see how a classroom can become a landscape of promise. Ten-year-old George is black. He is a gifted writer and, fortunately, is placed in the classroom of Ms. Donovan, a white, first-year teacher who is sensitive and caring and who is appalled by the attitudes of her fellow teachers. Ms. Donovan describes her experiences:

My class consisted of fifth- and sixth-grade students....When I was told that I would be getting a new student in mid-December, the teacher's lounge reverberated with negative comments: "Now you will have a chance to compare black and white students, and you'll see how terrible these black students are." "You're lucky we only have a few at this school....They can't read, barely even speak, you'll see." All this was said to me before I even met the new student. I was appalled by my colleagues' comments. I knew racism existed in the teacher's lounge but not to this degree.

George has already been assigned to remedial reading, taught by Mrs. Crim. Ms. Donovan is concerned about this placement, as Mrs. Crim has on previous occasions made derogatory remarks to her about students in poverty, describing them as "all the bad, low-skilled kids...[who] come from broken homes....They are either hillbillies or blacks from the poor section where those run-down apartments are...and that means trouble." George, however, according to Ms. Donovan, is a warm and friendly child who adjusted quite easily to her classroom routines and who has a gift for poetry:

> As a group project, the fifth graders were designing and publishing their own book. When George first joined the class, he was somewhat intimidated by the group project. But once the other students realized that he had such a creative sense of phrasing, they asked him to write for the book. And for a class assignment on personification he produced this poem, which was selected as the book's opening page:

> > The willow tree became a harp
> > in the gentle fingers of the wind.

> In passing I mentioned the poem to Mrs. Crim, the remedial reading teacher, and told George to show her his work because I felt it was very good. He returned quickly and did not say a word to me about what her reaction had been. Since she said nothing to me about his visit, I finally asked her if she was not impressed with his creativity. "Oh, it was nice," she responded. Then with her usual cynicism she asked, "Do you think George really made up that poem or did he copy it?"

Ms. Donovan also describes the difficult situation of George and his single mother, who works late at night and is forced to leave George alone at home:

> I asked George if it would be possible to reach his mother by telephone and he said, "Yes, but she often sometimes works until nine at night." I began to call in the evening as late as 10 P.M.; I could not reach her. I asked George if he was alone at home at night, and he said, "Yes, but it's okay. I'm used to it." I was becoming increasingly concerned. I mentioned to another teacher that George's mother was at work until late, and he responded, "How do you know she's at work? She might be out on the streets. You know what these black women are like—the more kids they have, the more money they get from AFDC." I tried to explain to him that George's mother worked, and from all records it appeared he was an only child. He simply smiled and said, "I can't believe you're so naive."

While George is seen as a child of promise in the eyes of Ms. Donovan, whose eyes will see George next year? And will sixth grade become a landscape of condemnation in which George is reduced to a category of otherness, framed by his race and his poverty?

Ms. Donovan's classroom was unusual within that school setting, where class bias and racial prejudice ran rampant. I have also observed other good classrooms where teachers were sensitive to poor children's needs, where bias and racism were confronted, and where caring teachers made a significant impact on their students' lives in multiple ways. However, I intentionally chose to illustrate harsh and insensitive school worlds because they do exist and we need to pay attention to them; they chronicle the making of early educational failure and a continuing assault on young lives. Teachers do not live above their culture. Why expect them to critically transcend what legislators, judges, doctors, and college professors do not? Teachers, like other professionals, are often participants in the pervasive discrimination that blights young lives and begins the "pattern of inferior education, of low standards and expectations [that] continues through secondary schools and culminates in failures, dropouts and pushouts," that has long characterized a pedagogy of the poor in the United States.[33]

Despite the fanfare of educational reform, school restructuring, and higher standards of accountability, poor children continue to experience failure disproportionately in their early school years,[34] and most federal remedial programs yield dismally predictable outcomes. An analysis of costs and funding also consistently reveals that educational programs for poor children have been designed to provide the minimum amount of the least expensive instruction allowed under federal and state guidelines.[35] Head Start, the most successful early intervention program for poor young children, has long been flawed by its restricted access, creating a stratified, two-tier form of early schooling, as well as the general failure to provide services for all income-eligible children; only 36 percent of preschool children in need were served in 1993, with four-year-olds making up the major constituency.[36] While early intervention programs such as Head Start do serve critical family support needs, they do not begin to solve the crisis in child care, since most current programs run only four days a week for half a day, and the majority of children in need are excluded from these programs because they have been chronically underfunded and continue to be so. Furthermore, the most recent report released by the Inspector General's Office reviewing federally funded early childhood centers in different states across the United States found severe health and safety violations in each of the states investigated and concluded that lack of regulation and monitoring was a critical cause.[37] How does one regulate and monitor when there are no funds to provide for inspections, when each state has different standards of care, and when no national child care system exists?

Like poor mothers, poor children are cheap. They are part of "the great American disease," in which insignificant lives belong on the horizons of indifference and forgetfulness.[38] The alarming record of the United States in failing to address the housing, health, nutritional, safety, and educational needs of the more than 14.6 million children living in poverty has spawned a plague of savage inequalities, where "the immense resources which the nation does in fact possess go not to the child in the greatest need but to the child of the highest bidder."[39]

Savage Distributions and the Future

What, then, do childhood and motherhood mean to the citizens of the other America? A pervasive sense of invisibility? Cheap "benefits" for cheap women and cheap children? Welfare reform that assaults their daily lives? The Murrayesque vision of eliminating food stamps and subsidized housing and building mass orphanages for the babies of the poor? At present, state after state continues to enact punitive coercive legislation against single mothers and their children—the denial of benefits for additional children, the reduction of welfare grants when mothers or their children fail to attend school, the Bridefare and Healthfare policies, the time limits on welfare benefits, embraced by both Democrats and Republicans who vow with bipartisan resolve to eliminate "welfare as we know it." These kinds of proposals represent assaults on families. Women are being forced into "workfare" with a two-year welfare limit. After the two-year limit is up, they and their children are threatened with the terror of the "final cut," if the shaky ground of gendered low-skill job training, minimum-wage work, lack of child care, and unaffordable housing have failed to bear their scanty fruits of success.

All these punitive policies are grounded in a wellspring of historical sensibilities that has framed single motherhood as pathological. It may not be scarlet letters that we affix to the bosoms of errant women like Nathaniel Hawthorne's Hester Prynne; rather, the postmodern version may be more diffuse—the shaming and displaying of recipients in supermarket queues, in welfare offices, in shelters, in public sidewalk evictions. Surveillance is the tool by which we discipline and punish, and the degrading welfare/workfare system maintains the omnipresent "panopticon" eye as all the technology of a modern state is put to serve in the documentation and regulation of poor women's lives.[40]

Yet, as we listen to the stories of single mothers confronting the dailiness of destitution, there are clear, practical, social measures that would alleviate some of the chronic suffering of their families. Universal health insurance is one of them, although the current health care crisis that faces more than thirty-eight million uninsured Americans, and millions more underinsured, is denied as a crisis by many in Congress who oppose Clinton's health care reform proposals. School-based teen clinics and child health clinics (in New York City and elsewhere) have impressive outcomes in terms of the health and welfare of their child and adolescent clients;[41] yet the future of these clinics is uncertain, and school-based teen clinics are under strong attack by the national Christian Coalition and by the political right wing, which forcefully oppose reproductive and abortion counseling, condom distribution, and AIDS education.

Another critical social issue is the lack of a national subsidized quality child care system, which, as we have seen, is a particularly acute need for single mothers. It is instructive to note how Western Europe has addressed this issue. S. B. Kamerman and A. J. Kahn point out that European countries have a long-established social infrastructure for families that includes child and family allowances, guaranteed minimum child-support payments, housing allowances for both low- and middle-income families, and almost universal child care for preschool children.[42] Policies for parents of infants and toddlers include paid job-protected leaves for five to six months on the average, as well as extended supplementary job-protected leave for six months to three years, as well as subsidized child care for toddlers. This stands in sharp contrast to the dearth of family entitlement in the United States, where in 1993 the Family and Medical Leave Bill was finally passed but which allows only twelve weeks of *unpaid* leave in companies with more than fifty workers. Paid leave, child allowances, and child support payments, administered as statutory family benefits, would clearly strengthen the chronic vulnerability of female-headed families.

Gertrude S. Goldberg and Eleanor Kremen's cross-national study of seven industrialized countries further points out the differences between "advanced welfare states" such as Sweden and "reluctant welfare states" such as the United States.[43] If we compare the lives of single mothers in Sweden and in the United States, the transatlantic contrast is startling. In Sweden, in addition to the universal child allowance, single parents receive advance maintenance-support payments for each child that ensure that neither child nor single parent is penalized for the absent parent's lack of support. Although 83 percent of support obligations from noncustodial parents is recovered by the Swedish government, the actual amounts collected are only 35 percent of the monies paid out in advance maintenance-support payments, which are set at uniform levels.[44] Social assistance is also available as a cash benefit to single mothers. The amounts vary according to need, which is defined by the Social Services Act of 1980 to make sure that each person has "a reasonable level of living." In 1988, for example, a single mother with two children, ages three and six, received a cash benefit of $808 (SEK 5050) plus housing costs.[45] In 1992, an American single mother with two children received an average AFDC monthly payment of $372 (excluding food stamps), with no housing allowance, no universal child allowance, no advance child maintenance support, no paid parental leave, and no affordable quality child care. That is why, despite the fact that one-fifth of families are headed by single parents in Sweden, 87 percent of single mothers participate in the labor force and why "abject poverty, homelessness, and social disorganization do not exist,"[46] and, conversely, why in the United States they do and continue to rise at alarming rates.

It is clear that the current system succeeds in maintaining and perpetuating child and family poverty and is complicit in the *unmaking* of a viable family life. The United States is now one of the most dangerous democracies to live in, if one is poor, female, and the mother of young children. It is also clear that, as the "social asphyxia" of poverty continues, the poverty industry is flourishing; T. Funiciello claims that this industry has become "a veritable fifth estate," in which countless middle- and upper-income people in corporations and the human service professions have built their careers as the direct beneficiaries of poverty.[47] How logical is it, then, once poverty is produced, to define it, to research it, to index it, to manage it, and to declare war on it and its victims? Yet, the war on poverty has always been the wrong war. The real war that needs to be named and fought is the war against the savage distributions of the political economy. It is not "welfare as we know it" that needs reform but "wealth concentration as we know it," in which U.S. corporations have "pillaged the economy...where the spoils reaped by business in the past decades are unprecedented."[48] And, in confronting the constructed disenfranchisement and continuing squalor that private greed and unlimited privilege have brought millions of U.S. citizens, it is pertinent to examine tax welfare for the rich, where, for example, the millionaire's (or the top 1 percent of families') effective federal tax rate has dropped considerably from a rate of 85.5 percent in 1960 to less than 35 percent today.[49]

And what of corporate welfare, and legislative welfare, and perks-in-high-office welfare? It is, after all, a matter of naming and framing the world, as Humpty Dumpty informed Alice:

"When I use a word...it means just what I choose it to mean—neither more nor less."
"The question is," said Alice, "whether you can make words mean so many different things."
"The question is," said Humpty Dumpty, "which is to be master—that's all."[50]

The power of language and the power to define one's victims; cheap mothers and cheap children, consigned to the hem of life: the geography of privilege is all-encompassing, mapping the savage distributions—*them and us*. Lives on the edge: they matter little in the other America.

NOTES

This chapter was originally published in *Sage Race Relations Abstracts* 19, no. 4 (1994), 3-29.

1. Adolph Reed, "The Underclass as Myth and Symbol: The Poverty of Discourse about Poverty," *Radical America* 24, no. 1 (1992): 21.
2. For a discussion of the myths of family, see Michael Mitterauer and Rachel Sieder, *The European Family* (Chicago: University of Chicago Press, 1982); Sidney W. Mintz and Susan M. Kellogg, *Domestic Revolutions: A Social History of American Family Life* (New York: Free Press, 1988); and Stephanie Coontz, *The Way We Never Were: American Families and the Nostalgia Trap* (New York: Basic Books, 1992). For a discussion of single motherhood and the status of single mothers, see Linda Gordon, *Heroes of Their Own Lives* (New York: Penguin, 1988); and Valerie Polakow, *Lives on the Edge: Single Mothers and Their Children in the Other America* (Chicago: University of Chicago Press, 1993).
3. Robert Fuchs, *Abandoned Children* (Albany: State University of New York Press, 1984).
4. Isabell Sawhill, "The Underclass: An Overview," *Public Interest* 96 (Summer 1989): 5.
5. Children's Defense Fund, "Child Poverty Hits Record Levels," *CDF Reports* 14, no. 12 (1993): 11.
6. Children's Defense Fund, *The State of America's Children, 1992* (Washington, D.C.: Children's Defense Fund, 1992).
7. National Law Center on Homelessness and Poverty, *No Way Out* (Washington, D.C.: National Law Center on Homelessness and Poverty, 1993).
8. See James Jennings's "Persistent Poverty in the United States: Review of Theories and Explanations," *Sage Race Relations Abstracts* 19, no. 1 (1994): 5-34, for a comprehensive overview and discussion of poverty theories—from poverty as pathological to poverty as structured, racialized, and gendered. See also Michael B. Katz, *The Undeserving Poor: From the War on Poverty to the War on Welfare* (New York: Pantheon, 1989).
9. Reed, "The Underclass as Myth and Symbol," 24.
10. The following stories are drawn from Polakow, *Lives on the Edge*. All names and identifying characteristics have been changed to protect confidentiality.
11. Victor Hugo, *Les Misérables* (New York: Penguin, 1862, 1897).
12. Charles Murray, "The Coming White Underclass," *Wall Street Journal*, 29 October 1993.
13. James Garbarino, "The Meaning of Poverty in the World of Children," *American Behavioral Scientist* 35, no. 3 (1992): 227.

14. Nancy Dubrow and James Garbarino, "Living in the War Zone: Mothers and Young Children in a Public Housing Project," *Child Welfare* 68, no. 1 (1988): 11.

15. James Garbarino, Kathleen Kostelny, and Nancy Dubrow, "What Children Can Tell Us about Living in Danger," *American Psychologist* 46, no. 4 (1991): 376-83.

16. National Law Center on Homelessness and Poverty, *No Way Out.*

17. Iris J. Lav, Steven D. Gold, Edward Lazere, and Robert Greenstein, *The States and the Poor: How Budget Decisions Affected Low-Income People in 1992* (Washington, D.C.: Center on Budget and Policy Priorities, 1993).

18. This holds true for single-parent working families, despite the earned-income benefit provisions in the law.

19. Murray, "Stop Favoring Unwed Mothers," *New York Times*, 10 January 1992.

20. Fuchs, *Abandoned Children.*

21. George F. Will, "A Moral Environment for the Poor," *Washington Post*, 30 May 1991.

22. Heidi I. Hartmann and Roberta M. Spalter-Roth, "The Real Employment Opportunities of Women Participating in AFDC: What the Market Can Provide," paper presented at the Women and Welfare Reform Conference, Institute for Women's Policy Research, Washington, D.C., October 1993.

23. Lav et al., *The States and the Poor.*

24. KidsCount in Michigan, *Child Care and Early Education in Michigan: A Status Report* (Lansing, Mich.: KidsCount in Michigan, 1993).

25. National Law Center on Homelessness and Poverty, *No Way Out.*

26. Will, "A Moral Environment for the Poor."

27. Elise F. Jones et al., *Teenage Pregnancy in Industrialized Countries* (New Haven, Conn., and London: Yale University Press, 1986).

28. Reed, "The Underclass as Myth and Symbol."

29. Children's Defense Fund, "Births to Teens," *CDF Reports* 14, no. 7 (1993): 7-10.

30. Claudia Dreifus, "Joycelyn Elders," *New York Times Magazine*, 30 January 1994.

31. The following classroom observations are selected from Polakow, *Lives on the Edge.* All names and identifying characteristics have been changed to protect confidentially.

32. W. Norton Grubb and Marvin Lazerson, *Broken Promises: How Americans Fail Their Children*, 2nd ed. (Chicago: University of Chicago Press, 1988), 207.

33. Kenneth Clark, "Foreword," in *America's Shame, America's Hope: Twelve Million Youth at Risk*, ed. R. C. Smith and C. A. Lincoln (Chapel Hill, N.C.: Charles S. Mott Foundation, 1988), iv.

34. Michael S. Knapp and B. Turnbull, eds., *Better Schooling for the Children of Poverty*, vol. 1 (Washington, D.C.: U.S. Department of Education, 1990).

35. Richard L. Allington, "Effective Literacy Instruction for At-Risk Children," in *Better Schooling for the Children of Poverty*, vol. 1, ed. M. S. Knapp and B. Turnbull (Washington, D.C.: U.S. Department of Education, 1990), 1-19.

36. Children's Defense Fund, *The State of America's Children: Yearbook 1994* (Washington, D.C.: Children's Defense Fund, 1994).

37. Department of Health and Human Services, 1993.

38. Barbara Kingsolver, *Animal Dreams* (New York: HarperCollins, 1990).

39. Jonathan Kozol, *Savage Inequalities: Children in America's Schools* (New York: Crown, 1991).

40. Michael Foucault, *Discipline and Punish: The Birth of the Prison* (New York: Vintage, 1979).

41. *New York Times*, 8 December 1993.

42. Sheila B. Kamerman and Alfred J. Kahn, "A U.S. Policy Challenge," in *Child Care, Parental Leave, and the Under 3s: Policy Innovation in Europe*, ed. Sheila B. Kamerman and Alfred J. Kahn (New York: Auburn House, 1991), 1-22.

43. Gertrude S. Goldberg and Eleanor Kremen, *The Feminization of Poverty: Only in America?* (New York: Greenwood Press, 1990), 7.

44. Sheila B. Kamerman, "Women, Children, and Poverty: Public Policies and Female-headed Families in Industrialized Countries," in *Women and Poverty*, ed. Barbara C. Gelpi et al. (Chicago: University of Chicago Press, 1986), 41-63; Goldberg and Kremen, *The Feminization of Poverty*.

45. This figure is cited in Goldberg and Kremen, *The Feminization of Poverty*, based on their personal communication with Bergita Akerlind, Socialstyrelsen, 8 August 1988.

46. Ibid., 144.

47. Therese Funiciello, *Tyranny of Kindness: Dismantling the Welfare System to End Poverty in America* (New York: Atlantic Monthly Press, 1993), xvii.

48. Robert Cloward, "The Workfare Hoax," presented at the Women and Welfare Reform Conference, Institute for Women's Policy Research, Washington, D.C., October 1993.

49. Kevin Phillips, *Boiling Point: Democrats, Republicans, and the Decline of Middle-Class Prosperity* (New York: Random House, 1993), 110.

50. Lewis Carroll, *The Annotated Alice* (New York: Bramhall House, 1960), 269.

DISCUSSION QUESTIONS

1. Discuss the argument that not much has changed in the discourse about poverty or single parenthood during the past century.

2. How does the author critique the argument that poverty is a "private" affair?

3. Analyze the "racialized" nature of the attack on single-parent families in poverty.

4. Critique the argument that "family breakdown" is the major cause of poverty, using the information and analysis provided by the author.

5. How do governmental programs aimed at single-parent families facilitate or depress social and economic mobility?

6. Discuss the significance of child care as a fundamental element in the struggle against poverty.

FOR FURTHER READING

Children's Defense Fund (1994) *The State of America's Children: Yearbook 1994*. Washington, D.C.: Children's Defense Fund.

Coontz, S. (1992) *The Way We Never Were: American Families and the Nostalgia Trap*. New York: Basic Books.

Katz, Michael (1989) *The Undeserving Poor: From the War on Poverty to the War on Welfare*. New York: Pantheon.

Kozol, Jonathan (1991) *Savage Inequalities: Children in America's Schools*. New York: Crown.

Mintz, Sidney W., and Susan M. Kellogg (1988) *Domestic Revolutions: A Social History of American Family Life*. New York: Free Press.

Polakow, Valerie (1993) *Lives on the Edge: Single Mothers and Their Children in the Other America*. Chicago: University of Chicago Press.

Chapter Fourteen

Race, Family Values, and Welfare Reform

Bonnie Thornton Dill, Maxine Baca Zinn,
and Sandra Patton

The national tempest in the United States over family values shows no signs of abating. Though most reasonable people acknowledge that the causes of contemporary family change are complex, public discourse is still polarized and simplistic. In the past two decades, conservatives have galvanized public opinion and public policy around an explanation of social decay rooted in the "breakdown of the family" and a decline in "family values." Progressives, on the other hand, have challenged this perspective by calling on substantial bodies of theory and research to demonstrate that changes in family life are global and primarily the result of structural, economic, and political changes that have led to major cultural shifts. And though progressives offer compelling evidence that shifting social and economic conditions are more important than declining moral standards in the creation and perpetuation of current shifts in family life, their arguments have not prevailed. Instead, in the 1990s, the conservative narrative has become broadly accepted as a way of explaining social, economic, and cultural dislocations in the U.S. landscape. Their story is one that blames single mothers and immigrants for such social ills as poverty, crime, drug abuse, and gang violence. It has become entrenched in mainstream political discourse as policy analysts and politicians have promoted these simplistic causal connections as explanations for broad socioeconomic dislocations and as justifications for dismantling the U.S. social welfare system.

At the heart of this national debate are issues of race that are only partially addressed in the progressive critique and widely exploited in the conservative narrative. In this chapter, we seek to extend the progressive challenge in three ways: first, by examining the way in which race and racial narratives are drawn on and function in contemporary public discourse regarding family values and welfare reform in the United States; second, by showing how an analysis of racialized patterns of family formation sharpens our understanding of structured inequalities; and third, by extending the discussion of race to include both black and Latino families and demonstrating a multiracial discussion of race introduces new complications into the discussion of family values and welfare reform.

We begin by outlining the conservative narrative about family values and identifying the ways that race and gender stereotypes are embedded and exploited in their discourse. We then turn to a discussion of progressive responses to the family values and welfare reform discourse, focusing on the ways in which the progressive challenge could be extended and strengthened by explicitly incorporating race into the analyses. Next, we seek to expand the progressive critique, first, by examining the way in which racial narratives function in the family values debate; second, by identifying the ways in which race structures families; and third, by examining data on family dynamics among Latinos and blacks, in order to create a more comprehensive picture of race in the family values debate. Finally, we turn to welfare reform itself and argue that the demonization of black and Latina women is part of a racialized attack on the welfare system—one that seeks to control their fertility and their work and, ultimately, to reduce the presence of poor women of color in the society.

Our Analytical Approach

Our analytical strategy in this paper combines sociological and descriptive analyses with narrative analysis. This seems particularly appropriate in trying to shed light on issues that are rooted in social life but have been portrayed and given meaning through a variety of forms of language, symbols, and representations that are highly contested in contemporary U.S. society. Narrative analyses of policy argue for the importance of recognizing that public policy dialogues are, indeed, *public* discussions situated in complex discursive, legislative, and sociopolitical histories. Legislative agendas do not exist in isolation from popular culture and public opinion, and, in our view, it is necessary to explore the relationships between shifts in public policy and widespread media narratives in order to fully understand the relations of power at work in such social shifts. As Graeme Turner explains, "What is clear is that the world comes to us in the shape of stories."[1] The political narratives embedded in public policy agendas draw on sociological data and interpretations of those data that reflect broader social stories about race, gender, family, class, and citizenship that are widely available in public discourse. The philosopher Robert Gooding-Williams argues that such representations should be read as sociopolitical allegories. His analysis suggests that we must ask, What is the social function of a particular racial representation? What does this representation of race signify beyond the particular meanings conveyed within the given text?[2] And of course, we must also seek to answer the question, Why has this narrative appeared here and now? The cultural studies scholar Hazel Carby suggests that "these narrative genealogies, in their production of this symbolic power, have significant political resonance when they are produced in response to a perceived crisis in the formation of a society."[3] Thus, Carby argues that popular narratives, in their allegorical power to signify sociopolitical "truths," function ideologically as justifications for oppression and inequality.

In this chapter, we examine the social function of racialized political narratives that blame poor single and immigrant mothers for social ills like drug addiction, poverty, crime, and gang violence. Using examples of these narratives from different points in U.S. history, we trace these themes into the present and argue that contemporary discourse on welfare reform and family values has served as justification for the passage of punitive social policies that seek to regulate the lives of low-income women of color and white women whose sexual and reproductive behavior deviates from the middle-class nuclear family norm.

While we draw on critical race theory, cultural studies, family demography, and the work of political economists, our approach is most fundamentally grounded in multiracial feminism. This perspective is an attempt to go beyond a mere recognition of diversity and difference among women to examine structures of domination, specifically, the importance of race in understanding the social construction of gender. Despite the varied concerns and multiple intellectual stances that characterize the feminism of women of color, they share an emphasis on race as a primary force for situating genders differently. It is the centrality of race, of institutionalized racism, and of struggles against racial oppression that link the various feminist perspectives within this framework.[4]

The Conservative Narrative

The conservatives, or, as they sometimes call themselves, the "pro-family" forces, believe that the traditional nuclear family is the basis of social organization and cohesion in the United States. This family form, in their view, is the one in which children are best socialized to become good citizens and in which men and women perform the roles essential to creating and maintaining social order and continuity from one generation to the next, as wives and mothers, husbands and fathers: "As the Institute for American Values [a conservative think tank] writes in its mission statement, the two-parent family, based on a lasting monogamous marriage, is the most efficacious one for child rearing."[5] Thus, in this view a lack of family values among the "underclass"—evidenced by the supposed immorality of single women bearing "illegitimate" children—causes poverty. Much of their argument turns on the notion of a "culture of poverty" that causes and perpetuates joblessness, welfare dependency, laziness, immorality, drug addiction, and crime. It is posited as the antithesis of family values—the ostensible source of middle-class stability. This narrative not only stands in direct opposition to the progressive perspective but also serves to deflect attention from economic dislocations, discrimination in the labor market, disinvestment in inner cities, and decreasing social supports for low-income families. It does this by citing a lack of hard work and family values as the cause of welfare dependency and poverty.

The critical race feminist Nathalie A. Augustin describes the contemporary narrative of the women who receive Aid for Families with Dependent Children (AFDC):

> The "welfare mother" is a deviant social creature. She is able-bodied, but unwilling to work at any of the thousands of jobs available to her; she is fundamentally lazy and civically irresponsible; she spends her days doing nothing but sponging off the government's largesse. Despite the societal pressure to be gainfully employed, she enjoys her status as a "dependent" on the state and seeks at all costs to prolong her dependency. Promiscuous and shortsighted, she is a woman who defiantly has children out of wedlock. Without morals of her own, she is unlikely to transmit good family values to her children. She lacks the educational skills to get ahead and the motivation to acquire them. Thus, she is the root of her own family's

intergenerational poverty and related social ills. She is her own worse enemy. And she is Black.[6]

While the narrative about family dissolution is associated primarily with stereotypes of black women and families, racist and misogynist imagery of poor Latino families is fundamental to anti-immigrant campaigns. With rare exceptions, little connection is made between immigration and family values. Yet the link reveals a distinctive form of racism embedded in conservative pro-family rhetoric where there is said to be "too much of the former and too little of the latter."[7] When it comes to Latino immigrants, conservatives pathologize the values they champion and recast strong families as a menace to society. The immigration scholar Pierrette Hondagneu-Sotelo describes how stereotypes of Latino immigrants as breeders of large families were used in California's 1994 campaign to pass Proposition 187:

> The protagonists...were poor, pregnant immigrant women who were drawn to the U.S. to give birth in publicly financed county hospitals, allowing their children to be born as U.S. citizens and subsequent recipients of taxpayer-supported medical care, public assistance and education. In this scenario, immigrant families constitute a rapidly expanding underclass draining education and medical resources in the United States.[8]

Common to each of these narratives is a "bad mother," one who is seeking public funds or services to support and maintain her family and has no legitimate claim to these resources because she does not conform to traditional family values. These racialized representations of poor women guided the construction and passage of Proposition 187 in California and the Personal Responsibility and Work Opportunity Reconciliation Act of 1996 that repealed AFDC and denied benefits to legal immigrants.

The unspoken narratives embedded in this discourse draw on tenacious social myths of black family "pathology"—signified by single-parent families—infecting white women and causing a so-called epidemic of illegitimacy. It is through an assumed racialization of sexual and reproductive deviance that, in both popular and political discourse, *single mother* has come to signify *black single mother*. Sexual deviance from the patriarchal middle-class nuclear family—for white women as well as for women of color—is racialized through social narratives that link supposed black family pathology with illegitimacy, poverty, and social dysfunction.

The conservative narrative is the most recent edition of a very old story. There is a long history in the United States of social disdain for poor and single mothers, and in the nineteenth and early twentieth centuries discourse about deserving and undeserving poor women was linked to issues of race and citizenship. These earlier ideologies are reinvoked in the contemporary discourse on welfare reform and family values. In fact, part of their appeal and ready acceptance comes from the fact that they draw on ideas that are deeply rooted in American social thought.

The Progressive Challenge

For progressives, the traditional family is not a given. Rather, family forms are socially and historically constructed, not uniform arrangements that exist for all times and places.

One of the central points of contention between conservatives and progressives in these discussions concerns the causal relationships among family structure, poverty, and social problems. Three strands of thinking figure prominently in the progressive critique of family values. While they often overlap, the first emphasizes gender, the second emphasizes class, and the third emphasizes family structure.

Mainstream Feminist Perspectives

Although there is no single feminist perspective on families, it is fair to say that feminism has been at the forefront of efforts to clarify our understanding of family life. Feminists have long worked for the recognition of diverse forms of family and household arrangements, demonstrating that family forms are socially and historically constructed, not monolithic universals that exist across all times and all places. They have argued that the social and legal arrangements that govern family life are not the result of unambiguous differences between women and men. Feminists have drawn attention to the disparities between idealized and real patterns of family life, to the myths that romanticize "traditional" families in defense of male privilege, and to the fact that only a small minority of families and households has ever resembled the sentimentalized form. In challenging the dichotomy between public and private spheres, feminists have deepened our understanding of the social conditions surrounding women's family experiences.[9]

An important conclusion from the vast feminist literature on changing families is that family forms once thought to be natural and immutable are declining throughout the industrial world. Conditions of postindustrial capitalism are contributing to the demise not of the family but of an arrangement that Judith Stacey calls "the *modern* family"—an intact nuclear household composed of a male breadwinner, his full-time homemaker wife, and their dependent children.[10] This model is being replaced by rising levels of female-headed households and the growing impoverishment of women and their children. According to Stacey, marital instability and women-centered household arrangements are becoming endemic facts of life all around the world. According to Kristin Luker, "Out-of-wedlock births increased just as all industrialized societies were cutting welfare spending, so the assumption that welfare promotes such births is not borne out by the facts."[11] Stacey calls these new family forms "post-modern" because they do not fit the criteria for a "modern family."

Political Economy Perspectives

Progressive economists have contributed another strong challenge to the rhetoric of family values. Less concerned with gender relations in family life and more concerned with market forces and class formation, this work is a variant of feminist thought that directs attention to the close connections between family life and global economic developments. These thinkers call on macrostructural economic changes to explain why families are far different from what they used to be. Agreeing that families are more diverse and more easily fractured, that family members spend less time together, and that parents have less influence over their children, many political economists reason that "the current economic system is no longer congruent with traditional nuclear family values."[12] Economic realities, including men's declining wages and the pressures on women to work outside the home, mean that the family is an institution both in flux and under pressure.

As the need for certain kinds of labor diminishes, more and more working-class and middle-class families are the victims of economic dislocations. Families are profoundly affected when their resources are reduced, when they face economic and social marginalization, and when family members are unemployed or underemployed. As Lester Thurow explains, the traditional family is being destroyed by a modern economic system. Families are under attack

> not by government programs that discourage family formation (although there are some) and not by media presentations that disparage families (although there are some), but by the economic system itself. It simply won't allow families to exist in the old-fashioned way, with a father who generates most of the earnings and a mother who does most of the nurturing. The one-earner middle-class family is extinct.[13]

The argument that changes in the economy and the class structure undermine family stability is widespread within the social sciences and family studies. William Wilson's contention that supportive forces in the larger society have undergone major shifts and undermined family stability is the exemplar, but "there is no shortage of evidence of the impact of economic hardship on the family."[14] Although this position rests on growing structural inequalities rather than on the behavior of individuals or families or on their moral standards, this analysis does not discount the role of values in producing family change: "Values follow economic realities."[15] Or, as the economist David Gordon put it, "values matter, but jobs matter, at least as much if not more."[16]

Family Demography Perspectives

Conservatives believe that declining family values threaten the collective good. Yet when they say *family values*, they often mean *family structure*, or, more precisely, *nuclear family structure*. The question "What difference does family structure make?" is posed by sociologists and demographers, often quantitative social scientists. Although they do not usually engage in ideological debates about the relationship between values, single-headed households, and social problems, these scholars provide powerful evidence that social conditions are the shapers of family arrangements. This body of work empirically challenges the preoccupation with family structure as the cause of social pathologies.

By disentangling family structure from socioeconomic background, education, race, and other variables, research in this vein reveals that family structure is paramount in determining the life chances of children. Furthermore, there is a relationship between family structure and poverty.[17] Still, despite the correlation between family structure and family resources, we cannot conclude that single-parent households are the "root cause of poverty."[18]

This research finds that family structure is an increasingly important axis of racial inequality, especially between black and white children.[19] Yet it also shows that child poverty cannot be reduced to family structure for either blacks or Latinos. In the words of Sara McLanahan and Gary Sandefur, "If there were not single parents, Black children would still have much higher poverty rates."[20] To put it more precisely, for African Americans, "emulating the white family structure would close only about one-half of the income gap."[21] If Puerto Rican children lived in nuclear families, their poverty would be reduced from 41 percent to 24 percent (in other words, half is due to family structure). But poverty rates would be reduced only slightly if Mexicans and Cubans had the nuclear family structures of non-Latino white children.[22]

For feminists, progressive economists, and family demographers alike, a variety of social and economic forces has contributed to the decline of traditional family arrangements. Feminists such as Judith Stacey and Iris Marion Young have drawn from all three clusters of thought to reveal two overarching flaws in the family values position.[23] First, it reverses the relationship between family and society by treating the family as the cause of social conditions, rather than as a reflection of them. Second, it ignores the structural reasons for family breakdown.

The works of mainstream feminists, progressive political economics, and family demographers offer an extensive critique of the conservative rhetoric of family values. Each stream of work moves in different directions. Still, the critiques are similar in that they all show the link between larger economic forces and family patterns. All three argue that family life is being reconfigured more by severe structural problems than by a shift in values. Moreover, progressive scholars have taken important steps in exposing the racial scapegoating that lies at the heart of the conservative construction of family values.

Race and the Family Values Debate

Of particular importance to many progressive scholars are the racial images in the national discussion. Each body of literature recognizes that family breakdown is often a thinly veiled attack on the black urban underclass and that single motherhood is "often a code word for Black single mother."[24] For example, Ruth Sidel confronts the myth that most poor, single, childbearing women are black,[25] and Judith Stacey notes that racial anxiety about family structure is as old as the United States itself:

> Racial anxiety predates [Daniel Patrick] Moynihan's incendiary 1965 report. It reaches back a century to xenophobic fears about high fertility rates among Eastern and Southern European immigrants...[and] it reaches back much further into the history of colonial settler fears of diverse sexual and kinship practices of indigenous cultures.[26]

Progressive critics of family values are especially successful in unmasking the color-evasive language of family moralists who long for a return to a mythical time when "normal" values of "normal" Americans were sacrosanct and the law of the land.[27] Stacey interprets former Vice President Dan Quayle's criticism of Murphy Brown as an ill-fated attempt to reconstruct "Willie Horton in Whiteface":

> Without resorting to overtly racist rhetoric, the image conjured up frightening hoards of African American welfare "queens" rearing infant fodder to sex, drugs, and videotaped uprisings, such as had just erupted in Los Angeles.[28]

This pattern of discussing racial anxieties that deceptively appear to be race neutral is explained by Kristin Luker in her discussion of the ostensible *epidemic* of teenage pregnancy:

> The debate, in centering on teenagers in general, thus combined two contrasting features of American society: it permitted people to talk about African Americans and poor women (categories that often overlapped) without mentioning race or class; but it also reflected the fact that the sexual behavior and reproductive patterns of white teenagers were beginning to resemble those of African Americans and poor women—that is, more and more whites were postponing marriage and having babies out of wedlock.[29]

Although progressive scholarship has not been silent about race, its treatment of the concept is unsatisfactory. Three limitations prevent the progressive critique from fully exposing the racial dimensions within the pro-family position. First, while it is true that the images of low-income single mothers draw on long-held stereotypes and controlling images of black and Latina women as breeders and bad mothers and that this is a classic process of scapegoating the least powerful in times of economic crisis and social change, these patterns exist as part of broader social narratives. It is important not only to identify these narratives but to reveal the factors that make them so widely accepted and easily understood in an effort to examine the functions they serve in our society.

Second, the progressive framework does not reflect current conceptualizations of race as a macrostructural force, comparable to gender and class, that situates families differently and produces—indeed, *requires*—different arrangements. Progressives contend that the conservative view of social reality is steeped in racial prejudice that becomes a "kind of family Darwinism" that is blind to larger economic forces.[30] Such exposure of the racial bias in pro-family positions is crucial, but it does not go far enough in addressing the importance of race in shaping family life.

The third limitation rests on combined empirical and theoretical problems stemming from a black-white treatment of race. Progressive discourses on family values devote almost exclusive attention to African Americans. Except in some small clusters of scholarship by family demographers, Latinos and other people of color are ignored. Their invisibility in the national discussion is surprising since Latinos are rapidly approaching the epicenter of the current family crisis. Latinos now have the highest poverty rate in the United States. In addition, Latinos now make up the largest category of minority children in the country. These economic and demographic changes are introducing new complications into the family values debate. Yet they are invisible in most progressive literature.

Racial Narratives and Personal Responsibility

Evelyn Brooks Higginbotham uses the concept of "metalanguage" to describe the pervasiveness of racial representations in social relations in the United States. Race, she says, "speaks about and lends meaning to a host of other terms and expressions, to myriad aspects of life that would otherwise fall outside the referential domain of race....It blurs and disguises, suppresses and negates, its own complex interplay with the very social relations it envelops."[31] Race is both text and subtext in the family values discussion. The images of unrestrained childbearing, freeloading, idleness, delinquency, crime, violence, abandonment, abuse, gangs, and lack of love are all associated with single mothers on welfare and inscribed on the bodies of black women nationally, Latina women—especially on the West Coast and in the Mexican border states—and Native American women in the West. In fact, a major source of the power and appeal of welfare reform is its plan to discipline and control the behavior of black and Latina women, other women of color, and, by example, white women. Placing these arguments in historical perspective illuminates how their emphasis on individual morality and personal choice masks the relationship among public discourse (that is, the social narratives and representations that shape our public debates on the issue), public policy, and the economy.

Feminists have been subject to conservative criticism, in part, for our emphasis on the social structure and the economy as *producing* diverse family forms. Those who argue for family values, on the other hand, are seen as emphasizing individual behaviors and personal responsibility. These latter arguments are constructed in such a way that social structure, as a force that *produces* certain behaviors and reinforces certain values, is essentially discredited and seen as part of a widespread failure of individuals to take responsibility for themselves. Yet what the historical analysis shows is that these ideas are themselves social products and that values are modified and even corrupted in their interaction with social structures. In our view, individual behavior must be considered in the socioeconomic context in which people's life choices are made; poverty drastically circumscribes the means through which people are able to fulfill personal values and aspirations, whatever they may be. However, drawing on the concept of a culture of poverty and a view of feminism as a form of female self-indulgence and selfishness, conservatives and centrists characterize the growth of poor single-mother families in personal, moral, and cultural terms, rather than structural and economic ones.

This association of poverty, family structure, and morality is not new. According to Michael Katz, it accompanied the transition to capitalism and democracy in early-nineteenth-century America, justifying the "mean-spirited treatment of the poor" and helping to "ensure the supply of cheap labor in a market economy increasingly based on unbound wage labor."[32] As Mimi Abramovitz has pointed out:

> The rise of the market economy brought forward a new individualistic and moralistic explanation (of poverty) which focused instead on the characteristics of the poor...(locating) the problem in lack of labor discipline, lack of family discipline, and the provision of relief itself.[33]

This view of poverty works in tandem with the quintessential ideology of capitalism: the myth of the American Dream, in which success is determined by personal responsibility, hard work, and good morals.

The themes that Abramovitz and Katz identify in the early-nineteenth-century arguments appear again in contemporary welfare reform discourse. The predominant explanatory system among conservatives and centrists correlates lack of a strong work ethic, laziness, present-time orientation, sexual licentiousness, and the prevalence of single-mother families with a culture of poverty that perpetuates an endless cycle of intergenerational poverty. Today, concern about lack of labor discipline has a particularly gendered construction. For example, black male unemployment is seen as the primary cause and its solution as the means of ending the rise of single-mother families among low-income black people. Latino men are seen as posing a different kind of breach in labor discipline because their unbridled desire to work in the United States is characterized as a threat to the employment opportunities of native workers. For women, work requirements have been initiated in response to the stereotype image of the black "welfare queen," who refuses to work and has babies just so that she can get more resources from the state, and the Latina woman whose stereotypic large family is seen as requiring too much undeserved support from the state. The criticism of the alleged lack of family discipline focuses primarily on women and has only recently been extended to absent fathers. For example, black single mothers are seen as unrepentantly defying traditional values regarding female sexual activity, family formation, and family structure by not marrying and by having children out of wedlock. Latinas are seen as using their childbearing as a way to illegally attain the rights and privileges of U.S. citizenship for their children, if not for themselves. These images have helped to sustain public support for provisions in the welfare reform legislation that seek to control women's fertility and reassert the values of proper family functioning and patriarchal governance over low-income women. In fact, these images have justified naming the welfare reform legislation of 1996 the Personal Responsibility Act.

Such cultural explanations for social inequality are used as a means of obscuring structural and economic causes of poverty. This, too, is a very old story. African American families and cultures have, throughout U.S. history, been alternately and sometimes simultaneously pronounced pathological, destroyed, and vanishing. The interwoven issues of black families and cultures—and questions concerning their existence, structure, and social viability—were the central concerns in the social debate between the sociologist E. Franklin Frazier and the anthropologist Melville J. Herskovitz that occurred in the 1930s and 1940s.[34] Frazier's thesis that slavery had destroyed "the black family," leaving an abnormal matriarchal family system, was the foundation of the 1965 Moynihan report.[35] Moynihan's articulation of black matriarchal families as a "tangle of pathology" was central in recent conservative and centrist arguments about the supposed epidemic of "illegitimacy" and welfare reform.

> Carla Peterson and Rhonda Williams explain: "Today, it seems that both culture and nature conspire to damn poor women in general, and poor Black women in particular. The horror of today's welfare reform lies in the truths masked by narratives of culture, nature, race, and gender.[36]

In short, in public discourse, what culture masks is power. The culture-of-poverty explanation, so widely accepted among conservatives and centrists alike, obscures the role of the state in perpetuating and enforcing inequality, even while placing the blame for the continuation of poverty on individuals and families.

The emphasis on personal values and the culture of poverty masks the interests, of the state in, and its need for, a ready, willing, and available workforce and for a patriarchal family structure that controls and directs the fertility, sexuality and child rearing, and employment behavior of women. We disagree with an approach to poverty that focuses on values, obscuring the power relations involved in the state's treatment of poor families. Our concern is with the ways that social narratives about family values and single-mother families function in both popular and political discourse as explanations of and justifications for the passage of public policies designed to police poor women's reproductive choices and to ensure the continuing availability of a low-wage workforce. In other words, we are concerned with connections among public discourse, power relations, and the political economy.

Race as Social Structure

Over the past decade, a considerable amount of attention has been devoted to race as a primary axis of inequality for situating families differently.[37] Instead of focusing on economic conditions alone, this emergent framework for studying families argues that racial inequality is also part of the larger structure in which families are embedded. Along with class and gender, race is a hierarchical structure of opportunity and oppression that has profound material consequences for family formation. The long-standing diversity of family forms by race is produced in part by an unequal distribution of social opportunities in U.S. society.

Some of the most influential work linking family formation with racial patterns of social relations is found in a conceptual framework called multiracial feminism. Grounded in multiple, interlocking hierarchies, what Patricia Hill Collins calls the matrix of domination,[38] this perspective underscores the pervasive nature of race in shaping the experiences of women and men throughout society. At the same time, this framework acknowledges how race is shaped by a variety of other social relations, especially class and gender.[39]

This perspective offers a useful set of analytic premises for thinking and theorizing about family life. It views families in relation to a racially organized social structure that provides and denies opportunities and therefore influences the way families in different social locations organize themselves to survive. One of the crucial lessons of multiracial feminism is that "race has always been a fundamental criterion in providing the kind of work people do, the wages they receive, and the kind of legal, economic, political and social support provided for their families";[40] "groups subordinated in the racial hierarchy are often deprived of access to social institutions that offer supports for family life."[41] As Collins contends, "actual families all live somewhere, and that somewhere in the United States is typically segregated."[42]

When we examine how families are positioned within intersecting inequalities, we have a better grasp of family diversity. People experience the family differently depending on their social, class, race, ethnicity, age, and sexual orientation, and from their experiences they construct different definitions of what families are and ought to be. Multiracial feminism has furthered our understanding of the racialized connections between normative family structure and social support. The family that conservative writers uphold as "legitimate" is a product of socially structured opportunities. It emerged as a result of social and economic conditions that no longer operate for most Americans and that never were operative for many poor Americans and people of color. From the original settlement of the American colonies through the mid-twentieth century, families of European descent often received economic and social supports to establish and maintain families.[43] Following World War II, as Stephanie Coontz points out, the G.I. Bill, the National Defense Education Act, the expansion of the Federal Housing Authority, and Veterans Administration loan subsidy programs, and government funding of new highways, provided the means through which middle-class whites were able to achieve the stable suburban family lives that became the ideal against which all other families were judged.[44] These kinds of support have not been widely available to people of color and, until quite recently, were actively denied them through various forms of housing and job discrimination. A careful reading of U.S. family history makes it clear that family structure is the result of far more than economic transformations.[45]

Today's economically based reorganization of U.S. society is reshaping family structure through distinctive racial patterns. Families mainly headed by women have become permanent in all racial categories, with the disproportionate effects of change most visible among racial ethnics. While the chief cause of the increase in female-headed households among whites is the greater economic independence of white women, the longer delay of first marriage and the low rate of remarriage among black women reflects, in part, the labor force problems of black men.[46] Thus, race and gender create different routes to female headship, but whites, blacks, and Latinos are all increasingly likely to end up in this family form.[47]

Latino Families and the Limits of Family Structure

Family solidarity is commonly thought to be a defining feature of the Latino population. In both the popular images and in social science literature, Latinos are regarded as "traditional" in their family convictions and behaviors.[48] Even though research shows that Latinos are not monolithically familistic, nor are their family relations uniformly traditional, "current literature is characterized by a redundancy in accounts of Latino families."[49]

The traditional Latino family archetype has always been controversial. In the earliest research on Mexican-origin families, structural functionalism and its variant, cultural determinism, attributed negative outcomes to strong family values. Mexicans were *criticized* for the strength of their family ties. Their lack of social progress was blamed on a way of life that kept them tied to family rather than open to economic advancement. During the 1960s and 1970s, many scholars vigorously refuted explanations of cultural deficiency in Mexican families, showing that family life was not deviant, deficient, or disorganized. Instead, what were once viewed as culturally deficient Mexican family lifestyles reflected adaptive responses to hardships of poverty and minority status.[50]

A new twist on the social adaptation approach has emerged in response to the family values debate. Several scholars have expressed the view that familism facilitates adaptation in difficult social settings and that strong family orientations serve Mexican immigrants in ways little understood by social scientists and policymakers. For example, David Hayes Bautista and his colleagues found that Mexican immigrants arrive in the United States imbued with rich family values, high rates of family formation, and high labor force participation.[51] According to these researchers, "since Latinos have large families they are quite committed to fulfilling their parental roles and assuring familial obligations."[52]

Other scholars have asserted not only that strong family values facilitate immigrant adaptation, but that Latinos are better able than other groups to withstand economic hardship. Large webs of close-knit kin, a strong propensity to marry and raise large families, and, above all, "strong" family values are said to be cultural strengths that are now absent in black communities. For example, in finding that poor Mexicans in Chicago often work at two jobs, one researcher concluded that they had an intense commitment to the marital bond and to work, whereas blacks did not, presumably because of cultural differences between the two populations.[53]

Such interpretations about Latinos having strong family values and better family demographics are meant, no doubt, to challenge conservative assumptions that "Latinos as a whole have joined inner-city blacks to form one, vast, threatening underclass."[54] However, they perpetuate racial stereotypes. In their zeal to refute the negative outcomes of culture for Latinos, they use the logic of cultural determinism to "imply that Blacks and other groups do not have strong family values or a work ethic, and ironically, they ultimately reinforce the model itself."[55]

A better line of attack is to use the Latino experience to show that we cannot blame the family for social inequality. Two developments belie conservative assumptions about family. The first brings a new perspective to the discussion about the two-parent family and the impact of family structure on family well-being. The second reveals that social and economic conditions are reconfiguring living arrangements even among groups with strong commitments to marriage as the basis for family life.

Whether Latinos (or some Latino groups) have stronger family values and live in close-knit family arrangements is a question for further research. But the fact remains that the family convictions and behaviors attributed to Latinos have not prevented them from becoming the poorest racial category in the United States. As the demographers Lichter and Landale conclude, "although Latino families typically 'play by the rules,' they often remain poor."[56] These researchers found that, while substantial variation exists across Latino groups, parental work patterns are more important than family structure in accounting for poverty among Latino children. "The vast majority of Latino children live in two-parent families and almost one-half of all poor Latino children live in married-couple families, compared with 17 percent of poor African American children."[57] The conventional wisdom about the association between family structure and poverty does not hold up for Latinos. Hence, policies designed to strengthen the family will not be enough to alleviate poverty among Latinos.

Another paradox of the Latino presence in the United States underscores the importance of social and material conditions in shaping attitudes, behaviors, and family patterns. Despite high official rates of intact family characteristics upon their arrival in the United States, these characteristics are weakened in successive generations. Through the 1980s and 1990s, Latino rates of female-headed households have risen. Furthermore, research shows that life in the United States exposes immigrants (even those with strong family networks) to the current social context that gives rise to high rates of single parenthood and divorce. Although marriage is idealized in many Latin American countries, and there is a stigma attached to being divorced,[58] the U.S. social context produces family patterns that are part of a worldwide trend toward increasing maritally disrupted family structures. This generational trend is true for all immigrant groups.[59]

"Illegitimates," "Illegals," and Welfare Reform

Although black and Latina women are characterized differently in the family values debate, each group is demonized and their behavior depicted as threatening the basic values of American society. In the case of blacks, the central threat is single-parent families that produce "illegitimate" children, who according to the conservative and centrist narrative are likely to become unruly citizens. In the case of Latinas, the threat is undocumented immigrants who give birth in the United States and create unwanted citizens, who then become a conduit of government resources to families of "illegal" residents. Interestingly, in both cases and for quite different reasons, the family behavior of women is the focal point for criticism and complaint. For example, in his role as one of two primary Republican advisers on welfare reform in the 104th Congress, the conservative policy analyst Charles Murray testified to the House Subcommittee on Human Resources:

> "My proposition is that illegitimacy is the single most important social problem in our time—more important than crime, drugs, poverty, illiteracy, welfare or homelessness because it drives everything else. Doing something about it is not just one more item on the American policy agenda, but should be at the top."[60]

This social vision was then codified in the language of the welfare legislation passed in 1996, which itemized a long list of "negative consequences of raising children in single-parent homes," including such statements as, "Young women who have children before finishing high school are more likely to receive welfare assistance for a longer period of time"; "Children of teenage single parents have lower cognitive scores, lower educational aspirations, and a greater likelihood of becoming teenage parents themselves." On the basis of this preamble of problems, the bill states:

> Therefore, in the light of this demonstration of the crisis in our Nation, it is the sense of the Congress that prevention of out-of-wedlock pregnancy and reduction in out-of-wedlock birth are very important Government interests and the policy contained in part A of title IV of the Social Security Act (as amended by section 103(a) of this Act) is intended to address the crisis.[61]

Although Republicans were not successful in pushing through the most draconian version of the Personal Responsibility Act, the federal system of AFDC has been dismantled. Entitlements to federal benefits have been ended through the allocation of block grants to facilitate state-run assistance programs. The version of the bill that President Bill Clinton eventually signed into law places a five-year lifetime limit on benefits, requires able-bodied adults to work after two years, requires minors to be enrolled in school and living at home or with a responsible adult, requires unwed mothers to cooperate in identifying paternity, disallows support to anyone convicted of a felony drug charge, and cuts benefits to families of children with disabilities.

Although derogatory images of blacks were most prominent in public discussion of welfare reform on a national level, negative images of Latinos and other immigrants fueled debates in the states and paved the way for denying benefits to legal immigrants nationwide. The discussion surrounding California's Proposition 187 exemplify the xenophobia and anti-immigrant sentiment that resulted in the initial denial of public resources to legal immigrants as part of welfare reform.

As is evident in the language of the legislation itself, illegitimacy and single-parent families are seen as the cause of poverty and social ills; thus, it is argued, the prevention of out-of-wedlock pregnancy and the promotion of two-parent families will be in the best interest of the nation.

Although these social problems are unproblematically cited here as outgrowths of family forms that deviate from two-parent nuclear families, feminists and other progressive scholars, as pointed out earlier, typically explain such family difficulties as the consequences, not the causes, of poverty. As Judith Stacey states in her critique of the body of literature that has served as the basis for a new orthodoxy regarding the relative merits of two-parent over single-parent families:

> Most research indicates that a stable, intimate relationship with one responsible, nurturant adult is a child's surest route to becoming the same kind of adult. In short, the research scale tips handily toward those who stress the quality of family relationships over their form.[62]

The ideas of Charles Murray figure prominently in the shift in public dialogue from an acceptance of the centrist scholarship that suggests that single-parent families are harmful to children to the conservative argument that out-of-wedlock births are at the root of most contemporary social problems. In his discussion of the rising percentage of "illegitimate" births to black women (he cites 68 percent in 1991), Murray draws on one of the central theses of the 1965 Moynihan Report on black families—that single mothers are incapable of properly socializing and disciplining their sons—to explain what he sees as the social chaos of inner cities:

> But if the proportion of fatherless boys in a given community were to reach such levels, surely the culture must be *Lord of the Flies* writ large, the values of unsocialized male adolescents made norms—physical violence, immediate gratification and predatory sex. That is the culture now taking over the black inner city.[63]

Poor black women are a central concern in this narrative, not simply because as women they are seen as behaving in ways that are socially unacceptable but also because they are mothers and the primary socializers of young children. In their role as mothers, they are continually portrayed as "unfit." As the political writer Richard Cohen explained, "We fear our children, not because there are too many of them, but because too many of them lack fathers."[64]

On the surface, the concern about single-parent families among blacks appears to contrast sharply with the growth of immigrant families in the United States. After all, female-headed households are neither as prevalent statistically among these groups nor part of the dominant image of Latinos. Nevertheless, Latinos, along with blacks, became a primary target of national and local legislative efforts to reduce the provision of welfare benefits.

In his essay "Poor Suffering Bastards: An Anthropologist Looks at Illegitimacy," published in the conservative Heritage Foundation's journal *Policy Review* in 1994, the foundation fellow David W. Murray uses a striking rhetorical ploy that reveals a kind of narrative link between the issues of illegitimacy and illegality:

> Here is the pertinent meaning of the *"legitimacy"* of children: Legitimacy is nothing more nor less than the orderly transfer of social meaning across the generations. Remember that children are the ultimate *illegal aliens*. They are undocumented immigrants to our world, who must be socialized and invested with identity, a culture, and an estate. By conferring legitimacy marriage keeps this process from becoming chaos.[65]

In an important essay in which she analyzes California's Proposition 187 campaign, Pierrette Hondagneu-Sotelo argues that the anti-immigrant narrative took an important turn with this campaign. Instead of drawing on themes found in earlier anti-immigrant narratives that had generated considerable public response in the past, such as unfair job competition and "inassimilable" cultural differences, she argues that contemporary rhetoric

> targets women and children because it is they who are central to making settlement happen. Viewed in this manner, the 187 campaign is less about illegal immigration and more about rejecting Latino immigrants and their U.S.-born family members as permanent members of U.S. society.[66]

Hondagneu-Sotelo argues that this attack on the use of public resources by immigrant Mexican women and children is directed mostly toward alleviating public anxiety about the rapid increase in the Latino immigrant population in California and is less concerned with their actual use of public assistance. In fact, she cites a number of studies that document the claim that immigrants are considerably less likely than the native-born to receive public assistance.[67] The real difference between this anti-immigrant campaign and earlier ones, she contends, results from the shift on the part of immigrant Mexicans from a sojourner or temporary, work-focused pattern of engagement in the United States to a pattern of establishing permanent communities and settlements throughout California. Women, she argues, are key to this settlement pattern because they are able to find relatively stable, nonseasonal jobs; they build community through their interactions with each other and other families; and they are more likely than men to seek out and utilize the resources that make permanent settlement possible.[68]

Reforming the Children of "Unfit" Mothers

The idea that racial or cultural diversity—either native-born or immigrant—is a threat to the nation has a long venerable history in the United States. Gwendolyn Mink has eloquently and convincingly argued that motherhood became pivotal in mediating issues of diversity and citizenship in the United States as early as the late nineteenth century:

> By welding motherhood to woman's citizenship, women's politics problematized claims for gender equality. It further compromised the possibility of racial equality when it offered

motherhood as the solvent for diversity in America. Arguing for policies tied to gender difference, women's politics interposed women reformers as managers of racial difference. This politics promoted an uplifted universal motherhood, one that would achieve both uplift and universality through the assimilation of Anglo-Saxon norms. Assimilated motherhood was women reformers' weapon against the blows to democracy dealt by poverty and multiculturalism.[69]

The contemporary conservative narrative picks up some of these same themes in its argument that "legitimate" nuclear families are necessary for the good of the nation. As George Will explains: "Democracy depends on virtues that depend on socialization of children in the matrix of care and resources fostered by marriage."[70] In contrast to women reformers of the late nineteenth century, at least one theme in conservative thought has abandoned the idea that low-income mothers can be uplifted and assimilated.

Once again it is the work of Charles Murray, this time in collaboration with Richard J. Herrnstein, that lays out an argument used to justify this conclusion. In their misleading and controversial book, *The Bell Curve: Intelligence and Class Structure in American Life*, they argue that IQ determines economic and social success and that the global economy is based on the manipulation of information.[71] Thus, the future economic viability of the United States is dependent on those citizens with high IQs whom they refer to as the "cognitive elite." From their perspective, "productive" citizens are defined not by hard work but, rather, by superior intelligence. Unproblematically accepting the belief that IQ tests accurately and objectively measure intelligence, they argue that African Americans are less intelligent than other racial groups, and they state that on average blacks score fifteen points lower than whites on IQ tests. Using these skewed data to account for racial stratification, they conclude that poverty among blacks is due to genetic inferiority rather than to discrimination and oppression.[72] In their circular logic, they claim that socioeconomic location is also evidence of intelligence, thereby inferring that all poor people have low intelligence. Not surprisingly, they contend that women with low IQs typically have "illegitimate" children; furthermore, given the hereditarian logic of their argument, they conclude that those children inherit their mothers' limited capacity for mental achievement and are destined to live on the margins of society, never achieving for themselves, forever draining government resources.

In their view, intelligence is so predominantly shaped by genetics (they concede a small measure of influence to environment) that social programs, such as Head Start, are doomed to failure. Yet they provide one glimmer of hope for these children: adoption. According to Herrnstein and Murray, adoption is the only social intervention radical enough to raise the IQs, and thus the chances for economic success, of poor, illegitimate children. The added bonus, they explain, is that "in terms of government budgets, adoption is cheap; the new parents bear all the costs of twenty-four-hour-a-day care for eighteen years or so."[73] They continue:

> If adoption is one of the only affordable and successful ways known to improve the life chances of disadvantaged children appreciably, why has it been so ignored in congressional debate and presidential proposals? Why do current adoption practices make it so difficult for would-be parents and needy infants to match up? Why are cross-racial adoptions so often

restricted or even banned?...Anyone seeking an inexpensive way to do some good for an expandable number of the most disadvantaged infants should look at adoption.[74]

Although on the face of it this argument may seem too draconian to be taken seriously, two years after those questions were written and published, the legislative infrastructure to support such policies was put in place. In the same week the Personal Responsibility Act was signed into law, legislation was also signed that provides a substantial tax deduction to couples who adopt and that bars federally funded adoption agencies from considering race in the adoptive placement of a child. It is no accident that these bills were passed at the same time. In fact, up until the final version of the welfare reform bill, the legislation to remove all restrictions to transracial adoption was part of the Personal Responsibility Act and was located in the section designed to combat the so-called epidemic of illegitimacy.

Adoption, and specifically transracial adoption, then, becomes another potential weapon in the war against illegitimate/illegal children and their mothers. The conservative narrative that constructs the mothers of these children as incapable of raising worthy citizens is already poised to be used to justify implementation of a policy that would remove the children from their birth mothers and place them in the homes of married, white, middle-class couples who are expected to do the job appropriately.[75]

In an editorial on welfare reform and adoption that was published prior to *The Bell Curve*, Murray argues that the state should actively intervene to remove children from mothers who refuse to abide by regulations that require welfare recipients to work: "What about women who can find no support but keep the baby anyway? There are laws already on the books about the right of the state to take a child from a neglectful parent."[76] There is, of course, extensive legal precedent for removing children from the homes of neglectful parents. There is also a long history in which these provisions have been used most frequently against poor women and women of color. At issue, of course, has been the definition of the term *neglect*. In antebellum Virginia, as Victoria Bynum has argued, provisions such as these were used to remove children from the mothers of free black women and from white women who had children out of wedlock, especially those who had children by black men.[77] According to Bynum, the explicit grounds on which these children were removed were primarily that they were poor and their mothers could not provide adequately for them. Implicit, however, was the fact that their mothers lived outside the control of acceptable white male authority in an explicitly racist and patriarchal social order. Although it is clearly beyond the scope of this chapter to trace the history of the relationship among mothers' social and economic status, child custody, and race, we point it out here to show that, while Murray's proposals may sound extreme to some, they are not without legal, historical, and social precedent.

Conclusion

Taken together, welfare reform legislation and the public discourse that has surrounded it can be read as a sort of *cultural eugenics* geared toward both the regulation of poor women's reproductive capacities and the social construction and socialization of economically productive citizens.[78] When compared to the eugenics movement of the early twentieth century, which sought to prevent white "race suicide" through the control of fertility among poor women and women of color, the insidious racial agenda of the recently passed legislation seems clear. The sociologist Kristin Luker discusses women's sexuality and "illegitimacy" in the context of the eugenics movement:

> Whether passive victim or willing participant, the young woman who was sexually active, particularly outside marriage, and particularly when intercourse led to an out-of-wedlock birth, was perceived as deviant, unfit. And the problem did not end with her: her child represented the antithesis of reformers' hopes for societal improvement, by becoming yet another link in a chain of unfitness. Born to an immature and presumably unfit woman, the illegitimate child evoked reformers' worst fears for future generations.[79]

In the early years of this century, these social fears translated to movements for eugenic sterilization and birth control among poor women and immigrants. In the post-Holocaust and post-civil-rights-movement era, such racist and classist inclinations must adopt a more "race-neutral" veneer. While essentialist racism—the pseudoscientific explanation of the supposed inferiority of nonwhite people—was the "legitimating" knowledge that drove the eugenics of the early twentieth century, in the contemporary moment cultural determinism has joined biology as the engine of racial oppression. The earlier focus on biological heritability led to efforts at curtailing the "excess" fertility of undesirables; in a framework dominated by the culture of poverty, social engineering can be envisioned in many ways, among them reducing illegitimacy, discouraging immigration by denying social resources to both legal and undocumented immigrants, and intervening in the socialization of children through the promotion of policies such as transracial adoption.

While most of these policies have been critiqued by progressives, it is only through an analysis that extends race beyond a black-white dualism and treats it as a dynamic, macrostructural force comparable to gender and class that one can fully expose the ways in which the U.S. legacy of racial exclusion and oppression permeates contemporary discourse on family values and public policy. For example, by including Latinos in this discussion we can document that family values and family structure matter far less than conservatives claim. We also broaden our understanding of how gender, race, and family values intersect, by revealing the ways that women, as child bearers and as mothers, are particularly subject to scrutiny and stereotype, regardless of whether they are married or unmarried. In fact, in the cases of both blacks and Latinos, stereotypes of women have been used to galvanize public support for policies to control their reproductive, productive, and family behavior.

The multiracial feminist perspective that has guided this analysis has directed us to challenge the discussion of family values and the well-being of children by raising questions of which children and which family forms are privileged and, thus, whose values are enforced and fostered by social institutions. It acknowledges the differences in cultural and racial locations, the variations in access to resources, and the resulting differences in family strategies. In addition, it points us toward an examination of the cause-and-effect relationship among families, poverty, social institutions, and values, demonstrating that families are shaped through interaction with social structures. A discussion of family cannot effectively begin with values if values are seen only through the lens of individual choice and morality. We argue that the choices women make about values and morality are strongly influenced by race, class, gender, and financial resources. The stereotyping, blaming, and scapegoating of women, particularly women of color, that too frequently accompany such discussions privileges white middle-class families and sabotages attempts at addressing the needs of low-income families. This occurs in part because racial animosity and suspicion remain a fundamental (and largely unaddressed) aspect of U.S. culture. As a society, we can eradicate the scourge of racism only when we are fully cognizant of the ways it permeates and shapes our discourse and our public policies.

NOTES

This chapter was published in *Sage Race Relations Abstracts* 23, no. 3 (1998).

1. Graeme Turner, *Film as Social Practice* (New York: Routledge, 1988).

2. Robert Gooding-Williams, "Look, a Negro!" in *Reading Rodney King/Reading Urban Uprising*, ed. Robert Gooding-Williams (London: Routledge, 1993).

3. Hazel Carby, "Encoding White Resentment: Grand Canyon—A Narrative for Our Times," in *Race, Identity, and Representation in Education*, ed. Cameron McCarthy and Warren Critchlow (New York: Routledge, 1993), 236.

4. Maxine Baca Zinn and Bonnie Thornton Dill, "Theorizing Difference from Multiracial Feminism," *Feminist Studies* 22 (Summer 1996): 321-31.

5. Arlene Skolnick, "Family Values: The Sequel," *American Prospect* 32 (May-June 1997): 86-94.

6. Nathalie A. Augustin, "Learnfare and Black Motherhood: The Social Construction of Deviance," in *Critical Race Feminism: A Reader*, ed. Adrein Katherine Wing (New York: New York University Press, 1997), 144.

7. Ruben Rumbaut, "Ties That Bind: Immigration and Immigrant Families in the United States," in *Immigration and the Family*, ed. Alan Booth (Lawrence Erlbaum, 1997), 1.

8. Pierrette Hondagneu-Sotelo, "Women and Children First: New Directions in Anti-Immigrant Politics," *Socialist Review* 25, no. 1 (1995): 173.

9. Bonnie Thornton Dill, Maxine Baca Zinn, and Sandra Patton, "Feminism, Race, and the Politics of Family Values," Report from the Institute for Philosophy and Public Policy (Summer 1993).

10. Judith Stacey, *In the Name of the Family: Rethinking Family Values in the Postmodern Age* (Boston: Beacon Press, 1996).

11. Kristin Luker, *Dubious Conceptions: The Politics of Teenage Pregnancy* (Cambridge, Mass.: Harvard University Press, 1996).

12. Lester D. Thurow, "Changes in Capitalism Render One-Earner Families Extinct," *USA Today*, 27 January 1997, 17A.

13. Ibid.

14. Quoted in Arlene Skolnick and Stacey Rosencrantz, "The New Crusade for the Old Family," *American Prospect* 18 (Summer 1994): 64.

15. Thurow, "Changes in Capitalism," 17A.

16. David Gordon, "Values That Work," *Nation*, 17 June 1996, 16.

17. William P. O'Hare, "A New Look at Poverty in America," *Population Bulletin* 51, no. 2 (September 1996): 347.

18. Sara McLanahan and Gary Sandefur, *Growing Up with a Single Parent* (Cambridge, Mass.: Harvard University Press, 1994), 3.

19. Daniel T. Lichter and Nancy S. Landale, "Parental Work, Family Structure, and Poverty among Latino Children," *Journal of Marriage and the Family* 57 (May 1995): 347.

20. McLanahan and Sandefur, *Growing Up with a Single Parent*, 85.

21. Andrew Hacker, "The Racial Income Gap," in *The Meaning of Difference*, ed. Karen E. Rosenblum and Toni-Michelle C. Travis (New York: McGraw-Hill, 1996), 309.

22. Lichter and Landale, "Parental Work," 347.

23. Stacey, *In the Name of the Family*; Iris Marion Young, "Making Single Motherhood Normal," *Dissent* 41 (Winter 1994): 88-93.

24. McLanahan and Sandefur, *Growing Up with a Single Parent*.

25. Ruth Sidel, *Keeping Women and Children Last* (New York: Penguin, 1996), 29.

26. Stacey, *In the Name of the Family*, 72.

27. Sidel, *Keeping Women and Children Last*, 29.

28. Stacey, *In the Name of the Family*, 72.

29. Luker, *Dubious Conceptions*, 86.

30. Valerie Polakow, *Lives on the Edge: Single Mothers and Their Children in the Other America* (Chicago: University of Chicago Press, 1993), 39.

31. Evelyn Brooks Higginbotham, "The Metalanguage of Race: Reflections on Race, History, and Feminist Theory," *Signs: Journal of Women in Culture and Society* (Winter 1992): 255.

32. Michael B. Katz, *The Undeserving Poor: From the War on Poverty to the War on Welfare* (New York: Pantheon Books, 1989), 14.

33. Mimi Abramovitz, *Regulating the Lives of Women: Social Welfare Policy from Colonial Times to the Present* (Boston: South End Press, 1989), 144.

34. Franklin E. Frazier, *The Negro Family in the United States* (Chicago: University of Chicago Press, 1939); and Melville J. Herskovitz, *The Myth of the Negro Past* (Boston: Beacon Press, 1941).

35. Daniel Patrick Moynihan, *The Negro Family: The Case for National Action* (Washington, D.C.: U.S. Department of Labor, 1965).

36. Carla Peterson and Rhonda M. Williams, "The Color of Memory: Interpreting 20th-Century U.S. Social Policy from a 19th-Century Perspective," Intersections: A Series of Working Papers of the Consortium on Race, Gender, and Ethnicity (April 1997), 10.

37. Maxine Baca Zinn, "Social Science Theorizing for Latino Families in the Age of Diversity," in *Understanding Latino Families: Scholarship, Policy and Practice*, ed. Ruth Zambrana (Thousand Oaks, Calif.: Sage, 1995), 177-87; Maxine Baca Zinn, "Family, Feminism, and Race in America," *Gender and Society* 4, no. 1 (1990): 68-82; Bonnie Thornton Dill, "Fictive Kin, Paper Sons, and Compadrazgo: Women of Color and the Struggle for Survival," in *Women of Color in U.S. Society*, ed. Maxine Baca Zinn and Bonnie Thornton Dill (Philadelphia: Temple University Press, 1994), 149-70; Patricia Hill Collins, *Black Feminist Thought: Knowledge, Consciousness, and the Politics of Empowerment* (Boston: Unwin Hyman, 1990); Patricia Hill Collins, "African American Women and Economic Justice: A Preliminary Analysis of Wealth, Family and Black Social Class," unpublished paper, 1997; Evelyn Nakano Glenn, "From Servitude to Service Work: Historical Continuities in the Racial Division of Paid Reproductive Labor," *Signs: Journal of Women in Culture and Society* 18, no. 1 (1992): 1-43.

38. Collins, *Black Feminist Thought*.

39. Baca Zinn and Dill, "Theorizing Difference from Multiracial Feminism."

40. Dill, "Fictive Kin, Paper Sons, and Compadrazgo," 166.

41. Baca Zinn, "Family, Feminism, and Race in America," 74.

42. Collins, "African American Women and Economic Justice," 18.

43. Bonnie Thornton Dill, "Our Mothers' Grief: Racial Ethnic Women and the Maintenance of Families," *Journal of Family History* 13, no. 4, (1988): 415-431.

44. Stephanie Coontz, *The Way We Never Were: American Families and the Nostalgia Trap* (New York: HarperCollins, 1992).

45. Bonnie Thornton Dill, Maxine Baca Zinn, and Sandra Patton, "Feminism, Race, and the Politics of Family Values."

46. William Julius Wilson and Katherine Neckernan, "Poverty and Family Structure: The Widening Gap between Evidence and Public Policy Issues," in *The Truly Disadvantaged: The Inner City, the Underclass, and Public Policy*, ed. William Julius Wilson (Chicago: University of Chicago Press, 1986), 265.

47. Baca Zinn, "Family, Feminism, and Race in America," 129.

48. On popular images, see Richard Estrada, "Myths of Hispanic Families' Wellness," *Kansas City Star*, 10 September 1989, 51; on the social science literature, see William A. Vega, "The Study of Latino Families: A Point of Departure," in *Understanding Latino Families: Scholarship, Policy and Practice*, ed. Ruth E. Zambrana (Thousand Oaks, Calif.: Sage, 1995).

49. Vega, "The Study of Latino Families," 9.

50. Baca Zinn, "Social Science Theorizing," 180.

51. David Hayes Bautista et al., *No Longer a Minority: Latinos and Social Policy in California* (University of California at Los Angeles: Chicano Studies Research Center, 1989).

52. Patricia Zavella, "Living on the Edge: Everyday Lives of Poor Chicano/Mexicano Families," in *Mapping Multiculturalism*, ed. Avery F. Gordon and Christopher Newfield (Minneapolis: University of Minnesota Press, 1996), 369.

53. Ibid., 363-64.

54. Frances Fukuyama, "Immigrants and Family Values," *Commentary* (May 1993): 29.

55. Zavella, "Living on the Edge," 370.

56. Lichter and Landale, "Parental Work," 347.

57. Ibid.

58. Scott Turner, "Single Parenthood Hurts Immigrants' Economic Gains," *Population Today* 24, no. 5 (May): 4-5.

59. Rumbaut, "Ties That Bind."

60. Charles Murray, "Testimony," House Ways and Means/House Subcommittee on Human Resources, 104th Congress, "Welfare Revisions," *Federal Document Clearinghouse Congressional Testimony*, 29 July 1994.

61. Public Law 104-193, Section 101.

62. Stacey, *In the Name of the Family*, 60.

63. Murray, "Testimony."

64. Richard Cohen, "Dealing with Illegitimacy," *Washington Post*, 23 November 1993, editorial page.

65. David W. Murray, "Poor Suffering Bastards: An Anthropologist Looks at Illegitimacy," *Policy Review* 68 (Spring 1994): 10 (emphasis added).

66. Pierrette Hondagneu-Sotelo, "Unpacking 187: Targeting Mexicans," *Immigration and Ethnic Communities: A Focus on Latinos*, ed. Refugio I. Rochin (East Lansing, Mich.: Julian Samora Research Institute, 1996), 93.

67. Ibid., 95.

68. Ibid., 98.

69. Gwendolyn Mink, *The Wages of Motherhood: Inequality in the Welfare State, 1917-1942* (Ithaca, N.Y.: Cornell University Press, 1995), 102.

70. George Will, "Underwriting Family Breakdown," *Washington Post*, 18 November 1993, editorial page.

71. Richard J. Herrnstein and Charles Murray, *The Bell Curve: Intelligence and Class Structure in American Life* (New York: Free Press, 1994).

72. For critiques of this work, see Steven Fraser, ed., *The Bell Curve Wars: Race, Intelligence, and the Future of America* (New York: Basic Books, 1995); Joseph L. Graves Jr. and Amanda Johnson, "The Pseudoscience of Psychometry and *The Bell Curve*," *Journal of Negro Education* 64, no. 3

(Summer 1995): 277-94; Russell Jacoby and Naomi Glauberman, eds., *The Bell Curve Debate: History, Documents, Opinions* (New York: Times Books, Random House, 1995); Joe L. Kincheloe, Shirley R. Steinberg, and Aaron D. Gresson III, eds., *Measured Lies: The Bell Curve Examined* (New York: St. Martin's Press, 1996).

73. Herrnstein and Murray, *The Bell Curve*, 416.

74. Ibid.

75. Sandra Patton, *Birth Marks: An Interdisciplinary Ethnographic Study of Transracial Adoption*, Ph.D. dissertation, University of Maryland, College Park, 1997.

76. Charles Murray, "The Coming White Underclass," *Wall Street Journal*, 17 November 1993, editorial page.

77. Victoria Bynum, "On the Lowest Rung: Court Control over Poor White and Free Black Women," *Southern Exposure* (November-December, 1984): 6.

78. Patton, *Birth Marks*.

79. Luker, *Dubious Conceptions*, 36-37.

DISCUSSION QUESTIONS

1. Why do the authors contend that public discourse about family values is "simplistic"?

2. Describe the various "schools of thought" and approaches utilized in the literature to analyze the status of families.

3. How is public discourse about family values racialized, and why?

4. What are the major explanations and models for understanding changes in family structure in the United States? How do these explanations reflect ideology?

5. How are scholarship and research limited in exploring certain facets of family structural developments?

6. How are particular definitions of various family structure dynamics and situations utilized for political or ideological purposes?

FOR FURTHER READING

Collins, Patricia Hill, *Black Feminist Thought: Knowledge, Consciousness, and the Politics of Empowerment* (Boston: Unwin Hyman, 1990).

Coontz, Stephanie, *The Way We Never Were: American Families and the Nostalgia Trap* (New York: HarperCollins, 1992).

Dill, Bonnie Thornton, "Fictive Kin, Paper Sons, and Compadrazgo: Women of Color and the Struggle for Survival," in *Women of Color in U.S. Society*, ed. Maxine Baca Zinn and Bonnie Thornton Dill (Philadelphia: Temple University Press, 1994), 149-70.

Hacker, Andrew, "The Racial Income Gap," in *The Meaning of Difference*, ed. Karen E. Rosenblum and Toni-Michelle C. Travis (New York: McGraw-Hill, 1996), 309.

Luker, Kristin, *Dubious Conceptions: The Politics of Teenage Pregnancy* (Cambridge, Mass.: Harvard University Press, 1996).

Mink, Gwendolyn, *The Wages of Motherhood: Inequality in the Welfare State, 1917-1942* (Ithaca, N.Y.: Cornell University Press, 1995).

Moynihan, Daniel Patrick, *The Negro Family: The Case for National Action* (Washington D.C.: U.S. Department of Labor, 1965).

Sidel, Ruth, *Keeping Women and Children Last* (New York: Penguin, 1996), 29.

Skolnick, Arlene, "Family Values: The Sequel," *American Prospect* 32 (May-June 1997): 86-94.

Stacey, Judith, *In the Name of the Family: Rethinking Family Values in the Postmodern Age* (Boston: Beacon Press, 1996).

Chapter Fifteen

Women in the Welfare Rights Struggle

Jackie Pope

The decade of the 1960s was one of struggle by a number of groups to obtain basic human rights. During the course of these activities, participants went through personal transformations, and sometimes the groups themselves changed. This chapter explores the efforts of a large number of poor urban women on welfare who organized to improve the quality of their lives, to redefine welfare as a right rather than a privilege, and to obtain what they were entitled to by law.[1] The Brooklyn Welfare Action Council (B-WAC) was created to coordinate the efforts of neighborhood groups of welfare rights advocates. At its peak in 1968, B-WAC was the largest union of welfare recipients in America, with almost eight thousand individual members and forty-eight welfare rights groups under its auspices. Membership was predominantly black, with smaller numbers of whites and Hispanics.

I describe how B-WAC came to be organized, the principles and strategies it employed, its accomplishments, its effect on individual lives, and the combination of forces that eventually led to its demise. It was linked, through the involvement of a small number of priests and nuns, to a radical movement within the Catholic Church, a movement growing out of the Second Vatican Council, under Pope John XXIII, that exhorted the clergy to focus on the needs of the poor. It was also a part of the national welfare rights movement that emerged in the mid-1960s, relatively autonomous but formally linked to the National Welfare Rights Organization (NWRO).

The welfare rights movement was unusual in that it was a movement primarily of poor women, many of them minority, who were able to overcome the obstacles of poverty, ill health, and stigma to organize and fight for their rights under the law. Some of the women participated as leaders not only in local welfare rights groups but also in the Brooklyn coordinating group and as paid officials at the national level in NWRO.[2] The role of the Catholic clergy was that of catalyst or broker, because it sought to empower poor people. At the same time, priests and nuns acted as supporters, initially providing valuable resources such as funding, meeting places, and information.[3]

On the national level, organized welfare recipients, also overwhelmingly women, fought and lobbied for legislation on issues of welfare reform, health care, housing, and food stamps. On the local level, they developed strategies and tactics that gained increased financial benefits for their members. Personal transformations took place as the women became more politically mature and skilled. Their involvement in militant organized actions became legendary. Unlike the female leadership of many other local social movement organizations, B-WAC's leaders were tapped for paid movement positions at the national level. Ironically, the promotion of these local leaders left a resource gap in B-WAC, hastening its decline. A changing national mood and the defeat of President Richard Nixon's Family Assistance Plan, an attempt at welfare reform, also contributed to the demise of B-WAC.

The Economic, Political, and Welfare Environment in the 1960s

President John F. Kennedy signed the Public Welfare Amendments to the Social Security Act on July 25, 1962, providing for increased federal funds to enable states to expand job training, placement, and casework services to welfare recipients. The law's proponents saw it as an effort to personalize the system and to put able-bodied people to work. Opponents viewed the law as a method of changing the person to fit the system, leaving the system's weaknesses intact.[4]

In 1965, in Lyndon B. Johnson's administration, the Economic Opportunity Act (EOA) was passed and the Office of Economic Opportunity (OEO) established. The act was considered a major weapon in the War against Poverty, and OEO in fact developed a number of programs, such as Volunteers in Service to America (VISTA), Job Corps, Operation Head Start, and a Community Action Program.

This War against Poverty, as the EOA was popularly called, reached New York City neighborhoods amid considerable fanfare and provided limited numbers of first-time white-collar jobs for their residents. Hope for the future spread when low-income people saw next-door neighbors staffing community programs. Until that time, most administrators (regardless of ethnic background) lived outside the area. This change of policy was appreciated because, observed Mr. Daniels, a former department community organizer, "services improve when staff and residents are users."[5] However, critics of the programs pointed out that, while well-meaning, the services often did not reach the people needing them most.

Welfare recipients on the economic bottom availed themselves of some of the new services but did not share the general euphoria. Their lives remained virtually unchanged. With few skills, little training, and limited formal education, women on welfare realized they were moving further away from the mainstream of American life. They watched other classes making progress. "In our isolation, we blamed ourselves and complained about welfare-related problems," said Ms. Delta, a welfare rights and community activist.[6] Society as a whole remained disdainful of people on public assistance. Sympathizing with welfare recipients would have meant acknowledging that America's cultural and economic systems had serious flaws. Still, the election of John Lindsay as mayor of New York in 1965 brought hope to the poor of the nation's largest city, since his campaign had addressed the concerns of low- and grant-income people.

Public Assistance in New York City

In 1964 the categories for public assistance, all of which required a means test to establish eligibility and benefit level, were administered by the New York State Department of Public Welfare through thirty welfare centers across the city. By 1965 aid to dependent children, by then called Aid to Families with Dependent Children (AFDC), had become the largest of the public assistance programs. A New York State Department of Social Welfare booklet from 1965 stated that public assistance would be granted to any needy children under the age of eighteen to enable them to remain with their families. If the children continued in high school or in other formal training programs, then welfare assistance was available to age twenty-one. Pregnant women were entitled to prenatal care and delivery and also to special dietary needs, food, clothing, shelter, and other supplies they might require.

Ever since colonial times, the biggest expenditure of public relief funds has been for widows, orphans, and children born out of wedlock. In modern times, however, parents or other relatives have had to provide extensive information to welfare officials about all possible sources of funds in order to establish need and eligibility.

Since benefit levels were not set by the federal government, AFDC grants varied greatly from state to state. They were lowest in southern states, with Alabama's benefits set at $2,124 per year for a family of four in 1969.[7] New York City was at the other end of the spectrum, with yearly payments for a family of four, including rent, totaling $3,408.[8] The U.S. Department of Labor noted that urban renters of that family size required $5,915 a year to live above the poverty line in 1967. Consequently, New York's welfare grants were 42 percent below the poverty line, while Alabama's were 64 percent below the line. Moreover, New York State law authorized additional funds to meet numerous special needs (e.g., furniture, clothing, washing machines, paint, costs for camp, and air conditioners for asthmatics).

Few New York City clients knew of such provisions, and rarely did they apply for or receive additional money for any reason. As we shall see, organizers of recipients would use these "special needs" regulations as a tool for recruiting purposes. Special grants would increase for families receiving AFDC between 1963 and 1968, the crucial years of organizing welfare recipients. This strongly suggests that expanded benefits for poor families were at least partially the result of the welfare rights activism to be described.

Whether in New York or in Alabama, having one's welfare application approved by administrators involved delay and aggravation. Applicants normally made several trips to the welfare center with birth or death certificates, utility bills, and school and medical records. Acceptance to the welfare rolls did not end a life of hardship. Welfare recipients paid a high psychological price because of the degrading and patronizing process at the welfare centers. Scenes in New York City offices varied little from those in other states before 1967, with rude behavior accepted as part of the price of public assistance. Caseworkers' attitudes mirrored the nation's prejudices against individuals they believed did not have a fully developed work ethic. In seventeenth-century tradition, services were often provided in a manner geared toward making the client's life as uncomfortable as possible. This strategy of trying to force recipients to obtain employment might have been useful had clients had alternatives, but most of them were unemployable. They either lacked work experience or were responsible for the care of children or disabled adults. The small number of employable people on welfare were unskilled; few had high school diplomas. For example, employable persons constituted only 3.8 percent of those on welfare in 1965; of that number, 14.9 percent had never worked.[9]

Despite such statistics, welfare authorities were determined to keep public assistance rolls down. Thus, in June, July, and August 1963, 45 percent of the applications were rejected. Five years later, analysis of the rates for the same months revealed a 21 percent decrease in the number rejected—and this despite a 55 percent increase in applications. Total grants rose almost 500 percent between 1963 and 1968.[10]

The denial of aid, even temporarily, posed hardships. Seeking loans from friends and relatives on public assistance or working in low-paying jobs were the only recourse. These loans tended to be paid back as soon as grants were received, but generally utilities and other bills had to be left unpaid, creating deepening financial difficulties.

Theory, Reality, and Practice of the Welfare System

A report issued in 1964 by the New York City Department of Welfare cited its official mandate as threefold: first, to meet the common human needs of those unable to help themselves; second, to return persons to gainful employment or assist them toward self-support and a maximum of self-care; and third, to prevent dependency.[11] Women who had survived ten to fifteen years on welfare grants maintained, however, that the system did not adhere to its mandate. They agreed with Frances Fox Piven and Richard A. Cloward's claim that relief policies are cyclical, liberal, or restrictive depending on the problems of regulation in the larger society with which government must contend; that America's response to people in financial crisis has been to create a system of constituent dependency; and that the unspoken mandate is to maintain social and political order and reinforce the work ethic.[12]

Women on welfare decried forced and temporary low-wage employment that provided little opportunity for advancement and no job security. In contrast to the typical American reward system, welfare mothers could not increase their income by accepting work. Instead, welfare grants were taxed at a high rate and AFDC mothers' allotments were reduced if they entered the labor market. The tax rate of 67 percent of earnings was a disincentive to seeking paid work. When a job ended, readjustments by the department were slow; often the recipients had to endure hardships until their money arrived. Further, a mother's employment decreased available parental supervision, creating additional problems.

Clients who were knowledgeable could seek redress through a "fair hearing," but statements of lawyers, clergy, and social workers were required to support their claims of hardship. When budget complaints subsided temporarily, department policy required staff to assume that clients had obtained funds from other sources. This was a signal to begin new investigations for possible unreported income.

These problems were common knowledge among AFDC mothers, standing as a warning against volunteering for any work program recommended by the department. Ninety percent of the women interviewed confirmed the practice of not accepting employment unless certain of leaving the welfare rolls completely. Earning subsistence-level wages guaranteed the women a double life—half in the labor force mainstream and half on public assistance through supplementary grants. One still remained a welfare recipient—poor, stigmatized, and, frequently, a discriminated-against woman of color.

Catalysts for Organized Change

Several women from Brooklyn attended the first NWRO conference in the District of Columbia in 1966 and returned home determined to establish local welfare rights organizations. Their efforts, supported by liberal Catholic clergy, bore fruit. Within one year, storefront welfare rights centers existed in almost every low-income Brooklyn community. Nuns and priests lent personal support as well as funds to enable clients to create and run their own organizations.[13]

A Survey of Community Needs

In the course of conducting a survey of community needs and problems, in 1966, a group of Roman Catholic teaching nuns became friendly with women on welfare. Despite their usual suspicion of strangers, poor black women in Brooklyn welcomed these representatives of a powerful church. It was an eye-opening experience for the nuns when they heard the women describe the horrors of a welfare existence: stolen checks that were not replaced for weeks, delayed approvals for relocation that resulted in apartments being lost or tenants evicted, and routine refusals of special allowances for shoes or winter coats.[14] The survey revealed that insufficient funds, inadequate housing, lack of child care centers, recurrent fires, and inadequate sanitation and police services topped the list of problems.[15] Daily reports of their parochial school students supported these findings. The nuns had tried to help these children and their families on an individual basis but soon recognized this as a short-term solution. They concluded that people on welfare had to organize for collective action.[16]

Such thinking was radical even in the liberalized church environment at that time. The nuns were determined to develop the principles set forth by the Second Vatican Council (known as Vatican II).[17] They were mindful of the council's mandate that church activism should focus on the needs of the poor and were influenced by the humanistic social dynamics of the 1960s. They came to interpret welfare organizing as an empowerment effort, respecting the desire of poor people and people of color to help themselves.

The nuns first proceeded independent of the parish priest. However, aware of the pragmatic demands of convent life and of the limitations on women in the church hierarchy, they decided to enlist the participation of a priest. A new priest had arrived at Our Lady of Sorrows in Brooklyn's Bedford-Stuyvesant section a few weeks after the completion of the survey. Father Carl Stevens had acquired a reputation as a man of action, concerned about the plight of low-income people. Strongly distrustful of officials and politicians, Father Stevens joined Sisters Mary, Joan, and Ruth in organizing the people on welfare. They compiled information from neighboring parishes where priests had achieved some successes in assisting tenants. The nuns and the priest believed that similar tactics could be effective against the Department of Public Welfare.

The Catholic Church and Social Change

Many of Brooklyn's Catholic nuns and priests interpreted the pronouncements of Vatican II literally and liberally. They believed that service to low-income people included sharing their pain and helping them to meet their needs. And so the churchwomen enthusiastically spearheaded an organizing drive that was to have a national impact.

Convincing Father Stevens to join their efforts had been easy, as he was a man looking for a cause. Two years later, with another priest, Father Robert Matthews, Father Stevens submitted a proposal to broaden parish work. In it, the priests expanded their concept of theological responsibilities to include direct confrontation of the political and economic issues faced by community people. They had faith in and respect for people's ability, regardless of class, race, or gender. Lacking formal organizing experience, they acted on their religious beliefs and faith in organizing for community empowerment. Only later, in 1968, did they receive training at Saul Alinsky's Chicago institute, the Industrial Areas Foundation, and develop their theory. The late Saul Alinsky was a legendary community organizer and sociologist based mainly in Chicago. In the mid-1950s, he established a privately funded institute for community organizers. Its graduates, supported mainly by churches, operated throughout the country.

The Alinsky model provided poor people with a way to increase their share in the distribution of wealth and to strengthen their voice in the political process. Alinsky believed the local self-reliant and community-based organization to be the only antidote against the dangerous trend of increasing political centralization, bureaucratization, corruption, and manipulation of information.[18] Whether the clergy advocated everything Alinsky espoused is unknown, but in the 1960s in Brooklyn they applied and tested most of his tenets.

Challenging the Welfare Bureaucracy

In the first week of February 1966, the nuns moved into and refurbished a decrepit storefront. They had begun by surveying the neighborhood to determine the residents' needs. They encouraged women on welfare to attend a community meeting, offering child care as an inducement. A week later, with Father Stevens as chair, twenty women and their children attended the first of many meetings at the storefront. Initially skeptical about Father Stevens's knowledge of the welfare system, they came to appreciate his information about their lawful rights and the functioning of the system. Former AFDC mothers recall that their interest was sparked because they felt that they had found a group focused specifically on their concerns. They learned that the social services department was legally bound to provide for certain basic needs and that those found eligible had the *right* to special monetary grants.

This procedure was known as "being brought up to minimum standards." Many recipients reported at the meetings that they had never owned such basic things as measuring spoons, blankets, or adequate clothing. They learned from the priests the meaning of being considered the "undeserving poor," finding out that suburban women on welfare were treated with greater respect and dignity as the "deserving poor," often receiving larger grants to cover work- or school-related expenses. Group discussions raised the political consciousness of the city women and fueled their desire to confront the department. This was a big step for people who had never before considered standing up to welfare authorities.[19]

The enthusiasm of that first meeting extended to subsequent ones. Word about the need to organize welfare recipients spread throughout the community of priests. Father Matthews joined Father Stevens to organize welfare rights organizations (WROs) throughout Brooklyn. The public legitimation of their complaints by the Catholic Church proved another vital mobilizing force, as welfare mothers were coming to realize the vulnerability of the welfare system.

As their first act of client administration, the WRO women agreed to manage the storefront office when the nuns were absent. This simple act of taking control of their own organization added new feelings of self-worth. The women felt their time and skills were needed. The women volunteers' main responsibility in political organizing was to help others compile complete and accurate standard forms, to answer phones, and to recruit interested recipients.

The First Demonstration

Bolstered by the knowledge that the power of the Catholic Church was behind them, the women prepared for action. At the first meeting, Father Stevens had fueled their resolve by distributing forms that described the "minimum standard." These forms listed every item a family had a right to own. By the time the meeting ended, one respondent observed, she had begun to believe that welfare was a right rather than a privilege and that changes in the Department of Public Welfare could be made.[20] This view, however, was in direct conflict with that of the majority of Americans, who did not regard welfare as a right.

A week after the first session, Father Stevens and twenty-five welfare mothers, armed with their forms, confronted officials at the Livingston welfare center in downtown Brooklyn and demanded that checks be ready the next day to enable them to purchase their "special needs." Contrary to usual practice, and much to the women's surprise, checks were ready when the protesters returned the following morning. Instead of the expected long, hard fight, each woman received about $100. They had acted collectively instead of individually and had won against the powerful welfare bureaucracy. The event proved to be a major organizing lesson, showing that early success could reinforce interest and spur the recruitment of others.

More welfare recipients, almost all black women, visited the storefront office as word of the victory spread. The nuns began to transfer responsibility for daily operations to the welfare rights women. By the end of three months, the welfare mothers not only were in charge of the storefront but had become experts in helping others to complete forms, accompanying them to the welfare centers, and even making referrals to other service programs. The nuns had reached across religious, class, and racial lines and succeeded in helping a number of poor women to organize for a better life.

Two years later, the three nuns left their order and moved to another city to teach and organize. But first they witnessed an important political outcome of their efforts. In May

1966 recipients voted to establish a formal welfare rights group, naming it the Neighborhood Action Center (NAC). It was the forerunner of forty-eight centers organized under the auspices of Fathers Stevens and Matthews. The NAC elected officers, including a woman president who would later become the first chair of the borough-wide welfare rights union, B-WAC.

The Early Days of B-WAC

The proliferation of storefront centers, expansion of membership, and increased demonstrations highlighted the need for a unifying and coordinating body—a boroughwide council or executive committee. Forty-eight storefront centers, representing almost every Brooklyn neighborhood, had been established. After a series of meetings, the women and their church supporters decided, in 1967, to create such a coordinating council. All welfare rights groups in Brooklyn were informed about the organization and urged to contribute their views to an ad hoc planning committee. This was the birth of B-WAC. It was funded by Catholic Charities of Brooklyn with an initial budget of $5,000 plus an additional staff salary of $5,000. By 1971, the budget had increased to $12,000.[21] Total grants disbursed by Catholic Charities for all the WROs between 1967 and 1971 was approximately $500,000. Some federally funded community action programs joined the council, but the centers organized by Fathers Matthews and Stevens remained the strongest force.

As the movement expanded, internal problems began to surface. Some local WRO groups feared loss of autonomy and opposed the federation. Others worried about creating a bureaucracy that mirrored the institutions they were pledged to change. The Citywide Coordinating Council, headquartered in Manhattan, and B-WAC's parent group, NWRO, located in Washington, D.C., expressed qualms about the growing power of the Brooklyn group. These concerns were not grounded in reality, because B-WAC's president had strong loyalties to Manhattan's Citywide and to NWRO. While it cooperated on most issues, B-WAC did occasionally refuse to support certain actions or decisions of the large movement, sometimes by withholding membership dues from NWRO.

The priests' role was again vital in B-WAC's formation and development. The responsibilities of Fathers Matthews and Stevens included lobbying, fund-raising, and scheduling speaking engagements for the welfare rights women, with their honoraria going to the council. Arranging a meeting with the bishop was another step in gaining recognition for the recipients. The women's self-confidence and self-respect increased, and, in turn, the public image of the welfare rights coalition was strengthened. The clergy negotiated across the class, race, and gender barriers that would have been insurmountable in society that devalued women's—especially poor women's—political activism, views, and demands. Once gaining access to powerholders, the women were eloquent in presenting their own case.

Brooklyn differed from other areas where white male organizers dominated decision making and leadership, for the priests were dedicated to recipient empowerment. Members of B-WAC were well informed because members discussed, voted on, planned, and organized all activities. If they decided against an action, then it was abandoned, regardless of the priests' position on the issue.[22] Demonstrations not approved by B-WAC received almost no support in the borough. Hundreds of loyal and disciplined members proved to be the organization's primary strength. Leadership training for and by people receiving public assistance was another important factor in its success.

A Constitution and New Headquarters

B-WAC was initially housed in the downtown Brooklyn offices of Catholic Charities' social action department. It soon moved to a large rent-free, three-story Victorian house obtained by Father Matthews in a more centrally located area. In November 1967 a constitution was drafted and approved by the membership that became a model for all Brooklyn groups.[23] The former president of NAC was elected B-WAC's first president. With Catholic Charities' funding, the organization hired two staff members, a young black woman and a Jewish male VISTA worker, as coordinator and office manager, respectively. It then increased its demonstrations and confrontations with the welfare departments.

Major Demonstrations

The first action to obtain minimum standard grants, described earlier, was designed not only to reward those who participated but also to enhance group solidarity.[24] In this confrontation, B-WAC members had learned the importance of unity. None had left until all had received their checks. This success attracted new members and volunteers to the movement. Minimum standard drives became routine, institutionalized organizing lessons for new members and training for client representatives. Mothers who had once feared the welfare department's response to their demands often found themselves, a few days later, representing others with similar problems. As advocates and protectors, they challenged officials and demanded to be treated fairly and courteously. Their self-confidence increased as they became astute political activists. One respondent described the situation: "We were used to begging; we never demanded anything. Welfare rights enabled us to walk into a welfare center unafraid, dignified, and secure in the knowledge that our needs would be met."[25]

The State's Response to Special-Needs Demonstrations

Having participated in minimum-standards demonstrations, the group found other protest actions less difficult. The Brooklyn women campaigned for and obtained funds for various needs: costs of laundry; graduation; layettes; confirmation, camp, gym, and spring clothes; and washing machines. Former recipients recalled their frustrations and their children's suffering before, when they had lacked money for simple but essential items. Now their children could participate in gym classes, attend camp with the required clothing, be confirmed, and take part in graduation ceremonies.

The very success of the special-needs demonstrations, however, created other problems. Awareness of the special allocations drew hundreds of members and nonmembers to the welfare centers. In an unsigned article, a caseworker depicted the rising confusion at one welfare center in April 1968, starting with the 6 A.M. arrival of the welfare mothers and their children. Hundreds of these recipients endured long hours of waiting for service, as they tried to take care of their crying babies.[26]

This scene was, of course, partly the result of welfare rights organizing. Hundreds of nonmembers who heard about clothing grants went to the department independently to request them. Others continued arriving with multiple problems, such as evictions, fires, or burglaries. While the collective demands of WRO members were being addressed by caseworkers and supervisors, other individuals with emergencies were forced to wait. Although WROs' disruptive strategies against the bureaucracy succeeded, the price for other clients and for staff was sometimes psychologically high; resentment from nonmembers was substantial. The state legislature eventually came to the Welfare Department's rescue by eliminating the movement's major organizing tool—the special-needs grant. New York State enacted the first flat grant in 1969. Under the new law, the basic needs of recipients were now covered by only one grant, with the exception of shelter, fuel, utilities, and a few other items. This dealt a serious blow to the mobilization of welfare mothers.

As legislators attempted to change the system, criticism of welfare mounted. Two years earlier, Nicholas Kisburg of the International Brotherhood of Teamsters had begun to voice concern with the existing system. Although the welfare allowances were acknowledged as being abysmally low, the welfare family of four still had a larger take-home income than the same family whose head earned $1.50 an hour. The solution to this crisis, in Kisburg's view, was to federalize the welfare system. Many others, from liberals to conservatives, proposed welfare reform and called for a guaranteed annual income. Although Congress debated President Nixon's Family Assistance Plan and several other national welfare reform proposals in the late 1960s and early 1970s, none became law. In the meantime, B-WAC expanded its protests into the private as well as the public sector.

The Credit Campaign Strategy

The only financial credit generally available to those on welfare came from loan sharks or small neighborhood businesses that charged usurious interest rates. In response, and facing the loss of special needs as an organizing lever, B-WAC initiated a campaign for the extension of department store credit to people on public assistance or having fixed incomes. The B-WAC membership voted to challenge general credit policies and specifically targeted those of Korvettes, a department store that many poor people frequented.

According to plan, B-WAC officers first attempted to negotiate for the extension of credit—and were ignored by Korvettes officials. On November 21, 1968, protests began. Demonstrations were staged inside and outside Korvettes in Brooklyn's major shopping area. The outcome of this collective action was that each woman obtained between $25 and $100 of personal credit. In the aftermath of the Korvettes demonstrations, a higher-priced department store, Abraham and Strauss, voluntarily opened credit negotiations with B-WAC. By December, both stores had developed and instituted procedures to review credit applications submitted by people on welfare. Shortly after that, all grant-income recipients (those on pensions, Social Security, and disability) were encouraged to apply for credit.

The victory for B-WAC had involved the use of diverse, unique, and theatrical strategies. For instance, the owners of Korvettes were contacted by B-WAC's middle-class supporters—members of Friends of Welfare Rights Organization (FWRO)—on the golf course, at their private clubs, and at their places of worship, where they asked for support.[27] FWRO members also agreed to raise the credit issue at stockholders' meetings. In addition, B-WAC members received special training in sessions that were dress rehearsals for protest action. Members were assigned special roles and responsibilities: outside the store, some were picketers, messengers, marshals, leafleteers, and spokespersons. Inside the store, welfare rights mothers acted as "customers," sometimes as "angry customers"; at other times they role-played expressing or giving sympathy to those annoyed by the disruption. Some were asked to be "real" customers or to fill in as part of crowds, as a backdrop to the militants and moderates.

Members impersonating customers selected hundreds of dollars' worth of goods and took them to cashiers, who tallied the items on the register. When requests for payment were made, the "customer" produced her welfare ID card and said, "Charge it to the Welfare Department." The cashier was impelled to call for assistance in order to clear the register of the mock charge. Such actions resulted in long lines at the cash registers throughout the store. "Irate customers" standing in line with numerous expensive items voiced their displeasure about the delay. Other "customers in the crowds" grumbled loudly about the store's incompetence to unsuspecting legitimate customers. All this commotion at rush hour proved too much for Korvettes' personnel. The store manager, later joined by the company's regional representative, invited B-WAC's leaders to meet and negotiate. At the same time, the management called in the police. The women left to avoid arrest, as previously planned. When the police arrived, everything had returned to normal except for the piles of unbought clothing that surrounded most cash registers. B-WAC "customers" still browsed unnoticed alongside actual purchasers, waiting for the police to leave and the signal to begin the demonstration anew. Then the whole process recommenced. When negotiations began in earnest, "moderates" agreed to discontinue the inside demonstrations. Late in the evening, welfare members left Korvettes but vowed to return the next day if their demands were not met. These actions continued for five days.

Demonstrators met to evaluate the results of their actions following each action, discussing strengths and weaknesses late into the night. Besides moving the women toward a political analysis of the process of creating change, the sessions also helped demonstrators and staff prepare for questioning by members, for according to B-WAC rules members had to be informed promptly of the results of any major action. B-WAC members debated and voted on every decision and demonstration. The give-and-take of their often heated and acrimonious debates had some very positive effects. Members became well informed and knowledgeable about issues. In fact, Brooklyn welfare rights participants were sometimes viewed as independent, arrogant, and opinionated. This resulted from the serious consideration of each person's comments and remarks at B-

WAC meetings, a process that led to empowerment for women who had been pejoratively labeled as "lumpen proletariats" by intellectuals and "brood mares" by a U.S. senator.

Regardless of the intensity of their internal conflicts, the Brooklyn women remained publicly united, acting as one on nearly every issue. Those deviating from an agreed-on strategy had to justify their behavior at B-WAC's next meeting, a formidable and usually no-win task. B-WAC's women inspired admiration, awe, and envy within the national movement. They were "out there," somewhat "crazy," and "really together." A humorous episode that occurred during an NWRO conference in 1968 illustrates this. When B-WAC's president left the conference hall, word spread among Brooklynites that B-WAC members had been insulted by someone. As a result, every B-WAC member got up and left the hall, following the president. The session was halted while NWRO officials tried to determine the cause of the walkout. Meanwhile, B-WAC members discovered that their president had simply gone to the women's room. When she looked around, the room was filled with B-WACers and, eventually, with conference officials wanting to know why Brooklyn had "walked out."

Brooklyn's credit demonstration, watched closely by welfare clients everywhere, precipitated other protests across the nation. Actions against Sears, Roebuck and three of New York's major department stores resulted in extensions of credit to welfare recipients and national publicity. Success, however, brought forth other reactions.

Government Reaction to Welfare Protests

Organizers, members, and theorists had underestimated the government bureaucracy's strength and resiliency and were surprised by its reaction and its efforts to regain control. Welfare rights organizations had succeeded in transferring millions of dollars from welfare agencies to low-income people. Now an increasingly conservative government attempted to eliminate loopholes that had been used by the movement. As pointed out earlier, replacing minimum standards with one-time grants (flat grants) removed a major organizing tool and effectively halted further mobilization. This caught advocates unprepared and without a contingency plan. They realized too late that this backlash forecast the turning of the political tide and the ultimate demise of their movement.

B-WAC was doubly devastated. Its president and staff had been invited to move to Washington, D.C., to work in NWRO's national office, leaving a leadership vacuum that was hard to fill. Even had the leaders remained, it is very doubtful that the earlier momentum could have been maintained in the absence of a supportive political climate. The environment was rapidly becoming more hostile to the demands of the poor, especially poor women. B-WAC's resources and support rapidly shrunk, hastening its demise. In this, it followed the path of most organizations of poor people: a volatile, short-term structure organized around a single issue and dependent on outside support for funds.

The Debate over Strategies

A number of intellectuals who had been involved in the national welfare rights movement as supporters or theorists entered the debate about what had gone wrong in organizational strategies. Richard Cloward, for example, acknowledged that the organizing skills and street protests of the Brooklyn group had substantially expanded the benefits of its members. He maintained, however, that too much energy had been put into building a membership organization and institutionalizing the group. According to him, continued street demonstrations would have been more effective.[28] In introspect, he felt that the movement should have been an organization of the *poor*, a coalition of various types of groups, rather than being limited to welfare clients.

Although Cloward's evaluation of street protests has some merit, he did not consider the risk of burnout when people are continually in the front lines. Nor did he suggest how interest and high energy levels could have been maintained during prolonged confrontations. Another flaw in the arguments of those who call for continued protest with minimum organization is the question of whether protesters could have continued to be mobilized over extended periods of time. Finally, relying on small and vulnerable protesting cadres may invite violence by the police. Cloward argues that large numbers of politicians elected by low-income people would protect the demonstrators against harm by the establishment. He opposes institutionalizing a movement yet advocates the use of traditional institutions, specifically the electoral system, to secure power and protection. Had welfare rights groups become institutionalized in the 1970s, perhaps they could have played a key role in the voter education and registration drive among the poor in the 1980s. Several participants in this debate, however, contend that relying on leaders in the establishment, elected or not, simply maintains the dependent role that those protectors sought to destroy.

Conclusion

In the mid-1960s, women receiving public assistance from the state challenged traditional views of poverty and demanded structural changes in the provision of social welfare. During a relatively short period, women mobilized thousands of recipients in the struggle. Collectively, thousands of women dependent on the state created and ran B-WAC, a unique social movement organization, bringing social change into the lives of individuals and the welfare system. This organization was unusual because it was managed by women on welfare and because of its large size. B-WAC's members in the early years made up almost one-third of the NWRO membership.

Brooklyn's welfare rights movement followed the pattern of most lower-economic-class protests. It lasted just a few years during a time when the political climate remained relatively tolerant of protest. The momentum was impossible to maintain as the state reacted and clamped down. The elimination of special grants reduced the incentives for protest and organizational commitment. Membership dropped dramatically.

The reasons for the decline of this local grass-roots movement are numerous and complex. First, there was disillusionment regarding the ability to attain the long-range legislative goal of a guaranteed annual income. Second, the dominating political philosophy had rapidly shifted from liberal to more conservative solutions to the problems of poverty and welfare. Third, public opinion had become less accepting of political protest and unconventional movement organizations. Finally, the deep-rooted stigma attached to welfare recipients, especially mothers, remained entrenched, limiting support for the movement. Most of the client leaders interviewed agreed that welfare rights members were left with difficult and limited options. They could continue the demonstrations and mobilization and invite arrests; they could reconsider and change their initial objectives; or they could cease operating. Although there were varying views, there was general agreement that disruptive tactics had to be abandoned and attempts made to build an institution.

Frances Fox Piven, one of the movement's theorists, agreed that interminable mobilization was unrealistic. Yet she cautioned that imitating middle-class associations would operate against poor people's interests, for grass-roots institutions require flexibility and innovation. She believed that the infusion of new ideas and recruits often ceases when longtime members consolidate their own power. An excessive amount of organizational energy tends to be used in lobbying for support. Piven continued to have faith in the power of street demonstrations.[29]

The Catholic Church played a major role in shaping the direction of the Brooklyn welfare rights movement and its members' political views. Politically and religiously progressive, the Church men and women had, nonetheless, facilitated a traditional atmosphere. They helped many people to enhance the quality of their lives within the confines of the system. Their doctrine had been one of helping others to help themselves. Nevertheless, when the political tides shifted and the movement began to decline, the Catholic diocese took over full administrative responsibilities for the centers. They became neighborhood service centers staffed by professionals. The Church thus reflected the government's reversal of its original but short-lived policy of encouraging maximum feasible participation by indigenous people.

On the whole, the clergy concentrated on guiding recipients into the cultural and economic mainstream and teaching them how to negotiate rather than to change the system. The priests' idealistic but pragmatic tactics for ending poverty altered and enhanced the lives of individuals and families, while theorists such as Piven and Cloward concentrated on raising the political consciousness of clients and others regarding the inequities of the welfare system.

According to welfare rights leaders, their fundamental concern was to provide new opportunities for their children, since many believed it was too late for themselves. However, one result of the protest efforts was that most of the seventeen former leaders interviewed subsequently left the welfare system. Fifteen moved off the welfare rolls and no longer receive public assistance. All returned to and completed high school; four accumulated several college credits; and two received master's degrees. None of the leaders' sons and daughters, and only one grandchild, was on welfare. Their children were high-school graduates, and most attended college.

Today, despite the movement's demise, many of its leaders and members remain politically active in diverse ways. Ideologically, they are still committed to confronting issues that have a negative impact on poor people's lives. They have continued to be involved in various community causes, including block associations, school and planning boards, welfare recipient councils, and political clubs. All interviewed believed that B-WAC had inspired and changed many individuals.

The more immediate economic results for poor people are clear. During a three-month period in 1968, New York City grant income recipients received approximately $42 million in additional payments, compared with $1.3 million in 1963. Public assistance applications were accepted 81 percent of the time in 1968, but only 65 percent in 1963.[30] In sum, protest actions brought expanded benefits to the poor in the state.

In addition, institutional changes in the welfare system resulted in some important and enduring gains. Among them were the establishment of state procedures for fair hearings, the elimination of residency requirements, and the elimination of most home visits. Other gains were a move toward granting credit for people on fixed incomes, the seeds of a national voter education drive, and the development of community paraprofessionals. On the other hand, it seems clear that the one-dimensional nature of welfare rights impeded advances beyond these issues. The movement focused mainly on the economics of poverty and specifically on welfare reform, to the exclusion of other factors such as racism and sexism. That is, poverty was not attacked in a holistic manner.[31] To address the fundamental causes of poverty would have required far more resources than those available to B-WAC and the national welfare rights movement.

B-WAC's small core of active members joined the mainstream, while the majority of recipients experienced only limited personal advancement. But, despite scorn from many groups, the women activists achieved a measure of self-respect and confidence. They were minorities in the truest sense—five times, if one considers they were women, black and Hispanic, middle-aged, many fat, and economically disadvantaged recipients of public aid. Despite these obstacles of gender, class, race, and age, collectively they were able to overcome their isolation and stigma and to act aggressively and politically to better their lives. They proved that fundamental freedoms in a democratic society must not be limited to people with access to powerholders. The meaning and political impact of B-WAC was summarized succinctly and dramatically by one of its members:

> I learned I am somebody. Welfare rights meant a right to life—it freed me from emotional slavery. I am a person you can't push aside, I have the right to be. Welfare rights showed me that my counterparts are all around; knowing this, I no longer felt alone. Welfare rights lives, I and other people are still active, struggling for a better life. PTAs, school boards, even political clubs have former welfare rights members, and we continue pushing the welfare rights agenda. B-WAC lives in the minds of everyone remotely associated with it. An organization for and by poor people, a women's movement that addressed real survival issues. Its concepts and promises live in us and our children.[32]

NOTES

This chapter was originally published in Guida West and Rhoda Lois Blumberg, *Women and Social Protest* (New York: Oxford University Press, 1990), 57-74.

1. This study is based on forty-seven in-depth interviews from 1980 to 1984 with movement activists, mostly women who had been mothers receiving Aid to Families with Dependent Children (AFDC) in Brooklyn during the 1960s.

2. Ronald Lawson and Stephen Barton, in "Sex Roles in Social Movements: A Case Study of the Tenants Movement in New York City," *Signs: Journal of Women in Culture and Society* 6, no. 2 (1980): 230-47, argue that, more often than not, male leaders are elected for paid positions in social movements.

3. See also the discussion of the role of the white Protestant churches in the National Welfare Rights Movement in Guida West, *The National Welfare Rights Movement: The Social Protest of Poor Women* (New York: Praeger, 1981); also the analysis of the role of "outsiders" in Gary Marx and Michael Useem, "Majority Involvement in Minority Movements: Civil Rights, Abolition and Untouchability," *Journal of Social Issues* 27 (1971): 81-104.

4. Much of the material in this section is based on Walter Trattner, *From Poor Law to Welfare State: A History of Social Welfare in America* (New York: Free Press, 1974).

5. Personal interview, July 1983. All identities of interviewees have been disguised to protect them.

6. Personal interview, June 1982.

7. *Bedford-Stuyvesant-New York Recorder*, January 3, 1969. In Alabama, a family of four on AFDC received a monthly check for $177 for food, shelter, and clothing. Although federal funds accounted for 83 percent of the grant, Alabama refused to contribute matching funds, forfeiting $11.6 million in federal moneys in 1967 alone.

8. City of New York, Department of Welfare, 1963-68.

9. U.S. Department of Labor, Employment and Training Division, Regional Manpower Administration Notice #1-72.

10. City of New York, Department of Welfare, June, July, August 1963-68.

11. The present title for the public assistance office is the Human Resources Administration, Department of Social Services.

12. Frances Fox Piven and Richard A. Cloward, *Regulating the Poor* (New York: Pantheon, 1971).

13. The nuns were from the Sisters of St. Joseph order, which numbered two thousand nuns nationally. Seventeen of them taught at Our Lady of Victory School in Brooklyn's Bedford-Stuyvesant neighborhood. The students at their school were primarily African American and Caribbean.

14. Mailboxes were regularly burglarized and checks stolen in low-income neighborhoods. At times, people lost all benefits for failing to respond to a Welfare Department letter or notice that had never been received.

15. The survey conducted by the nuns was referred to in interviews but was not made public, nor is it presently available.

16. Sister Tina, personal interview, May 1983.

17. Vatican II was a council of the Catholic Church's highest officials, convened in Rome from 1962 to 1965 by the pope to reestablish and modernize religious guidelines for its clergy and lay people.

18. See Manuel Castells, *The City and the Grass Roots* (Berkeley and Los Angeles: University of California Press, 1983) for an excellent discussion of community-based organizations.

19. See also discussions of this process of individuals and groups learning about their rights prior to moving into direct confrontation with welfare authorities in Frances Fox Piven and Richard A. Cloward, *Poor People's Movements: Why They Succeed, How They Fail* (New York: Pantheon, 1977); Susan Handley Hertz, *The Welfare Mothers Movement: A Decade of Change for Poor Women?* (Washington, D.C.: University Press of America, 1981); Lawrence N. Bailis, *Bread or Justice: Grass Roots Organizing in the Welfare Rights Movement* (New York: Heath, 1974); and West, *The National Welfare Rights Movement*.

20. Personal interview.

21. B-WAC's expenditures increased sixfold when the organization was conducting leadership training classes, peaking at $33,000 in 1969.

22. Personal interview with Hulbert James, 1982; see also Bailis, *Bread or Justice*; and West, *The National Welfare Rights Movement*.

23. Only welfare recipients were eligible to hold offices in the council, according to its constitution.

24. Many social movement theorists place much significance on self-serving behavior as a motivation for activism. Yet the women in the welfare rights groups quickly subordinated self-interest to the larger community's cause, a phenomenon said to be common among female activists regardless of class. Eric Hirsch, "The Creation of Political Solidarity in Social Movement Organizations: A Critique of the Resource Mobilization Approach," unpublished report (n.d.), 19, supports this observation: "Self-sacrifice in pursuit of...emergent group interests seems to be relatively common....Self-sacrifice—to which they [women] are socialized—begins almost with the decision to join a group."

25. Personal interview with Maggie Halstrum.

26. *The Tablet*, July 16, 1968.

27. Friends of Welfare Rights Organization members were professional, mainly white middle-class or wealthy individuals sympathetic to the plight and goals of clients. They contributed time and money to the organization and made contacts and speeches for the organization. In almost every welfare rights group—local, state, and national, except B-WAC—FWRO members were permitted to hold office or vote.

28. Richard Cloward, personal interview, fall 1983.

29. Frances Fox Piven, personal interview, fall 1983.

30. City of New York, Department of Welfare, *Monthly Statistical Reports*.

31. For a discussion of an implied holistic approach to poverty and social planning, see Herbert Gans, *People and Plans: Essays on Urban Problems and Solutions* (New York: Basic Books, 1968).

32. Personal interview with Ms. Wise, summer 1983.

DISCUSSION QUESTIONS

1. Discuss the origins of the Brooklyn Welfare Action Council (B-WAC).

2. What were the underlying principles of B-WAC?

3. Analyze the nature and effectiveness of the strategies employed by B-WAC.

4. Explain the reasons for B-WAC's demise. What are the implications for contemporary political mobilization on the part of poor people?

5. Discuss potential changes for individuals who participated in the welfare rights struggle.

6. Discuss the author's argument that political powerlessness is the major determinant of the quality of life of welfare recipients.

7. Explain the emergence and demise of the welfare rights movement. How is this similar to the fate of the civil rights movement?

FOR FURTHER READING

Gans, Herbert, *People and Plans: Essays on Urban Problems and Solutions* (New York: Basic Books, 1968).

Hertz, Susan Handley, *The Welfare Mothers Movement: A Decade of Change for Poor Women?* (Washington, D.C.: University Press of America, 1981).

Trattner, Walter, *From Poor Law to Welfare State: A History of Social Welfare in America* (New York: Free Press, 1974).

West, Guida, *The National Welfare Rights Movement: The Social Protest of Poor Women* (New York: Praeger, 1981).

Part V

Poverty, Race, and the Distribution of Jobs

Chapter Sixteen

The Working Poor
Lousy Jobs or Lazy Workers?

Marlene Kim

Most Americans believe that if one works hard, one should not be poor. Yet the working poor constitute one of the fastest growing segments of the impoverished population, and their number is expected to increase.[1] According to the official government definition of poverty, which compares family income to a minimum standard of living, the number of working poor is between seven and nine million Americans. This number doubles, however, when alternative definitions of poverty are used.[2] Despite the importance of this population, there remains a substantial debate about why these workers are poor. A critical part of this debate is whether they are poor because they choose to work too few hours or because the labor market fails to provide them with adequate wages and full-time, steady employment.

Bradley Schiller, for example, believes that the working poor are poor simply because they do not work enough hours.[3] If they worked full-time year-round, he argues, they would lift themselves out of poverty. Others, however, argue that the cause of the working poor is more complex and due to inadequate jobs that fail to provide full-year or full-time work or to jobs that pay wages that are too low.[4] Mary Jo Bane and David T. Ellwood, for example, argue that even if they worked more hours, the working poor would remain poor.[5]

The outcome of this debate is critical for effective policy formation. If the working poor are poor because they choose to work too few hours, there is little role for public policy except to encourage more hours of work. If, on the other hand, the working poor are working as many hours as they can, but structural forces beyond their control force them into poverty, government policies and support could be essential. This chapter examines the extent to which working additional hours would reduce poverty among the working poor and whether the working poor are able to work such additional hours. I find that few of the working poor would be able to work enough hours to earn their way out of poverty: most command wages that are so low that working full-time and year-round would still leave them poor. In addition, of those who could rise above poverty if they worked full-time year-round, many simply cannot work these hours. The next section explains the data and the definitions used. Subsequent sections present the empirical results and policy implications.

Measuring Poverty

The Current Population Survey (CPS), published in March 1994, is used for this analysis because it provides the most current national data set that contains poverty and work measures, as well as a large sample of the working poor. The CPS is a national data set collected by randomly sampling approximately fifty-seven thousand U.S. households. The working poor are defined as those age eighteen or older who worked at any time during the previous calendar year in 1993 and who are poor. Poverty status is determined by using the official government poverty thresholds, which measure whether family income is adequate for a given family size.

There is considerable debate regarding how to measure poverty accurately. John E. Schwarz and Thomas Volgy, for example, argue that those with incomes of up to 200 percent of the poverty threshold should be considered poor.[6] Most researchers, however, report those who are below 100 percent or 125 percent of the poverty threshold. Because of the range of measures used, I report those who are below 100 percent, below 125 percent, and below 150 percent of the official poverty line in the tables presented. In order to facilitate reading the text, however, I often present the results using only one of these measures. When this occurs, the measure used is those below 125 percent of the poverty level.

Table 16.1A shows some of the characteristics of the working poor. In 1993, 12 percent of adults worked but were below 150 percent of the poverty threshold; 9 percent of working adults were below 125 percent of the poverty line. In comparison, for all adults—working and not working—27 percent were below 150 percent of the poverty line, and 21 percent were below 125 percent of the poverty threshold (see Table 16.1B).

As Charles Murray and others argue, working indeed reduces the likelihood of being poor.[7] Of those who worked at any time during 1993, 14 percent were still poor (defined as below 125 percent of the poverty level; see Table 16.1B). In comparison, 35 percent of the adults who did not work were poor. In addition, as Table 16.2 illustrates, the more hours worked, the fewer the number of the poor. Of those who usually worked full-time (thirty-five or more hours per week), 9 percent were poor (6 percent were below the official poverty rate, and 3 percent were between 100 percent and 125 percent of the poverty level); this compares with a poverty rate of 32 percent for those who worked ten or fewer hours per week. Among those who worked year-round, 6 percent were poor. This number rose to a poverty rate of 32 percent among those who worked 13 or fewer weeks.

On average, the working poor worked full-time (thirty-five or more hours per week), but they did not work a full year (fifty or more weeks per year). The working poor worked, on average, two-thirds of a full year. Although this supports Murray's and Schiller's contention that most of the working poor fail to work full-time year-round, it does not necessarily follow that increasing the number of work hours will substantially reduce the extent of poverty. One must first examine to what extent working less than a full year contributes to the poverty of the working poor—in other words, whether the working poor would remain poor even if they worked a full year.

TABLE 16.1A
Characteristics of the Sample—The Working Poor

	Those Who Are Below		
	150%	125%	100%
	Percent of the Poverty Line		
Working poor population (percent of adults who worked and were poor)	12	9	7
Percent of the working poor[a]			
who were disabled	7	8	8
who were age 60 or older	8	7	7
who faced a layoff	1	0.5	0.5
who were involuntarily employed part-time	21	22	23
who were single parents with children under 6	3	4	4
Percent of those who were working poor[b]			
who faced a layoff	18	13	9
who did not face a layoff	12	10	7
who were single parents with children under 6	40	36	30
who were not single parents with children under 6	12	9	7
who were disabled	7	5	4
who were not disabled	13	10	7
who were elderly	3	3	2
who were not elderly	15	12	9
Percent of workers who were members of the working poor[c]			
who were single parents with children under 6	62	56	46
who were not single parents with children under 6	18	14	10
who were disabled	31	25	19
who were not disabled	18	14	10
who were elderly	16	12	8
who were not elderly	19	14	10

[a]This table reads as follows: of the working poor population, 7 percent are disabled, measured at 150 percent of the poverty threshold.
[b]This table reads as follows: of adults (working and not working) who are disabled, 7 percent are among the working poor, measured at 150 percent of the poverty threshold; of all adults (working and not working) who are not disabled, 13 percent are members of the working poor, measured at 150 percent of the poverty threshold.
[c]This table reads as follows: of adult workers who are disabled, 31 percent are among the working poor, measured at 150 percent of the poverty threshold.

TABLE 16.1B
Characteristics of the Sample—Poverty Rates

| | Those Who Are Below | | |
| | 150% | 125% | 100% |
	Percent of the Poverty Line		
Poverty rate of all adults (those who worked and didn't work)	27	21	16
Poverty rate of adults who worked	18	14	10
Poverty rate of those who did not	43	35	26

TABLE 16.2
Distribution of the Working Poor across Poverty by Hours and Weeks Worked

| | Distribution Relative to | | | |
| | Below 100% | 100%-124% | 125%-149% | 150+% |
		Percent of the Poverty Threshold		
Usual weekly hours worked in 1993				
10 or fewer	24	8	8	61
11-19 hours	23	3	5	68
20-34 hours	15	5	5	75
35+ hours	6	3	3	89
Weeks worked in 1993				
13 or fewer	24	8	8	60
14-26 weeks	22	5	3	69
27-39 weeks	20	6	5	69
40-48 weeks	13	5	6	77
49+ weeks	4	2	3	91

NOTE: This table is read as follows: of those who worked 10 or fewer hours per week, 24 percent were below 100 percent of the poverty level; 8 percent were between 100 percent and 124 percent of the poverty level; 8 percent were between 125 percent and 149 percent of the poverty level; 61 percent were above 149 percent of the poverty level. Numbers across rows may not sum to 100 percent due to rounding.

Working One's Way Out of Poverty?

The first question examined here, therefore, is "What proportion of the working poor could rise above poverty if they worked full-time and year-round?" To estimate this, I calculated "potential earnings" for each of the working poor in my sample. Potential earnings is an estimate of total earnings for each worker, assuming that he or she works 2,080 hours—forty hours per week and fifty-two weeks per year—at his or her current (1993) wage rate. I then added the difference between potential and actual earnings to family income. This procedure allowed me to calculate for each of the working poor in 1993 the income he or she would have earned if he or she had worked full-time year-round. By comparing this new income level with the poverty threshold for each worker's family size, I was able to determine whether working full-time and year-round would have contributed enough earnings to enable the worker to live above poverty. I then tallied these responses for the entire sample. Workers who were self-employed or working without pay were excluded from this analysis.

As Table 16.3A illustrates, working additional hours would have reduced the poverty rate of workers, but most of the working poor would have remained poor even if they had worked full-time and year-round. Of those who were below the official poverty threshold, 52 percent would have remained poor. Of those who were below 125 percent of this threshold, 61 percent would still have been poor. And of those who were below 150 percent of the poverty threshold, 68 percent would have remained poor. Thus, slightly more than half to just over two-thirds of the working poor would have remained poor even if they had worked full-time and year-round.

TABLE 16.3A

Poverty Status of the Working Poor If They Had Worked Full-Time, Year-Round

	Those Who Would Be Below		
	150%	125%	100%
	Percent of the Poverty Line		
Those who would be poor even if they worked full-time, year-round	68	61	52

NOTE: This table is read as follows: of adults who were below 100 percent of the poverty level, 52 percent would still be below this poverty level, if they worked full-time and year-round.

Why Still Poor?

Most of the working poor would have remained poor even if they had worked such hours because of the low wages they earned. Table 16.3B illustrates this. Those who would have remained below 150 percent of the poverty level earned on average $6.45 per hour; those who would have risen above 150 percent of the poverty level had they worked additional hours earned wages that averaged $9.20 per hour. Research indicates that some workers fall into poverty after losing a relatively high-paying job due to downsizing or company closures.[8] These workers are forced to settle for lower wages, fewer benefits, and subsequent poverty. Others who never had the fortune of employment in a relatively high-paying job are simply unable to escape a history of low-paying employment.[9] Lack of skills and education partly account for the inability of these workers to find more lucrative employment. But this is exacerbated by the disappearance of well-paying jobs with benefits that were once available to those at the bottom end of the income distribution—often those whose formal educations ended with a high school diploma.[10]

TABLE 16.3B
Average Wages Received by the Working Poor

	Those Who Would Be Below		
	150%	125%	100%
	Percent of the Poverty Line		
Average wages for those who would not be poor if they worked full-time year-round	$9.20	$8.46	$7.69
Average wages of those who would remain poor even if they worked full-time year-round	$6.45	$6.43	$6.51

Why Not Work More Hours?

Although most of the working poor would have remained poor even if they had worked full-time year-round, a fair number—32 percent to 48 percent—would have risen above poverty. It is crucial to understand why these workers failed to work more hours, since doing so would have made a significant difference in their living standards. The second question examined, therefore, was, "Why don't the working poor who could rise above poverty if they worked more hours work more hours?" The answer appears to be that many cannot.

Before examining the evidence, however, it is important to remember that, when investigating whether or not one can work additional hours, one is treading on controversial and difficult terrain. This is because this issue reflects society's expectations about who should work and about acceptable reasons for not working. These expectations change over time, moreover, so that at any one point in time there is likely to be less than unanimous agreement. Yet, despite a certain amount of disagreement, public policy has nevertheless addressed who is expected to work, and this social consensus manifests itself in the social benefit programs we provide as a nation. Because an in-depth analysis of who should work full-time and year-round is beyond the scope of this chapter, I assume that those who are unable to work full-time year-round are those who have been excused from doing so (rightly or wrongly) as reflected in our public policies.

Historically, these have included four groups: the disabled, the elderly, single parents with young children, and the unemployed. The first three have been excused from working full-time and year-round because as a nation we simply have not expected them to work these hours. The disabled are not expected to work such hours because their physical capacities often limit the type and amount of work they can perform (and, of course, because they face greater difficulty getting hired). The elderly are also excused from working full-time and year-round, even though many are capable of working these hours. But because society does not expect one to work one's entire lifetime (retirement is a certainty for most workers), no one condemns a retiree for failing to work, even if he or she is healthy enough to do so and is drawing upon tax revenues to subsidize his or her retirement. Our social policies have mirrored these expectations: the existence of Social Security and SSI benefits attest that we do not expect the elderly or the disabled to work full-time year-round to support themselves and their families.

The recent change of Aid to Families with Dependent Children (AFDC) from an entitlement to temporary assistance reflects changing expectations about the next group that has traditionally been excluded from working full-time and year-round: single parents with young children. At one time, when single parents were mostly widows and were perceived as victims of misfortune (their husbands' death), and when most women did not work for pay, these widows were not expected to work. The establishment of AFDC reflected this social consensus; the benefit was intended to provide for these women and their children so that the widows did not have to work for pay. But the recent elimination of this program indicates how much this consensus has changed. Today, since most women with children are now working, single parents are expected to work, at least part-time. In addition, because relatively fewer single parents are widows, and relatively more have never been married, they are viewed less as victims of misfortune (through death or divorce) and more as a population that consciously chose to become single parents.[11] Due to this ambivalence in social expectations, I report my findings about single parents, as I do with each of the four groups, separately.

Of course, demand-side constraints also limit the number of hours one can work during a year. Historically, an acceptable reason for not working full-time and year-round has been the lack of available jobs. There simply are not enough jobs to employ everyone who wants to work, especially those with fewer skills, who are more likely to be the working poor.[12] As a nation, we have accepted the lack of full-year employment as a reason for missing periods of work; the existence of our unemployment insurance system reflects this consensus.

Like single parents, however, the unemployed have been accused of being unwilling to work and lax about searching for jobs. Although one can certainly argue that those who are laid off may have been slack workers or could have found another job more quickly, layoffs often reflect decisions that are beyond a worker's control. The resulting consequence—entering the ranks of the working poor—although for some it may in part be voluntary, certainly contains an element of involuntariness as well. For this reason, I include those who are laid off among those who are unable to work a full year.[13]

These four groups—the disabled, elderly, single parents with young children, and those who have been laid off—are examined in Table 16.1A. It is interesting to note that the strong social consensus that the disabled and the elderly cannot or need not work results in these two populations' being *underrepresented* among the working poor. Of disabled adults (working and not working), only 5 percent were members of the working poor, compared to 10 percent of nondisabled adults. Of all adults sixty years old and older (working and not working), only 3 percent were among the working poor, compared to 12 percent of the nonelderly adult population. What these numbers reflect is that the disabled and the elderly are underrepresented among the working poor because they do not work and therefore are not counted as a member of the working poor.[14] Thus, the strong social consensus that the disabled and the elderly should not work is reflected not only in the social programs we offer but also in their own workforce behavior.

Table 16.1A also shows that those in the two remaining groups, single parents with young children and those facing demand constraints (measured as those who were laid off), were more likely to be among the working poor. Those in single-headed families with young children were four times more likely (36 percent compared to 9 percent) to be members of the working poor than were other adults (see Table 16.1A). Workers who faced a layoff were slightly more likely (13 percent compared to 10 percent) to be members of the working poor than were those who were not served layoff notices.

Now to answer the question I posed: "Why don't the working poor who could rise out of poverty if they worked more hours work more hours?" To examine this, I calculated the proportion of the working poor who could rise above poverty after excluding each of the four groups discussed—the elderly, the disabled, single parents with young children, and those who faced layoffs.

Table 16.4 shows the results. Each line shows the proportion of the working poor who could escape poverty if they worked more hours when the four groups are excluded from working full-time year-round. For example, excluding the disabled and the elderly from working full-time year-round leaves 26 percent of the working poor who (by working more hours) could have risen above 150 percent of the poverty level. Of those who were under 125 percent of the poverty level, 33 percent could have earned their way out of poverty.

If, in addition to the elderly and the disabled, one excuses those who were laid off from working full-time year-round, the proportion of the working poor who could have risen above poverty if they had worked more hours remains 26 percent at 150 percent of the poverty line and 40 percent at 100 percent of the poverty line, and it declines only one percentage point, to 32 percent (from 33 percent) at 125 percent of the poverty line (see Table 16.4). Thus, because those who were laid off constitute a small fraction of the working poor population—less than 1 percent—excusing them or not excusing them from working year-round did not alter the results substantially.

Eliminating single parents with children from the calculations also had little effect. Whether or not one expects single parents with young children to work full-time year-round makes little difference in the results, since this population is a small part (3-4 percent) of the working poor. If we add these workers to those (the disabled, elderly, and those who are laid off) who are excused from working full-time and year-round, we find that the proportion of the working poor who could have risen above poverty if they had worked additional hours falls only one percentage point (to 25 percent) at 150 percent of the poverty line, remains at 32 percent at 125 percent of the poverty line, and declines one percentage point, to 39 percent, at 100 percent of the poverty line (see Table 16.4).

TABLE 16.4

Percent of the Working Poor Who Could Raise Themselves above Poverty
If They Worked Full-Time Year-round Excluding Certain Populations of Workers

	Those Who Are Below		
	150%	125%	100%
	Percent of the Poverty Threshold		
Excluding no one	32	39	48
Excluding those who are disabled	29	35	43
Excluding those who are disabled or elderly	26	33	40
Excluding those who are disabled, elderly, or on layoff	26	32	40
Excluding those who are disabled, elderly, on layoff, or single-headed families with young children	25	32	39
Excluding those who are disabled, elderly, on layoff, or working part-time due to slack work or lack of full-time employment	19	23	28
Excluding those who are disabled, elderly, on layoff, single-headed families with young children, or working part-time due to slack work or lack of full-time employment	18	23	28

NOTE: This table is interpreted as follows: of the working poor who were below 150 percent of the poverty line, 32 percent could have been above poverty if they had worked full-time year-round. If we exclude those who were disabled from working full-time year-round, 29 percent could have risen above poverty. If we exclude the disabled and elderly workers from working full-time year-round, 26 percent could have worked their way out of poverty.

It is instructive to examine how these results change if we exclude those who were involuntarily employed part-time as well. These workers either could not find full-time work or were working part-time due to slack work. Traditionally, these workers have not been included in our social policies, since the magnitude of the problem of involuntary part-time work is a more recent phenomenon. In addition, as with the unemployed, one can argue that these workers could have found full-time work if they had searched harder. However, the extraordinary growth of involuntary part-time employment (most of the growth of part-time work over the past ten years is due to growth in the number of *involuntary* part-time workers) indicates that many of these workers do want full-time work but were unable to find such work because opportunities for these jobs have fallen.[15] When these workers are added to those already excused from working full-time year-round, only 18 percent of those below 150 percent, 23 percent of those below 125 percent, and 28 percent of those below 100 percent of the poverty line could have escaped poverty by working more hours. Thus, adding involuntary part-time hours as a reason for not being able to work full-time year-round has a tremendous impact on the results.

In summary, when taking into consideration who should be expected to work full-time and year-round, between 19 percent and 28 percent of the working poor could have risen above poverty had they worked more hours, assuming that the elderly, the disabled, and those who were laid off or employed involuntarily part-time are unable to work such hours. Excusing single parents with young children from also working such hours reduces the proportion of those who could work their way out of poverty to between 18 and 28 percent of the working poor.

Despite the debate surrounding whether single parents with young children and those who are laid off should or should not be expected to work full-time year-round, the estimates are not much affected by the decision whether to include or exclude these groups. Because single parents and those on layoff are only a small proportion of the working poor population, excusing them or not excusing them from working more hours per year docs little to change the empirical results.

Overall, these results support findings from qualitative research on the working poor. Unpublished results from a study by Charles Craypo suggest that the working poor work less than full-time year-round for a reason—many are simply unable to work such hours, even if offered, due to family obligations, age, or health problems.[16] Sar Levitan et al. also find that constraints of health and family obligations tend to prevent the working poor from working more hours.[17] Thus, fewer than half the working poor could rise out of poverty if they worked full-time year-round, and many of them are prevented from doing so.

It is difficult without further data to assess why the 18 to 28 percent of the working poor who could have risen above poverty had they worked full-time year-round failed to work such hours. Qualitative evidence suggests that many of them cannot find year-round work, are unemployed, or are unable to work additional hours due to family responsibilities and inadequate child care. Unfortunately, the data do not include information on why these workers failed to work additional hours and whether and for how long they were unemployed. This is an important area that should be addressed by future research.

Conclusion

Charles Murray asked, in 1987, "Can any American who is willing to work hard make a decent living?"[18] The answer seems to be no. Although working clearly reduces the probability of being poor, which is consistent with previous claims, it is not a panacea. Most of the working poor would remain poor even if they worked fifty-two weeks out of the year, forty hours per week. In addition, of those who could climb out of poverty if they worked such hours, two out of five are either disabled or elderly workers or are unable to find full-time or full-year employment. Thus, it appears that most of the working poor *are* doing all they can to support themselves. Only between 19 percent and 28 percent of the working poor could potentially climb out of poverty by working full-time and year-round, assuming that enough jobs were available.

This has important policy implications. This research supports the findings in a growing body of literature that argues that working more hours is not a solution to poverty and that the working poor will not disappear if the government urges greater work effort. Instead, because most of the working poor are poor not because they choose to work too few hours but because their wages are too low and their jobs fail to provide full-time and year-round employment, government supports continue to be needed. Such supports include an increase in the minimum wage so that workers can earn enough to support their families. It also includes an expansion of income supports so that those who are employed part-time or part-year can live above poverty. These policies can consist of expanding the Earned Income Tax Credit (EITC) or instituting wage subsidies.[19] Under either of these policies, income levels (for the EITC) or wage levels (for wage subsidies) that allow families to live above poverty are determined. The difference between these minimal income or wage levels and a worker's actual income or wages is then refunded to the worker. In the case of the EITC, the worker receives a tax credit that can exceed his or her tax contributions. In this way the EITC can refund money through the tax system so that anyone who works will be above poverty. Wage supplements, which have never been tried, would operate through the worker's payroll system; a worker would receive a government-provided wage supplement in his or her paycheck along with the wages paid by his or her employer. The additional amount of this wage supplement would bring every worker above poverty.

Currently, a minimum-wage worker with three or fewer dependents who works full-time and year-round is above the official poverty level at the current level of the EITC. But because workers are likely to work less than full-time year-round, and because the official poverty level is argued to set too low a standard, many suggest expanding the EITC.[20] Expanding the EITC has been a preferred strategy over wage supplements, even though the two strategies are strikingly similar: both result in government supplements for workers who are low paid.[21]

Besides income policies, demand-side policies are also needed to create jobs for low-skilled workers. Education and training programs are needed to help these workers move into jobs that promise full-time and year-round employment and rising earnings streams. Although these policies may seem ambitious, by targeting the source of the problem—low wages, less than year-round or full-time work, and the inability of some of the working poor to work more hours and generate enough income to rise above poverty—they are far better remedies for the plight of the working poor than simply encouraging the working poor to work more hours. Rather than cutting these programs, we need to maintain them, and, given the growth in the number of the working poor, to expand them, in order to alleviate poverty among workers.

NOTES

This chapter was originally published in the *Journal of Economic Issues* 32, no. 1 (1988) with permission by the Association for Evolutionary Economics.

1. Sar A. Levitan, Frank Gallo, and Isaac Shapiro, *Working but Poor: America's Contradiction* (Baltimore: Johns Hopkins University Press, 1993); Richard K. Caputo, "Patterns of Work and

Poverty: Exploratory Profiles of Working-Poor Households," *Families in Society: The Journal of Contemporary Human Services* (1991): 451-60.

2. John E. Schwarz and Thomas Volgy, *The Forgotten Americans* (New York: Norton, 1992).

3. Bradley Schiller, "Who Are the Working Poor?" *Public Interest* (Spring 1994): 61-71.

4. Levitan et al., *Working but Poor.*

5. Mary Jo Bane and David T. Ellwood, "Is American Business Working for the Poor?" *Harvard Business Review* (September-October 1991): 58-66.

6. Schwarz and Volgy, *Forgotten Americans.*

7. Charles Murray, "In Search of the Working Poor," *Public Interest* 89 (Fall 1987): 3-19.

8. Schwarz and Volgy, *Forgotten Americans;* also see Charles Craypo, "Industrial Restructuring and the Working Poor in a Midwestern U.S. Factory Town," *Labour and Society* 16, no. 2 (Fall 1991): 153-174.

9. Levitan et al., *Working but Poor;* Craypo, "Industrial Restructuring"; Schwarz and Volgy, *Forgotten Americans.*

10. Gary Burtless, "Employment Prospects of Welfare Recipients," in *The Work Alternative: Welfare Reform and the Realities of the Job Market,* ed. Demetra Smith Nightingale and Robert H. Haveman (Washington, D.C.: Urban Institute Press, 1995): 71-106.

11. Murray, "In Search of the Working Poor."

12. Peter Edelman, "The Worst Thing Bill Clinton Has Done," *Atlantic Monthly* (March 1997): 43-58.

13. Discouraged workers—those who are without jobs, who want to work, but who do not look for jobs because they do not think any are available—are also not examined, since they cannot be identified in the data.

14. These numbers cannot be construed to indicate that these populations lack disadvantages in the labor market. Their very absence from the labor market may reflect their difficulties holding jobs or being hired. As Table 16.1A also shows, the disabled are clearly overrepresented among the working poor compared to all other workers: 25 percent of disabled workers were poor in 1993, compared to 14 percent of nondisabled workers. Thus, the disabled clearly suffer in the labor market from their physical limitations and from perceptions of these limitations by employers.

15. Chris Tilly, "Dualism in Part-Time Employment," *Industrial Relations* 31, no. 2 (1992): 330-347; Chris Tilly, *Half a Job: Bad and Good Part-Time Jobs in a Changing Labor Market* (Philadelphia: Temple University Press, 1996); also see Ronald G. Ehrenberg, Pamela Rosenberg, and Jeanne Li, "Part-Time Employment," in *Employment, Unemployment, and Labor Utilization,* ed. Robert Hart (Boston: Unwin Hyman, 1988), 256-87.

16. Craypo, "Industrial Restructuring."

17. Levitan et al., *Working but Poor*

18. Murray, "In Search of the Working Poor," 3.

19. See, for example, Schwarz and Volgy, *Forgotten Americans;* also Laurie J. Bassi, "Stimulating Employment and Increasing Opportunity for the Current Work Force," in Nightingale and Haveman, *The Work Alternative,* 137-56.

20. See Schwarz and Volgy, *Forgotten Americans;* also see Sheldon Danziger and Peter Gottschalk, *America Unequal* (Cambridge, Mass.: Harvard University Press, 1995); and, William J. Wilson, *When Work Disappears: The World of the New Urban Poor* (New York: Knopf, 1996).

21. Tax credits are perceived as more politically viable since the concept of tax credits is familiar and since plenty of other tax credits exist. In addition, using the tax system to create income floors is perceived as less intrusive than creating wage supplements, since the latter may create the perception that the government directly sets wages.

DISCUSSION QUESTIONS

1. What does the author mean by the term, *working poor?*

2. Explain how the author uses census data to describe the growth and characteristics of the working poor.

3. What is the author proposing about poverty and its relationship to work? What are the implications of this relationship?

4. In addition to the working poor, what other sectors exist within the population that is impoverished?

5. How does the author critique scholars and observers who suggest that poverty reflects an unwillingness to work?

6. What kinds of proposals are suggested by the author as a response to the problems of the working poor? How are these kinds of proposals developed or critiqued by other contributors in this text?

FOR FURTHER READING

Bane, Mary Jo, and David T. Ellwood, "Is American Business Working for the Poor?" *Harvard Business Review* (September-October 1991): 58-66.

Ehrenberg, Ronald G., Pamela Rosenberg, and Jeanne Li, "Part-Time Employment," in *Employment, Unemployment, and Labor Utilization*, ed. Robert Hart (Boston: Unwin Hyman, 1988).

Levitan, Sar A., Frank Gallo, and Isaac Shapiro, *Working but Poor: America's Contradiction* (Baltimore: Johns Hopkins University Press, 1993).

Schiller, Bradley, "Who Are the Working Poor?" *Public Interest* (Spring 1994): 61-71.

Schwarz, John E., and Thomas Volgy, *The Forgotten Americans* (New York: Norton, 1992).

Wilson, William J., *When Work Disappears: The World of the New Urban Poor* (New York: Knopf, 1996).

Chapter Seventeen

The Black Poor and the Politics of Expendability

Barbara Ransby

In the presidential election year 1996, as rhetoric about international terrorism heightened, the two major U.S. political parties united in a campaign of terror against poor and working-class people, especially poor black and brown people—a campaign consistent with the shifting economic needs of American capitalism. At a time when unemployment and underemployment were at epidemic proportions, we witnessed a callous erosion of the welfare state as we have known it for nearly two generations. The system was never ideal, but even the most basic services are now being eradicated. Government aid to the unemployed and to the working poor is being cut to a point where many more families will literally be living on the street without the most basic resources of food, shelter, and clothing. This elimination of a basic commitment to those in need corresponds to an economic shift that has virtually eliminated any real possibility for employment for millions of these very same out-of-work Americans.

A number of economists and analysts, most notably Jeremy Rifkin and Stanley Aronowitz, have described the devastating impact of the new technological revolution. Downsizing and the introduction of labor-replacing technology (that is, computer technology, automation, and biotechnology) have created a situation in which millions of jobs and prospective jobs in manufacturing and service industries are being rapidly erased. The impact of this retrenchment, which began at the low-skill job levels, has been hardest on black and Latino workers. Thirty percent of the manufacturing jobs eliminated by downsizing in 1990 and 1991 were jobs held by blacks. This economic trend, which has persisted for more than a decade with little abatement, means that there now exists a class of permanently unemployed men and women who are essentially surplus laborers in an increasingly "streamlined" economy.[1] These are the men and women to whom social scientists condescendingly refer as the "black underclass."

So, then, what do the Democrats and the Republicans propose to do with these excess proletarians? The solutions being advocated are alarming and raise serious challenges for Left and progressive forces as we attempt to construct a response tailored to the realities we are confronted with. A three-pronged legislative agenda graphically illustrates the virtual convergence of Democratic and Republican ideologies: the passage of a welfare bill that blames the poor for their own poverty and denies them basic resources for survival; a willingness to cut taxes and give additional resources to corporate elites; and, finally, the passage of the 1994 crime bill and the law-and-order campaign that inspired it. In essence, a major element of the solutions proposed to address this economic reality—although discussed in euphemistic terms by those in power—involves a redistribution of resources in favor of the wealthy and containment, coerced labor, and imprisonment for large sectors of the black and Latino urban poor. Clearly, the conditions for slave labor are returning.

Economic Terrorism against the Poor

The welfare bill passed into law in 1996 signals an unprecedented assault on the well-being and survival of millions of poor Americans. One feature of the bill is its imposition of rigid time limits on how long poor people can receive assistance (five years over an entire lifetime), and its elimination of the social obligation of state governments to try to meet the needs of their impoverished citizens. That is, the bill eradicates the notion that citizens are "entitled" to basic subsistence resources, despite the fact that they live in one of the richest countries in the world and that most of them have paid taxes to the same federal government that now denies them much-needed benefits. There are also economic penalties for women who have additional children while receiving welfare. And the doors of colleges and universities are closed even tighter to exclude the poor. The reduction of funds for job training and the elimination of programs that now enable welfare recipients to attend school in preparation for employment will deny them even the most remote chance to obtain the skills necessary to compete in the shrinking job market. Policy analysts estimate that welfare reform will cause an additional 2.6 million people, including 1.1 million children, to sink below the poverty threshold by the year 2000.[2]

The crux of the problem with the so-called welfare reform programs is the underlying assumption that the problem lies with the culture, behavior, and morality of the poor, rather than with poverty itself. The mandatory work requirement for welfare recipients after two years ignores the absence of real jobs for unskilled and undereducated workers and, instead, blames unemployed people for not being resourceful enough to find nonexistent jobs. In other words, it is poor people who are defective, not the economy. The alleged moral agenda of the current welfare reform crusade—to reduce out-of-wedlock births and instill a greater work ethic in the poor—applies higher moral standards to poor people than those adhered to by many of our public officials themselves. Moreover, the elitist assumption that poor people are lazy and irresponsible ignores the fact that most of these people have to work harder than most rich people just to survive. Daily life demands a certain resourcefulness, discipline, and stamina that are wholly ignored and discounted by the behaviorist arguments against the poor.

The Changing U.S. Economy

The promise by both major political parties of substantial tax cuts to the middle class—more like tax breaks for the wealthy—is the selling point of the social spending cuts we are currently witnessing. Despite the rhetoric of uplifting the poor by "cutting their dependency on government," the underlying economic objectives of the recent social policy initiatives are clear. And what are some of the economic motives at play? A book written nearly twenty-five years ago by Sidney Wilhelm, titled *Who Needs the Negro?* offers a hint.[3] In it, Wilhelm outlines the growing marginalization of black workers to the American economy, foreshadowing the even more pronounced developments two decades later. During the colonial and the early American periods, black labor was, of course, the unpaid labor on which the wealth and profit of the slave South and, by extension, much of the North, rested. Later, blacks were instrumental as exploited farm labor under the sharecropping system and, most recently, as indispensable factory workers in the industrial marketplace after the Second World War. Wilhelm wrote in 1970: "White America, by a more perfect application of mechanization and a vigorous reliance upon automation, disposes of the Negro: consequently, the Negro transforms from an exploited labor force to an outcast."[4]

Jeremy Rifkin in the United States and Ambalavaner Sivanandan in Britain, among others, argue persuasively that the scientific revolution we are experiencing today is bringing about even more dramatic changes—and is changing the very nature of labor and work as we know it.[5] Rifkin argues, as the title of his book, *The End of Work*, suggests, that the direction we are going in will ultimately render a certain section of the population permanently unemployed and wholly superfluous to the economy. The obvious social consequences of such a scenario are profound. He paints the following picture:

> Unemployment is rising (sharply) as transnational companies build state of the art high-tech production facilities all over the world, letting go millions of laborers who can no longer compete with the cost efficiency, quality control and speed of delivery achieved by automated manufacturing. In more and more countries the news is filled with talk about lean production, re-engineering, total quality engineering. post-Fordism, decruiting, and downsizing. Everywhere men and women are worried about their future.[6]

In response to the suggestion that this economic crisis is cyclical or temporary, Rifkin and his colleagues insist:

> In the past, when new technologies have replaced workers in a given sector, new sectors have always emerged to absorb the displaced laborers. Today all three of the traditional sectors of the economy—agriculture, manufacturing and service—are experiencing technological displacement. The only new sector emerging is the knowledge sector, made up of a small elite of entrepreneurs, scientists, technicians, computer programmers, educators and consultants.[7]

Abdul Alkalimat and others have written and spoken eloquently on the ways in which this scientific revolution and its economic reverberations have and will continue, directly and ominously, to shape social policy. The bottom line is that if certain sectors of the workforce and the potential workforce are no longer needed by an economy increasingly reliant on highly skilled computer experts, what becomes of those left behind by these changes? Even service-sector jobs, flipping hamburgers at local fast-food chains or changing bedpans at hospitals and nursing homes, are becoming harder to come by. Union busting, which began with Ronald Reagan's first administration in the early 1980s, has made decent-paying union jobs a thing of the past for all but the lucky few. My mother and father's generation could count on certain hard, grueling, backbreaking work as a ticket to a reliable income and a relatively decent life. No more. Government economic interventions over the past decade and a half have been increasingly and unabashedly geared toward the interests of the rich and upper middle class, offering more tax loopholes and tax breaks to those at the top of the economic pyramid and ushering in what some economists have labeled a "jobless recovery." In other words, economic improvements for corporate elites and nothing for unemployed workers.

These policies are fattening up elite strata already quite pampered by the state. While welfare for the poor is being slashed, corporate perks are growing. Even Bill Clinton's former secretary of labor, Robert Reich, has spoken critically of the undue benefits enjoyed by corporate elites as a result of government policy. In the 1950s, corporate taxes accounted for one-third of all federal revenues. That figure had been reduced to a mere 10 percent in 1995. Corporate agricultural businesses are heavily subsidized by the state, and many companies claim tax exemptions for a variety of things, including advertisement of their own products abroad. The "supply-side" economic policies espoused by the Republican nominee, Bob Dole, in the 1996 presidential campaign promised to shift the economic policy debate even more to the right and more in favor of big-business interests. The net result of all this is that the top 10 percent of the U.S. population now own nearly two-thirds of all the private wealth, and the top 1 percent own and control 40 percent.[8]

Of course, forcing the working class and the poor to bear the brunt of economic downturns is nothing new, but the widening and unmediated gulf between rich and poor, with less and less of a buffer in between, coupled with the growing insecurity of a certain stratum of professionals victimized by cuts in corporate bureaucracies, all represent significant shifts in the political and economic landscape. Historically, the notion of American exceptionalism has meant that most U.S. workers embraced an illusory "middle-class" identity and felt privileged and distinct from workers in other parts of the world. The economic and technological changes we are experiencing threaten to redefine that self-concept, offering both hopeful and frightening prospects for future political mobilizations. Middle managers who played by the rules and personified the American dream are being booted out of their jobs by downsizing. Many of them feel betrayed by a system they once believed in. However, that resentment can go in one of two political directions. These excess bureaucrats can either become more sympathetic to Left critiques of the social order or join the right-wing militia movement or the conservative Christian Coalition or endorse the thinly veiled fascism of someone like Ross Perot.

While surplus managers and professionals can look forward to loss of mortgages and eclipsed career ambitions, the prospects for the poor are much grimmer. At the same time that social service expenditures are being cut and, in the case of some programs, eliminated outright, prison construction is flourishing. In the state of Michigan, which led the way in spending cuts for services to the poor, a $200 million prison building project is under way. In Missouri, a $94 million prison is being constructed. And a $50 million bond campaign has been launched in Maryland to expand the state's prison system to accommodate overcrowding.[9] With this pattern of funding reallocation throughout the country, it seems clear where most politicians and bureaucrats plan to deposit the excess workforce.

Criminalization and Elimination Schemes for Poor Black People

In 1994 Bill Clinton, with Republican support, passed a repressive crime bill that moved the nation closer to a police state than ever before. In 1995, an alarming study by the Washington, D.C.-based Sentencing Project reported that there were more black men in U.S. prisons than white men, 43 percent and 42 percent, respectively, despite the fact that blacks constitute a mere 13 percent of the entire population. This means that the percentage of black men imprisoned is more than three times their representation in the population at large. Today five thousand of every one hundred thousand black men are in prison, as opposed to five hundred out of every one hundred thousand persons in the general population. Even more striking, one in every three black men between the ages of twenty and twenty-nine is either in prison or on probation or parole, in contrast to a mere 7 percent of their white counterparts. More black men are under the supervision of the criminal justice system in the United States today than were imprisoned in South Africa under the racist apartheid regime. And black women are not exempt from what the prisoner rights activist Angela Davis calls "the punishment industry." Incarceration rates for black women have risen 20 percent in the past decade.[10]

One response to these statistics might be to say that blacks are simply committing more crimes. The answer is not that simple. Although crime rates have gone down over the past twenty years, the incarceration rate has more than quadrupled, from two hundred thousand prisoners in 1975 to 1.6 million in 1996. This has largely been a result of stiffer and mandatory sentencing laws, greater reluctance to release prisoners on parole, the creation of new crime statutes, and the deinstitutionalization of mental patients, many of whom end up homeless and eventually incarcerated for one infraction or another. The United States now leads the world in imprisoning its citizens.

Much of this get-tough-on-crime and law-and-order hysteria has been carried out under the guise of the so-called war on drugs. And this is where racism comes into play most clearly. Black urban neighborhoods have been vilified as drug-infested jungles, inhabited by bloodthirsty savages who lack morals, civility, or conscience. This is not to deny the fact that crime is a real problem in poor inner-city communities. It is. Kids without jobs or education often turn to the ruthless business of drug trafficking, thereby mimicking the entrepreneurial spirit of capitalism. Like their legal counterparts, they kill, maim, and destroy people's lives in the process of making a profit. This grim fact notwithstanding, predatory crimes are still committed by a minute fraction of the black community, and the racism embedded in the antidrug laws and enforcement practices is still undeniable.

Particularly ominous, and quite telling, is the blanket criminalization of entire communities for crimes committed by a few, which suggests that the elimination of drugs is not the objective at all. Rather, containment and control of a potentially rebellious population seem a more plausible explanation. Parenthetically, this type of communitywide punishment is reminiscent of the treatment meted out to Palestinian communities during the intifada, in which whole neighborhoods were razed as retribution against rock-throwing youths. Some examples of this type of group punishment in the U.S. context can be seen in public housing projects where large numbers of the urban poor live. In many of these projects, quasi-military conditions now prevail. Residents have to walk through metal detectors and provide identification on demand. Housing police are often allowed to carry out what are termed "lockdowns" and "sweeps," which mean locking residents in their buildings at night and conducting random searches of apartments to identify so-called outsiders. More often than not, outsiders are individuals who are staying with public housing residents but who are not officially on the lease for that dwelling. This might be a homeless relative, a domestic partner not legally married to the resident, or children or siblings evicted from their own housing. Having an unlisted occupant in the apartment at the time of the sweep can result in the termination of a lease and the eviction of an entire family.

Such practices not only deny poor people basic civil rights but build tensions within extended families, deter people from helping one another in a crisis, and literally break down survival mechanisms employed by poor people in order to adapt to increasingly adverse conditions. It is important to note that, contrary to the notion that increased policing and repression apply solely to black men, black women and children are the primary residents of public housing in most major cities, and these housing projects increasingly resemble minimum-security prisons—at best. The criminalization of youth, with the emphasis on trying teenagers as adults, and the economically punitive measures against poor single mothers are additional facets of this larger trend of criminalizing the black urban poor.

Another component of the so-called war on drugs, the battle cry of the crime bill proponents, is the racially biased practice of imposing harsher sentences on those forms of drug use and sales that are most common in the black community, while handing out lighter sentences for comparable offenses committed most commonly by whites. Even though drug use among whites and blacks is estimated to occur at relatively the same rate, blacks get arrested five times as often. Another widely cited discrepancy is the fact that crack cocaine possession is met with much harsher sentencing than is the possession and sale of powder cocaine.[11] Crack is more common in the black community, and powder cocaine is more popular among wealthy whites. In fact, between 83 and 90 percent of those convicted of crack possession and sales are black.[12] There is a hundred-to-one disparity between powder cocaine and crack cocaine sentences as established under the 1986 Narcotics Penalties and Enforcement Act.[13] So, for very similar offenses, whites either get a shorter sentence compared to blacks or avoid jail altogether. The net result of biased sentencing, increased mandatory sentencing, and generally increased repression of poor and working-class black communities is that the entire black community is placed under surveillance and subjected to greater police harassment. Ultimately, of course, poor blacks are much more likely to end up in prison.

Another often ignored by-product of the trend of increased black imprisonment constitutes a reversal of many of the voting rights gains won by the civil rights movement of the 1960s. Prisoners, now mostly black, are essentially deemed noncitizens. Poor blacks, therefore, are being systematically disenfranchised and reduced to a noncitizen status reminiscent of slavery. Under slavery, every black person was deemed three-fifths of a person by the U.S. Constitution; today, thousands of black prisoners and former prisoners are not seen as persons at all. Nearly all states deny prisoners the right to vote, more than half deny voting rights to individuals on probation, and nearly a third deny even former offenders the ballot. Today, this racially biased disenfranchisement affects fourteen million Americans, disproportionately black.[14] In essence, therefore, conviction for a single crime can, in many instances, mean lifelong exclusion from the body politic.

Once you have a record, the authorities have information on you and a right to monitor you and restrict you in ways that they cannot vis-à-vis other fully fledged citizens. Ex-offenders are frequently hauled into police lineups or designated as suspects because they fit the description of some alleged lawbreaker. All of these factors help to strengthen the state's ability to control a population that has growing reasons to feel angry and rebellious.

Finally, there is the issue of the death penalty. Perhaps the most serious by-product of the current crime-fighting crusade is a push to make the death penalty more common, to streamline the appeals process, to deny death-row inmates the right of multiple appeals, and to implement quicker, more cost-efficient methods of execution. Capital punishment has always constituted a form of special treatment reserved for the poor and, disproportionately, the black poor. So it is not surprising that, even as we see policies that view poor black people as expendable, we also hear increased demands for the more liberal use of capital punishment. Of the three thousand inmates awaiting execution, 40 percent are African American, again a figure far exceeding black representation in the population. After decades of decreased popularity, the death penalty has risen as a part of the battle cry of the new campaign for law and order at any cost. More people were executed by the state in 1995 than in any year since the death penalty was reinstated in 1976. One of the most well-known inmates on death row is the political prisoner Mumia Abu-Jamal, whose case has helped to bring attention to the injustice of capital punishment, but this unfortunately has not won Mumia's freedom or that of dozens of other black political prisoners, like Geronimo Pratt, who have been languishing in U.S. prisons since the 1960s and early 1970s.[15]

Thus, the current political climate in the United States is one in which repression and criminalization of the poor are quite compatible with economic shifts that have created a superfluous class of workers. But how are such fascistic policies being carried out, seemingly with popular tolerance, if not support? Let me indicate, as an aside, that the current conservative Congress, led by the right-wing icon Newt Gingrich, was not elected by a majority of Americans. The majority of Americans either voted for candidates who lost or, even more telling, did not bother to vote at all. Nevertheless, some of the harshest social policies we have seen in generations are being carried out in the name of the American people. This policy agenda, which hinges on the denial of basic resources to and the mass imprisonment of poor black people, is fundamentally racist in its nature. And it is racism and its propagation in the mainstream media that allow such a program to be implemented, by politicians and bureaucrats of varied skin tones and by both major political parties.

I in no way subscribe to the ahistorical notion that the worse things get, the better the climate for radical social movements to develop. If this were the case, we would never have witnessed the development of fully fledged fascism in Europe or the emergence of Third World dictatorships today. But the sobering political and economic reality we are confronted with has led to a resurgence of organizing efforts among American leftists, especially black and Latino activists. Student and youth activism on American college campuses never died out completely, despite rumors to the contrary. Recent years have witnessed a renewed phase of campus organizing, which perhaps has even greater promise of making links with off-campus struggles. The union campaign by Yale University graduate students in 1996 garnered national attention and support from Left intellectuals and trade unionists alike. Shortly before that, Columbia University students led a militant campaign for an ethnic studies program, taking over university buildings and forcing the administration to bring New York City police on campus for the first time in more than a decade. The Columbia students also lent support to the clerical workers' strike at adjacent Barnard College, which occurred around the same time. And California students have led the fight against the state's reversal of affirmative action and its attacks on largely Latino immigrants, in the form of Proposition 187, which has become a national model for denying all public services, including health care and access to schools, to undocumented workers.[16]

Not all youth organizing is confined to the campuses. Hundreds of young people (most of whom were, in fact, students) participated in a union organizing drive in the summer of 1996 that was labeled Union Summer, reminiscent of the civil rights movement's historic Freedom Summer campaign of 1964. Some former student organizers have also made a priority of doing community-level youth organizing with high-school-age young people. The Southwest Youth Collaborative in Chicago is one example of this effort. Led by an African American organizer, Jonathan Peck, and a Palestinian activist, Jeremy Lahoud, the project carries out mass political education of youth and offers workshops on political organizing. One of the key issues on which they have done an impressive amount of work is the criminalization of youth.

On a national level, despite two decades of largely single-issue organizing campaigns, black Left forces are once again attempting to organize on a national level, some in interracial formations and some exclusively in the black community. A contingent of veteran black organizers and intellectuals has involved itself in and influenced the formation of such groups as the New Party; the Labor Party, which held a highly promising founding conference in 1996; and Committees of Correspondence, a group that grew out of the breakup of the Communist Party but has reached out to include other sectors of the progressive and Left communities.[17] Black Left intellectuals and organizers are talking to each other more these days as well, across organizational and ideological boundaries. Among the national dialogues, conferences, and summits that have taken place or are being planned are a national gathering of black radical activists in 1997; a National Black Leadership Summit, which involved some radicals and many mainstream leaders as well; and a number of black feminist initiatives, such as the New York-based Agenda 2000—A Black Feminist Network (formerly African American Agenda 2000) and the Washington, D.C.-based Black Women for Justice.

The political situation is serious, but not hopeless. The real challenge in this country at this juncture seems to be threefold. The first challenge is to build a national network, if not organization, to coordinate local and overlapping national efforts but to insist on antiracism and leadership by people of color as a priority to avoid the elitism and isolation that have plagued such efforts in the past. Second, blacks seriously need to create a constructive and inclusive conversation about the internal weaknesses of their own movement, historically and today. Paramount in the list of discussion items have to be the persistence of sexism and homophobia; the need to ally across the boundaries of the academy and the community; and the need to combat egocentrism and to hold even the most eloquent spokespersons accountable for what they say. Finally, blacks need to build on, and take more seriously, efforts at creating a sustained international alliance. The demise of socialist experiments and the socialist movement worldwide and the globalization and the increased cross-national operation of capitalism demand that poor people take this task to heart. The challenges of the twenty-first century are formidable, but the potential is tremendous.

NOTES

This chapter was originally published in *Race and Class* 38, no. 2 (1996): 3-12.

The author would like to acknowledge Abdul Alkalimat, University of Toledo (Ohio), for his contribution to this article.

1. Jeremy Rifkin, *The End of Work: The Decline of the Global Labor Force and the Dawn of the Post-Market Era* (New York: Putnam, 1995); Stanley Aronowitz and William DiFazio, *The Jobless Future: Sci-Tech and the Dogma of Work* (Minneapolis: University of Minnesota Press, 1995). For similar observations regarding the situation in Britain, see Ambalavaner Sivanandan, "All That Melts into Air Is Solid: The Hokum of New Times," *Race and Class* (January-March 1990); and Ambalavaner Sivanandan, "New Circuits of Imperialism," *Race and Class* 30, no. 4 (April-June 1989).

2. *New York Times*, 23 August 1996, A10.

3. Sidney Wilhelm, *Who Needs the Negro?* (Cambridge, Mass.: Schenkman, 1970).

4. Ibid., 162.

5. Rifkin, *The End of Work*; and Sivanandan, "All That Melts into Air." See also A. Sivanandan, "Heresies and Prophecies: The Social and Political Fall-out of the Technological Revolution," *Race and Class* 37, no. 4 (April-July 1996).

6. Rifkin, *The End of Work*, xv-5.

7. Ibid.

8. Chuck Collins, "Aid to Dependent Corporations: Exposing Federal Handouts to the Wealthy," *Dollars and Sense* (May/June 1995).

9. Richard V. Ayre, "The Prison Crisis: An Essay on the Social and Political Foundations of Criminal Justice Policy," *Public Administration Quarterly* 19, no. 1 (Spring 1995): 42-57; David Kaplan, "Prison Building Boom a Bust for Bankers," *Bond Buyer*, 6 April 1995.

10. These statistics were obtained in various forms from the following sources: Larry Gossett, "Bringing Balance to Our Justice System," *Seattle Times*, 24 June 1996, B5; Paul Finkelman, "The Crime of Color," *Tulane Law Review* 67 (June 1993); Ted Gest, "A Shocking Look at Blacks and Crime," *U.S. News and World Report*, 16 October 1995, 53; for statistics on prison populations in Britain and the *Criminal Justice White Paper* published by Home Secretary Michael Howard, see David Rose, "Back to the Chain Gang," *Observer*, 4 February 1996, 13.

11. Ronald Brownstein, "Why Are So Many Black Men in Jail?" *Los Angeles Times*, 6 November 1995, 5A.

12. Gary Fields, "Blacks Now a Majority in Prisons," *USA Today*, 4 December 1995, 1A; Larry Bivins, "Black Men in America: Prison Rates Rise," *Detroit News*, 8 October 1996.

13. Jefferson Morley, "Crack in Black and White: Politics, Profits and Punishment in America's Drug Economy," *Washington Post*, 19 November 1995, C01.

14. Andrew Shapiro, "Giving Cons and Ex-Cons the Vote," *Nation*, 20 December 1993. For more information, see Andrew Hacker, "Malign Neglect: The Crackdown on African Americans," *Nation*, 10 July 1995; Marc Mauer, "Americans behind Bars: A Comparison of International Rates of Incarceration," report issued by the Sentencing Project (Washington, D.C.: Sentencing Project, 1991); Robert Gangi, "Pataki's 'No Frills' Prisons Means Trouble for the State," *Buffalo News*, 14

March 1996, 3B; Clifford J. Levy, "Pataki Proposes a Ban on Parole in Violent Crimes," *New York Times*, 12 December 1995, A1.

15. For interviews with U.S. black political prisoners, see "Black America: The Street and the Campus," *Race and Class* 35, no. 1 (July-September 1993).

16. Some of this information is based my conversations and meetings with other activists. See also Robert Perkinson, "School Days: A New Voice at Old Blue," *Z Magazine* 9, no. 7-8 (July-August 1996).

17. For information on the newly formed Labor Party, see Adolph Reed Jr., "Building Solidarity," *Progressive* 60, no. 8 (August 1996) and "A Party Is Born," *Z Magazine* 9, no. 7-8 (July-August 1996).

DISCUSSION QUESTIONS

1. Why does the author accuse the two major U.S. political parties of a "campaign of terror" against poor people, particularly in communities of color?

2. How is the welfare state eroding or declining in the author's view, and what are the reasons for this development?

3. How is the problem of "excess proletarians" created, and how has the government responded?

4. How are poor people "criminalized," and what role does race play in this process, according to the author?

5. How do poor people in black and Latino communities respond to a politics of "expendability"?

FOR FURTHER READING

Aronowitz, Stanley, and William DiFazio, *The Jobless Future: Sci-Tech and the Dogma of Work* (Minneapolis: University of Minnesota Press, 1995).

Fields, Gary, "Blacks Now a Majority in Prisons," *USA Today,* 4 December 1995, 1A.

Morley, Jefferson, "Crack in Black and White: Politics, Profits and Punishment in America's Drug Economy," *Washington Post*, 19 November 1995, C01.

Rifkin, Jeremy, *The End of Work: The Decline of the Global Labor Force and the Dawn of the Post-Market Era* (New York: Putnam, 1995).

Wilhelm, Sidney, *Who Needs the Negro?* (Cambridge, Mass.: Schenkman, 1970).

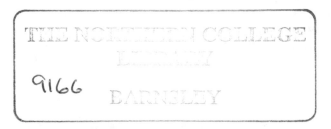